Women and Slavery in the Late Otto

Madeline Zilfi's latest book examines gender poli
lation in the Ottoman Empire. In a challenge to pre
that, throughout the eighteenth and nineteenth centuries, female slavery was not only central to Ottoman practice but also a critical component of imperial governance and elite social reproduction. As Zilfi illustrates through her accounts of the particular vulnerabilities of slave women, the failures of abolitionism in the Ottoman Middle East were due in large part to the overwhelmingly female character of the slave institution in the later centuries. The book focuses on the experience of slavery in the Ottoman capital of Istanbul, also using comparative data from Egypt and North Africa to illustrate the regional diversity and local dynamics that were the hallmarks of slavery in the Middle East during the early modern era. This is an articulate and informed account that sets the Ottoman system in the context of more general debates on women, slavery, and the construction of social dependency.

MADELINE C. ZILFI is Professor of History at the University of Maryland. Her previous publications include *The Politics of Piety: The Ottoman Ulema in the Post-Classical Age* (1988), and she is also the editor of *Women in the Ottoman Empire: Middle Eastern Women in the Early Modern Middle East* (1997).

Cambridge Studies in Islamic Civilization

Published titles are listed at the back of the book

Women and Slavery in the Late Ottoman Empire

The Design of Difference

MADELINE C. ZILFI

University of Maryland

CAMBRIDGE
UNIVERSITY PRESS

CAMBRIDGE UNIVERSITY PRESS
Cambridge, New York, Melbourne, Madrid, Cape Town,
Singapore, São Paulo, Delhi, Mexico City

Cambridge University Press
The Edinburgh Building, Cambridge CB2 8RU, UK

Published in the United States of America by Cambridge University Press, New York

www.cambridge.org
Information on this title: www.cambridge.org/9781107411456

First published 2010
Reprinted 2011
First paperback edition 2012

A catalogue record for this publication is available from the British Library

Library of Congress Cataloguing in Publication Data
Zilfi, Madeline C.
Women and slavery in the late Ottoman Empire : the design of difference / Madeline C. Zilfi.
p. cm. – (Cambridge studies in Islamic civilization)
Includes bibliographical references and index.
ISBN 978-0-521-51583-2 (hardback)
1. Women slaves – Turkey – History. 2. Slavery – Turkey – History. I. Title. II. Series.
HT1306.Z55 2010
306.3′6208209561–dc22 2009039049

ISBN 978-0-521-51583-2 Hardback
ISBN 978-1-107-41145-6 Paperback

Contents

List of illustrations

Preface and acknowledgments

Women and Slavery in the Late Ottoman Empire is a study of slavery in a particular time and place. It is in some respects, then, a local history. At its center is the city of Istanbul, capital of the Ottoman Empire, with the period of the eighteenth century through the 1830s as the time line for slavery's portrait there. Although the book has a specific geographical anchoring, any consideration of social practice in an imperial capital of Istanbul's size and stature is ultimately about more than the habits and byways of the city and its residents. To be sure, the capital cannot stand for the entirety of the empire, but as its largest city and administrative center, it was deeply implicated in the life and well-being of Ottoman subjects elsewhere.

Notwithstanding the book's microhistorical features, it is also intended to add to farther-reaching discussions regarding the place of slaveholding in human affairs beyond the Ottoman center and even beyond the Middle East. By exploring the social contours of the Ottoman trade as it functioned in the region of the capital, I have been interested in reconstructing this piece of the past for its distinctive roots, context, and temporal shifts, in short, for its own history. As with any history of "its own," however, the study is also implicitly – and here, sometimes explicitly – comparative. This is especially the case with regard to previous generations and other regions of the Mediterranean over which the Ottoman Empire was sovereign. The purpose of comparison, however, is not to provide a parallel story. Rather, it is to underscore the singular and not-so-singular features of this Ottoman Middle Eastern example of the practice of slavery.

I have also sought to engage with the growing body of historical writing on slavery in the Middle Eastern and Islamic past. In addressing the political dimensions of Ottoman slavery in the long eighteenth century, the book takes issue with two related histories, that of Middle Eastern and Ottoman slaveries, which foregrounds male and ethnic categories, and that regarding the Ottoman reform era, which, in neglecting the gendered parameters of Ottoman politics and early reformism, arrives at another, fundamentally male, story. The centrality of women and female slavery, as social realities and as representations of Ottoman sovereignty and its vulnerabilities in the period of the study, constitutes the core argument of the book and the main counterpoint to the conventional wisdom.

In arguing for the importance of gender – indeed, for its overriding importance in the place and period of the study – I also take issue with some of the perspectives of world-history narratives. The greater inclusiveness of world history and maritime and transnational formulations has shed welcome light on intercontinental linkages and legacies, nowhere more so than in the history of trade and the circulation of valued commodities in the early modern era. The study of slave trading has arguably been the primary beneficiary of world perspectives. Historians of Africa and the Americas especially have been involved in mapping and assessing the linkages and reciprocities among Africa and the Atlantic, Mediterranean, and Indian Ocean trades. Significant findings have crowned their inquiries but not without cost to local context and conjunctural change.

An insistence on detail and specificity is the usual historian's riposte to any attempt at universal history. Nonetheless, it speaks to abiding epistemological concerns. The privileging of continuities and commonalities tends to reinforce Eurocentric categories and premises or, in the case of slavery studies in particular, Atlantic-derived categories, most notably those of race and Africanness. Color was undeniably important in Middle Eastern and North African slavery in the period. Still, it did not hold the same value as in the Atlantic context, nor did race play the structuring role that it did in the Americas. In any case, blackness and Africanness are and remain unstable and subjective descriptors. Middle Eastern and North African bodies did not and do not comfortably fit the Atlantic frames of reference that characterize much of the conversation about world slavery inside and outside academe. Although *Women and Slavery in the Late Ottoman Empire* disputes such racial framing, its larger purpose is to attend to historical complexity in context and to the contingencies of social values and organization within that context.

I am indebted to the University of Maryland General Research Board for its generous and timely awards in support of the research for this book. I am most deeply appreciative of a yearlong grant from the National Humanities Center and the Tri Delta Foundation in 2005–6. The grant provided me with uninterrupted writing time at the National Humanities Center, the wonderful luxury of expert and attentive support staff, and the warm and vibrant community of fellow scholars in the humanities. My earlier work on social regulation and women in the Ottoman Empire, both of which are foundational to the present study, was made possible by grants from the U.S. Fulbright Program, which has been for me, since my graduate-student days, an indispensable portal to the study of the Middle East.

Note on transliteration

Modern Turkish usage has been followed here for Ottoman Turkish terms and names. Exceptions are made for words in the text that have been absorbed into English. Thus, when the choice has been mine to make (as opposed to bibliographical citations, quotations, and the like), *pasha* is written rather than *paşa*, *agha* rather than *ağa*, and so on. Otherwise, the spelling of Turkish words generally conforms to that employed in the *Redhouse Yeni Türkçe-İngilizce Sözlük/ New Redhouse Turkish-English Dictionary* (1968; repr., Istanbul, 1979). The number of diacritical marks has been further reduced, however, in the interests of readability but without, it is hoped, loss of meaning. For Arabic and Persian names and terms that are not a part of quoted material or bibliographical citations, a simplified system of romanization has been used.

Chronology

1703–30	**Reign of Ahmed III**
1711–18	Seesaw warfare with Russia, Venice, and Austria in Morea and the Balkans; Belgrade lost but later recovered in 1739
1718–30	Tulip Era, coinciding with grand vizierate of Nevşehirli, İbrahim Pasha, ends in deposition of Ahmed III and execution of İbrahim
1730–54	**Reign of Mahmud I**
1730–6	Loss of western Iran and Azerbaijan to Iran
1736–9	War with Russia and Austria
1743–6	War with Iran
1754–7	**Reign of Osman III**, focus on social regulation
1757–74	**Reign of Mustafa III**
1768–74	War with Russia
1772	Mansfield Decision in England: slaves brought to England by masters could not be taken back to the colonies as slaves or sold for export
1774–89	**Reign of Abdülhamid I**
1774	Treaty of Küçük Kaynarca with Russia. Independence of Crimea and northern shores of Black Sea from Ottoman rule. Russia formally annexes Muslim Crimea in 1783
1787	Renewal of war with Russia
1787	Society for the Abolition of the Slave Trade founded in Britain
1789–1807	**Reign of Selim III**
1798–1801	Invasion of Egypt by Napoléon Bonaparte; French occupation
1804	Serb revolt
1805	Mehmed Ali as governor of Egypt
1807	Rebels in Istanbul and environs depose Selim, crushing his New Order army
1807	British Parliament votes to abolish the African trade
1807–8	**Reign of Mustafa IV**
1808–39	**Reign of Mahmud II**
1821–30	Greek insurrection and creation of independent Greece

1826	Destruction of Janissaries
1833	Great Britain abolishes slavery in its Caribbean territories
1839–61	**Reign of Abdülmecid I**
1839	Gülhane Rescript and inauguration of Tanzimat Reform Era, 1839–76
1846	Ahmad Bey, Ottoman governor of Tunis, proclaims end of slavery in his realm in January
1846	Closure of Istanbul's Esir Pazarı, or central Slave Market, in December
1847	Ottoman decree abolishes African slave trade in Persian Gulf
1853–6	Crimean War: Britain, France, and Ottomans versus Russia
1856	Imperial Decree of 1856, with equalizing provisions for religious minorities
1857	Ottoman prohibition on African slave trade, but uprisings in Hijaz result in exemption for much of Arabian Peninsula
1861–76	**Reign of Abdülaziz**
1862–8	Hundreds of thousands of Circassians, many of them slaves, flee Russian conquest of Caucasus to settle in Ottoman Empire
1863	Emancipation Proclamation in United States, effective January
1865	Thirteenth Amendment to U.S. Constitution bans slavery
1870	Fifteenth Amendment to U.S. Constitution extends voting rights to males of all races
1876	Proclamation of First Ottoman Constitution, with electoral rights for Muslim and non-Muslim males
1876	**Reign of Murad V, deposed**
1876–1909	**Reign of Abdülhamid II**
1877	British-Egyptian Convention for the Suppression of the Slave Trade
1880	Anglo-Ottoman Convention to end the African trade
1890	Ottoman Empire signatory to International Brussels Act forbidding African trade
1909–18	Young Turk era
1914–18	World War I and dismemberment of Ottoman Empire
1923	Establishment of Turkish Republic, Mustafa Kemal Pasha (Atatürk) as first president

CHAPTER 1

Empire and imperium

> For the rulers, what is necessary is to protect the Muslim social order and to maintain the obligations and principles of Islam among the people.
>
> – Katib Çelebi (d. 1659), *The Balance of Truth* (London, 1957)

> Take necessary care to summon all the local imams to the *shari'ah* court and admonish each of them in the strongest terms to broadcast to the people of the residential quarters that the punishments of wrongdoers will be carried out without mercy.
>
> – Command to the *kadı* of Istanbul, 1743[1]

Imperial Istanbul

In the seventeenth and eighteenth centuries, Istanbul claimed a population of some four hundred thousand inhabitants. The capital of the Ottoman Empire since 1453, it was by turns the glory and despair of its rulers and peoples. More than once in the early modern era it seemed ungovernable. The city drew men and women from every province as well as from beyond the empire's borders. It was cosmopolitan by early modern standards but no melting pot. Migration to Istanbul was life changing for most new arrivals, but it did not change everything. Living in the city was seldom enough to erase distinctive origins and social demeanor or the attitudes that came with them. At many moments in its history, most of Istanbul's residents had been born elsewhere. Even when native to the capital, the majority were archetypal urban villagers. Urban in name, they remained intimately bound to rural associations and mores and to family members left behind in the home region. For residents of Istanbul, this most pluralistic of Continental European cities, getting on and getting along required competition and cooperation. The Ottoman state was concerned with choreographing both.

Istanbul underwent dramatic expansion between the fifteenth and sixteenth centuries. Thereafter, growth was more a matter of fits and starts. The interplay of rural flight and urban calamity saw to the more erratic pattern of the seventeenth and eighteenth centuries. Neighborhoods differed in their experience of

[1] İstM 2/184, fol. 150a (1156/1743).

Fig. 1. "Fountain and Market at Tophane [in Istanbul]." Julia Pardoe, *The Beauties of the Bosphorus* (London, 1838).

newcomers, affluence, poverty, and disorder. Most were economically mixed, with rich and poor living side by side, although economic stratification in the eighteenth century increasingly undermined that cohesion. Many neighborhoods reflected ethnic and confessional self-ghettoization. The city as a whole, however, had an overwhelmingly male appearance and sensibility. Men, the visible sex, dominated the streets, the markets, and the public buildings.

The residential home of the sultan and the seat of government, Istanbul was a company town, both the empire personified and the core domain of male rulership. That being said, the city's precise gender ratio in the seventeenth and eighteenth centuries is indeterminable.[2] The state's interests until the end of the nineteenth century lay in the empire's tax base and manpower potential. Its surveys counted economic households and male adulthood but not the gender distribution of the population.[3] In the absence of true censuses in the period of the study, it is difficult to know if men's demographic share was congruent with their cultural weight.[4] Their cultural weight was heavy indeed.

[2] The ratio of men to women was about five to four in 1844, according to figures given by J. H. A. Ubicini, *Letters on Turkey: An Account of the Religious, Political, Social, and Commercial Condition of the Ottoman Empire*... (1856; repr., New York, 1973), 1:24.

[3] The tax registers (*tahrirs*) occasionally recorded women, usually widows, who headed households.

[4] On Istanbul's population and migration patterns in the nineteenth century, see Alan Duben and Cem Behar, *Istanbul Households: Marriage, Family, and Fertility, 1880–1940* (Cambridge, U.K., 1991), 24–5; according to the (flawed) census of 1885, the city's population was 873,565

Over the centuries, waves of new arrivals, free men and women as well as forced settlers, many of them foreign captives, poured into the city. It was the influx of voluntary arrivals, however, that ensured Istanbul's megacity demographic. Foremost among these were young men. Many were poor and unmarried and remained so. Others cobbled together a living and established Istanbul families. Muslim migrants considered themselves especially fortunate if they secured employment within the ranks of officialdom or as protégés linked to individual officeholders. The grander the officeholder, the greater were the prospects for favor seekers. Non-Muslims (T., *zimmi*s, Ar., *dhimmi*s) looked for similar connections and protectors, especially among their own coreligionists, some of whom at the highest levels enjoyed the patronage of Muslim officials.

Both Muslim and non-Muslim migrants counted themselves decidedly unfortunate if they found themselves swept up in the regime's population-culling drives. Newcomers to the city, even those of some years' habitation, were sometimes expelled en masse, victims of periodic campaigns to reduce surplus labor and ease pressures on the capital's resources.[5] Very often it was Istanbul's policing capability that required relief, as migrant flows were predominately male, and male unemployment was an all-too-familiar trigger of urban unrest.

The successful migrant was a sponsored migrant. Newcomers who had kin, compatriots, or other willing patrons already residing in the city stood the best chance of making some small corner of the capital their own. Maintaining the health of one's supporting networks entailed demonstrations of loyalty as well as the willingness to act or stand attendance when called on. As Sabean found for Continental Europe, sub-subsistence was an all-too-common living standard in the period.[6] A majority of Istanbul's inhabitants were very likely engaged in a life-or-death struggle to secure their economic footing. Family solidarity, compatriot sponsorship, and other dependencies, vertical and horizontal, were not a lifestyle choice but the foundations of urban survival. Hierarchical attachments in particular held great promise for social promotion, but patrons could not always be found.

Sultan Mahmud II (1808–39), whose reign is famous for its alteration of Istanbul's social landscape, set about his reforms by abolishing the Janissary corps and remaking the Ottoman army in a new Western-looking image. Until 1826 and the destruction of the Janissaries in June of that year, Istanbul was distinguished, and chronically troubled, by its enormous military and paramilitary population.

(192). See also Ubicini, *Letters on Turkey*, 1:24; Kemal H. Karpat, *Ottoman Population, 1830–1914: Demographic and Social Characteristics* (Madison, Wis., 1985).

5 For these processes in the late eighteenth century, see Betül Başaran, "Remaking the Gate of Felicity: Policing, Migration, and Social Control in Istanbul at the End of the Eighteenth Century, 1789–1793," Ph.D. diss., University of Chicago, 2006.

6 David Warren Sabean, *Kinship in Neckarhausen, 1700–1870* (Cambridge, U.K., 1998), 97.

Thousands of active-duty soldiers and guardsmen were barracked in the capital and its suburbs. Their numbers were supplemented by several thousand irregulars, including pensioners and other formal and informal affiliates of the Janissaries, Bostancıs, and other imperial corps.[7] Contingents of soldiers functioned as police, shore patrol, and fire brigade. The Janissaries' monopolistic grip on vital municipal services compounded their political leverage as a corporate body and that of individual corpsmen as social actors. Over time, the economic lives of corps enrollees had become intermingled with the vocations and interests of shopkeeper commerce.[8] Many were themselves more tradesman than soldier. Not surprisingly, these kinds of civic and civilian linkages further enhanced the attractions of military affiliation for economically and socially hungry young men, whether or not they were new to the capital.

The three thousand or more young men studying in Istanbul's hundreds of religious colleges (*medreses*), whether part-time, full-time, or sometimes, constituted the empire's future religious leadership. As aspiring *ulema*, these students of Islamic jurisprudence and *shari'ah* law hoped to launch their careers by gaining appointments as entry-level *medrese* professors or religious-court judges (*kadıs*).[9] Career posts were at a premium, however. The number of students and unemployed graduates of the *medreses* by far exceeded available employment, even in the junior ranks. The majority of office seekers had to make do with the most meager postings, if they managed to stay in the profession at all. Many gave up the ghost and settled for whatever jobs they could find, selling something or assisting those who did. Until then, young diploma holders marked time in hopeful attendance on the senior men of the profession. Even greater numbers of youths waited for years just to take the diploma examination (*rüus imtihanı*).[10] Despite the shrinking of the empire's borders and the disappearance of the offices and benefices of lost or war-scarred provinces, the central system continued to swell with new graduates during the eighteenth century and through the reign of Mahmud II. In doing so, it made promises that it could not keep.

[7] *EI2*, s.v. "Istanbul," by Halil İnalcık, esp. 242–3; for an analysis of the social connections and paradoxes of the Janissaries in history and historiography, see Cemal Kafadar, "Janissaries and Other Riffraff of Ottoman Istanbul: Rebels without a Cause?" in Baki Tezcan and Karl K. Barbir, eds., *Identity and Identity Formation in the Ottoman World: A Volume of Essays in Honor of Norman Itzkowitz* (Madison, Wis., 2007), 113–34.

[8] Donald Quataert, "Janissaries, Artisans and the Question of Ottoman Decline, 1730–1826," in Donald Quataert, ed., *Workers, Peasants and Economic Change in the Ottoman Empire, 1730–1914* (Istanbul, 1993).

[9] Madeline C. Zilfi, "The *İlmiye* Registers and the Ottoman *Medrese* System Prior to the Tanzimat," in J.-L. Bacqué-Grammont and P. Dumont, eds., *Collection Turcica III: Contributions à l'histoire économique et sociale de l'Empire Ottoman* (Louvain, 1983), 309–27.

[10] On educational bottlenecks in the eighteenth century particularly, see Mehmed Raşid, *Tarih-i Raşid* (Istanbul, 1282/1865), 4:47–51; Küçük Çelebizade İsmail Asım, *Tarih-i Asım*, vol. 6 of Raşid, *Tarih-i Raşid*, 603–5; Tatarcık Abdullah, "Nizam-i Devlet hakkında Mütalaat," *TOEM*, no. 41 (1332/1916–17), 272–3.

Ulema and would-be *ulema* rivaled the military in terms of corporate interests and political influence, if not in sheer numbers. *Ulema* hierarchs, who oversaw personnel and promotions, were the official religious career's chief beneficiaries. Those at the pinnacle of the profession – the grand muftis, or *şeyhülislam*s, the chief justices of the army (*kadıasker*), and city judges – were first-line recipients of the career's direct compensations. They also had priority claim on its stock of patronage. Through supernumerary appointments and emoluments, they kept relatives and clients dependent, if not economically whole. Individual students and novice *ulema* – typically young men from adolescence to their midtwenties – were a source of political and personal support for their career superiors. Collectively, they were also a potential source of opposition.

As in the case of soldiery in the pre-Mahmudean, Janissary-dominated military order, the status of student (*danişmend*) carried with it official standing and a certain social dignity. Apart from scions of the great *ulema* families, however, students were penurious almost by definition. They also lacked the coercive means available to armed soldiers. Students, nonetheless, possessed a certain power of numbers. Depending on the issue at hand, they could tap into like-minded social elements, many of which represented family or compatriot connections and related social networks. Residential clustering in the *medrese*s and boarding houses (*bekâr odaları*) of Istanbul's Old City neighborhoods facilitated students' capacity for rousing their fellows to collective action. At various times in the early modern era, with and against their own *ulema* leadership, activists mobilized the student population to help topple an unpopular vizierial regime. Sometimes, alongside the Janissaries and other strategic allies, they threatened the sultan himself.

In everyday urban life, the men of the *medrese*s tended to be a conservative force. Their vocational commitment to the study of Islamic law and the sclerotic *medrese* curriculum inclined them toward that disposition. Nonetheless, study of the law did not guarantee hidebound conservatism in every regard. Nor can it be said that *ulema* circles as a whole, or even the *ulema* elite, embraced one and the same politics. Throughout the eighteenth and nineteenth centuries, some of the most distinguished members of the various reform parties were products of the *medrese*.[11] Still, much of the support for conservatism regarding gender relations and the position of the non-Muslim minorities could be found among *medrese* students and in the ranks of their *ulema* teachers and mentors. *Shari'ah* law provided an ideological framework for the opposition to much social change. When the static premises of Islamic jurisprudence, as taught in the *medrese*s, were coupled with the students' and religious

[11] Uriel Heyd, "The Ottoman 'Ulemā and Westernization in the Time of Selīm III and Maḥmūd II," *Scripta Hierosolymitana* 9 (1961): 63–96; Şerif Mardin, *The Genesis of Young Ottoman Thought: A Study in the Modernization of Turkish Political Ideas* (1962; repr., Syracuse, N.Y., 2000), 216–18.

supernumeraries' chronic economic vulnerability, the likelihood of their opposition to religious egalitarianism and democratizing trends increased. It does not surprise that the sultanic and vizierial proponents of social laws – particularly laws regulating consumption practices and the social position of women and the non-Muslim minorities – could avail themselves of the manpower as well as the vocabulary of religious institutions.

Despite Istanbul's immense size – the most populous city in Europe and West Asia for much of the early modern period – as well as its multiple ethnicities and religions and the daily traffic of thousands of residents and sojourners, urban mayhem was remarkably rare. Official posts and emoluments proliferated in the seventeenth and eighteenth centuries. Most of these opportunities fell to Istanbul's inhabitants. Although helping to contain some of the forces of urban instability, they were ultimately unable to keep up with demand. They had an even less salutary effect on the provinces, more and more of whose revenues were diverted to the capital's special interests. The practice of collective liability for the behavior of one's fellows – guildsmen, neighbors, coreligionists, and the like – accelerated the detection of crimes and social misdeeds and helped stave off disturbances.[12] The dispersion of policing responsibilities to neighborhood notables complemented the vigilance of ordinary residents. Through its own civilians, Istanbul achieved a level of intercommunal quiet that was rare elsewhere in Europe.

Ottoman social norms, the general adherence of its urban populations to differentiating rules of apparel, deference, address, and comportment, were the product of communal conditioning and state regulation. The absence of a clear-cut distinction between offenses against Islamic law (*shari'ah*) and offenses against custom and usage also opened up pliable space for state intervention in the interests of the prescribed social order.

Seeing like the Ottoman state

The empire's fading international position in the seventeenth and eighteenth centuries forced a readjustment of the rationales underlying state claims to legitimacy. The affirming role of military imperatives, particularly in the form of expansionist expeditions against neighboring states, lost its luster after the seventeenth century. Expansion had become a practical impossibility in any case. The military dynamic increasingly gave way to a more internalist vision of dynastic legitimacy and of the central elites' role in the legitimation

[12] Abdullah Saydam, "Kamu Hizmeti Yaptırma ve Suçu Önleme Yöntemi Olarak Osmanlılarda Kefâlet Usûlü," in Kemal Çiçek and Abdullah Saydam, *Kıbrıs'tan Kafkasya'ya Osmanlı Dünyasında Siyaset, Adalet ve Raiyyet* (Trabzon, 1998), 98–115; Tahsin Özcan, "Osmanlı Mahallesi Sosyal Kontrol ve Kefalet Sistemi," *Marife* 1, no. 1 (2001): 129–51; *EI2*, s.v. "Kafāla," by Y. Linant de Bellefonds; Ferdan Ergut, *Modern Devlet ve Polis: Osmanlı'dan Cumhuriyet'e Toplumsal Denetimin Diyalektiği* (Istanbul, 2004), 48–54, 86–104.

project.[13] In the eighteenth century, as foreign enemies ate away at the empire's territories, the state's diminished martial stature was offset by a compensatory investment in the domestic order and the empowering authority of social control.[14]

The empire was, on many levels, conceived as domestic space. As nonforeign, nonalien terrain, its allocation in the form of governorships, service fiefs (*timar*s), and philanthropic benefices (*vakf*s) was, in theory at least, the prerogative of the ruling sultan. The capital itself was a uniquely branded sovereign property. Istanbul was more narrowly domestic – the more so as the empire continued to contract in the eighteenth century and thereafter – as it was home to the imperial family. The Ottoman dynasty was, after all, a family that ruled an empire on three continents, yet possessed no real residential house or home outside of Istanbul and its environs. The palace and lodges of Edirne and the palace-villas of the Bosphorus and Golden Horn, even when not the usual flimsy kiosks, were still in Istanbul's backyard.

Istanbul was effectively the province, the personal fiefdom, of the sultan.[15] His was an overarching dynastic household governed by sultanic dictate, *shari'ah* prescription, and male priority. The capital, the throne room of the empire, increasingly came to embody the imperial system's first and last line of defense against enemies inside and out. The punctilios of personal and public comportment, the dos and don'ts of intercommunal contact, and the rules and roles of the Ottoman gender system were devised mainly within the capital. They were certainly most closely watched there. The Ottoman way was often really, and sometimes merely, Istanbul's practice. Although the language of social order had always been an important component of Ottoman legitimation, in the eighteenth century it assumed pride of place in sultanic discourse. The regime literally and figuratively retreated from conquest to defense of the realm.[16]

The imperial social formation that the rulership sought to secure, and the relationships of power that it tasked itself to reproduce, were formulated in agonistic terms. They represented more theory than fact, although they were widely held to be, or to have been in some golden past time, reality. Their significance lies in their recurring invocation and enduring appeal in these early modern centuries, when their terms were most sharply contested.

13 The term, though not the application of "seeing like the state," is borrowed from James C. Scott, *Seeing Like a State: How Certain Schemes to Improve the Human Condition Have Failed* (New Haven, Conn., 1998).

14 Madeline C. Zilfi, "A *Medrese* for the Palace: Ottoman Dynastic Legitimation in the Eighteenth Century," *JAOS* 113, no. 2 (1993): 190–1.

15 Nora Seni's important study, "Ville ottomane et représentation du corps feminin," *Les Temps Modernes* 41 (1984): 66–95, argues that "public" space was in fact conceived of as an extension of the ruler.

16 See the introduction and individual articles in Hakan T. Karateke and Maurus Reinkowski, eds., *Legitimizing the Order: The Ottoman Rhetoric of State Power* (Leiden, 2005); see also Zilfi, "A *Medrese* for the Palace," 184–91.

Five broad dualities or polarities both prescribed and purported to describe the lineaments of the well-ordered society. In each pair, differences were construed hierarchically. The alleged inferiorities or inabilities of one member of the pair served to justify its subordination, and in some interactions its subservience, to the other. The rationales behind the discriminations varied not only between pairs but, in historical terms, also in the context of particular crises or exigencies. In general, justifications relied on a mix of Islamic religious principles, reflecting the more expansive formulations of *shari'ah* law rather than the Qur'an by itself, as well as on custom and the legislative rulings (*kanun*s) of the sultans .

In the first and most comprehensive of these dualities, classical Islamic theorists posited for the world at large a religio-political portrait of worldly space. Lands under non-Muslim dominion, styled the "Abode of War" (*Dar el-Harb*), were held to be subordinate to the superior "Abode of Islam" (*Dar el-Islam*). The latter term denoted Muslim-ruled territories, particularly those under Sunni Muslim governance. The epitome of Sunni governance in the early modern era, as even its rivals conceded, was the Ottoman Empire. A premise of hostile or conflictual difference underlay the demarcation of a Muslim interior and non-Muslim exterior. Although Shiite Iran was periodically depicted as a non-Muslim entity, the representation came and went according to the degree of belligerence between the two states.[17] The quintessential non-Muslim powers in the period were the Christian states of Europe and Russia.

Like all prescriptions of stark difference, the worldly bifurcation between a realm of warfare and a realm of peaceful rule was more a rhetorical strategy than a grounded practice. Indeed, the concept of a third way, the Abode of Peace, or Conciliation (*Dar el-Sulh*), offered ideological reinforcement for the Ottomans' essentially pragmatic foreign policy throughout their history.[18] Like their counterparts in the Islamic past, Ottoman leaders over the centuries treated conflict with one or another non-Muslim power as entirely consonant with the divinely ordered scheme of things. However, war was not universally regarded as necessary or inevitable.[19] There were always peace parties as well

[17] See Karen M. Kern, "The Prohibition of Sunni-Shi'i Marriages in the Ottoman Empire: A Study of Ideologies," Ph.D. diss., Columbia University, 1999, regarding the Ottoman ban on Sunni-Shiite marriage as evidence for the enduring importance of the Sunni-Shiite divide; on this point and on the ambiguities in Ottoman-Shiite relations with regard to enslavement practices, see Chapter 4 in this volume.

[18] Cemal Kafadar, *Between Two Worlds: The Construction of the Ottoman State* (Berkeley, Calif., 1995), 79–80; Frederick M. Denny, *Islam and the Muslim Community* (San Francisco, 1987), 11; Khaled Abou El-Fadl, "The Use and Abuse of 'Holy War,'" review of *The Holy War Idea in Western and Islamic Traditions*, by James Turner Johnson, *Carnegie Council Resource Library*, at http://www/cceia.org/viewMedia.php/prmID/216; although for the more bifurcated view, see Rifa'at 'Ali Abou-El-Haj, "Ottoman Attitudes toward Peace Making: The Karlowitz Case," *Der Islam* 51 (1974): 131–7; Viorel Panaite, *The Ottoman Law of War and Peace: The Ottoman Empire and Tribute Payers* (New York, 2000), 486–7.

[19] Virginia H. Aksan, *An Ottoman Statesman in War and Peace: Ahmed Resmi Efendi, 1700–1783* (Leiden, 1995), 195–200; see also Aksan, "Ottoman Political Writing, 1768–1808," *IJMES* 25 (1993): 53–69, regarding the changing use of classical postulates.

as war parties among Ottoman decision makers. The power of the paradigm nonetheless lay in its uncomplicated us-versus-them psychological appeal. In dark times, its deep popular resonance made it a potent instrument for mobilizing public opinion.

Inside the empire, differences in religion, gender, and estate supplied the raw materials with which social stratification was fashioned. In the logic of the second dualism, the sovereignty of Islam as the true faith and official religion of the empire achieved practical reality in Muslims' positioning as the social as well as the moral superiors of non-Muslims. In the architectural plan of the capital, the city's highest elevations were crowned by mosques endowed by the Ottoman sultans. In the social ordering of the populace, Muslim preeminence and the symbolic place of the ruler were inscribed on the material environment. A hierarchized allocation of status goods and appurtenances – not all goods by any means but those designated for the Muslim ruling classes – signified Muslim privilege, even though poor Muslims could not have afforded their cost. In most quotidian interactions, however, the duality of Muslim and non-Muslim was a matter of small differences rather than clear-cut superior-inferior ranking.

Apart from state injunctions regarding appropriate Muslim and non-Muslim attire, each of the individual religious communities, Muslim, Christian, and Jewish, laid claim to its own historically preferred garb, modes of address, foodways, and family systems, among other distinctions. Each community was also able to exercise near-complete self-regulation in its religious and civil affairs through its own religious leadership.[20] The several religious leaderships were as interested as was the central state, arguably more so, in the maintenance of communal boundaries.[21] Visual distinctions helped to reify identities where doctrinal debates were not everyday conversation. Dissimilarities of dress and comportment denoted the boundaries of the different confessions. For Muslim and non-Muslim religious leaders, their daily livings and the promise of the hereafter depended on the religious conformity of their flocks. Sartorial demarcations gave color and shape to the communicants and community that religious shepherds were struggling to preserve.

In the third assignment of social value and place, the predominately Muslim *askeriye*,[22] the ruling order of civil, religious, and military officials and their dependents (*askeri*s), stood in a superior relationship to *reaya*, the

[20] For an introduction to the operation and limitations of confessional autonomy, see Benjamin Braude and Bernard Lewis, eds., *Christians and Jews in the Ottoman Empire: The Functioning of a Plural Society* (New York, 1982); also Molly Greene, ed., *Minorities in the Ottoman Empire* (Princeton, N.J., 2005); Daniel Goffman, "Ottoman *Millet*s in the Early Seventeenth Century," *New Perspectives on Turkey* 11 (1994): 135–58.

[21] Abraham Marcus, *The Middle East on the Eve of Modernity: Aleppo in the Eighteenth Century* (New York, 1989), 41–3.

[22] In the centuries that are the focus of the present study, *askeri*s almost always were Muslims, but this was not always the case; see Halil İnalcık, *The Ottoman Empire: The Classical Age 1300–1600* (London, 1973), 69–114; İ. Metin Kunt, "Transformation of *Zimmi* into *Askerî*," in Braude and Lewis, *Christians and Jews*, 1:55–67.

Ottoman equivalent of commoners. The *reaya* comprised folk whose livelihoods, through their own labor or that of their guardians, derived from nonofficial, nongovernment occupations. *Reaya* numbers included the wealthy, the penniless, and every stratum in between, although most were impoverished or nearly so. They were mainly male and female peasants, but also pastoralists and town dwellers. Some *reaya* made a handsome living as merchants, manufacturers, seafarers, and herdsmen; Ottoman subjects did not have to be Muslims or government employees to possess large houses and incomes and to have slaves and servants to labor for them.

Reaya were also of all religions – although by the nineteenth century, the term had come to be applied almost exclusively to non-Muslims, especially Christians. Ottoman conceptions of a circle of equity in the governance of human affairs posited reciprocity and interdependence between *askeri*s, officers of the state (literally "the military"), who in their lay or religious capacities defended faith and realm, and *reaya*, who produced wealth through the mundane labors of farm, pastureland, and city.[23] Like the European maxim, "'the priest prays, the knight defends, the peasant works,'"[24] the Ottoman construct underscored the interdependency and necessity of fixed social roles. As with lord and peasant in Europe, the complementarity of social estates did not constitute a relationship of equality. For the fulfillment of each estate's role in the Ottoman model, the direction of authority and coercion led from the *askeri*s to the *reaya*, and not vice versa.

The distinction between the official and common social orders entailed different compensations as well as different functions. *Askeri*s were entitled to certain tax exemptions and to social preferment. This last included, for office-holding *askeri*s in the highest ranks, rights of command. For *askeri*s generally, as representatives of imperial authority and favor, there was also an expectation of, if not a right to, deference from *reaya*. For *reaya*, whose nonofficial vocations earned them their commoner designation, liability to taxation and circumscribed social latitude were their lot so long as they were counted as *reaya*.[25]

As a product of the state's imagination, the *askeri-reaya* divide did not carry the force of religious sanction. It had no scriptural foundation, nor did it have the advantage of reflecting consistent social reality. Rather, it represented a fiscal mapping of society's taxable and nontaxed elements. Its principal purpose was to regulate the two identities to ensure a complement of

[23] Mardin, *Genesis*, 95–102; Gottfried Hagen, "Legitimacy and World Order," in Karateke and Reinkowski, *Legitimizing the Order*, 65–6. Among the individuals who were not public officials in the strict sense but received exemptions, government stipends, and *askeri* standing were descendants of the Prophet Muhammad, although any descendant might also be *askeri* by dint of office holding in the military or *ulema*.

[24] Qtd. in Michael Mann, *The Sources of Social Power* (Cambridge, U.K., 1986–), 1:384.

[25] Halil İnalcık, "Osmanlılarda Raiyyet Rüsûmu," *Belleten* 23 (1960): 575–610; Ahmet Mumcu, *Osmanlı Devletinde Siyaseten Katl* (Ankara, 1963), 55.

reaya – producers of goods, services, and revenues – sufficient for the provisioning of the empire. "Provisioning" the empire meant sustaining society's interdependent components. The health of the productive *reaya* sector secured the upkeep of the ruling elements – soldiers, statesmen, bureaucrats, and Muslim and non-Muslim religious functionaries – who were thereby enabled to fulfill their requisite roles.

In this visionary universe of Ottoman theory, "the Sultan's subjects were divided into two separate classes (*sınıf*) . . . the ruling class . . . and the lower class, completely under their authority."[26] As social description, the very tidiness of a two-class model is suspect. The legal-administrative boundary between *askeri* and *reaya* disguised a more complicated and fluid reality. A rigid divide was untenable as living practice, much less heritable practice, given the social and geographical mobility that, in many periods, characterized Ottoman society.

Perhaps more than anything, the nightmarish death tolls and premature mortality of the early modern era made cradle-to-grave assignments of social place impossible, even undesirable, to uphold. According to many commentators, careers open to talent were in any case part of the Ottoman social ethic. In the view of the sixteenth-century Habsburg envoy Ogier de Busbecq, the sultan "pays no attention to wealth or the empty claims of rank" when selecting officials.[27] Although Ottoman recruitment was not the wide-open meritocracy that Busbecq imagined, countless children and grandchildren of taxpaying subjects, Muslim and even non-Muslim, ascended to *askeri* status over the centuries. Some fought, some studied, and some married their way into the entitled ranks. Most probably did so with a hand up from insider patrons. Social recruitment had to be flexible for the empire to replenish its leadership ranks in the wake of death and disaster.[28] The paradox of sponsored mobility, of course, lay in the authorities' own ambivalence. Again and again in the seventeenth and eighteenth centuries, the state had to have recourse to *reaya* males to meet its military and other personnel needs. As the evidence of the memorialist literature makes clear, however, it did so all the while insisting that the *reaya* population remain in its place. The seventeenth-century sage Koçi Bey observed that if commoners acquired a taste for bearing weapons and riding on horseback, they would never go back to being simple *reaya*.[29]

26 Attributed to Grand Vizier (Mehmed) Fuad Pasha (d. 1869), in [Grégoire] Aristarchi Bey, *Législation ottomane, ou, recueil des lois, règlements, ordonnances, traités, capitulations et autres documents officiels de l'Empire Ottoman* (Constantinople, 1873–88), 2:25, qtd. in Gökçen Alpkaya, "Tanzimat'ın 'Daha az Eşit' Unsurları: Kadınlar ve Köleler," *OTAM* 1, no. 1 (Haziran 1990), 1. Fuad Pasha was seeking to describe the imperial political order as it existed before the nineteenth-century reforms that he helped put in place.

27 Ogier Ghislen de Busbecq, *Turkish Letters* (London, 2001), 39.

28 On the exceptionalisms and ambiguities underlying tax exemptions and *askeri* status conferral in practice, see Hülya Canbakal, *Society and Politics in an Ottoman Town: 'Ayntāb in the Seventeenth Century* (Leiden, 2007), 63–76.

29 Zuhuri Danışman, ed., *Koçi Bey Risalesi* (Istanbul, 1972), 7.

But as his own testimony makes clear, many had done exactly that and others were pursuing the same course.

The passage of individuals from *reaya* to *askeri* status, even when under state or elite sponsorship, troubled those who swore by the efficacy and rectitude of dichotomy. Underlying much of the grumbling, however, were personal economic interests as much as high-minded principle. Insofar as the military-administrative and religious elites were concerned, the diluting effect of unregulated mobility was the bugbear of those already in the fold. The privileged were particularly worried that they would not be able to bequeath their status to their offspring. Without it, their sons faced the challenges of a level playing field and competition from talented outsiders. The inroads of variously defined outsiders – provincials, Turkish and Kurdish villagers, those without ties to the current Istanbul elite – were a recurring complaint of political memorialists (Koçi Bey among them) and chroniclers as well. The musings of the Istanbul literati on the state of the empire literally underwrote the legitimacy of social hierarchy, as well as the literati's own place within it.[30]

The *askeri-reaya* duality was further belied by the state's own legal and fiscal practice. Various nonelite groups and individuals occupied a medial status between the two supposed legal poles. By serving in semiofficial capacities, carrying out tasks in support of one or another state function, they became "privileged *reaya*."[31] Although the presumptive *askeri* was Muslim as well as male, some non-Muslims shared in the elite's perquisites. Among these official exceptions were Muslim and Christian *reaya*, villagers and city dwellers, who guarded and maintained frontier outposts. Christians and Jews who served as volunteer firefighters in fire-prone Istanbul occupied a similar place. Such individuals, when recognized by the state, enjoyed some tax forgiveness, though not the remaining complement of *askeri* prerogatives.[32] The Greek Orthodox overseers of Ottoman Moldavia and Walachia enjoyed princely stature and

[30] Rifaat Abou Hadj [Rifa'at 'Ali Abou-El-Haj], "The Ottoman Nasihatname as a Discourse over 'Morality'," in Abdeljelil Temimi, ed., *Mélanges Robert Mantran* (Zaghouan, 1988), 26–8, and his *Formation of the Modern State: the Ottoman Empire Sixteenth to Eighteenth Centuries* (Albany, N.Y., 1991), 58.

[31] For the term and its usage, see Colin Heywood, "A *Buyuruldu* of A.H. 1100/A.D. 1689 for the Dragomans of the English Embassy at Istanbul," in Çiğdem Balım-Harding and Colin Imber, eds., *The Balance of Truth: Essays in Honour of Professor Geoffrey Lewis* (Istanbul, 2000), 125–44. For specific kinds of exemptions, see Canbakal, *Society and Politics*, 63–8; Linda T. Darling, *Revenue-Raising and Legitimacy: Tax Collecting and Finance Administration in the Ottoman Empire, 1550–1660* (Leiden, 1996), 83.

[32] For examples and disputes regarding these roles, see Osman Yıldırım, Vahdettin Atik et al., eds., *83 Numaralı Mühimme Defteri (1036–1037/1626–1628): Özet, Transkripsiyon, İndeks, ve Tıpkıbasım* (Ankara, 2001), 18, 23–4, 81–2; see also Charles White, *Three Years in Constantinople, or Domestic Manners of the Turks in 1844* (London, 1846), 1:24; Halil İnalcık with Donald Quataert, eds., *An Economic and Social History of the Ottoman Empire, 1300–1914* (Cambridge, U.K., 1994), 660–1; and Gülnihâl Bozkurt, *Gayrimüslim Osmanlı Vatandaşlarının Hukukî Durumu, 1839–1914* (Ankara, 1989), 23.

wealth as the sultan's deputies.[33] Christian and Jewish religious figures, including students and acolytes, were typically exempted from taxation. In addition, the most senior non-Muslim exemplars, among them the Greek Orthodox patriarch and members of the city's rabbinical council, enjoyed dignifying marks of status as appointees and representatives of the sultan's authority.

And then there were the local non-Muslims employed by the various foreign embassies now resident in the capital. Technically, local diplomatic employees remained subjects of the Ottoman Empire. However, their employment afforded them diplomatic privileges, including exemption from local laws and taxes. Men serving as dragomans (*tercüman*), embassy translators, along with their "sons and servants" constituted a troubling hybridity in the eyes of their fellow Ottomans, including their own coreligionists. These holders of diplomatic patents (*berat*s), born and/or bred in the Ottoman Empire, continued to make their homes and livelihoods in the empire's bounds. Yet as patentees, they walked among their fellow subjects immune from the legal and fiscal impositions of the homeland.[34]

Low-status and ill-paid Muslim functionaries – untitled government clerks, soldiers, and novice *ulema*, among others – were functionally *askeri*, but in material and social condition, they were worlds apart from their moneyed and empowered *askeri* superiors. Moreover, they lacked the wherewithal to compete in concrete terms with affluent *reaya*, whether Muslim, Christian, or Jewish. Economic distinctions, always a bitter pill to swallow, were all the more so if the rich were not generous or if they were perceived as not of one's own kind. If occupants of the low *askeri* ranks hoped to transform theoretical superiority into palpable social power, they would have to acquire material or symbolic means to combat competing marks of distinction.

The line between slave and free constituted the fourth of the binaries by which the distribution of social power was in theory calculated. The line was carefully drawn as a matter of legality. Slaves suffered different punishments from those levied on free persons, and crimes against them were weighed differently. Slaves were to be treated in a humane fashion, but the law permitted cruelties against them, including capture and enslavement; alienation from the parental family; and like insensible property, sale or transfer.[35] By law, the free were not subject to such handling, although free individuals were no strangers to dependency, social estrangement, and physical jeopardy. The core of the distinction was the slave's singular liability to the – on the

[33] H. A. R. Gibb and Harold Bowen, *Islamic Society and the West* (London, 1950–57), 1, pt. 1:168–73.

[34] Maurits H. van den Boogert, *The Capitulations and the Ottoman Legal System: Qadis, Consuls and Beratlıs in the 18th Century* (Leiden, 2005), 94–8, 112–15; *EI2*, s.v., "Imtiyāzāt – The Ottoman Empire," by Halil İnalcık; Salahi R. Sonyel, "The Protégé System in the Ottoman Empire," *Journal of Islamic Studies* 2 (1991): 56–66; Fatma Müge Göçek, *Rise of the Bourgeoisie, Demise of Empire: Ottoman Westernization and Social Change* (New York, 1996), 92–7.

[35] See Chapter 4 in this volume.

whole – unmediated will of another. As with the other paired categories, however, the distinction was not so clear cut in the actual social spaces in which slave and free encountered one another. But in contrast to the way in which the other pairs were formally represented, elite discourse was in itself inconsistent on the meaning of slavery and that which might constitute its opposite.

Literary production as well as official government pronouncements obscured as much as accentuated the line between free and unfree. In poetic convention, aristocratic patrons were portrayed as helplessly in thrall to slave beloveds. The amorous verse attributed to Sultan Süleyman I (1520–66), addressing his slave concubine Hurrem (Roxelana) as "my shah" and "my sultan" and himself as "your slave to command" and "your love's slave" are extravagant examples of the metaphor.[36] Inversions of a more concrete sort were the stuff of wartime dispatches, when high-placed Ottomans found themselves enslaved in foreign lands with their onetime slaves as their new keepers. Within the empire, former slaves whose owners had provided them with a trade or an endowment went on to become employers of the freeborn and sometimes owners of slaves themselves.[37]

Indeed, in the context of human relationships, the polarity between free and unfree was rarely articulated in absolute or even oppositional terms.[38] The dichotomy of pure difference was more commonly reserved for humankind's relationship to the divine, the absolute power of God with respect to God's creatures. Nonetheless, the connotations of divine absolutism, the suggestion of perfect mastery and perfect compliance, particularly in the idiom of lord/master vis-à-vis slave/servant, spilled over into other relationships, notably that of monarch to his subjects as well as Sufi sheikh to acolyte and owner to slave.

The master-slave usage was a cornerstone of Ottoman ideology. Its authority was reflected in Sultan Süleyman I's declaration, "I am the slave of God and sultan on earth."[39] Affirming the sultan's worldly posture, one that Süleyman's

36 "I am a slave [*bende*] at your command and you are shah and sultan to me"; Kanuni Sultan Süleyman, *Divan-i Muhibbi* (Istanbul, 1308/1890–1), 4, albeit using the genteel *bende* for "slave" or "absolute servant." For similar usage by Sultan Abdülhamid I in the eighteenth century, see M[ustafa] Çağatay Uluçay, *Padişahların Kadınları ve Kızları* (Ankara, 1980), 109. For other examples, see Talat S. Halman, *Süleyman the Magnificent Poet* (Istanbul, 1987), 30, 73. Walter G. Andrews and Mehmet Kalpaklı, *The Age of Beloveds: Love and the Beloved in Early-Modern Ottoman and European Culture and Society* (Durham, N.C., 2005), 140–4, offer a general discussion of these sorts of usages in Ottoman verse and learned literature.

37 Ron Shaham, "Masters, Their Freed Slaves, and the *Waqf* in Egypt (Eighteenth-Twentieth Centuries)," *JESHO* 43, no. 2 (2000): 162–88.

38 The representation of rulers and ruled in stark terms was nonetheless a recurring trope in political rhetoric, as in the Young Turk–era declaration, "We shall no longer be conquerors and slaves, but a new nation of freemen," qtd. in Ernest Edmondson Ramsaur, *The Young Turks: Prelude to the Revolution of 1908* (Princeton, N.J., 1957), 93, referencing a report by John Macdonald (*Turkey and the Eastern Question*).

39 "Ben Allah'ın kuluyım. Bu cihan mülkünde sultanım." See M[ihail] Guboglu, *Paleografia şi Diplomatica Turco-Osmană: Studiu şi Album* (Bucharest, 1958), 133 and 167, fac. 8. Cf. İnalcık, *Ottoman Empire*, 41, for a slightly different rendering.

successors also claimed, it laid down a behavioral model for the subject population. If the "sultan on earth" is God's slave/servant (*kul*), must not the sultan's subjects be slaves or servants to God? The prescriptive notion of subjects' servitude, even servility, was a keynote of Ottoman political rhetoric. It was a fixture of imperial decrees (*ferman*), in the sultan's direct address to and about his subjects, although in the case of orders to government officials, the language of slave/servant was juxtaposed with the formal titles and the honorifics that went with them.[40] The importance of the term *kul* and the difficulties of its meaning were underlined in the Imperial Command Lectures (*Huzur Dersleri*) of 1796, when *ulema* discussants of that year's Qur'anic selection spent a full two hours on that one word.[41]

Apart from scriptural debate, the seeming ambivalence of Ottoman discourse with regard to slave and free was not a function of blind inconsistency. Rather, it was tacit recognition of the instability of the slave condition. Given the high incidence of manumission in the Ottoman Islamic environment, slavery possessed – at least in the abstract, if not always in the eyes of slaves themselves – the appearance of impermanence. And, too, slavery was fundamentally relational. Being someone's slave did not mean being everyone's slave. The sultan's officials were, like his ordinary subjects, subservient to him whether or not they were actually enslaved persons. As representatives of his imperial person – again, whether or not they were actually enslaved persons – they were deputy sovereigns with respect to the ruled masses of lower and middling persons. Nonroyal owners likewise imparted something of their own class and status to their slaves and servants.

The use of the single, highly laden term *slave* (and its Indo-European cognates) is not entirely appropriate to Ottoman realities. Everywhere in the world that slavery existed, slaves' liabilities and vulnerabilities varied according to the wealth and temper of individual masters, the role of religious and state institutions, and the nature of employment, among other things. In the Ottoman Islamic case, nomenclature made for an added complication. The Ottomans had numerous terms for human property. The different terms that have come to be translated and understood as *slave* – *esir*, *abd*, *kul*, *bende*, *rıkk*, *köle*, *kölemen*, *kul*, *gulam*, *karavaş*, and *cariye*, among others – suggest some of the different legal conditions attached to one or another kind of owned being. The chapters that follow, however, argue that the theoretical and legal differences between them were far less significant – to the individual slave and to society as a whole – than the contingent practices that bound them to an owner, whether master or mistress and whether royal, elite, or common.

[40] For this point and a study of authoritarian discourse, see Gilles Veinstein, "La voix du maître à travers les firmans de Soliman le Magnifique," in Gilles Veinstein, ed., *Soliman le Magnifique et son temps* (Paris, 1992), 127–44.

[41] Ebül'ulâ Mardin, *Huzur Dersleri* (Istanbul, 1951–66), 1:74–5. See also İ. Metin Kunt, *The Sultan's Servants: The Transformation of Ottoman Provincial Government, 1550–1650* (New York, 1983), 41–2, on the practical usage of *kul* as "sultan's [male] servant."

In many regards, the most enduring yet paradoxically fragile social difference was that posited between men and women. Women's putative physical and moral weaknesses rendered them subject to men. As a general rule, women were economically dependent on men and derived their social position from their relationships to male family members. The wives and daughters of *askeri*s shared the status of their husbands and fathers. Unless women possessed wealth of their own and were of an age and disposition to remain unmarried, social expectations would have them bound to the authority of males, not only to obvious seniors like fathers and grandfathers but also to arguable compeers like husbands and brothers, and even to juniors, such as adult sons.

The view of women as dependent, lesser beings – a view rendered timeless by the official tendency to pronounce on a flawed, generic womankind (*taife-i nisvan*) – was taken for granted, in the air as it were. The weight of the designation in social relations and state policy derived from its wide discursive availability. It appeared in Qur'anic and *hadith* citations and sermons from the pulpit, as well as in poetry and everyday maxims.[42] One cannot know which Qur'anic and *hadith* passages regarding women consistently enjoyed most currency. There is little doubt, however, that decontextualized scriptural snippets played an important role in authorizing women's social marginalization. One of these was the Qur'anic verse calling on the wives of the Prophet Muhammad "to remain in your houses," an admonition commonly proposed for all women as a "model of emulation."[43] In the realm of popular sayings of uncertain provenance, "women are long of hair but short of brains" was a favorite period adage.[44] To be sure, popular literature's socially and ethnically more variegated company of bards and storytellers provided respite from high culture's misogynist drumbeat. Folk tales and popular verse allowed for worthy and spirited female figures, young and old, along with the usual crones and vixens.[45] The more negative formulations of the urban canon, however, have enjoyed the greater popular and historiographical recognition.

[42] Madeline C. Zilfi, "Muslim Women in the Early Modern Era," in Suraiya N. Faroqhi, ed., *The Cambridge History of Turkey* (Cambridge, U.K., 2006), 3:226–55; Leslie P. Peirce, *The Imperial Harem: Women and Sovereignty in the Ottoman Empire* (New York, 1993), 84, 179. On the need to deconstruct the notion of a monolithic Islamic opinion regarding women's place in society, see Maya Shatzmiller, *Her Day in Court: Women's Property Rights in Fifteenth-Century Granada* (Cambridge, Mass., 2007), 107–12, who argues that Islamic medical discourse was far more positive regarding women's sexual and legal personhood than were Islamic philosophical texts and Greek medical and philosophical texts.

[43] Barbara Freyer Stowasser, *Women in the Qur'an, Traditions, and Interpretation* (New York, 1994), 115–18; *The Koran Interpreted*, trans., A. J. Arberry (New York, 1955), 33:32–3.

[44] Ahmed Cevdet (Pasha), *Tarih-i Cevdet* (Istanbul, 1309/1891), 11:281; cf. Joseph von Hammer, *Geschichte des Osmanischen Reiches* (Pest, 1827–35), 7:317.

[45] Sarah Atış, "Telling Tales in the Mirror of Culture: A Comparison of Aarne Tale Type 709, 'Snow White,' and Eberhard-Boratav Tale Type 167, 'Nar Tanesi,'" Türk Dil Kurumu, *3. Uluslar Arası Türk Dil Kurultayı, 1996* (Ankara, 1999), 133–42; Mark Glazer, "Women Personages as Helpers in Turkish Folktales," in İlhan Başgöz and Mark Glazer, eds., *Studies in Turkish Folklore, in Honor of Pertev N. Boratav* (Bloomington, Ind., 1978), 98–109; İhsan Kurt, "Atasözlerinde Aile," in Ezel Erverdi, Hakkı Dursun Yıldız, İsmail Kara et al., eds., *Sosyo-Kültürel Değişme Sürecinde Türk Ailesi* (Ankara, 1992), 2:626–49.

The pervasiveness of misogynistic tropes across Europe as well as the East testifies to the potency and cultural suppleness of gendered metaphors. As in the Ottoman milieu among both Muslims and non-Muslims, in the Christian polities of Europe, the discourse of the flawed female was ubiquitous. Equally at home in scripture, exegesis, high verse, and doggerel, it had in fact gained new virulence in Europe's early modern era.[46] In both Ottoman society and Europe, the selfless labor, wisdom, mettle, and forbearance of flesh-and-blood women belied the incapacities ascribed to their gender. All in all, though, these counterexamples did little to dislodge sweeping negative stereotypes.

Like other designs of difference, the Ottoman gender hierarchy proved useful in more than one social setting. It was indispensable to those seeking justification for the exclusion of women from – among other honors and endeavors – public authority and the educational, vocational, and patronage pathways that led to it. However, in contrast to the slave/free or *askeri/reaya* dichotomies, the derogation of women and femaleness was more constant and more virulent in these later Ottoman centuries. Only the divide between Muslim and non-Muslim drew comparable fire in the period, but as will be discussed more fully in Chapter 2, the similarities between the two rhetorics are less revealing than the differences.

Not surprisingly, rigid gender hierarchization as social practice was difficult to sustain against the pressures of real-life events and psychologies. Not all families, much less all family decisions, hewed to patriarchal lines. In the bosom of the family, notions of male superiority could not always trump commonsense appraisals of female kin. Notwithstanding personal and individual adjustments of this sort, and with or without concerted state intervention to uphold the gender order, the discourse on women as lesser beings enjoyed bedrock longevity in the culture at large, serving the communal purposes of religio-political order and male primacy.

The institutionalization of female disadvantage through gender segregation, discriminatory labor practices,[47] physical sequestering and the exclusion of women from venues of publicly recognized authority, fell most heavily on young, marriageable women. The fecund female was essential to patriarchalism. Her sexuality nonetheless posed a threat to patriarchal order and its female-centered notions of honor, hence the institutionalization of male ownership of women's reproductive capacities through marriage and concubinage.[48] Still, adult men were not alone in profiting from the system. Senior

46 Olwen Hufton, *The Prospect Before Her: A History of Women in Western Europe* (1995; repr., New York, 1998), 28–61, 348; Bonnie S. Anderson and Judith P. Zinsser, *A History of Their Own: Women in Europe from Prehistory to the Present* (1988; repr., New York, 2000), 1:27–51, 67–84, 431–44; Judith M. Bennett, "Misogyny, Popular Culture, and Women's Work," *History Workshop Journal* 31 (1991): 166–8.

47 Madeline C. Zilfi, "Servants, Slaves, and the Domestic Order in the Ottoman Middle East," *Hawwa* 2, no. 1 (2004):1–33.

48 See Judith M. Bennett, "Women's History: A Study in Continuity and Change," *Women's History Review* 2, no. 2 (1993): 173–84; Pavla Miller, *Transformations of Patriarchy in the West, 1500–1900* (Bloomington, Ind., 1998); Gerda Lerner, *The Creation of Patriarchy*

women – senior by virtue of status, wealth, or age – were helpmates and in some circumstances coarchitects of gendered disadvantage. In more general terms, women usually came into their own as figures of authority with childbearing and with advanced age.[49] As they grew older, especially on the marriage of a son, they might be able to collect further on the "patriarchal bargain" that promised (though did not always deliver) male protection and financial support in return for female submissiveness.[50] Even if a son did not abide by patrilocal norms, if he was unable or unwilling to dwell with wife and children under the paternal roof, his mother presided over the younger and otherwise junior women of the family, including servants, slaves, daughters, and young female relatives. The power of most senior women derived from their relationship to senior males. Senior men and women together, however, shared in households and family regimes that relied on the cooperation and assent of both.

The enshrinement of male superiority retained its force throughout Europe and the Middle East. In the Ottoman East, however, the role of public authority in reifying notions of female incapacity and reproducing masculine bias was arguably more singular and powerful throughout the early modern era. The ways in which this was so – the discussion of which will be taken up more fully in subsequent chapters – raise a number of related questions. How, for example, are we to understand the imperial commitment to the prescribed gender order? In the context of an Ottoman commitment, in what particular regards, and under what conditions, were the central-state elites and elements of ordinary society supportive of women's subordination? How did women's subordinate position relate to the other dichotomies that informed Ottoman Muslim identity? What are the implications of Ottoman gender relations and gender politics for the social meaning of political reforms, given the latter's connotations of modernity and betterment? What inferences can we draw about the mind of the Ottoman reformer and the changing parameters of privilege, priority, and eventually rights in the emerging reform era of the nineteenth century?

Patriarchal patterns

The Ottoman fixation on social order and hierarchy was modeled on the durable image of the stern yet just patriarch-father. As the enthroned sultan mirrored divine authority, male heads of families and households drew strength and authorization from the religiously imbued example of the sovereign. The

(Oxford, 1986), on these points and on historical patriarchy generally; and see Chapter 4 in this volume.

49 On women's life stages and the exercise of power, see Leslie P. Peirce, "Seniority, Sexuality, and Social Order: The Vocabulary of Gender in Early Modern Ottoman Society," in Madeline C. Zilfi, ed., *Women in the Ottoman Empire: Middle Eastern Women in the Early Modern Era* (Leiden, 1997), 169–96.

50 Deniz Kandiyoti, "Bargaining with Patriarchy," *Gender and Society* 2, no. 3 (1988): 274–90.

Ottoman system of rule was not a full-blown, classical or biblical patriarchy investing the real or metaphorical father with the right to dispose of the property and persons in his all-powerful charge. The law, both *shari'ah* and sultanic *kanun*, mediated between householder and family, between subjects in their relations with each other, and most important between subjects and ruler. Variations in wealth also created alternative modes of distinction and routes to advantage. Nonetheless, the righteousness of paternal, and ultimately male, dominion was an embedded societal value.

Ottoman male dominion cannot be said to have constituted a single normative ideal unvarying across all landscapes and classes. One can speak of multiple patriarchal forms, each supportive of male priority in norms of social conduct, the distribution of power, and large and small habits of rule. Each, however, was differently inflected by the specifics of personal circumstance and historical time.[51] The high patriarchalism of the sultan and his deputies overshadowed and in most regards trumped the small dominion of the male peasant householder and his urban counterparts. The life circumstances of the common orders, deferential to their betters and often only nominally in charge of their own kin, bore little resemblance to the patriciate's suites of dependents, slave ownership, and emblematic goods. The distribution of wealth, the great unacknowledged in Ottoman prescriptions of social worth and privilege, in fact cut through and destabilized all of the prescribed polarities.

Despite the implied incongruence of dual or even multiple patriarchies, the variant forms were intimately related and derived meaning and possibility from one another. Each tapped into the same normative repertoire of religious and customary ideals of male priority and masculine virtue. Whether as hegemonic rulership or male-dominated familism, patriarchal modes were ultimately interdependent, each shoring up the other's claims to legitimacy and control.[52] Ordinary male heads of household – as well as those who aspired to be such – and male heads of state exercised authority over very different dominions. The one, however, was oxygen to the other.

The postulates of gender asymmetry in the context of the Muslim population underscored the universality and fundamental unity of male Muslim domination and advantage. The fraternalism and male comradeship entailed by the collective privileging of male Muslims were buttressed by males-only imperial ceremonies and audiences. They were further supported by male egalitarian worship in the mosques and by the spiritual and social brotherhood of Sufi affiliations. Male community, however, was always strained by real-life material and positional differences. Qur'anic tenets and Ottoman

[51] The discussion of patriarchal types draws from Deniz Kandiyoti, "Bargaining with Patriarchy"; Jeff Hearn, "From Hegemonic Masculinity to the Masculinity of Men," *Feminist Theory* 5, no. 1 (2004): 49–72; Sylvia Walby, *Theorizing Patriarchy* (Oxford, 1990).

[52] Hearn, "From Hegemonic Masculinity," 55–6. On the limitations of the distinction drawn by Weber and others between patrimonialism and patriarchalism, see James A. Bill and Robert Springborg, *Politics in the Middle East* (Boston, 1979), 151–2.

ruling principles were unequivocal regarding spiritual equality among all Muslims and social equality among Muslim males. However, economic and status differences argued for a different social story, as did individual family decision making.

For subjects of the empire who were male and Muslim, stratification within the Muslim community was perhaps most volatile in the juncture between religion and vocation. Male Muslims in high state office – the executive elite of viziers, metropolitan *kadı*s, bureau chiefs, military commanders, and the like – stood at the pinnacle of the Ottoman social hierarchy. As such, they had access to an enviable array of emoluments and privileges. Their lower-ranked and less remunerated counterparts partook of some of the same intangibles. However, they lacked the economic well-being of their betters and their horizons were more limited. They were unlikely to rise to grandee rank or security without luck and patronage. As for the tangibles of clothing, housing, and servants, the lower ranks also saw themselves as pitifully disadvantaged relative to wealthy Christians and Jews.

The professional and material disgruntlement of the lower ranks surfaced in the politicization of the underemployed and undercompensated in the various official careers. Such men were ripe for recruitment in popular demonstrations and upheavals. Their dissatisfactions were also a major force behind the confessionally charged tensions of the eighteenth and early nineteenth centuries. As a general rule, with respect to material security and legal position, men and women of the lower orders were at greater risk than the wealthy and the connected of either gender. Especially if they lacked patronage or direct membership in one of the official careers, they were also often at greater personal risk than wealthy Christians and Jews.

The extent to which the gender system's salutary effects were equally distributed across the male Muslim community's occupational groups and statuses is clearly open to question. The way in which particular women acquired stature and advantage through the system is even less straightforward. The chapters that follow are concerned with the social power of the male-female dichotomy, for its impact on women certainly but for its meaning to men's lives and masculine identity as well.

Despite official sanctioning, the five binaries were never fully substantiated, not when the Ottoman state was expanding in the fifteenth and sixteenth centuries, or in the eighteenth and nineteenth centuries, when Muslim lands and peoples were most beset. They are perhaps best understood as a stock of resonant imaginaries. They were available to those who believed them valid and essential, as well as to those whose credence was more contingent and opportunistic. In practice, they reflected a general though far-from-universal truth.

The boundaries laid down by the binary formulas constituted the backbone of moral programming. The contexts in which human interactions occurred, however, made for more ambiguity than bounded models could envision.

Overlaps and subcategories were always in play – the wealthy Christian or Jew might have Muslim employees and clients, the foreign slave concubine was often served by free natives, the wealthy widow had male as well as female dependents. Individual men's and women's relational statuses and social identities added fluidity and often unpredictability, not only to interactions between individual subjects but also to the conduct and expectations of officialdom and public in their moments of contact. If the eighteenth and nineteenth centuries' rhetorics of dissatisfaction are reflective of real change taking place in society, perhaps in earlier times, deviations and exceptions from idealized rules had occurred at tolerable levels. Or, a reassuring environment of imperial growth and self-confidence even into the seventeenth century had made them seem so.

The political ecology of the late eighteenth and early nineteenth centuries strained the old pieties to the breaking point. The disjunctures between norms and reality became more pronounced and increasingly more difficult to rationalize, although there is no denying that the old truths had staying power. Although they were an anchor for those who were unsettled by unsettled times, none survived intact through the crisis decades and reform era, and one or two arguably did not survive at all. The following three chapters consider the intersections of gender, slavery, and elite identity in the late eighteenth and early nineteenth centuries and suggest the new and old fault lines of social contestation in the emergence of Ottoman modernity.

CHAPTER 2

Currents of change

"It is well known that since my accession I have done my duty in accordance with the holy law and exerted myself to safeguard the subjects whom God has put in my charge."

– Sultan Mahmud II, June 1826[1]

"Infidel Sultan! God will punish you for your blasphemies. You have brought ruin on the world of Islam."

– Sheikh Saçlı, to Sultan Mahmud II[2]

A new world order

Ottoman subjects born in the early eighteenth century would have felt uneasy and very likely estranged had they been transported to the Ottoman world of the 1830s. Even Istanbulites accustomed to the capital's dynamic diversity; the ebbs and flows of its innumerable ethnic and confessional groups; the cavalcades of merchants, migrants, and foreign and home-grown freebooters, all of whom made Istanbul foreign and transient as much as domestic and urban, would have recognized that a shift in relations of power had occurred.

If the eighteenth-century Ottoman visitors lacked a clear sense of the empire's old territorial spread, they might have had difficulty fathoming the scale of Ottoman retrenchment in the early nineteenth century. From the atmosphere of disquiet and the impact of Muslim refugees and tales of gore from the Morea, the Danubian provinces, and eastern Anatolia, however, they would have soon understood that whole provinces had been lost without hope of recovery and that enemy armies were able to camp within miles of Istanbul. The increased presence and social assertions of Europeans in the capital and other imperial cities would have sounded additional alarms about the country's precarious footing. The new look of many Ottoman urbanites, Muslim and non-Muslim, male and female, offered striking evidence of the distance made by the passage of time. New clothing usages – the abandonment of

[1] Qtd. in Cevdet, *Tarih-i Cevdet*, 12:158.
[2] Qtd. in Recai G. Okandan, *Âmme Hukukumuzun Ana Hatları* (Istanbul, 1957), 63.

some, the adoption of others–including the European-style attire of Mahmud II, his ministers, and the new post-Janissary soldiery after 1826 – would have been jarring and inexplicable. Even Mahmud's own contemporaries could not entirely reconcile themselves to their trousers-clad, turbanless monarch. Like them, visitors had cause to wonder what the emperor's new clothes meant for the empire's Ottoman Islamic identity and for their own.

The period from the late eighteenth century through the mid-nineteenth century witnessed some of the most fateful events in the Ottoman Empire's some six hundred years. It competes with the high-tide century of the early empire, between the reigns of Mehmed II the Conqueror (1451–81), and Süleyman I the Magnificent (1520–66) – encompassing the Ottoman conquest of Constantinople (1453), the incorporation of the Arab lands (1517), and the first attempt on Vienna (1529) – with empire-changing events of its own. Among these, one can count the Treaty of Karlowitz (1699), marking the Ottoman shift to defense and diplomacy in relations with the European powers, the Russian seizure of Muslim Crimea (1774–83), the brief but portentous French occupation of Egypt (1798–1801), the Greek War of Independence (1821–9) and its Balkan domino effects, and the subsequent era of state reform and reconstruction under Mahmud II and his successors.

Headline political events underpin the preoccupations of Ottoman contemporaries and historians of later, postclassical Ottoman history. The contraction of imperial territory, resources, and autonomy between the late seventeenth century and the demise of the empire in 1918 is the core of those reflections. Signs of Ottoman economic weakness had been apparent to insiders and outsiders since at least the start of the eighteenth century. It was only after 1770 or so, though, that Europe could be said to dominate the commerce – if not yet the economy – of the Ottoman Mediterranean. The process by which the empire became a subordinate zone in a European-dominated world economic network was more rapid and thoroughgoing in some regions than in others. Modern historians continue to debate the application of dependency and semicolonization to the entirety of the empire. For the most part, though, they agree with the verdict of incorporation and with a chronology that places its definitive onset in the last quarter of the eighteenth century.[3]

Notwithstanding the importance of geopolitics, economy, and the empire-to-nation paradigm of Turkish history, a nonteleological view locates the big stories in domestic society between roughly 1750 and 1850 in the social

[3] For the Ottoman economy in these decades, see Mehmet Genç, "Ottoman Industry in the Eighteenth Century: General Framework, Characteristics and Main Trends," in Donald Quataert, ed., *Manufacturing in the Ottoman Empire and Turkey, 1500–1950* (Albany, N.Y., 1994), 59–86; Suraiya Faroqhi, *Subjects of the Sultan: Culture and Daily Life in the Ottoman Empire* (London, 2005), 225–7. See also Immanuel Wallerstein, *The Modern World-System II: Mercantilism and the Consolidation of the European World-Economy, 1600–1750* (New York, 1980); Reşat Kasaba, *The Ottoman Empire and the World Economy: The Nineteenth Century* (Albany, N.Y., 1988); Roger Owen, *The Middle East in the World Economy, 1800–1914*, rev. ed. (London, 1993).

and ideational currents of the period. Broad challenges to relationships of authority, expressions of individualism, the embrace of secularist principles of state formation and social identity and, toward the end of the period, the stirrings of a discourse of rights, shaped and were in turn shaped by the buffeted existence of the Ottoman state as empire. The articulation of the new ways of being and the contestation that these engendered established a dialectic of modernizing change and conservative resistance that would preoccupy succeeding generations as well.

Reforms and reformers

These transformative trends were most fully realized between the last decades of the nineteenth century and the demise of the Ottoman Empire in the early twentieth century. However, the period from the late eighteenth century to the mid-nineteenth represented an attitudinal and material point of convergence that made the advancement of Ottoman modernity possible. Historiographical treatments of the sultans Selim III (1789–1807) and Mahmud II depict them as the earliest, albeit imperfect, authors of the move toward a modernizing state. Selim is faulted for grand plans and political ineptitude, while Mahmud is credited with clearing away the old – for good or for bad – more than with establishing the new. Both, however, are distinguished from their predecessors as political reformers, builders of a constituency and a framework for the more sweeping changes that lay ahead.[4]

Most representations of the early reform period take their cue from the structural dimensions of the two rulers' policies, especially as they affected state institutions, relations with the West, and the status of non-Muslim peoples. Women and gender scarcely figure in their considerations. As the book seeks to show, however, concerns about women, masculinity, and power were dynamic components of this earliest stage in the reform era.

Sultan Mahmud, more than Selim, broke with the past. Although Mahmud is perhaps best known for the so-called auspicious event, the name given to the destruction of the politically murderous and, by 1826, militarily hopeless Janissary corps, his subsequent reforms took a more constructive turn. The empire's quasi-permanent embassies in European capitals became more widespread and genuinely permanent during his reign. Scores of students were dispatched to Europe to study. The first newspaper, the official *Gazette*

[4] On the two reigns, see Stanford J. Shaw, *Between Old and New: The Ottoman Empire under Sultan Selim III, 1789–1807* (Cambridge, Mass., 1971); Shaw, *History of the Ottoman Empire and Modern Turkey* (Cambridge, U.K., 1977), 1:217–79; Stanford J. Shaw and Ezel Kural Shaw, *Reform, Revolution, and Republic: The Rise of Modern Turkey, 1808–1975*, 2:1–54; see also Enver Ziya Karal, *Selim III'ün Hat-tı Hümayunları* (Ankara, 1946); Yaşar Şahin Anıl and Meltem Gencer, *Sultan İkinci Mahmut* (Istanbul, 2006); Erik J. Zürcher, *Turkey, A Modern History* (London, 1993), 23–51; Caroline Finkel, *Osman's Dream: The Story of the Ottoman Empire 1300–1923* (New York, 2005), 389–446.

Fig. 2. "A Scene in the Tcharchi [Covered Bazaar]." Julia Pardoe, *Beauties of the Bosphorus* (London, 1838).

of Events (*Takvim-i Vekayı*), began publishing. The Translation Bureau within the embryonic Ministry of Foreign Affairs and specialized civil and military academies were established to enhance the expertise and professionalism of state personnel.[5] The real aim of change, though, was survival. It was hoped that the new army and a rationalized administration would prevent further foreign and domestic encroachments on imperial sovereignty and the authority of the central government.

The crushing of the Janissaries and uprooting of their political networks prepared the way for the cultivation of a loyal central leadership. There was irony in the Janissaries' fate, of course, because the original corps' slave composition had, for centuries, been thought to ensure that very loyalty. The Janissaries of the early days, it was said, had been utterly reliable. They had "from their youth been reared and nourished with the bread and salt of the sultan," and they returned the favor by giving their all "for the well-being of their sovereign."[6] Even in the sixteenth century, those days were gone. The decision to rid the empire of the Janissaries found broad support in the nineteenth century, but the implementation of the decision took a heavy toll in public confidence and elite stability.

The end of the Janissaries in 1826 was in fact a bloodbath. Deaths numbered in the thousands in the definitive assault on the Janissary barracks, and manhunts, exiles, and confiscations of property went on for weeks.[7] To rebuild confidence in the regime and especially to allay the fears of potential allies in the civil and military elites, Mahmud declared an end to the capricious executions that placed the upper echelons of public service at such a high risk. The elites' worries in that regard were not at an end, however. In 1837, the apparent execution of Mahmud's longtime favorite, the accomplished statesman Pertev Pasha, was a shocking reminder that the monarch's guarantees needed shoring up. That Pertev's death produced such consternation, however, signaled the change in expectations now stirring in the ruling orders.[8] It marked a sharp break from the submissiveness with which such falls from grace had been greeted in the past. Indeed, the condemned usually went to their deaths with remarkable sangfroid.

In a further nod to the concept of rights, Mahmud renounced the practice of arbitrary property seizures (T., *müsadere*; Ar., *musadara*).[9] Although the

[5] See Carter V. Findley, *Bureaucratic Reform in the Ottoman Empire: The Sublime Porte, 1789–1922* (Princeton, N.J., 1980), esp. 132–50.

[6] Yaşar Yücel, ed., *Kitâb-i Müstetâb* (Ankara, 1974), 8.

[7] Finkel, *Osman's Dream*, 434–40.

[8] On Mehmed Said Pertev Pasha, see Mardin, *Genesis*, 157–61, who views Pertev's death as a watershed in spurring officials to seek reassurances about their own security.

[9] Uriel Heyd, *Studies in Old Ottoman Criminal Law*, ed. V. L. Ménage (Oxford, 1973), 264; Rudolph Peters, *Crime and Punishment in Islamic Law: Theory and Practice from the Sixteenth to the Twenty-first Century* (Cambridge, U.K., 2005), 33; Karl K. Barbir, "One Marker of Ottomanism: Confiscation of Ottoman Officials' Estates," in Tezcan and Barbir, *Identity and Identity Formation*, 135–51; and *EI2*, s.v. "Maliyye," by Carter V. Findley.

Fig. 3. "Two Janissaries in Their Dress of Ceremony." Octavian Dalvimart, *The Costume of Turkey* (London, 1804).

practice was not rooted in Islamic law, estate confiscation was confirmed by administrative usage and the sultan's *kanun* decrees. As a matter of law and custom, confiscation was linked to the slave status of some state servitors and the right of the slave master – in this case, the sultan – to claim as his own the material possessions of his human property. Although the slave component of the ruling elites had not amounted to a majority even at the system's height in the sixteenth century, and the number of elite slaves as officials and soldiers declined further in the seventeenth and eighteenth centuries, the line between the sultan's free or freed servitors, on the one hand, and his designated slaves, on the other hand, became blurred in the face of the sultan's authority. Absolute obedience to the autocrat's will was expected of all state officials, whether legally free or slave. The entirety of military-administrative officialdom consequently took on some of the encumbrances of slave servility, including the uncertainty of estate accumulation.

In principle, only the estates of disgraced military and administrative officials were liable. However, when the treasury was particularly strained, pretexts could always be found for bending the rules. In the latter half of the eighteenth century and well into Mahmud's reign, imperial accountants were known to show up at the doors of those who had served the empire honorably, even heroically. When the august Grand Vizier Koca (meaning "the Great") Ragıb Pasha passed away in 1763, "peacefully and in good odor," his associates were tortured to reveal the whereabouts of his treasures.[10] Ragıb, the freeborn son of a free Muslim bureaucrat, fit none of the categories by which confiscations were usually justified. He, or rather his heirs and household, nonetheless fell victim to the predicament of the public servant as quasi slave.

With wars and state projects depleting the treasury in the late eighteenth century, the estates of wealthy private individuals, especially those with business ties to the government, were increasingly defined into vulnerability.[11] Rich estates deriving from government contracts could be chalked up to ill-gotten gains and legitimized as targets. Sultan Mustafa III (1757–74), a notorious abuser of the official caste, among other victims, was said to have regarded confiscations as a kind of rightful inheritance of monarchy. The Austrian internuncio considered Mahmud II to be operating on the same principle, despite Mahmud's pronouncements.[12] In fact, to varying degrees, the empire was pure patrimony to every sultan. When it suited their purposes, all forms of imperial wealth, such as the offices by which state officials amassed power and riches, were on loan and revocable. The reform era, beginning with Mahmud's midreign initiatives, altered that premise but only slowly and with deplorable setbacks.

The ban on confiscations was especially welcomed by the well heeled and well placed. Of these, the primary beneficiaries were the central government elites, but the monarchy was also served. For the military-administrative cadres who were the frontline victims of estate confiscation, the ban meant greater security for family wealth and status.[13] Insofar as the regime was concerned,

[10] Sir Henry Grenville, *Observations sur l'état actuel de l'Empire Ottoman*, ed. Andrew S. Ehrenkreutz (Ann Arbor, Mich., 1965), 46–7; [François] Baron de Tott, *Memoirs of Baron de Tott* (1785; repr., New York, 1973), 1, pt. 1:186–7; Ahmed Rasim, *Resimli ve Haritalı Osmanlı Tarihi* (Istanbul, 1326–30/1908–12), 2:912; *İA*, s.v. "Râgıb Paşa," by Bekir Sıtkî Baykal; Norman Itzkowitz, "Mehmed Raghib Pasha: The Making of an Ottoman Grand Vezir," Ph.D. diss., Princeton University, 1959. On the fall of once-favored Halil Hamid Pasha (executed in 1785), see Findley, *Bureaucratic Reform*, 102–3, 145–6; see also Hasan Yüksel, "Vakıf-Müsadere İlişkisi (Şam Valisi Vezir Süleyman Paşa Olayı)," *Osmanlı Araştırmaları* 12 (1992): 399–424. For sixteenth- and seventeenth-century examples, see Klaus Röhrborn, "Konfiskation und Intermediäre Gewalten im Osmanischen Reich," *Der Islam* 55, no. 2 (1978): 345–51.

[11] Regarding private estates and confiscations, see White, *Three Years*, 1:104–12; see also Göçek, *Rise of the Bourgeoisie*, 92. For non-Muslims in positions of trust, the risks were as great as for the Muslim officials whom they served; see, e.g., Thomas Philipp, *Acre: The Rise and Fall of a Palestinian City, 1730–1831* (New York, 2001), 159–63.

[12] Grenville, *Observations*, 45; Rasim, *Resimli ve Haritalı*, 2:904, 912; Mardin, *Genesis*, 158.

[13] Mardin, *Genesis*, 157.

the ending of arbitrary confiscations acted as a disincentive to corruption and to the elites' notorious dog-eat-dog infighting. It was intended to lay the groundwork for a more stable and merit-driven officialdom. Although the ban was occasionally violated by its own imperial maker, it was reaffirmed in the famous Gülhane Rescript of 1839, the document that set the stage for the Tanzimat reform era (1839–76). Together with the sultanic issuance known as the Reform Decree (Hatt-ı Hümayun) of 1856, Gülhane presaged the First Ottoman Constitution, promulgated in 1876.[14]

In the language of Gülhane, all Ottoman subjects, regardless of religion or station, were to be on an equal footing with respect to their possessions. "Every one shall possess his property of every kind, and may dispose of it freely, without let or hindrance from any person whatsoever." In the case of convicted criminals, dispossession was also recognized as a collective injustice: "[T]he innocent heirs of a criminal shall not be deprived of their hereditary rights as a result of the confiscation of the property of such a criminal."[15] The latter principle was applauded by those who had reason to worry about the slippery definition of criminality under authoritarian rule.

Although Sultan Mahmud's declaration a decade earlier had been aimed at government employees, the 1839 rescript issued by his son Abdülmecid I (1839–61) appeared to reach out to the realm. Gülhane's implementation was ultimately disappointing, but its egalitarian promise found new life in the Reform Decree of 1856.[16] The 1856 decree, also a product of Abdülmecid's reign, was a bolder version of its predecessor, beginning with its opening clauses: "The guarantees that have been promised and granted . . . in my Imperial Rescript read at Gülhane, and in accordance with the worthy Tanzimat, regarding the security of life, property, and the preservation of honor for all my imperial subjects, without exception, in every religion and sect, are hereby confirmed and reaffirmed."[17]

In the end, neither proclamation lived up to the high hopes placed in it, yet each provided significant openings in political and intellectual life. The role of the two in creating a more egalitarian society may have been only a qualified success, but they both inaugurated unprecedented debate on the meaning of freedom and the nature of political belonging. By enlarging the

[14] On the reforms and reform era, in addition to Mardin, *Genesis*, see İlber Ortaylı, *İmparatorluğun En Uzun Yüzyılı* (Istanbul, 1983); Roderic H. Davison, *Reform in the Ottoman Empire, 1856–1876*, 2nd ed. (New York, 1973); Şevket Pamuk, *A Monetary History of the Ottoman Empire* (Cambridge, U.K., 2000); *Tanzimat I: Yüzüncü Yıldönümü Münasebetile* (Istanbul, 1940); Zürcher, *Turkey*.

[15] J. C. Hurewitz, ed., *The Middle East and North Africa in World Politics: A Documentary Record*, 2nd rev. ed. (New Haven, Conn., 1975), 1:48.

[16] The uneven course of egalitarian reform is discussed in Carter V. Findley, "The Acid Test of Ottomanism: The Acceptance of Non-Muslims in the Late Ottoman Bureaucracy," in Braude and Lewis, *Christians and Jews*, 1:340–68; see also Roderic H. Davison, "Turkish Attitudes Concerning Christian-Muslim Equality in the Nineteenth Century," *AHR* 59 (1954): 844–64.

[17] Translated from the Turkish text at http://www.tbmm.gov.tr/kultur_sanat/yayinlar/yayin001/001_00_005.pdf. See also Hurewitz, *Middle East*, 1:65.

realm of communications and creating a constituency for reform, they also ensured that change, however it was defined, would remain at the center of public consciousness.[18]

The initiatives of the 1820s and 1830s that laid the foundations for the Tanzimat and its discourse of rights were pursued under a cloud of lost wars – against Greek separatists and their Great Power allies, and several times over against Russia and the rebellious Ottoman governor of Egypt, Mehmed Ali Pasha (d. 1849). The human and material ravages of warfare were grim in themselves, but most foreign embroilments also carried a price tag in costly commercial concessions. A particularly far-reaching example, the 1838 Anglo-Ottoman Convention of Balta Limanı, promised the ending of Ottoman monopolies and granted valuable free-trade privileges to Great Britain. The agreement helped secure British intervention against Mehmed Ali Pasha, though at the eventual cost of exposing already-precarious Ottoman producers to unbuffered competition.[19]

The "imperialism of free trade" all but guaranteed that the Ottoman Empire would be a dependent state in the age of European paramountcy.[20] In a sense, free trade was merely a – if not the – last straw in a century-long struggle over the widening social and economic impacts of European power. The French ambassador's boast in the 1780s that the Ottoman Empire had become "one of the richest colonies of France" was wishful thinking in more ways than one.[21] However, it exposed the trajectory of Ottoman economic well-being. The pressure of European manufacturing and commercial mechanisms, the displacement and downsizing of local production, the rising demand for European consumer goods, and official and popular responses to European and European-perceived patterns of consumption were recurring motifs in Ottoman domestic politics. They were earliest and most directly experienced in the urban environment, especially in coastal cities like the capital.

The new European empires made no secret of the partnership between commerce and flag. Where the European merchant ventured, his country's firepower was usually close behind. The sultans and ministers of the eighteenth century failed to see the writing on the wall for Ottoman economic independence. Various sultans combated what they could see of the problems facing the empire. Throughout the century, though especially from the 1770s

[18] Şerif Mardin, "Some Notes on an Early Phase in the Modernization of Communications in Turkey," *CSSH* 3, no. 3 (1961): 250–71.

[19] On these measures, see Şevket Pamuk, *The Ottoman Empire and European Capitalism: Trade, Investment, and Production, 1820–1913* (Cambridge, U.K., 1987), 18–21; *New Perspectives on Turkey*, no. 7 (1992), for its several articles on free trade. Regarding regional variations, see also Sarah Shields, "Take-Off into Self-Sustained Peripheralization: Foreign Trade, Regional Trade and Middle East Historians," *TSAB* 17, no. 1 (1993): 1–23.

[20] John Gallagher and Ronald Robinson, "The Imperialism of Free Trade," *Economic History Review*, 2nd ser., 6, no. 1 (1953): 1–15.

[21] Edhem Eldem, *French Trade in Istanbul in the Eighteenth Century* (Leiden, 1999), 259, citing Marie-Gabriel de Choiseul-Gouffier (d. 1817); cf. *EI2*, s.v. "Imtiyāzāt – The Ottoman Empire," by Halil İnalcık.

on, the death tolls and refugee flows of combat gave unique urgency to military reconstruction, or at least to a preoccupation with military matters. Eighteenth-century monarchs from Ahmed III (1703–30) to Selim III sought to put the military, particularly the land forces, on firmer footing. To the extent that the sultans of the time conceived of the economic at all, even the most distracted of them were impelled to address the symptoms, if not the causes, of an economy going wrong. Habituated to a moralistic optic, the autocracy trained its sights on borders and boundaries, especially the comings and goings of its subjects. There were significant differences among reigns, but to a man, the sultans of the period swore by the utility of social disciplining, most notably in the matter of status transgressions.

The moral economy of the authoritarian

Ottoman rulers acted forcefully against contraventions of social place and ordering, but they chose carefully in decisions on when to act on behalf of private interests. The authorities, for example, did not energetically pursue delinquent husbands who had abandoned wives and children or had neglected to pay support stipends. Yet in the equally private matter of slave fugitivism, public heralds and runaway-slave hunters were eager to restore the absconded property to their owners. Husbands were morally and legally obligated to support their families, but unless they were tracked down by private individuals – usually members of the family – they were seldom, if ever, the object of a state dragnet. Runaway slaves and those who harbored them were guilty of a private crime against the property rights of the slave owner. However, the owner shared with the ruling regime a larger social interest. Both were threatened by the breach in obedience, and both had a strong interest in seeing it repaired.

With the proliferation of market relations in the eighteenth century, the regime increasingly struck out at deviations from what might be called legalized custom. These were habits of public propriety and deference prescribed by long usage, the self-regulating practice of neighbors and coreligionists, and institutional formalization through imperial commands. European power and intentions – Westernism and Westernization, as Berkes characterized the phenomenon – provided a potent frame within which a host of social tensions and grievances came to be understood and articulated.[22] On the streets and in the corridors of power, attention was increasingly drawn to subjects and nonnative residents who appeared to be advantaged or emboldened by European attachment. The poor, the transient, and others of the lower orders were, as always, strictly surveilled for nonconformity. The middling social orders and rising bourgeois elements, however, became newly central to ruling-class anxieties, and the regime reacted accordingly.

Of the merchants, tradespeople, and others who gave observable evidence of European ties or tastes, many were non-Muslims, particularly Christians. In

[22] Niyazi Berkes, *The Development of Secularism in Turkey* (New York, 1998), 29, 63, 71.

the popular mind, the appearance of European affinities on the part of Ottoman subjects posed a danger to both society and the apparatus of state. It could hardly have been otherwise, given the empire's geopolitical precariousness and domestic troubles. And, in fairness to the Ottoman populace, one has to say that the elite mind on issues of social order was sufficient of itself to view social presumption, with or without European trappings, as actionable insubordination. For many Muslims of all classes and status groups, the growing prominence of indigenous non-Muslims smelled of comeuppance and disloyalty, even treason.

Before the Tanzimat era, the central authorities seldom put energy or resources into the economics underlying their budgetary woes. A few sultans decided to fight import imbalances by rejuvenating domestic manufacturing. In addition to Mahmud II's experiments with military provisioning, the silk and textile initiatives variously undertaken during the reigns of Ahmed III, Mustafa III, and Selim III come to mind.[23] More consistently, economic offensives, if they can be called that, took a legalistic and regulatory form, in an effort to stanch the demand for imported and scarce goods. Bursts of social regulation wrapped in moral outrage became staples of the period from the mid-eighteenth century through the reign of Mahmud II.

By the 1820s and 1830s of Mahmud's reign, the effects of ruinous defensive wars and economic disablement had imposed a cumulative burden on the state fisc and on the economic position of important segments of society. At a similarly low point a hundred years earlier, peace had been sustained for more than a generation and the economy had shown surprising vibrancy. After 1770, there was no such respite from war and no real recovery.

Social friction and the regime's unpopularity in Selim's and Mahmud's times intensified in reaction to the growing prosperity of native non-Muslims. Non-Muslim subjects' ties to one or another European power – as formal protégés or patent holders (*beratlıs*) enjoying the extraterritorial legal status of foreign embassy personnel or as favored merchants, translators, and brokers – also increased, although in those early decades of European extraterritorial projections, Ottoman perceptions of the number of the privileged often exceeded the reality.[24] The general unease about change, together with the higher taxes and prices that came on the heels of specific policies, gave rise to an assortment of complainants. Dissenting elites and economically pressed members of the

23 Genç, "Ottoman Industry," 59–86; Eldem, *French Trade*, 268–9.

24 A point made by van den Boogert, *The Capitulations*, 110–12; see Ahmed Refik [Altınay], *Hicrî On İkinci Asırda İstanbul Hayatı (1100–1200)* (Istanbul, 1930), 74–6. During the nineteenth century, the number of patent holders in many locales increased exponentially; see Göçek, *Rise of the Bourgeoisie*, 92–7; İnalcık and Quataert, *An Economic and Social History*, 838; Alexis Alexandris, "The Greek Census of Anatolia and Thrace (1910–1912): A Contribution to Ottoman Historical Demography," in Dimitri Gondicas and Charles Issawi, eds., *Ottoman Greeks in the Age of Nationalism: Politics, Economy, and Society in the Nineteenth Century* (Princeton, N.J., 1999), 69; Steven T. Rosenthal, *The Politics of Dependency: Urban Reform in Istanbul* (Westport, Conn., 1980), 25.

Fig. 4. Sultan Mahmud II, 1808–1839, by Henri Schlesinger. Mahmud in a portrait commissioned after his clothing reforms. Photo, Jean-Gilles Berizzi. Réunion des Musées Nationaux/Art Resource, New York.

popular classes were not natural allies. Their different socioeconomic vantage points, however, often cohered around a scripturally tinged moral message in defense of social and institutional conservatism. The portrayal of domestic politics as a struggle between Islam, embodied in the Ottoman state and its society, and the West, embodied in Europe, including Russia, resonated with broad segments of the public. It could hardly have been otherwise, given the post-Karlowitz reality in which these domestic dramas were taking place.

Mahmud's assault on the socially entrenched Janissaries, his adoption of Western or Western-appearing administrative techniques, and his infatuation with Western styles of masculine dress and sociability won him implacable foes within the urban elites and populace as well as among provincials. For many, Mahmud was the infidel sultan (*gavur Padişah*), a label that he could scarcely ignore. Not only was the accusation bruited about by pro-Janissary diehards and religious conservatives, but a certain Sheikh Saçlı spat it at him in public view, in the heart of the capital.[25] Notwithstanding the religious idiom of popular dissent, the regime's practical shortcomings offered plenty of scope for displeasure.

By the time of Mahmud's death in the summer of 1839, his overhauled military and bureaucracy were still feeling their way. Building an army from the ground up was a monumental undertaking. Mahmud and his advisers had chosen to dub the new replacement army the "Trained, Victorious Troops of [the Prophet] Muhammad" to allay conservative reservations about its Western look and training. Whatever its name or uniform, however, the army was hard pressed to field enough men, let alone trained men, to operate effectively on the many fronts that opened up in the late 1820s and the 1830s.[26] The empire's borders continued to shrink, and internal challenges from one of Mahmud's own governors, Mehmed Ali Pasha of Egypt, went unchecked. The rationalization of the bureaucracy and the introduction of Western-style technical schools were piecemeal and tentative. Nonetheless, significant changes were well under way by the end of Mahmud's reign. They would prove to be the foundations of the more ambitious and successful elaborations that lent their name – Tanzimat, or "new orderings" – to the era of rehabilitation that followed.

Perceiving disorder

More than anything else, the visual ambiance of the urban would have decided how visitors from the past measured the distance between what they had known and what they were witnessing in the 1820s and 1830s. The built environment

[25] Okandan, *Âmme Hukukumuzun*, 63; Ubicini, *Letters on Turkey*, 1:8–9.

[26] Avigdor Levy, "The Officer Corps in Sultan Mahmud II's New Ottoman Army, 1826–1839," *IJMES* 2 (1971): 21–39. On Mahmud's military and other aspects of his reign, see Shaw and Shaw, *History of the Ottoman Empire*, 2:1–54; Virginia H. Aksan, *Ottoman Wars, 1700–1870: An Empire Besieged* (Harlow, U.K., 2007), 343–98.

of Istanbul had not appreciably changed. Imposing mosques still dominated the city's hills and thoroughfares. Their ubiquity across the face of the city – most of them founded by royal and ruling-class patrons out of the wealth of conquest – was daunting. In this age of loss and retrenchment, though, their omnipresence might have suggested cultural defensiveness. The age of triumphal piety was over.

Churches and synagogues were as plentiful and as unobtrusive as before. The principal markets and bazaars still functioned, as crowded as ever and probably more so. The merchandise on display, however, revealed new kinds of goods, especially new varieties of French, British, and Indian fabrics.[27] Istanbul's shorelines showed signs of energetic suburbanization and the presence of new, or newly showy, wealth. Both the Golden Horn and the Bosphorus Straits were liberally sprinkled with grandees' residences and imperial palaces where there had been few before.[28] The more striking differences, however, manifested themselves at street level, in material and behavioral signs of an alteration in social relationships and cultural outlooks.

Expanding commercial relationships with Europe and new patterns of trade, together with sanctioned and unsanctioned cross-cultural borrowings, fostered new forms of sociability and affiliation. The challenge to traditional social subordinations and to the symbolic structures that reinforced them was not wholly without precedent. In the distressing circumstances of the time, however, the scale of the challenge suggested something novel. It pointed to revolutionary permanency rather than temporary aberration. Formal systems for ensuring social conformity along with informal schooling in social discipline within families, neighborhoods, guilds, and religious communities had been broadly effective in more stable times. They were profoundly undermined by the economic and political disturbances of the eighteenth and early nineteenth centuries.

The erosion of traditional assumptions about the normative social order anticipated the emergence of a more secular and confessionally egalitarian society, but the road to that future was blocked by resistance on the part of a variety of social forces. The apprehensions of the ruling elites and like-minded confederates with regard to the body social bordered on obsession

[27] Eldem, *French Trade in Istanbul*, 34–70; İnalcık and Quataert, *An Economic and Social History*, 727–8, 732; Katsumi Fukusawa, *Toilerie et commerce du Levant, d'Alep à Marseille* (Paris, 1987).

[28] Shirine Hamadeh, *The City's Pleasures: Istanbul in the Eighteenth Century* (Seattle, Wash., 2007); Tülay Artan, "Architecture as a Theatre of Life: Profile of the Eighteenth-Century Bosphorus," Ph.D. diss., Massachusetts Institute of Technology, 1988. On similar patterns in Cairo, see Nelly Hanna, *Habiter au Caire: La maison moyenne et ses habitants au XVIIe et XVIIIe siècles* (Cairo, 1991), 72–8; André Raymond, "The Residential Districts of Cairo's Elite in the Mamluk and Ottoman Periods (Fourteenth to Eighteenth Centuries)," in Thomas Philipp and Ulrich Haarmann, eds., *The Mamluks in Egyptian Politics and Society* (Cambridge, U.K., 1998), 207–23; André Raymond, "Architecture and Urban Development: Cairo during the Ottoman Period, 1517–1798," in John Spagnolo, ed., *Problems of the Modern Middle East in Historical Perspective* (Reading, U.K., 1992), 211–27.

in this period of convergence. In the complex design of Ottoman society, the configuration of its social parts was profoundly relational. A shift in one of its foundational relationships threatened the integrity of the whole. As the situation of non-Muslim subjects changed, that of other regulated marginals was bound to be affected. The Ottomans themselves considered the problem to be one of balance and imbalance.

Different regions of the empire, with their individual demographies, economies, and political configurations, experienced the period's domestic and international watersheds with different degrees of intensity. The anonymous author of a reform-minded tract in the seventeenth century was perhaps overstating Istanbul's influence when he proclaimed it "the root" feeding all its provincial "branches."[29] Nonetheless, Istanbul was both capital and urban exemplar. Moral lapses in its precincts and the measures to combat them often had empirewide resonance.

Efforts to reequilibrate the imbalances that threatened the accustomed order assumed a variety of direct and indirect forms. Many were legislative. Imperial edicts and regulations sought to command society into an order whose dominant stratum not only was Muslim and male but also was bound to the ideal of multigenerational *askeri* households and lineages. Over the course of the eighteenth century, for example, Ottoman administrative practice had bolstered patrimonial families and households by effectively tenuring in the male dependents of senior officeholders. Sons of high *ulema*, bureaucrats, and military men could count on a stipended place in the elite, untaxed ranks. Nepotistic entitlement had historically been a begrudged reality in the distribution of state offices. By the eighteenth century, it had acquired the veneer of official sanction, becoming more deeply embedded in the several career vocations of state service.[30]

Among the mounting number of patrician lineages – virtual dynasties of executive-level officials – those of *ulema* hierarchs were the most numerous and enduring. *Kişizade ulema* – literally the sons of an *ulema* "somebody" – rose higher and faster thanks to the preferential promotions of nepotistic careerism. With few historical exceptions, the *ulema* as a body also enjoyed immunity from the confiscations and executions that hung over the heads of military and administrative officers.[31] In the topmost echelons of the elites as a whole, relatively few men were executed or materially dispossessed, even in the hard decades of the late eighteenth century. Bandits and rebels, of course,

[29] Yaşar Yücel, *Osmanlı Devlet Teşkilâtına dair Kaynaklar* (Ankara, 1988), 115 ("Kitâbu Mesâlihi'l-Müslimîn").

[30] Joel Shinder, "Career Line Formation in the Ottoman Bureaucracy, 1648–1750: A New Perspective," *JESHO* 16 (1973): 217–37; Norman Itzkowitz, "Eighteenth Century Ottoman Realities," *SI* 16 (1962): 73–94; Madeline C. Zilfi, "Elite Circulation in the Ottoman Empire: Great Mollas of the Eighteenth Century," *JESHO* 26 (1983): 318–64.

[31] Mumcu, *Osmanlı Devletinde Siyaseten*, 125–31; Röhrborn, "Konfiskation," 345–51; Madeline C. Zilfi, *The Politics of Piety: The Ottoman Ulema in the Postclassical Age (1600–1800)* (Minneapolis, 1988), 113–15.

were less scrupulous about honoring the custom. Nonetheless, a wider view of the *askeri* class and its fortunes puts the behavior of the regime itself in a fairly murderous light. The world of the Istanbul elites was a small one, highly factionalized, it is true, but Istanbul-focused and self-protective as a caste. The fate of unlucky peers, especially within the crème de la crème of the Istanbul-born, loomed large, even if a few enemies rejoiced. The number of victims arguably mattered less than the example, and the example was worrying. It is little wonder that the sultan's servants sought guarantees for their lives and property. Even given the competitive nature of politics, it is surprising that elite self-interest and the goals of the regime should effect change only as late as the mid-nineteenth century.

Whatever the frequency of confiscations, the notion of public servants' private wealth was tenuous, as Ottoman officialdom well knew. Wealthy families of every ilk adopted various strategies to secure their holdings. Investing abroad, keeping property liquid and hidden, and dispersing assets among relatives were among the most common strategies. Muslim families of means often sought the protection of *ulema* status by ensuring a *medrese* education for at least one son. His holdings, including what he might have from his father, were relatively safe under the *ulema*'s umbrella of exemption. Legal recourse via the malleability of *shari'ah* practice also served elite accumulation by providing legal cover for intergenerational transfers. Wealthy individuals, office-holders or not, male or female, could safeguard their heirs' inheritances by applying – some would say bending – the laws on *vakf*, eleemosynary endowments. The eighteenth century saw a precipitous rise in the number of benefactors who shielded family wealth through the creation of ostensibly pious foundations.[32]

As a practical matter, the most blatant challenges to male Muslim authority, particularly to the dominance of the official male elites, arose from the economic ascent of non-Muslim men and their dependents. Many who attracted disapproving notice were newly wealthy or gave the appearance of moving materially and psychologically beyond Ottoman prescription. In addition to their participation in the conspicuous, consumerist trade with Europe, non-Muslims were observed taking on – and thus competing in the market for – status accoutrements. The most visible of these were items of dress associated with the authorities. The usage rankled the Muslim public as much as it did the ruling orders. Moreover, many non-Muslims were simply regarded as lacking in the deference expected of a conquered and religiously inferior people. The eighteenth century and the years thereafter were, on the whole, a dispiriting

[32] Bahaeddin Yediyıldız, *Institution du vaqf au xviiiè siècle en Turquie* (Ankara, 1985), 13–19; Hasan Yüksel, "Vakfiyelere göre Osmanlı Toplumunda Aile," in Erverdi, Yıldız, and Kara, *Sosyo-Kültürel Değişme*, 2:476–85; Margaret L. Meriwether, *The Kin Who Count: Family and Society in Ottoman Aleppo* (Austin, Tex., 1999); Beshara Doumani, "Endowing Family: *Waqf*, Property Devolution, and Gender in Greater Syria, 1800–1860," *CSSH* 40, no. 1 (1998): 11–12.

age for the erstwhile Muslim conquerors. Perhaps they had need of a more convincing show of humility from their subordinates.

The wealth and pretensions of Christian and Jewish merchants owed less to the gifts and obligations of the patrimonial command economy than to a complex of market forces and foreign interventions. Non-Muslims' growing assertiveness, as it seemed, was laid to their real and perceived reliance on aggressive European "protectors." For their part, rising elements of the Christian and Jewish populations sought release not only from the state's financial exactions and demeaning social directives but also from the fees and restrictions imposed by their own confessional communities.[33] Short of immigration, the swiftest escape route from both sets of authorities passed through European commercial wealth and connections.

Women and non-Muslims were linked together in the regulatory imagination. They were targeted differently, but the clothing and social presence of the two alternated as objects of legislative interest. Fatima Mernissi's much-quoted characterization of "the infidel without and the woman within" as the double threat "to the Muslim order" is relevant here, although its fit with the Ottoman Empire warrants adjustment.[34] It was not only the emergence of a dynamic and ambitious non-Muslim bourgeoisie in this precolonial period that was of concern. The very density of the indigenous Christian peoples in the home provinces of Rumelia, Anatolia, and metropolitan Istanbul speaks to the importance of the native non-Muslim population, specifically the dialectics of non-Muslim subjecthood and Muslim self-perceptions. To be sure, the European powers were a lethal threat from without, but indigenous non-Muslims were, like women, very much within the Ottoman realm.

Women and indigenous non-Muslims were the twin pillars on which male Muslim superiority of the time rested. The two were not precise social equivalents. Femaleness was understood as a biological category and, given the technologies of the day, permanent. The male dancers who were favorite entertainers at court played at being female, but their transvestism and impersonations did not subject them to being governed as women. Religious affiliation, the attribute of "not Muslim," could be shed at will; conversion to Islam was frequent and, in the case of males in particular, celebrated by the Muslim community. Given the potential for European intervention in favor of non-Muslims – males directly and their female dependents through them – non-Muslims were increasingly able to evade the impositions of traditionalists, whether Muslim or their own coreligionists. Women as women had no foreign patron to offer either extraterritoriality or gunboats to support defiance of the laws and mores of their native land.

33 Ron Shaham, "Jews and the Sharī'a Courts in Modern Egypt," *SI* 82 (1995): 124–5.

34 Qtd. in Deniz A. Kandiyoti, "Emancipated but Unliberated? Reflections on the Turkish Case," *Feminist Studies* 13, no. 2 (1987): 319; see also Leila Ahmed, *Women and Gender in Islam* (New Haven, Conn., 1992), 128.

Hegemony and proprietorship

The sumptuary legislation that dominated the moral campaigns of the eighteenth century had a structural and dispositional precursor in the Istanbul-centered Kadızadeli tempests of the previous century. In immediate origins and ramifications, the seventeenth century's religiously inspired discord differed from what was to come. However, dichotomized lines of argument and a preoccupation with Islamic authenticity featured in both. Their programmatic structures suggest a common moral attitude toward social change and hierarchy. The differences between the two periods and their approaches to moral rigor also command our interest. The emphases of the later period point to the salience of the Westernized framing in which Ottoman and Islamic vulnerability increasingly came to be understood in society. Ottoman failures, hardship, and unrest from the eighteenth century on were invariably perceived as the consequence of Western power and machinations.

Before the late eighteenth century, before European hegemony inserted itself into Ottoman consciousness, social conflict tended to spring from the near politics of local grievances and local resource allocations. The Kadızadeli disturbances that shook Istanbul in the seventeenth century exemplified just such contestation. The movement was named for the charismatic preacher-theologian Kadızade Mehmed (d. 1635), whose strict orthodoxy turned mosque congregants into enthusiastic disciples. In the fifty or so years that the Kadızadelis and like-minded activists had the ear of the Muslim public, they depicted government corruption and societal disorder not as untoward missteps but as transcendent ills. At the root of these ills, they saw not the swollen and swaggering military corps but religious practitioners, the Sufis primarily and the sympathetic *ulema* who consorted with them, defended them, and rewarded them with emoluments and influence.

The ideas promoted by Kadızade and later exponents pitted Muslim against Muslim, often violently, over the expressional limits of Sunni Islamic religiosity and the substance of piety. The Kadızadelis declared themselves opponents of religious innovation (Ar., *bid'a*), which they equated with the boundary-bending rites of certain Sufi orders and the intercessionary impulses of popular religion.[35] The Kadızadelis' acid test of right religion amounted to a list of condemnable innovations, about twenty in number, according to contemporaries. These ranged from the music- and dance-like worship services of the Halveti and Mevlevi Sufi orders to the use of new substances like coffee and tobacco, all of which Kadızade and his followers regarded as deviations from Sunni orthodoxy. To drive these concepts home, the Kadızadeli method was direct confrontation. For the most part, confrontations were verbal, but at various

35 Kātib Chelebi [Katib Çelebi], *The Balance of Truth*, trans. Geoffrey L. Lewis (London, 1957). On the group's religious and socioeconomic interests, see Madeline C. Zilfi, "The Kadızadelis: Discordant Revivalism in Seventeenth-Century Istanbul," *JNES* 45, no. 4 (1986): 251–69.

moments, they devolved into physical assaults. The call to believers to commit their individual energies to the "enjoining of right and prohibiting of wrong" (Ar., *al-amr bi'l-ma'ruf ve al-nahy 'an al-munkar*) had, for centuries, been a proof text of puritanical enthusiasm.[36] The Kadızadelis employed it liberally.

The Kadızadelis' emblematic byword, *innovation*, was a historically laden term for beliefs and practices that had arisen since the era of the Prophet Muhammad (d. 632). By denouncing innovation, Kadızadeli exponents staked their claim to a pristine, uncorrupted Islam.[37] Their position struck many contemporaries as blind, if not absurd, on its face. Because, at their most extreme, the Kadızadelis rejected any qualifying distinction between good innovations and bad, detractors joked that their ban on anything unknown in the Prophet's day meant the end of underwear and spoons.[38] As the judicious historian Katib Çelebi commented at the time, "Scarcely any of the sayings or doings of any age are untainted by innovation."[39] In later years, *Şeyhülislam* Yenişehirli Abdullah stressed the validity of good or useful innovation in sanctioning the first Ottoman printing press and in affirming the acceptability of certain innovative religious practices.[40] Centuries of Islamic exegesis and practice endorsed such perspectives on change, but the Kadızadelis in their day were undeterred.

The question of the acceptability – ultimately the religious licitness – of new elements, whether ideational or material, was a recurring problem in Islamic life and religious discourse. The seventeenth century's rejectionist wave added a new chapter to an already-long story. Regardless of the fate of those whom their contemporaries called Kadızadelis, the struggle over innovation and the new had a life of its own. As developments in the eighteenth and nineteenth centuries would prove, conservative reaction against perceived departures from Islamic norms was not confined to any single movement or historical moment. Apart from turmoil in their own time, the Kadızadelis added to future conversations by rekindling interest in the works of anti-innovation exemplars. Chief among these were the pious catechist Birgili Mehmed ibn Pir Ali (d. 1573) and the Hanbali theologian Taqi al-Din Ahmad Ibn Taymiyya (d. 1328). The writings of the two were and remained mainstays of conservative thinking.[41]

[36] *Qur'an* 3:100; Michael Cook, *Forbidding Wrong in Islam: An Introduction* (Cambridge, U.K., 2003); Zilfi, *Politics of Piety*, 137–8, 174–5; Marc David Baer, *Honored by the Glory of Islam: Conversion and Conquest in Ottoman Europe* (Oxford, U.K., 2008), 115–19.

[37] *EI2*, s.v. "Bid'a," by J. Robson; Muhammad Umar Memon, ed. and trans., *Ibn Taimīya's Struggle against Popular Religion* (The Hague, 1976).

[38] Mustafa Naima, *Tarih-i Naima* (Istanbul, 1280/1863–4), 6:226.

[39] Katib Çelebi, *Balance of Truth*, 90.

[40] Yenişehirli Abdullah, *Behcet el-Fetava ma Nukul* (Istanbul, 1266/1849), 551–2.

[41] The convenient shorthand of *conservative* and *anti-innovation* does not do justice to the complex and contested views associated with Birgili (also known as Birgivi) Mehmed and Ibn Taymiyya. See *EI2*, s.v. "Ibn Taymiyya," by H. Laoust; Wael B. Hallaq, *Ibn Taymiyya against the Greek Logicians* (Oxford, U.K., 1993); Michael Cook, *Commanding Right and Forbidding Wrong in Islamic Thought* (Cambridge, U.K., 2001), 323–30; Dina Le Gall, *A Culture of Sufism: Naqshbandīs in the Ottoman World, 1450–1700* (Albany, N.Y., 2005); Zilfi, *Politics of Piety*, 131–2, 137, 143–6.

In the seventeenth century, the Kadızadelis' particular message resonated with important clienteles, among them religious functionaries, especially those in the lower ranks, and students, whose tuition the preachers shared with the regular *medreses*. But the student population, like the *ulema* and other religious functionaries, was far from being in lockstep with Kadızadeli puritanism. The movement did possess muscular manpower, with support drawn from the military corpsmen who served the palace. The ability to attract a military following was, in part, a consequence of the advantageous geography of Kadızadeli preachers' imperial appointments. As sermonists at Istanbul's preeminent mosques, including in various years Aya Sofya, Sultan Ahmed, and Süleymaniye, they were within shouting distance of Topkapı Palace as well as most of official Istanbul. Palace officers and military corpsmen who dwelled in or near the palace were a crucial audience and allies, although many among them were attached to pro-Sufi factions or moved opportunistically between the two sets of combatants. Sultans from Murad IV (1623–40) to Mehmed IV (1648–87) as well as sundry viziers piggybacked on the movement's coercive momentum when it suited their purposes. Their purposes usually had to do with tamping down political dissent more than riding herd on sinners, but the palace, in line with centuries of dynastic self-promotion, was happy to conflate political opposition with sin.[42]

Kadızadeli preachers employed the language of Islamic universality, of timeless truths and all-encompassing reality, but their practical focus was the here and now of imperial Istanbul. The mix of motivations of the equally mixed groups that have been labeled "Kadızadeli" defies precise analysis at this point. The leadership's intentions were nonetheless fairly straightforward. They sought to command the empire's religio-moral voice and, not incidentally, the religious institution's material prizes. Like activists elsewhere on the political spectrum, the Kadızadelis portrayed the empire's ills as the consequence of moral failure. The popular saying of the period, "fish stink from the head," captures their synecdochic vision. Pollution and purification of the community and faith, they contended, flowed from the top down, from the establishment *ulema* and others who thwarted their spiritual and worldly ambitions. Kadızade Mehmed himself, drawing from a popular folk saying, pronounced from the pulpit that whipping society's large oxen had the double advantage of frightening the small into obedience.[43]

[42] On the various waves of Kadızadeli activity and alliances, see Necati Öztürk, "Islamic Orthodoxy among the Ottomans in the Seventeenth Century with Special Reference to the Qādī-zāde Movement," Ph.D. diss., University of Edinburgh, 1981; Semiramis Çavuşoğlu, "The Kadızadelis: An Attempt of Şeri'at-Minded Reform in the Ottoman Empire," Ph.D. diss., Princeton University, 1990; Zilfi, *Politics of Piety*, 138–81; Baer, *Honored by the Glory of Islam*, 63–119 and passim.

[43] Zilfi, *Politics of Piety*, 137. Cf. the statement attributed to the eponym of the Mujaddidi line of the Naqshbandi (*Nakşbendi*) Sufi order, Ahmad Sirhindi (d. 1624): "'the virtuousness of kings is the virtuousness of the subjects, their corruption is the corruption of all the subjects,'" qtd. in Butrus Abu-Manneh, "The Naqshbandiyya-Mujaddidiyya in the Ottoman Lands in the Early 19th Century," *WI*, n.s., 22 (1982): 14.

Aggressive puritanism had its limits, however. From the movement's beginnings early in the century to its apparent dissolution in the 1680s, its various spokesmen identified their prey with political repercussions in mind. They hurled their charges of corruption and unbelief widely but selectively. They were careful to absolve their own high-placed patrons in the palace and military-administrative cadres. Sufism was the constant, nearer enemy. Other adversaries tended to be targets of opportunity, taken up or ignored depending on the inclinations of individual preachers.

In their texts and targets, the Kadızadeli disturbances were mainly, though not exclusively, internal Muslim affairs. During the second half of the seventeenth century, in the second and third waves of activist orthodoxy, preachers like Üstüvani Mehmed (d. 1661) and Vani Mehmed (d. 1685) and their followers were keen to prevent any weakening of the boundaries between Muslim and non-Muslim. They expended more energy on the soft Sunnism of the Sufi-inclined, but they just as vehemently attacked concessions to the religious minorities. And, as Baer has convincingly shown, Vani Mehmed and his allies sought to make their uncompromising policies an instrument for the conversion of the Christian and Jewish minorities.[44] Indeed, according to the Armenian chronicler Kömürcüyan, Vani declared himself in favor of any sort of persecution to bring about the conversion of the minorities or their annihilation.[45] Nonetheless, the burden of the Kadızadeli program, starting with lists of innovations to be stamped out and the individuals deemed responsible for the disarray of religion and state, were matters for the Muslim community to decide for and about itself.

Sporadic outbreaks of the controversy appeared elsewhere in the empire, apparently traveling into Egypt and Syria via the Turkish-speaking communities residing in the provinces.[46] For the most part, though, the waves of Kadızadeli disturbances were intramural struggles in every sense. The epicenter of the controversy from start to finish was Istanbul's Old City, whose neighborhoods lay within the old Byzantine walls. This was the stronghold of the Islamic capital of the Islamic Empire. The disputants who kept the debate alive over the decades, all men of religion, organized attacks on taverns and

[44] Baer, *Honored by the Glory of Islam*, 81–118; Zilfi, *Politics of Piety*, 149–56.

[45] Eremya Çelebi Kömürcüyan, *İstanbul Tarihi: XVII. Asırda İstanbul*, ed. and trans. Hrand D. Andreasyan (Istanbul, 1952), 45.

[46] Barbara Flemming, "Die Vorwahhabitische Fitna im Osmanischen Kairo 1711," in *İsmail Hakkı Uzunçarşılı'ya Armağan* (Ankara, 1976), 55–65; Rudolph Peters, "The Battered Dervishes of Bab Zuwayla: A Religious Riot in Eighteenth-Century Cairo," in Nehemia Levtzion and John O. Voll, eds., *Eighteenth-Century Renewal and Reform in Islam* (Syracuse, N.Y., 1987), 93–115; Derin Terzioğlu, "Sufi and Dissident in the Ottoman Empire: Niyāzī-i Misrī (1618–1694)," Ph.D. diss., Harvard University, 1999; Le Gall, *A Culture of Sufism*, 155; Barbara Rosenow von Schlegell, "Sufism in the Ottoman Arab World: Shaykh 'Abd al-Ghanī al-Nābulsī (d. 1143/1731)," Ph.D. diss., University of California, Berkeley, 1997, 80–102.

coffeehouses during the seventeenth century. Their main battleground, however, was religious space – mosques, *medreses*, Sufi lodges, saintly tombs, and shrines. They declaimed from the mosques, sought to rally the *medreses*, and censured Sufi lodges and devotional shrines. If a religious structure was to stand, it was not to house practices and practitioners in opposition to Kadızadeli ideals.

Kadızadeli conceptions of religious and spiritual boundaries had important interfaith implications even when interfaith relations were not directly at issue. Muslim self-identity, what it meant to be a Muslim, and the straightness of the straight path were contentious matters. The Kadızadelis' narrow religiosity drew a tight, essentially antisocial circle around what it was to be Muslim, imperiling the expansive metropolitanism of Ottoman religious policy at its best. The Kadızadelis' righteous Muslim possessed a single-minded appetite for religious purity that overrode ties to family and rejected cordiality or even civility toward those who did not subscribe to the same views. For the Kadızadelis, strict adherence to *shari'ah* law, as they themselves defined the law's permissions and prohibitions, would restore right religion. Lacking it, given the popular appeal of such innovations as saint worship – especially in the form of tomb visitations and prayer – and of syncretistic Sufi tenets, the Islam of the Kadızadeli imagination would lose its identity as a practice and as the true and supreme faith.

The ecclesiastical aspect of the seventeenth-century controversy was in sharp contrast to patterns of disturbance in the eighteenth century. The streets and marketplaces that had barely seemed to register with Kadızadeli preachers became the flash points of eighteenth-century anxieties. The authorities in the eighteenth century and the social elements on which they relied reacted against the rising tide of a newly dangerous public. Until the Janissaries were removed, political commentary was shot through with calls to renovate the military. At the same time, public opinion and the state's social concerns were also directed downward. The disciplinary gaze increasingly shifted away from ruling groups and institutions to street level and the ordinary public. Eighteenth-century policing became increasingly entangled with a seemingly recalcitrant public. Official admonitions that were heralded to the neighborhoods and markets reveal deep apprehension about the ways that social and cultural nonconformity – expressions of personal tastes and new group solidarities and the economic keys to such behaviors – undermined existing structures of dominance.

If the object of Kadızadeli revivalism had been an orthopraxic *Homo religiosus*, the preoccupation of eighteenth-century rectifiers was social man and woman. Seventeenth-century confrontations had their roots in religious performance and, except for the occasional coffeehouse or tavern, the topography of the sacred. The incendiary sites of the eighteenth century were essentially profane. They were unscripted space or, one might say, multiply scripted, by the diverse populations that crossed paths on the streets and by the forces that sought to direct those who ventured there for business or pleasure. Although streets and markets were not an entirely new terrain, they were newly contextualized and construed, as were many other imperial concerns in the age of European ascendancy.

The religious minorities, particularly males, and the urban female population, particular Muslim women, were the feared but fragile elements that stirred official and popular consternation. They were not a Habermasian "public," not a sphere of private individuals joined in civil counterpoint to state authority,[47] but when individuals among them failed to conform to state or communal dictates, their behavior was treated as insubordination, if not aggression. Peaceful resistance to customary rules and practices hinted at the emergence of an unwholesome and unauthorized social force. In the eyes of the regime and of those who sought comfort in the discomfort of women and non-Muslims, the nonconformity of women and non-Muslims, society's preferred others, was a danger rather than just an annoyance. Containment of that danger took on special urgency in the heartland of the empire. For many Muslims among Istanbul's elites and commoners, male Muslim identity, normative Ottoman identity, became more stridently invested in the subordination of women and the religious minorities.

Concerns about the changing visibility of women and non-Muslims reached their height in the period between the late eighteenth century and the second quarter of the nineteenth century. The mirror of those concerns was the sumptuary legislation that poured out of the central state. The regulatory emphasis exposes an apparent paradox of period rulership – the resort to customary rules (*kanun-i kadim, kaide-i kadime*) with respect to social subordinates in contrast to the reputation of the sultans as forward-looking reformers. The legislation's linguistic and substantive cadences over the course of these decades suggest the masculinist premises of the struggle over consumerism, fashion, modesty, and social deference. They also reflect the rhetorical and ultimately the constitutive framework in which the reformist debates of these and succeeding decades were confined. The linkages between perceptions of women's social personhood, the halting progress toward confessional egalitarianism, and the lingering place of slavery in the body social are illuminated by the social understandings embodied in the regime's sumptuary legislation and formal utterances.

47 Jürgen Habermas, *The Structural Transformation of the Public Sphere: An Inquiry into a Category of Bourgeois Society*, trans. Thomas Burger (1989; repr., Cambridge, Mass., 1991), esp. 1–27.

CHAPTER 3

Women and the regulated society

> Persons who are not grandees may not wear long robes [*kaftan*] as they are prohibited... especially for those who go about on foot, whether Janissaries, the slaves of grandees, or others, the wearing of robes is a grave offense.
>
> – Anonymous, "Kitâbu Mesâlihi'l-Müslimîn ve Menâfi`l'l-Müminîn"[1]

> You may with ease... know the quality of any man you meet by the particular ornaments of his restrained appearance.... Those look great among the Turks, who really are so.
>
> – Aaron Hill, *A Full and Just Account of the Present State of the Ottoman Empire (1733)*[2]

Popular law

In Gottfried Keller's parable *Kleider Machen Leute*, a poor tailor is taken for a man of consequence when he puts on a fashionable velvet cloak. The social confusion set in motion by the clever tailor's transformative garb plays on themes familiar to many cultures. In Keller's story, the deception is revealed by a jealous neighbor, and the tailor is ostracized.[3] In the imperial Near and Middle East, including the Ottoman Empire in the eighteenth and nineteenth centuries, sartorial transgressions were official business, a matter of law as well as custom. Members of the ordinary public, disliking unlawful pretenders, were active agents in the detection of wrongdoers. Members of the governing orders, backed by the full weight of the law, had even more powerful instruments for ensuring compliance. And they were keen to employ them, as sartorial offenses occurred at their particular – or at least ostensible – expense. The dialectical relationship between Muslim aristocratic privilege and lower-class moral economy is a concern of this chapter.

1 Yücel, *Osmanlı Devlet Teşkilâtına*, 95.

2 Aaron Hill, *A Full and Just Account of the Present State of the Ottoman Empire in All Its Branches*... (London, 1733), chap. 12.

3 Gottfried Keller, *Kleider Machen Leute* (Stuttgart, 1986). The tailor, however, is redeemed by a loyal fiancée and his own talents.

The history of sartorial regulation in the Ottoman context opens a window onto the ancien régime's struggle to manage both the newly debased circumstances of the empire in the world and the domestic contestations that those changed circumstances sparked. At first glance, sartorial legislation seems merely a single, rather narrow slice of the broader field of social legislation. Even social legislation taken as a whole – in the regulation of prostitution; migration; gambling; travel; peddling; cursing; drink and drunkenness; and in the seventeenth century particularly, smoking and coffee consumption – seems to promise only limited insight into the mind of the state or society. Yet these sorts of governances were reflections of the larger Ottoman discourse of identity and community. And in the "draped universe"[4] that was the project of Ottoman sartorial law, apparel, as costume, uniform, disguise, fashion, street wear, underwear, gift, robe of honor, corporal covering, and symbolic coverture, prevailed over housing, transport, and alimentation as the principal delineator of social place and relationships of power.[5]

Far from being ineffectual or obsolescent protests against change, Ottoman clothing laws lasted as strong state policy into the twentieth century.[6] Their durability alone commands the historian's attention. Although we are primarily concerned with the late eighteenth and early nineteenth centuries here, the persistence of sartorial laws among the Ottomans calls for comment on the longer term. Rigorous clothing restrictions survived, albeit sporadically, across hundreds of years and across the different politics, attitudes, and governing styles of many Ottoman monarchs and lay and religious executives too numerous to count. Such differences, as in the period of this study between strict conservative rulers and later reformers and modernizers, were considerable. Even so, the laws persisted. But just as the histories of rulers and policies tell of distinctions between regimes and leaderships, the edicts and ordinances that we call sartorial legislation were also historically inflected. The ways that the laws varied or remained constant over time point to continuities and ruptures not only in the project of social regulation but also in the motivations and mentalities that gave rise to the laws. The why that lies behind the legislation is inseparable from the particularities of individual issuances and their makers. The what of the legislation, the substance of its claims, bears not only on the question of material possessions and their display but also on the relationship between regulated and regulator in the context of ownership, rights of possession, and legal personhood. The modalities of clothing regulation offer a singular vantage point from which to calculate the interconnections between

4 The term is borrowed from Lisa Golombek, "The Draped Universe of Islam," in Pricilla O. Soucek, ed., *Content and Context of Visual Arts in the Islamic World* (University Park, Pa., 1988), 25–38.

5 On the relative insignificance of housing as a social and economic investment, see Doğan Kuban, *Istanbul: An Urban History* (Istanbul, 1996), 299–300.

6 And, with the Turkish Republic and the other successor states in the Muslim world, into the twenty-first century.

clothing and politics. They also suggest the conceptual framework in which the laws' human targets, overwhelmingly women and religious minorities, were understood.

Fashioning the regime

Like its imperial Islamic predecessors, the Ottoman Empire from at least the sixteenth century was a land in which street attire was social skin and a declaration of identity. Variations in outerwear labeled men and women as members of a particular confession and often of a particular ethnic, regional, or vocational subgroup. Some distinctions were self-imposed by and for the affected group. Others were mandated by the state. Most were combinations of self-identification and outsiders' impositions. Like residential clustering by religion, the genesis of clothing usages and their transmission to other times and places were the consequence of different imperatives and impulses.

Specific sartorial forms and configurations lacked the fixity that individual generations ascribed to them and that religious and political authorities frequently sought to impose. Precisely when the Ottoman Empire determined to inaugurate – or fix in place – a vestmental code is unclear.[7] The search for the first state codes takes one to the fifteenth and sixteenth centuries, when Ottoman rule was being established over disparate peoples. The sultans looked to imperial antecedents for usable techniques of governance. What surfaced as law under one sultan or another, however, was less a comprehensive clothing system than a repertory of boundaries and guidelines.

By the eighteenth century, regulated colors, styles, and materials had a long and checkered history. Invocations of timelessness – such-and-such attire has been the custom *kadimden*, "since bygone days" – sought to archaize what were often recent dicta. All clothing elements from head to foot had, in reality, been subject to modification over the centuries. Changes were often slight, at least to the modern eye accustomed to seasonal hemlines and décolletages. Some fashionable apparel fell out of use or was subject to ban only to receive approval later as "traditional," if not required, attire.[8] Since the beginning of the empire, European modes and materials, some of them adaptations of Ottoman and Islamic motifs, had circulated with varying degrees of acceptance. In the preindustrial age, most European clothing items were luxury imports. On economic grounds alone they were subject to regulation. Whatever the century, though, Istanbul was consumer, producer, and conduit for the diffusion of

[7] On this point, see Yavuz Ercan, "Osmanlı İmparatorluğunda Gayri Müslimlerin Giyim, Mesken ve Davranış Hukuku," *OTAM* 1, no. 1 (1990): 117.

[8] For example, in addition to the fez (see Chapter 6 in this volume) is the up-and-down history of the *çarşaf*, the one-piece female covering that became popular in the late nineteenth century; see R. Bulut, "İstanbul Kadınlarının Kıyafetleri ve II. Abdülhamid'in Çarşafı Yasaklaması," *Belgelerle Türk Tarihi Dergisi*, no. 48 (2001): 33–5; Fanny Davis, *The Ottoman Lady: A Social History from 1718–1918* (New York, 1986), 197–201.

fashion in the eastern Mediterranean and beyond.[9] Within the empire, it was also the great exporter of regulation.

Variously shaped and sized caps, kerchiefs, sashes, shirts, and braiding, put together in innumerable combinations of fabrics, told of different ethnicities, denominations, and ecologies. Long-term residence in Istanbul tended to homogenize provincialisms into the capital's broader categories of religious-community affiliation. The village costumes of Ottoman Muslim women, whether Anatolian or European, were adapted to Istanbul styles if they could be afforded and if the women in question had to venture much outside their own communal milieu. Similarly, the distinctive headdresses of Greek islanders usually gave way to Istanbul's Greek Orthodox fashions. Sephardic and Karaite Jewish apparel, like the congregations to which the various Jewish populations belonged, tended to meld after the seventeenth century. It remained acceptable for immigrants to keep to regional clothing, so long as standards of modesty and propriety were upheld. Istanbul's inhabitants themselves absorbed elements of "outsider" dress, with Abkhazian, Tatar, Russian, Syrian, Iranian, and Italianate currents variously showing up in Istanbul wardrobes.[10]

In the meeting between law and praxis, Islamic sumptuary laws generally adhered to two imperatives, though the Ottoman regime was arguably most adamant about them after the seventeenth century. The first of these, tracing back to the early Islamic centuries and caliphal Damascus, stipulated that, in public space, the population be marked by clear distinctions (Ar., *ghiyar*) between Muslims and non-Muslims. The second principle, the insistence on the hierarchy of those distinctions, visually reinforced the superiority of Islam. Hierarchical ranking served notice that membership in the dominant faith brought with it superior social status. And superior status was supported and manifested by preferential access to certain superior or coveted goods.[11]

[9] The circularity and internationalism of fashion and materials in the period are detailed in Louise W. Mackie, "Ottoman Kaftans with an Italian Identity"; Charlotte Jirousek, "Ottoman Influences in Western Dress," in Suraiya Faroqhi and Christoph K. Neumann, eds., *Ottoman Costumes: From Textiles to Identity* (Istanbul, 2004), 219–29 and 231–51.

[10] See Nureddin Sevin, *On Üç Asırlık Türk Kıyafet Tarihine bir Bakış* (Istanbul, 1973), 102; İsmail Hami Danişmend, *İzahlı Osmanlı Tarihi Kronolojisi*, 2nd rev. ed. (Istanbul, 1971–2), 3:360; von Hammer, *Geschichte*, 7:54–5; Defterdar Sarı Mehmed Paşa, *Zübde-i Vekayiât* (Ankara, 1995), 742. On Ottoman women's dress and its construction in the early modern era, see Jennifer M. Scarce, *Women's Costume of the Near and Middle East* (London, 2003); see, especially for developments in the nineteenth century, Nancy Micklewright, "Public and Private for Ottoman Women of the Nineteenth Century," in D. Fairchild Ruggles, ed., *Women, Patronage, and Self-Representation in Islamic Societies* (Albany, N.Y., 2000), 155–76.

[11] *EI2*, s.v.v. "Ghiyar," by M. Perlmann; "Hisba," by R. Mantran; "Libās," by N. A. Stillman and Y. Stillman; Gideon Weigert, "A Note on the Muhtasib and Ahl al-Dhimma," *Der Islam* 75 (1998): 331–7. Ercan, "Osmanlı İmparatorluğunda," 118–19, suggests that mandated distinctions were not hierarchical, as Muslims could as well be punished for dressing in non-Muslim garb. However, Şeyhülislam Ebussuûd's opinions pinpoint Muslims' fault in such cases as the manifestation of unbelief (*kufr*), not in the trespass on Christian or Jewish prerogatives; M. Ertuğrul Düzdağ, *Şeyhülislâm Ebussuûd Efendi Fetvaları Işığında 16. Asır Hayatı* (Istanbul, 1972), 118. See also A. S. Tritton, *The Caliphs and Their Non-Muslim Subjects: A Critical Study of the Covenant of 'Umar* (London, 1970); Madeline C. Zilfi, "Goods in the Mahalle: Distributional Encounters in Eighteenth-Century Istanbul," in Donald

The existence of these notions does not mean that they met with universal approval or application. To the contrary, their inconsistent application in both the Ottoman and pre-Ottoman eras suggests considerable diversity regarding the need and utility of confessional coding. Nonetheless, the religious pedigree of these ideas was available to those with an interest in leveling down the religious minorities or particular groups therein.[12]

In addition to personal dress, such things as housing heights, horseback riding in cities, and certain non-Muslim religious customs – bell ringing, processions, and public rites generally – were activities most subject to restriction in mixed quarters (*mahalle*) as existed in Istanbul.[13] Religious propagandizing and proselytizing were Islamic prerogatives.[14] To the strictly orthodox, and to others simply resentful of others' good fortune, prominence in public was tantamount to proselytizing. Foreign embassy personnel, however, had extraterritorial rights to elements of conspicuous display. Among other things, they could wear their own national costume, although many who wished to avoid notice or harassment preferred so-called Oriental dress and requested the right to wear Ottoman prestigious garb commensurate with their diplomatic status.[15] Apart from exemptions for nonsubjects of the empire, the implementation of clothing regulations, like all prescriptive ordinances, tended to be a sometime thing. In locales where non-Muslims were a majority, impositions could be all but absent. Findings by Çiçek and Saydam regarding Cyprus, as well as contemporaneous accounts of Balkan village wear and Greek Islands attire generally, attest to the Ottoman Empire as a conglomeration of diversities despite the homogeneities touted in state ordinances.[16] Deviations from

Quataert, ed., *Consumption Studies and the History of the Ottoman Empire, 1550–1922* (Albany, N.Y., 2000), 297–8.

12 On the politics behind clothing restrictions on non-Muslims in early nineteenth-century Acre, see Philipp, *Acre*, 182–3.

13 Regarding building and other nonclothing restrictions, see Altınay, *Hicrî On İkinci*, 20, 83, 88–9; Ahmed Refik [Altınay], *Hicrî On Üçüncü Asırda İstanbul Hayatı (1200–1255)* (Istanbul, 1932), 9; Ahmed Refik [Altınay], *Onuncu Asr-i Hicri'de İstanbul Hayatı (961–1000)*, (Istanbul, 1333/1914–15), 193–208; Rakım Ziyaoğlu, *Yorumlu İstanbul Kütüğü, 330–1983* (Istanbul, 1985), 323; Yavuz Ercan, *Osmanlı Yönetiminde Gayrimüslimler* (Ankara, 2001); Ercan, "Osmanlı İmparatorluğunda," 123; Necati Aktaş et al., eds., *85 Numaralı Mühimme Defteri (1040–1041/1042/1630–1631/1632)* (Ankara, 2002), 340–1.

14 Until the later nineteenth century, when apostasy from Islam was decriminalized, conversion involving Islam and Muslims by law operated in only one direction, into Islam, not out of it. Conversion among only non-Muslims was a matter for the Christian and Jewish authorities to grapple with, unless public order or other pressures called for state intervention; regarding Christian and Jewish disputes, see, e.g., Ubicini, *Letters on Turkey*, 2:254–61; Robert Anhegger, "Osmanlı Devleti'nde Hiristiyanlar ve İç Tartışmaları," *Tarih ve Toplum* 8, no. 47 (November 1987): 17–20; Marcus, *Middle East*, 47–8; Bruce A. Masters, *Christians and Jews in the Ottoman Arab World: The Roots of Sectarianism* (Cambridge, U.K., 2001).

15 On the regulation of Western visitors' dress, see Matthew Elliot, "Dress Codes in the Ottoman Empire: The Case of the Franks," in Faroqhi and Neumann, *Ottoman Costumes*, 103–23.

16 Çiçek and Saydam, *Kıbrıs'tan Kafkasya'ya*, esp. 145–6; also Kemal Çiçek, "Living Together: Muslim-Christian Relations in Eighteenth-Century Cyprus as Reflected by the Sharī'a Court Records," *Islam and Christian-Muslim Relations* 4, no. 1(1993): 36–64; Traian Stoianovich, *Between East and West: The Balkan and Mediterranean Worlds* (New Rochelle, N.Y., 1992–5), esp. vol. 2. For a useful discussion and bibliography regarding dress, especially in the

Istanbul's norms are also a reminder of the capital's often singular relationship to social regulation.

Some of the clothing distinctions found in Istanbul and the region represented forms of dress that wearing communities accepted as their own for reasons too distant or convoluted to be explained other than as tradition. The leaderships of the minority communities were no different from their Muslim counterparts in endeavoring to fence off their respective flocks to keep them distinct and intact. Visual and, where possible, physical separation fortified confessional solidarity and, not insignificantly, helped justify each leadership's reason for being. The various religious authorities and the state had in common an antipathy toward popular fashion, equating it with moral laxity and prodigality. Thrift was a virtue next to godliness in all three faiths. It was also a preventative against indebtedness and neighborhood antagonisms.[17] Christian and Jewish leaders took pains to safeguard coreligionists from intercommunal squabbles and brushes with imperial laws, as punishments could explode into collective retributions, with the family or entire community rather than just the transgressor made to suffer.[18] Like residence patterns, language affinities, and religious rites, distinctive attire aided each community in the enforcement of its confessional and cultural expectations. It reminded coreligionists of their shared communal past as well as present-day obligations. That, at least, was one intention of sartorial requisites. It was a compelling reason behind each community's own self-definitions and self-policing in such matters.

Clothing distinctions had even broader utility within society as a whole. Military uniforms were a tactical necessity on the battlefield. In civilian life, in the management of the populace as social beings, distinctive dress was a boon to efficient policing. It facilitated the search for wrongdoers, if only by narrowing the field of suspects and enlisting the cooperation of the community. Those considerations were especially apt in the case of officials. Their jealously guarded dress could become evidence against them in the presence of crime. Because most urban violence could be laid at the doorstep of misbehaving soldiers and paramilitary sorts, uniforms and insignia were important giveaways if troublemakers were wearing them in their troublemaking hours and if others

Ottoman Arab world, see Yedida K. Stillman and Nancy Micklewright, "Costume in the Middle East," *Middle East Studies Association Bulletin* 26, no. 1(1992): 13–38. Isa Blumi, "Undressing the Albanian: Finding Social History in Ottoman Material Cultures," in Faroqhi and Neumann, *Ottoman Costumes*, 157–80, offers interesting observations on clothing usages in Albanian lands in the later nineteenth century.

17 See, e.g., Jacob R. Marcus, *The Jew in the Medieval World* (1938; repr., New York, 1974), 193; Mark Mazower, *Salonica, City of Ghosts: Christians, Muslims and Jews, 1430–1950* (New York, 2005), 187; Diane Owen Hughes, "Sumptuary Law and Social Relations in Renaissance Italy," in John Bossy, ed., *Disputes and Settlements: Law and Human Relations in the West* (Cambridge, U.K., 1983), 84.

18 Marcus, *Middle East*, 115–18; Ruth Lamdan, *A Separate People: Jewish Women in Palestine, Syria and Egypt in the Sixteenth* Century (Leiden, 2000), 106–9.

could be prevented from infringing on their attire. Indeed, when Janissaries and such "are in a brawl or mischief, they're known by their clothing; there's no need for inquiry or investigation. In fact, their headgear provides information, with no room for denial," and that, according to a seventeenth-century commentator, was a very good thing.[19]

Over the centuries and even year by year, the cycle of regulation and infraction, including intracommunal, or class, infractions, suggests that costume by fiat was a failed policy. In the eighteenth century's widening world of goods, regulation arguably stimulated the experimentation it sought to prevent. Sartorial requirements could make social ranks more visible, but they were far from successful in achieving enforcement. By the eighteenth century, in addition to prescribed coverage wear for women, mandatory attire for the memberships of the confessional communities and distinctive uniforms for imperial officials were entrenched usages. Nonetheless, strict enforcement until then had been episodic on the whole. The eighteenth century witnessed a sea change. Several regulatory blasts appeared at the turn of the century, but in the late eighteenth century and continuing into the nineteenth century, clothing restrictions found new vigor under royal auspices. The Ottoman upswing contrasts with the decline of sumptuary regulation elsewhere. In Western Europe, the same decades saw sartorial laws all but disappear, their usefulness against the triumph of market capitalism apparently at an end.[20] The longevity of Ottoman regulating was bound up with foreign and domestic pressures and constraints, including the uneven inroads of the market, but longevity was also a function of the changing preoccupations of lawmakers.

The regulatory remedy

From the point of view of the wearer, clothing could signify self-expression, obligatory attire, the limits of resources, the scope of aspirations, and much more. For the Ottoman regime and its ruling house, the empire's clothes were a means to publicize power, to pronounce its gradations, and to communicate its reach. By law and custom, only the sovereign and his deputies had the right to step out of their customary garb and adopt – for whatever reason – a

[19] Yücel, *Osmanlı Devlet Teşkilâtına* 23–4, 97. Primary and secondary sources on crime among Janissaries and other troops are too numerous to cite here. Studies on criminality in urban settings between the seventeenth century and the mid-nineteenth century include Eyal Ginio, "The Administration of Criminal Justice in Ottoman Selânik (Salonica) during the Eighteenth Century," *Turcica* 30 (1998): 185–209; Abdul-Karim Rafeq, "Public Morality in 18th-Century Ottoman Damascus," *Revue du Monde Musulman et de la Méditerranée* 55–6 (1990): 180–96; Dana Sajdi, "A Room of His Own: The 'History' of the Barber of Damascus (fl. 1762)," *Massachusetts Institute of Technology Electronic Journal of Middle East Studies* 4 (2004): 19–35; Eunjeong Yi, *Guild Dynamics in Seventeenth-Century Istanbul: Fluidity and Leverage* (Leiden, 2004), 141, 195.

[20] Alan Hunt, *Governance of the Consuming Passions: A History of Sumptuary Law* (New York, 1996), 28. See also Madeline C. Zilfi, "Whose Laws? Gendering the Ottoman Sumptuary Regime," in Faroqhi and Neumann, *Ottoman Costumes*, 125.

sartorial identity that was not, strictly speaking, their own. In the kind of clothing turnabout beloved by wary rulers everywhere in the premodern world, sultans often took to dressing down to survey their subjects. They did so out of suspicion and boredom as well as out of a sense of their own role as social judge and jury. Certainly they always professed to be acting in the name of justice. In the guise of ordinary policing authorities or tradesmen, they patrolled the streets, righting wrongs. The sultans' incognito adventures were an open secret among their palace servants and guardsmen. Other individuals less proximate to the royal person in affiliation or location – members of the workaday public and officials on duty beyond the palace – were not so fortunate. They would have had no warning that on this day, above all, rules, regulations, and decrees should be followed promptly and precisely.

Monarchical masquerades were a favorite instrument of weak or beleaguered monarchs. Two such monarchs, Osman III (1754–7) and Mustafa III (1757–74), ratcheted up the penalties and purview of sartorial surveillance. Their successors, Abdülhamid I (1774–89), Selim III (1789–1807), Mustafa IV (1807–8), and Mahmud II (1808–39), added further embellishments. After a relatively peaceful and prosperous half century, the reigns of Osman, Mustafa, and Abdülhamid became the occasion of plague, fires, earthquakes, warfare, and economic instability, all of which continued into the following decades. Like their forebears, the three monarchs were stubborn defenders of hierarchy and deference. Selim III and Mahmud II, the reformist sultans who succeeded them, had a more complicated relationship to the social system that they inherited.

In the terrible times in which these several rulers found themselves, fury at sumptuary transgressions, particularly sartorial breaches, was perhaps predictable. If a demonstration of sovereign authority was needed, it could be achieved far more readily against individual offenders than against foreign adversaries or homegrown rebels. Indeed, in the late eighteenth century, a witty Ottoman official, possibly the grand vizier himself, remarked that Janissary ruffians showed "'so much bravery'" battling hats in the non-Muslim neighborhoods of Galata but cowardice in combat on the Danube.[21] And in the wake of natural calamities, exemplary punishments could communicate to a terrified population that a propitiation of divine wrath was well in hand. But notwithstanding the incentive of specific crises, the sultans' shows of strength in sumptuary law and summary justice responded to an abiding preoccupation of their time, the instability of the Ottoman order and the struggle to rescue it.

The theme of an orderly, harmonious society runs through centuries of Ottoman profane and religious writings. Righteous order in accordance with

[21] Aksan, *An Ottoman Statesman*, 164, though with a somewhat different interpretation of the exchange between Baron de Tott and the vizier; see de Tott, *Memoirs*, 2, no. 1: 131.

MUSTAPHA III. (1757-1774.)

Fig. 5. "Mustapha III (1757–1774)." William J. J. Spry, *Life on the Bosphorus* (London, 1895).

Ottoman Islamic models – *nizam-i alem* – was a vital plank in the ideological platform on which the legitimacy of the ruling house rested.[22] The lifeblood of social order was the principle of bounded social latitudes (*hadd*), or everyone and everything in their place (*yerli yerinde*). Nowhere was the preoccupation with social order more pronounced than in the empire's cities. And in no city was social surveillance more intense than in Istanbul, heterogeneous metropolis and royal demesne.

In virtually every era and reign, men with pens and men with swords campaigned against disorder. The lack of order or the endangerment to good order (*nizam*) usually meant the transgression by individuals or groups beyond the bounds of their status and station (*haddini tecavüz*). Poets, chroniclers, statesmen, and moralists took up the theme, chastising by turns the governing classes, the orthodox, the rich, and this or that set of commoners for destabilizing the order that ought to be and, according to critics, used to be. In the seventeenth and eighteenth centuries, memorialists measured their own era against the paradise lost of the sixteenth century, especially the reign of Süleyman I, the Magnificent (1520–66), as Europe knew him. The Ottomans bestowed on him a different sobriquet, Kanuni, or the Lawgiver. With it, they commemorated not only Süleyman's legislative milestones but also the domestic peace that his lawmaking was believed to have made possible.[23]

Most – though not all – sumptuary laws were documents of economy. They spoke directly to consumers, producers, and suppliers about what buyers were managing to put on their backs or otherwise use, and how and where merchants and clothiers should or should not acquire regulated stuffs. Most laws were responses to specific problems of exchange – shortages, price gouging, adulterations, imitations, and the like – as a function of market processes or failures. In contrast to the myriad decrees and adjudications governing production – weights and measures, transport, taxes, division of labor, and guild operations generally – sartorial laws focused on the demand side, on individual consumers' supposed role in creating shortages and in driving up prices. In the command economy of sultanic authoritarianism, consumers could not be allowed to follow their passions. The imperial subject as consumer of goods possessed only such rights of usage as the hierarchical governing system allowed. And the system, which is to say the regime and its official and unofficial enforcers acting in the name of order and justice, sought to dictate needs and norms. Differences between the name and the reality of order and justice, however, are part of the story here.

22 See Hagen, "Legitimacy and World Order," 55–83; Boğaç A. Ergene, "On Ottoman Justice: Interpretations in Conflict (1600–1800)," *Islamic Law and Society* 8, no. 1 (2001): 52–87, regarding justice, legitimacy, and *nizam-i alem* as a historically contingent concept.

23 Halil İnalcık, "Süleyman the Lawgiver and Ottoman Law," *Archivum Ottomanicum* 1 (1969): 105–38. Also İ. Metin Kunt, "State and Sultan up to the Age of Süleyman: Frontier Principality to World Empire," and Christine Woodhead, "Perspectives on Süleyman," both articles in Kunt and Woodhead, *Süleyman the Magnificent*, 28, 166.

The eighteenth century's sartorial regulations reflected the struggle in the period between the growing market culture and the normative command economy. The leading edge of the struggle was the circulation of coveted goods, especially imports. For all their economic resonances, though, Ottoman sumptuary pronouncements were fundamentally ideological. Their makers typically had a particular version of social order in mind. Then, as in the present day, the concept of order had multiple connotations. Order, in some contexts, meant social peace. In others, it signified social arrangement and sometimes authoritative command. Indeed, a common Ottoman term for *order* in the sense of an issued command was *nizam*, the same word as that for societal order itself. The regime and the social system that supported it were invested in order in all its meanings. Individual appearance and personal mobility – the presentation of one's self – had everything to do with public peace, social arrangement, and political authority.

The regime promoted its social vision in many ways. Legislative commands were arguably the most comprehensive and most frequent advertisement of its social apprehensions. Sumptuary regulations offered a multicolored key to how the members of state-designated groups (e.g., women, Muslim women, non-Muslim women, high *askeri* officials, servants of dignitaries, non-Muslims as a whole, and *reaya* folk of all religions) should be in public. The legislative mode was negative. The words *prohibit* and *prohibition* (*men', memnu'*) were omnipresent in regulatory prose. Sumptuary regulations were chiefly about what not to do or to wear. They aimed to deter, to limit, or to eradicate altogether.

Cloth and clothing were at the eye of the eighteenth century's regulatory storm, but insofar as women were concerned, modes of transport, especially the ox-drawn wagon (*araba*) and oared commuter boats (*kayık*, *pereme*), came in for censure as well.[24] Like clothing, transport was linked to unwholesome possibility. The chief concern was women's physical mobility. The possibility of sexual dalliance was heightened when women escaped homes, guardians, and the watchful city, ostensibly for picnics and fresh-air excursions, but in any case away from the usual brakes on their freedoms and choices. Even when women traveled on foot to the markets or bazaars, the thought that they might be enjoying themselves outside house, home, and kinship was enough to enrage moralists.

Strict moralists were suspicious of entertainment and leisure – frivolity – on principle, but they were especially opposed to women's venturing outside "needlessly." In his *Vasiyetname* ("testament"), Birgili Mehmed, the spiritual

[24] Nejdet Ertuğ, *Osmanlı Döneminde İstanbul Deniz Ulaşımı ve Kayıkçılar* (Ankara, 2001). For particular ordinances, see Altınay, *Onuncu*, 59–60; Reşat Ekrem Koçu, *Osmanlı Tarihinde Yasaklar* (Istanbul, 1950), 30, on women hiring wagons in 1752. The ban on wagons by Sultan İbrahim (1640–8), whose sanity was in doubt, was aimed against traffic in the city and his own convenience rather than women's transport; İsmail Hakkı Uzunçarşılı, *Osmanlı Tarihi* (Ankara, 1973), 3:226.

exemplar of the Kadızadelis, listed only a handful of permissible occasions for women to leave their own homes. Religious obligations accounted for several of these. The list also gave a nod to the practicalities of life and death in allowing for women to tend to the collection or payment of debts and in recognizing that midwives and female corpse washers must sometimes go outside, but Birgili essentially saw women as captives of the family circle, especially of the males within it. With a male guardian's permission, women might move beyond the approved list, but even a husband's or a father's approval could not legitimize all such occasions in Birgili's eyes: A woman "should not be sent to be with non-relatives (*namahremler*), nor to their houses or weddings, nor to the public bath, nor to visit the sick if they are not intimate relatives (*mahremler*)." If she does so, "'the angels will curse her until she returns to her house,'"[25] What punishments the angels, or Birgili, would mete out to guardians who permitted such outings are not revealed.[26]

Women did break out of the circle of *mahrem* intimates with varying degrees of family consent. Conservatives' strictures on women venturing outside were generally more a matter of preference than of law. They were, in any case, premised on an unrealistic, even bourgeois, imaginary in which static families stood on rock-solid foundations of male bounty. Many women at some stage of their lives relied all or in part on their own labor. For every ordinary householder there was always water to fetch, for personal hygiene, household cleaning, and ablutions, in a society that placed a high premium on cleanliness. Those who made a living as laundresses, bathhouse attendants and proprietors, clothing finishers and piecework employees, cooks, servants, or wet nurses, and women who had ill, disabled, underemployed, or absent male protectors, had a different perspective about the need to be outside. Slave women, like male slaves, did what was required of them by their owners. Gender norms and appropriate conduct for female slaves were conditioned by their position at the intersection of the gender regime and the peculiar exemptions that came with the legal status of being owned persons. All of these women may have subscribed to society's gender ideals as fervently as any male pundit or wealthy dowager, but they were encased in a different reality.

When conservative – or perhaps more accurately ultraconservative – opinion was rendered into law, it was usually in response to a specific call for state intervention, such as when neighbors or townspeople witnessed what they considered female misconduct. Individuals could complain in person or by petition to the authorities, although typically groups of concerned citizens approached the nearest *kadı*, who would transmit the collective grievance of respectable folk (*ehl-i ırz*) to the executive authorities. Every century saw a

[25] A. Faruk Meyân, trans., *Birgivî Vasiyetnâmesi'nin Kâdızâde Şerhi* (Istanbul, 1977), 259. See Arberry, *Koran Interpreted*, 24:31, for the Qur'anic rule on permissible intimates (*mahrem*).

[26] The quotation refers to a saying (*hadith*) attributed to the Prophet Muhammad and liberally cited as such, as in *Birgivî Vasiyetnâmesi*, 259.

flurry of ordinances ensue from local quarrels. Many complaints had to do with the spatial relations of female commerce, women in transit as shoppers. Edicts warned female market-goers away from certain shops that were said to be havens for mixed-sex encounters or interconfessional mingling.

Throughout Europe as well as the Ottoman East, the layering of sex and religion was a reliable recipe for gaining the attention of the authorities. In the sixteenth century, in the Istanbul suburb of Eyüb, clotted-cream shops (*kaymakcıs*), the ice-cream parlors of the day, were the spatial culprits. "Women are going into the cream shops on the pretext of eating cream," the *kadı* of Eyüb wrote, "and they're sitting down with unrelated people [*namahrem*] and transgressing *shari'ah* law." Piling recrimination on recrimination, the *kadı* also noted that flute playing and dancing took place in and around such shops, which were mostly frequented by Christians. Lest the authorities miss the import of the situation, the *kadı* fixed the scene in religious context, how real or exaggerated is difficult to say. Such things were occurring not only in the revered shrine city of Eyüb, he reported, but also in the very neighborhood of the Holy Mosque of Eyüb, close by *medreses* and a Qur'anic elementary school (*mekteb*), with the music and dancing so loud that the recitation of scripture and the call to prayer could not be heard. The imperial decree that followed ordered the expulsion of the offending clientele and reminded the police that "negligence in this matter is impermissible."[27]

In the eighteenth and nineteenth centuries, with fashionable attire on the minds of both consumers and regulators, ribbon makers (*şeritçi*) and sundries shops (*tuhafçı*) eclipsed cream shops as problematic sites. By the mid-nineteenth century, though, the spatial dictum on female customers aimed to maintain a comprehensive shopping barrier between outside and in. According to ordinances of 1847 and 1861, for example, women were forbidden not only to sit down in shops but also to enter any shops at all.[28] The popularity of these locales, the gathering of unrelated people – presumably most of them women and presumably most of them actually interested in the goods on offer – in an interconfessional and sexually mixed tangle of buyers and sellers, threatened more than one tenet of propriety. When one considers the inconveniences and indignities of moving around premodern Istanbul – indeed, when one recalls the difficulties of modern Istanbul – one can think only that the number of shoppers in want of a rest far outnumbered any who fancied a flirtatious, much less a sexual, moment.

In the context of the nineteenth century, the chronology of the two midcentury prohibitions is suggestive of the complex and often contradictory politics of the decades we know as the reform era. The cited regulations, wrapped

[27] Altınay, *Onuncu*, 57–8. References to "police" in this study are intended only as shorthand for the military personnel in the premodern period who functioned as law enforcement officers; on the development of a civilian police force, see Ergut, *Modern Devlet ve Polis*.

[28] Anonymous, "Kadın-I," *Tarih ve Toplum* (1984): 37, 39, regarding restrictions issued in Ramadan 1263/August 1847 and Muharrem 1278/August 1861.

around gender and commerce, were products of the same political environment in which the divide between Muslim and non-Muslim was gradually but undeniably fading. The regulations remind us of the "silent male referent"[29] that imbues the categories and judgments – of egalitarianism, reform, and antireform – that Ottoman contemporaries employed about their own time and that later historians have frequently adopted. Confessional egalitarianism was an ongoing project of the Tanzimat era, but if it was sometimes ill-conceived and insincere, it was doubly so with regard to women and gender roles. Granted, the social laws had meaning, even if they served only to placate an aggrieved constituency. However, the parameters of women's sociability were profoundly at issue in a way that men's socializing and confessional intermingling were not. Certain groups in the male population continued to be represented as regulatory problems throughout the nineteenth century. They were monitored with similar diligence, but the categories that drew them to the attention of the authorities – the unemployed, vagrants and beggars, unregistered residents, bachelors, unlicensed purveyors – were fluid and inherently, if not always practically, transitory and escapable.

Most urban social laws of the eighteenth and early nineteenth centuries echoed the economic and moral tensions of previous centuries in their targeting of personal appearance and demeanor. Yet regulations in this later period reflected a newly charged, European-inflected mix of concerns. Among other things, there was palpable anxiety about the European provenance of goods and fashions. In quantity, issuances during the six reigns from Osman III through Mahmud II, roughly from the 1750s through the 1830s, made for a torrent in comparison with earlier times. In substance, they served notice on the population's attempts to transgress social boundaries. And they exposed the ruling orders' near hysteria about popular consumption, public display, and subject people's mobility, especially on the part of women and non-Muslim men.

The purview of sumptuary law customarily stopped at the threshold of the residential household. Islamic law and communal norms were hostile to official and social interrogations that trespassed on family or home life. Regulators directed their energies at publicly visible or audible usages.[30] The authorities were reluctant to inquire into the (usually) male-ordered familial realm in any case. Any man might be king under his own roof and to his own dependents. Except for the rarest imperially reserved furs and fabrics, any man might also dress like a king, or sultan, under his own roof, and his wife might play queen. Female heads of household of a certain age and level of wealth could command similar luxury and pretense. In public space, however,

[29] Zillah R. Eisenstein, *The Female Body and the Law* (Berkeley, Calif., 1988), 222.

[30] Mohsen Kadivar, "An Introduction to the Public and Private Debate in Islam," *Social Research* 70, no. 3(2003): 659–80; Roy Mottahedeh and Kristen Stilt, "Public and Private as Viewed through the Work of the *Muhtasib*," *Social Research* 70, no. 3 (2003): 735–48; Maribel Fierro, "Idra'ū l-Hudūd bi-l-Shubuhāt: When Lawful Violence Meets Doubt," *Hawwa* 5 (2007): 228.

rules of dress were expected to prevail. And in public space, only imperially designated persons, overwhelmingly male, were authorized to exercise rights of command over nonfamiliars. Clothing and transport symbolically spelled out those rights.

Unauthorized male subjects who publicly mimicked the regalia of entitlement and exemption may have done so in emulation of their rulers, as conspicuous consumers, in acknowledgment of a common aesthetic, or out of a sense of entitlement as their personal fortunes or connections blossomed.[31] All of these impulses played a role in the regulatory confrontations of the late eighteenth and early nineteenth centuries. Indeed, individuals usually acted out of an assortment of motives. Consciously or unconsciously, their sartorial forays threatened to render "illegible" the universe of goods by which the Ottoman ruling orders sought to project their political and social claims.[32] Douglas's insight regarding the fragility of groups – "a group's intended eternity is always at risk," its cohesion continually needing reinforcement – sheds light on the Ottomans' often ferocious response to sumptuary missteps.[33] Preventing Christians, Jews, women, and *reaya* from trespassing on *askeri* entitlements recalled non-Muslims, women, and all commoners to the allocations of power and their own inferior status. At the same time, it rallied the ruling orders, and those who supported their claims, around the shared ownership of entitlement.

Prescriptive edicts have been said to be most insistent when they are most seriously challenged. If quantity is any measure, the volume of laws in the eighteenth century and the first decades of the nineteenth century points to heightened social volatility in the capital city and elsewhere. Violations of clothing norms were a perennial, if intermittent, concern. The chroniclers inform us that they resurfaced as notable policies around the turn of the eighteenth century. Their emergence cannot be divorced from the doomsday climate surrounding the military and economic blows of the Karlowitz years, although the vizierial executors of the period were not of one mind regarding strict enforcement.[34] The venality and amour propre of individual officials often weighed more heavily than ideology or policy.

[31] Émile Durkheim, *Émile Durkheim on Morality and Society: Selected Writings*, ed. Robert N. Bellah (Chicago, 1973); Thorstein Veblen, *The Theory of the Leisure Class* (New York, 1994).

[32] On the legibility of society that such programs facilitate, see Scott, *Seeing Like a State*, 78. The discussion in these pages also draws from important works on consumerism and status, including Mary Douglas and Baron Isherwood, *The World of Goods: Towards an Anthropology of Consumption* (1979; repr., London, 1996); Hunt, *Governance of the Consuming Passions*; Alan Hunt, *Governing Morals: A Social History of Moral Regulation* (Cambridge, U.K., 1999); Daniel Roche, *The Culture of Clothing: Dress and Fashion in the "Ancien Régime,"* trans. J. Birrell (Cambridge, U.K., 1994); Hughes, "Sumptuary Law," 69–99.

[33] Douglas and Isherwood, *World of Goods*, 21.

[34] There were significant differences, for example, between Kalaylıkoz Ahmed and Daltaban Mustafa on the one hand and Amcazade (Köprülü) Hüseyn on the other hand; see Defterdar Sarı Mehmed, *Zübde*, 742, 745; von Hammer, *Geschichte*, 7:54–5, 107–13; Danişmend, *İzahlı*

The story changes for the post-1770 epoch, when European influence became domination and ever more defeats and scarcities battered imperial morale. The sharp increase in sumptuary issuances in the later period suggests a change in their importance and perhaps in their meaning. Until then, sumptuary promulgations had often coincided with particular crises, a fact that helps explain their spasmodic chronology before the late eighteenth century. As reactions to natural and man-made calamities, social regulations also tended to be intensifications rather than standing policy. The famous draconian decree of the Tulip Era, a period known for its relative indifference to social strictures, was of this kind, having been issued in wartime.[35] The frequency of regulations later in the century, however, does not reflect what historians of sumptuary law call "panic regulation,"[36] although war, fires, and plague were rife in these years. Rather, the cumulative effect of such unresolved and recurring calamities and downturns contributed to profound unease and disequilibrium; this was crisis of a prolonged, enduring kind. Not merely volume but also the ebbs and flows of regulatory targets mirror the new circumstances in which the ruling orders found themselves and a favorite instrument for managing them.

The edicts of the late eighteenth century called on a tried-and-true range of penalties for sartorial and other hierarchical infringements. Simple and relatively inexpensive measures such as fines, flogging, detention, and expulsion from the city or neighborhood were the most common punishments. The very act of seizure made for edifying street drama. As in the rest of premodern Europe, galley servitude and execution were always a possibility in cases of egregious offense. They loomed larger in Ottoman regulatory texts as the eighteenth century wore on. Corporal punishments, including exemplary executions, were intended to quash threats to the peace of the city, if not the peace of the realm altogether. While crime-and-punishment policies reveal much about official perceptions of disorder and offenders, they also highlight the multiple ways that the authorities sought to recalibrate existing social arrangements.[37] What such policies say about an Ottoman public

Osmanlı Tarihi, 3:50, 487. See also Eldem, *French Trade*, 231–2, for French reports about such differences.

35 Altınay, *Hicrî On İkinci*, 86–8. On the reign of Ahmed III (1703–30) and the tenure of his last grand vizier, Nevşehirli İbrahim Pasha (1718–30), see Ahmet Refik [Altınay], *Lâle Devri* (Ankara, 1973); Berkes, *Development of Secularism*; M. Münir Aktepe, *Patrona İsyanı (1730)* (Istanbul, 1958); Ahmet Ö. Evin, "The Tulip Age and the Definitions of 'Westernization,'" in Osman Okyar and Halil İnalcık, eds., *Türkiye'nin Sosyal ve Ekonomik Tarihi (1071–1920)* (Ankara, 1980), 131–45; Madeline C. Zilfi, "Women and Society in the Tulip Era, 1718–1730," in Amira El Azhary Sonbol, ed., *Women, the Family, and Divorce Laws in Islamic History* (Syracuse, N.Y., 1996), 290–303.

36 Hunt, *Governing Morals*, 18–20.

37 For social crimes and criminalizing in Istanbul in the period, see Başaran, "Remaking the Gate of Felicity," and Osman Köse, "XVIII. Yüzyıl Sonları Rus ve Avusturya Savaşları esnasında Osmanlı Devletinde bir Uygulama: İstanbul'da İçki ve Fuhuş Yasağı," *Turkish Studies/Türkoloji Dergisi* 2, no. 1 (2007): 104–23.

opinion – and about the composition of such a public – is relevant here, if difficult to assess.[38]

Many sumptuary ordinances were royal utterances, the public voice of the sultans. As such, however, they often sounded less like sovereign majesty than like preacherly vexation and guild disquiet. In what was very likely a guild-informed ordinance of the mid-eighteenth century, women were exhorted "not to go out on the streets with collars on their *ferace*s greater than a span [*sibir*], nor scarves [*yemeni*s] more than three squares, and they are not to use ribbons [*şirit*] that are more than a finger's width."[39] In regulatory blasts against the illicit consumption of silks, furs, foreign cloth, expensive cloth, and decorative touches, morality and economy were intertwined, and the public's stake in good order underscored. Over and over it was said that Christians, Jews, women, and others of the subordinate orders who had the means but not the right to such finery "must be prevented from profligate expenditure on clothing that exceeds their proper station."[40] Economically pressed elements in, especially, the Muslim commercial and religious sectors heard their own worries echoed in the sovereign's elucidation of the dangers of wasteful spending, unfair competition, and foreign imports.

Some segments among the unempowered and downwardly mobile acquired a measure of legislative representation in these sorts of directives. The commercial and religious sectors of the Muslim workforce, especially those in the lower reaches of the economy, personified the social and economic predicament of much of the urban population. They were far from representing the inclinations of the entire ordinary public, however. Given religious and/or status differences, no subset of the artisanry or clerisy represented the views even of its own profession. Members of competing guilds fought tooth and nail over goods that were too often in short supply. In guilds, members took their leaders to court.[41] Junior *ulema* who lacked effective patronage seethed at the advantages extended to the *ulema*-born.[42] Economic stratification was, to some extent, papered over by the gifts and favors of vertical patronage. Strains and tensions nonetheless remained, regardless of whether the wealthy overseers of one's vocational calling were coreligionists. Occupational and confessional solidarity did not always prevail in everyday life. Had they done so, the period's conflicts would have played out in far different ways. Many sumptuary infractions had to do with vertical infringements on hierarchy.

38 For a later period, see Bedri Gencer, "The Rise of Public Opinion in the Ottoman Empire (1839–1909)," *New Perspectives on Turkey* 30 (2004): 115–54.

39 Mustafa Sami, Hüseyn Şakır, Mehmed Subhi, *Tarih-i Sami ve Şakır ve Subhi* (Istanbul, 1198/1783), 34.

40 Mehmed Hâkim, "Hâkim Tarihi," Istanbul, TKS, Bagdat no. 231 (hereafter B231), fol. 234b.

41 Ahmet Kal'a et al., eds., *İstanbul Külliyâtı, İstanbul Ahkâm Defterleri: İstanbul Esnaf Tarihi 1* (Istanbul, 1997), 184–5, 227–8, 347–8; Câbî Ömer Efendi, *Câbî Târihi*, ed. M. Ali Beyhan (Ankara, 2003), 1:97.

42 Madeline C. Zilfi, "The Diary of a Müderris: A New Source for Ottoman Biography," *Journal of Turkish Studies* 1 (1977): 157–74; Zilfi, "Elite Circulation," 318–64.

Others resulted from horizontal jealousies, in ostensible social classes or cohorts. Other kinds of social quarrels reflected the intersections of class and confession, with disputes cutting through ethnic and religious groups in defiance of normative solidarities.[43]

Sumptuary ordinances were built on a template of four components. Each was usually repeated for emphasis and for clarity. The unschooled public had need of the repetition. So, too, did the high and low lay and religious figures who had to act on the rules and make them comprehensible to the population. Ordinances typically addressed the authorities responsible for communicating and carrying out the law's provisions, identified the offending parties who were the proximate cause of the issuance, described the offense and the nature of its harm to society – often juxtaposing transgressor and transgressed – and prescribed punishments and remedies. Very often, an edict's timing was triggered by the sultan's direct and angry observations of offending subjects or lax officials: "I have seen this with my own eyes." "I have heard and seen... womenfolk behaving shamelessly.... Why are you not attending to it?"[44]

Most regulations were blends of economic, religio-moral, and status complaints. Virtually all, regardless of their explicit message, were morally shaded. Sometimes the wrongdoing was flatly equated with sin. More often it was a matter of rule breaking – norm breaking, really – a violation of societal expectations of conformity. Capital punishment was sometimes explicitly threatened, but most penalties fell into the realm of discretionary inflictions – severe remonstrances. In effect, the severity of beatings and physical roughing up varied with the politics of the day and individual officers.[45] Whatever their targets and indictments, however, sumptuary laws promoted what we might call core Ottoman values. The public virtues and behaviors conveyed in the laws, which overwhelmingly applied to women and non-*askeri* males, situated the hierarchical social system and dynastic legitimacy within a matrix of *shari'ah* and sultanic (*kanun*) precepts. In the regulations' usual formulation, order as social tranquility and order as ordained social arrangement were mutually dependent core values.

Sumptuary legislation of the eighteenth and early nineteenth centuries, like all bodies of law, told an uneven and somewhat-disingenuous story. The ideals of propriety that it promoted were replete with contradictions and multiple agendas. The legislation's recurrent nature and panorama of material targets give evidence of manifold interests and social perspectives. Economic, social, political, and confessional differences, including conflicting worldviews and

43 Numerous examples of guild squabbles of these kinds, many of them against the confessional grain, appear in the registers of the *kadı* courts; for the eighteenth century, see İstM 1/25, fols. 2bff., 79a–79b, 101a–101b, 104b–106a, 111a; 1/32, no. 39; 2/178, 3b, 5a.

44 Sevin, *On Üç Asırlık*, 120; Necdet Sakaoğlu, "Osmanlı Giyim Kuşamı ve 'Elbise-i Osmaniyye,'" *Tarih ve Toplum* 8, no. 47 (1987): 38/294.

45 Émile Tyan, *Histoire de l'organisation judiciaire en pays d'Islam* (Paris, 1938–43), 2:424–8.

shades of belief within ethno-religious groups, account for the demand for legislation. Such differences also help explain the public's noncompliance and the official laxity that so often subverted the law in any case. Ottoman society showed remarkable consensus in the demand for order as social peace, but the population and its lay and religious governors differed over the measures required to achieve it. The proliferation or at least high visibility of infractions in the late eighteenth century points to heightened contestation over the meaning of order. Among Muslims, however, consensus with regard to women's secondary place and Muslim versus non-Muslim competition was more coherent, as was the discourse of order that sought to keep that consensus intact.

Cultures of complaint

Ottoman literatures of complaint were, in some respects, all of a piece. Statesmen, poets, and other literati who put their observations on paper between the seventeenth and nineteenth centuries typically focused on institutional failings and the inadequacies of leadership. There is a sameness about commentators' faultfinding. Most critiqued the Janissary corps, the land regime, the bloated bureaucracy, and official venality, among other things nominally in the purview of the central government. Whether solicited or unsolicited, memoranda of advice (*risale*, *layiha*) for the sultan ruminated on the imperial sources of imperial dysfunction. Problems were inevitably conceived as matters of top-down governance, whether military, bureaucratic, or personal. Solutions were formulated in statist terms, inevitably with a call for purposeful central government action.

Prior to the eighteenth century, uneasiness about the different peoples of the empire in terms of their mutual relationships did not rise to a sustained, high level of official consciousness. To be sure, discourses of order were mainstays of official and unofficial literatures. Imperial justice writs (*adaletname*s) of the seventeenth and eighteenth centuries were about justice, or most commonly the lack of it, but they mainly had in mind rural production, taxation, and the wretched condition of peasant producers.[46] As in reform memoranda, justice and order were narrowly framed. That is, justice and order were well-nigh one and the same, and the state alone seemed to be the creator of reality.[47]

In the seventeenth century, two remedial programs and, in effect, two moralities set the agenda for discussions about social order and urban living. That of poets and of litterateurs generally was conceived as an exercise in civic morality and personal discipline. The city's neighborhoods, guilds and

[46] See Halil İnalcık, "Adâletnâmeler," *Belgeler* 2 (1965): 49–145.

[47] Walter L. Wright, *Ottoman Statecraft: The Book of Counsel for Vezirs and Governors* (1935; repr., Westport, Conn., 1971), 76; Ergene, "On Ottoman Justice," 82–3; Hagen, "Legitimacy and World Order," 55–83.

laborers, civic luminaries, and merchants were deemed accountable and derelict, as were, inevitably, imperial administrators and police. The competing agenda, advanced by groups like the Kadızadelis, was conveyed in theological terms of orthodoxy and orthopraxy.[48]

The poet Üveysi's contrarian view of Istanbul – poetically dubbed "İslambol," "the plenitude of Islam" – as a hotbed of iniquity was typical of the literary critique. His "Advice on İslambol," composed in the 1620s, fulminates against the "traitors" who "fill all the offices of trust."[49] His charges have a generic ring, echoing the tropes of Ottoman and other poets before him. Üveysi's cynicism, however, is more than authorial posturing. His charges call to mind the mutinous terrors, rural upheaval, and regicide of his own anarchic era. In 1622, Sultan Osman II, "Young Osman," four years on the throne and still a teenager, was murdered by his own soldiers.[50] Executions and revenge killings followed. Üveysi's poem bears on these events and alludes to other scandals of the day – the diversion of warrior fiefs to sycophants, the rise of inept commanders "who everywhere bring anarchy and feud,"[51] and the alleged domination of state offices by Albanians and Bosnians. The ethnic derogation was meant to suggest the eclipse of merit by parvenu "outsider" cronyism.[52]

Üveysi's contemporary, the scholar-poet Nevizade Atayı (d. 1636), took a similar authorial stand against the perfidy and corruption of the powerful.[53] So, too, did their later counterpart Nabi (d. 1712), writing in what have been called "the disaster years," following the Ottoman defeat at Vienna in 1683 through the Treaty of Karlowitz of 1699.[54] The three poets vary in religion-mindedness and expressions of despair, but all make a plea for moral enlightenment.

48 Zilfi, "Kadızadelis," 251–74; Katib Çelebi, *Balance of Truth*; Ahmet Yaşar Ocak, "XVII. Yüzyılda Osmanlı İmparatorluğu'nda Dinde Tasfiye (Püritanizm) Teşebbüslerine bir Bakış: 'Kadızâdeliler Hareketi,'" *Türk Kültürü Araştırmaları* 17–21 (1979–83): 208–25.

49 E. J. W. Gibb, *A History of Ottoman Poetry* (1900–9; repr., London, 1958–67), 3:216; Günay Kut, "Veysi'nin Divanında Bulunmayan bir Kasidesi Üzerine," *Türk Dili Araştırmaları Yıllığı-Belleten* (1970), 172–3; Heinrich Friedrich von Diez, ed. and trans., *Ermahnung an Islambol, oder Strafgedicht des turkischen Dichters Uweissi uber die Ausartung der Osmanen* (Berlin, 1811), 9; cf. [Hatibzade Abdullatif] Latifi, *Evsaf-i İstanbul*, ed. Nermin Süner [Pekin] (Istanbul, 1977), for a sixteenth-century version of Istanbul's ills.

50 Gabriel Piterberg, *An Ottoman Tragedy: History and Historiography at Play* (Berkeley, Calif., 2003); Finkel, *Osman's Dream*, 196–205.

51 Gibb, *A History of Ottoman Poetry*, 3:216; Kut, "Veysi'nin," 173; Diez, *Ermahnung*, 13.

52 For ethnic rivalries in imperial politics, see Metin Kunt, "Ethnic-Regional (*Cins*) Solidarity in the Seventeenth-Century Ottoman Establishment," *IJMES* 5 (1974): 233–9; see also Cornell Fleischer, *Bureaucrat and Intellectual in the Ottoman Empire: The Historian Mustafa Âli, 1541–1600* (Princeton, N.J., 1986), 154–9, 253–7, regarding the intersections between ethnicity and geography in the late sixteenth century.

53 Tunca Kortantamer, "17. Yüzyıl Şairi Atayı'nın Hamse'sinde Osmanlı İmparatorluğu'nun Görüntüsü," *TID* 1 (1983): 64; see also Hatice Aynur, "Ottoman Literature," in Faroqhi, *Cambridge History of Turkey*, 3:496.

54 Ahmet Refik [Altınay], *Felâket Seneleri* (Istanbul: 1332/1916–17); Pavet de Courteille, *Conseils de Nabi Efendi à son fils Aboul Khair* (Paris, 1857); Tunca Kortantamer, "Nabi'nin Osmanlı İmparatorluğunu Eleştirisi," *TID* 2(1984): 83–116.

For the most part, their remedies are about earthly choices and judgments. Even Üveysi, the most insistent about divine recourse, situates his complaints in the here and now, as when he warns the sultan against false counsel: "Repose no confidence in yon Vezirs. . . . For those are foes to Faith and State. . . . A drove of brutes have come and set themselves in the vezirial seats."[55] It was a vintage indictment, but its forceful language was in keeping with events of the time.[56]

For all three poets, the powerful were ripe for moral rectification. In contrast to the Kadızadelis, however, none resorts to religious orthodoxy, at least in their best-known writings. They seem to have shared the view of their contemporary, the polymath Hezarfen Hüseyn (d. 1691), regarding this-world accountability: "Society is destroyed by injustice, not by irreligion."[57] Reform for these thinkers was grounded in traits of character like honesty, integrity, and selflessness in the service of religion and state. Although such attributes were inherent in Islamic ethical norms, they were not exclusively Islamic nor in themselves religious. In fact, the poets' proposed rectifications were disciplinary, the discipline of the self achieved by individual will and the obligatory corrections imposed by society or state. Social order and civic righteousness might emerge with or without a spiritual mentor or righteous ruler. More commonly in the Ottoman mind, however, strong leadership was essential. Its absence was thought to be a recipe for mayhem. As Evliya Çelebi remarked, citing a saying of the Prophet, "'Without a [ruler], people would devour one another.'"[58] The point could have been reinforced by any number of contemporary and historical calls for strong, top-down male leadership.[59]

As for the Kadızadelis, their worldly and religious grievances fed on socioeconomic conflict, including the efforts of their own preacher leadership to capture from the Istanbul establishment a bigger share of prestigious appointments.[60] In the capital, the pursuit of office and favor was always fierce, but it was hardest on newcomers and on provincials generally. It is not surprising that the movement – if the myriad advocates of strict constructionism can be so characterized[61] – found their leading voice among individuals born in the provinces. Kadızade Mehmed himself came to Istanbul from the town of Balıkesir in western Anatolia; Üstüvani Mehmed was a transplant from Damascus; and Vani Mehmed found fame as a preacher in eastern

55 Gibb, *A History of Ottoman Poetry*, 3:217; Kut, "Veysi'nin," 172; Diez, *Ermahnung*, 15.

56 For the long lineage and standardized lexicon of critiques of Istanbul and the empire, see the sixteenth-century examples in Lâtifi, *Evsâf-i İstanbul*, 15, 18–19, 40–1, 65–9; and Fleischer, *Bureaucrat and Intellectual*, 154–9, 175–9, 253–7.

57 *Dünya kufr ile yıkılmaz, zulum ile yıkılır*; Hezarfen Hüseyn (d. 1691), qtd. in Metin Kunt, Sina Akşin et al., eds., *Türkiye Tarihi 3: Osmanlı Devleti 1600–1908* (Istanbul, 1988), 264.

58 Robert Dankoff, *An Ottoman Mentality: The World of Evliya Çelebi* (Leiden, 2004), 83.

59 Zilfi, *Politics of Piety*, 88–9.

60 Zilfi, "Kadızadelis," 251–69.

61 Ocak ("XVII. Yüzyılda," 208–25) cautions against ascribing the cohesion of a movement to these disparate and still lightly studied events and actors.

Anatolia, in Erzurum by way of Van, before reaching Istanbul.[62] The religious and social message from the provinces was often more conservative and literalist than that represented by the Istanbul-bred men who dominated the quasi-ecclesiastical structure of Ottoman Islam. The economic conditions and law-and-order deficits in many easterly regions added an edge to the insider-outsider factionalism of capital politics.

Istanbul's hierarchical cosmopolitanism was not the inclusive pluralism usually meant by the term. Istanbul was nonetheless a mixed city of metropolitan proportions. About half of its population was non-Muslim, primarily Greek-speakers but also Jews of various origins and Armenians.[63] Many minority members were persons of great wealth and standing. Istanbul's structures of wealth and heterogeneous cultural ambience were a far cry from Erzurum or Balıkesir. It was arguably the continuing waves of provincial newcomers that fed social and cultural conservatism in Istanbul, especially with respect to strictures on women, Christians, and Jews.[64] Provincials were not the ultimate source of these views, but as new residents of this dynamically different city, they tried to make their new home more like the one they had left.

Seventeenth-century disorder

The two bodies of critique, worldly and otherworldly, possessed features in common beyond urban anxieties. Both identified society's chief offenders among the – implicitly male – rulership. However, maleness as an object of interrogation was passed over in silence. As the normative human category, "men" were an unproblematized reality. Men were seldom called on, much less reproached, in generic terms. State pronouncements from time to time directed men (*taife-i rical, taife-i zukur, erkek taifesi*) to monitor and supervise women, for whose comportment the *taife* of men had collective responsibility. More commonly, allusions to essentially male populations and propensities were stripped of gender references and offered up in associational or behavioral terms. Thus, it was not mankind's, much less men's, capacity for violence, dishonor, promiscuity, or cupidity that was to be supervised and controlled. Rather, male wrongdoing was laid to classes or castes or considered to be the product of individuals and social types – erring ministers, magistrates, sheikhs, Janissaries, *sipahi*s, bakers, merchants, tradesmen, bandits, or the urban literati's standard scapegoats, "Turks, Kurds, gypsies, and Iranians,"

[62] Zilfi, *Politics of Piety*, 129–81.

[63] Stanford J. Shaw, "The Ottoman Census System and Population, 1831–1914," *IJMES* 9 (1978): 325–38; Ubicini, *Letters*, 1:24; Robert Mantran, *Histoire d'Istanbul* (Paris, 1996), 44–9.

[64] Similar arguments continue into the present day regarding migrant flows into Istanbul, especially with respect to gender issues.

or "Türkmen nomads, mule drivers, camel herders, porters, depilatory dealers (*ağdacı*), highwaymen, pickpockets, and other such sorts."[65]

As for historical women of the seventeenth century, the literature makes relatively little mention of ordinary women's observed actions as a problem requiring concerted attention. The seventeenth-century traveler Evliya Çelebi often pronounced on women whom he had heard of or encountered himself. He had harsh words for some, but he also attested to admirable female demeanor. The women of the Tophane district of Istanbul, he noted, "comport themselves with the utmost propriety."[66] His frame of reference was the time-honored ideals of passivity and modest virtue, but he was something of a rarity among intellectuals of the time in occasionally granting that some women of the day met the standard.[67]

Although the poet-critics Nabi, Üveysi, and Atayı resembled essayists like Koçu Bey and Katib Çelebi in their statist assumptions,[68] the poets did not overlook the flaws and foibles of men and women outside official circles. Atayı's verse is studded with anecdotes about sexual impropriety of various sorts. Although never to the extent of Western male authors, poets and social critics depicted lesbianism and female sex romps along with the more usual allegations of female heterosexual promiscuity and insatiability.[69] The sexual misdeeds of certain male offenders, notably men in power who corrupted young boys, came in for more pointed denunciation. Such male-on-male vice is much the greater crime in both Üveysi's and Atayı's versified Istanbul. Nabi's fatherly counsel in his *Hayriyye* lacks the sexual detail for which Atayı is famous, except in advising his son on the best kinds of women with whom to form sexual liaisons. But as with Atayı, the conduct of women and ordinary folk, though deplored, were not central to these representations of contemporary rights, wrongs, and relationships of power.[70]

65 Yücel, *Kitâb-i Müstetâb*, 4; Danışman, *Koçi Bey Risalesi*, 23, 43. For this discourse in earlier centuries, see Fleischer, *Bureaucrat and Intellectual*, 153–9. On the dimensions of disparagement in the seventeenth century, see Marinos Sariyannis, "'Mobs,' 'Scamps' and Rebels in Seventeenth-Century Istanbul: Some Remarks on Ottoman Social Vocabulary," *IJTS* 11 (2005): 1–15.

66 Evliya Çelebi, *Evliya Çelebi Seyahatnâmesi*, ed. Tevfik Temelkuran and Necati Aktaş (Istanbul, 1976–82), 1:309; Robert Dankoff, ed. and trans., *The Intimate Life of an Ottoman Statesman: Melek Ahmed Pasha (1588–1662)* (Albany, N.Y., 1991), 98–9.

67 Cf. Fındıklılı Şemdanizade Süleyman, *Şem'dânî-zâde Fındıklılı Süleyman Efendi Târihi Mür'i't-Tevârih*, ed. M. Münir Aktepe (Istanbul, 1976–81), 1:3, 2a:36, 43, 69.

68 See Yücel, *Osmanlı Devlet Teşkilâtına*; *EI2*, s.v. "Kochu Bey," by C. Imber; *İA*, s.v. "Koçu Bey," by Ç. Uluçay; Bernard Lewis, "Ottoman Observers of Ottoman Decline," *IS* 1(1962): 71–87; A. Süheyl Ünver, "XVIIinci Yüzyıl Sonunda Padişaha bir Layiha," *Belleten* 33 (1969): 21–34.

69 İrvin Cemil Schick, "Representation of Gender and Sexuality in Ottoman and Turkish Erotic Literature," *TSAB* 28, no. 1–2 (2004): 90, 93. Andrews and Kalpaklı, *Age of Beloveds*, 167–74, on phallocentrism and insatiability as the more common heterosexual traits ascribed to women.

70 Diez, *Ermahnung*, 8; Kut, "Veysi'nin," 172; Kortantamer, "17. Yüzyıl Şairi Atayı'nın," 93–7.

The silence that erased historical women and female personality from the literary record of the period was broken by anecdotal acknowledgment of royal women. Their philanthropy and political activity were sometimes so prominent that their lives could not be disregarded. Chroniclers and poets praised queen mothers (*valide sultans*) and other women of the dynasty when they lived up to their sanctioned civic role, as maternal paragons or pious benefactresses. Approval was usually withheld from royal women, whether mothers, consorts, daughters, or sisters, who ventured too energetically – and perhaps too successfully – into dynastic politics.[71] A long line of powerful *valide*-regents – Nurbanu (d. 1583), mother of Murad III; Safiye (d. 1605), mother of Mehmed III; Kösem Mahpeyker (d. 1651), mother of Murad IV and İbrahim I; and Turhan (d. 1683), mother of Mehmed IV – inadvertently lent the term its negative cast.

Politics may have been the starting point of the *valide* critique, but gender was its foundation. That being said, men of all ranks and orders – Janissaries, courtiers, religious grandees, palace aghas, provincial strongmen – found it politically advantageous to ally themselves with these behind-the-scenes queens. For years at a time, powerful men sought their counsel and acted forcefully in their service, as grand viziers and sundry aghas did on behalf of Kösem, arguably the most famous of Ottoman mothers. When an outspoken preacher from the eastern provinces, a Nakşbendi sheikh called Saçlı ("long-haired" or "hairy") Mahmud, denounced Kösem and the power she wielded, he was bundled off to Süleymaniye's asylum. When he would not be silenced and continued to draw admiring crowds, he suffered the fate of many an uncompromising misfit and was expelled from the city.[72] All things considered, his punishment was light, a consequence either of Kösem's inclinations – she was fierce but known for compassionate philanthropy – or more probably of Mahmud's holy-man aura and his many sympathizers.[73]

Alliances with powerful women were not so taboo as political philosophers would have us believe. Otherwise, Kösem could not have remained a force for so long, and critics of an era reviled as a sultanate of women would have had less to grouse about. The point of contention with regard to the great *valides* of the seventeenth century was their exercise of power in the politics of dynastic

[71] For the roles and representation of royal women, see Peirce, *The Imperial Harem*; see also Gelibolulu Mustafa Âli, *Görgü ve Toplum Kuralları üzerinde Ziyâfet Sofraları (Mevâidü'n-Nefâis fi Kavâidi'l Mecâlis)*, ed. Orhan Şaik Gökyay (Istanbul, 1978), 1:81; Naima, *Tarih*, 5:106–22.

[72] Naima, *Tarih*, 5:315–16; von Hammer, *Geschichte*, 5:586.

[73] Sheikh (*Şeyh*) Mahmud, regarded in many quarters as a saintly ascetic, was said to be the nephew of another saintly figure, the famous Mahmud Urmevi, known as Urmiye or Rumiye Sheikh, a Nakşbendi whose vast following in eastern Anatolia worried Murad IV and led to the sheikh's death in 1639; Naima, *Tarih* 3:364–71. On Mahmud Urmevi's particular Nakşbendi line, see Le Gall, *A Culture of Sufism*, 73–80; also Dankoff, *Intimate Life*, 205–7, for Grand Vizier Melek Ahmed Pasha's admiring encounter with Urmevi when Melek was governor of Diyarbakir.

succession and rulership itself. There is little sense from historical accounts that their politicking was regarded as a source of social contagion with respect either to ordinary women or to the gendered order in society at large. Indeed, some chroniclers have as much to say about Kösem as a model benefactress – manumitting slaves by the dozen, feeding the poor, building mosques, and redeeming debtors – as about Kösem the presumptive sultan.[74]

The social legislation of the seventeenth century, admittedly still barely known, appears consonant with the discursive literature. Neither one was preoccupied with contemporary women's public behavior or with real women's transgressions or contagions, although particular women, notably female slave dealers, prostitutes, public scolds, and other law breakers did crop up in official documents as well as in unofficial literature. A definitive judgment on gender issues in the seventeenth century awaits further investigation. The near absence of women's clothing transgressions from the period's chronicles indicates relatively minor concern about sumptuary issues, although chroniclers may simply have been observing the statist conventions of the chronicle genre. The literati, including historians, moved in and around the ruling circles of the capital. They shared with the elites similar economic and cultural interests as well as the Olympian worldview of Istanbulites. For most of them, women, in more ways than one, occupied a remote cognitive field.

Awakening to society

As in the case of social legislation, so the general critique of the eighteenth century contrasts with that of the seventeenth century. In the eighteenth century, urban social issues began to attract ruling-class attention on a par with that devoted to imperial administration. The military and the budget were primary concerns and would remain so into the nineteenth century. However, the problems they represented were increasingly viewed in tandem with economic phenomena, with the behavior of consumers and producers of apparel the most public window on those concerns. State scrutiny increasingly turned to the public space of the municipality, to arenas of exchange and display. Bureaucrats, statesmen, and *ulema* intellectuals continued to agonize over the old institutional themes. Indeed, except for their individual emphases, Sarı Mehmed Pasha (d. 1717) sounded much like Koçi Bey (fl. 1640) and not unlike Tatarcık Abdullah (d. 1797).[75] But the conceptualization of the empire's

[74] Naima, *Tarih*, 5:106–22; *İA*, s.v. "Kösem," by M. Cavid Baysun; Peirce, *Imperial Harem*, 105–6, 247–52; Ahmed Refik [Altınay], *Kadınlar Saltanatı* (Istanbul, 1332/1913–14); von Hammer, *Geschichte*, 5:547; Baer, *Honored by the Glory*, 87.

[75] Cf. Wright, *Ottoman Statecraft*; Danışman, *Koçi Bey Risalesi*; Tatarcık Abdullah, "Nizam-i Devlet hakkında Mütalaat," 257–84; Yücel, *Osmanlı Devlet Teşkilâtına*, 163–6; Zilfi, *Politics of Piety*, 54–5, 212–14. See also Aksan, "Ottoman Political Writing," 53–69; Douglas A. Howard, "Ottoman Historiography and the Literature of 'Decline' of the Sixteenth and Seventeenth Centuries," *Journal of Asian History* 22 (1988): 52–77; Rhoads Murphey, "The

plight and the search for remedies accommodated rather different perspectives on social relations.

The militant puritanism championed by the Kadızadelis was implicitly, if not explicitly, disavowed after the ill-conceived attack on Vienna in 1683.[76] Nonetheless, the ideals of a righteous community and of disciplined conformity continued to have broad appeal among Muslim populations inside and outside the empire.[77] Among the ruling elites and in the population at large, the Nakşbendi Sufi movement held out hope for the fulfillment of both ideals. In Istanbul, it did so not with the arrogant opportunism of Vani Mehmed and the worst of the Kadızadelis but in the guise of a sober, *shari'ah*-minded Sufi order (*tarikat*) whose exemplars and friends found lasting though not uncontested celebrity in the empire.[78]

The *ulema*, statesmen, dynasts, intellectuals, and middle-strata individuals who found spiritual fellowship and direction in the Nakşbendi way were a varied lot. They differed in personal background and disposition as well as in the kind of benefit they hoped to gain from association with Nakşbendi sheikhs, rites, and fellow communicants. These lay friends – in contrast to the actual sheikhs and acolytes of the *tarikat* – frequented the order's lodges and ceremonies for all sorts of reasons, spiritual, convivial, political, and circumstantial. Many were friends of more than one Sufi order, taking part in discussions and rites in several orders' lodges and forming attachments to more than one order's sheikhs, as the spirit moved them. Some who associated with one or more Sufi orders remained attached for life. Others regretted their initial interest and moved on to different spiritual and socializing paths. Birgili Mehmed and Kadızade Mehmed early in their lives had sought instruction from Sufi mentors, Bayrami for the former and Halveti for the latter. Both not only dropped their association but also turned against the Sufism of the day, if not against Islamic mysticism entirely.[79]

In contrast to the emotive, Kadızadeli-targeted Sufism of the Halvetis and Mevlevis, the Nakşbendi order had come to be known in the capital region and

Veliyuddin Telhis: Notes on the Sources and Interrelations between Koçi Bey and Contemporary Writers of Advice to Kings," *Belleten* 43 (1979): 547–71.

76 War advocates like Vani Mehmed lost their palace patronage and ended their careers in banished obscurity, although Vani's banishment did not lack comfort and dignity; İsmail Hakkı Uzunçarşılı, *Osmanlı Devletinin İlmiye Teşkilâtı* (Ankara, 1965), 189; Zilfi, *Politics of Piety*, 157–8; Baer, *Honored by the Glory*, 226–7.

77 Flemming, "Die Vorwahhabitische Fitna," 55–65; Peters, "Battered Dervishes of Bab Zuwayla." In the later eighteenth century, the Wahhabi movement emerged from central Arabia to become the cutting edge of puritanical revivalism in the Arab provinces.

78 On the "renewed" (*Mücedded*) Nakşbendi order and its Halidiye (Ar., Khalidiyya) suborder in Ottoman lands, see Abu-Manneh, "The Naqshbandiyya-Mujaddidiyya," 2–36; Le Gall, *A Culture of Sufism*.

79 Katib Çelebi, *Balance*, 129; İbrahim Uşakizade, *Lebensbeschreibungen berühmter Gelehrten und Gottesmänner des Osmanischen Reiches im 17. Jahrhundert*, ed. Hans Joachim Kissling (Wiesbaden, 1965), 43–5; Katib Çelebi, *Fezleke-i Tarih* (Istanbul, 1286/1870), 2:64, 182–3; Nevizade Atayı, *Zeyl-i Şakaik* (Istanbul, 1268/1851–2), 179, 602–3, 759.

Anatolia for its erudite sheikhs, its close ties to ulema and lay hierarchs, and its establishment credentials in general. Still, the order was criticized over the years for encouraging or attracting a zealotry reminiscent of the Kadızadelis. At least one modern critic speaks of the combination of "fanatics" (*mutaassıb*) and men of distinction as a characteristic of the order's membership.[80] Most commentators of the time, however, reserved their criticisms for the actions of individuals rather than for the order itself. Among the most cited of such actions was the decision in 1680 by Beyazizade Ahmed – an adherent of the Nakşbendi order by avocation and the chief justice of the European provinces (*Kadıasker-i Rum*) by vocation – to carry out Istanbul's first and only stoning of an adulteress.[81]

As in other seventeenth-century societies that made adultery punishable by death,[82] Ottoman society leaned toward private resolutions or court-prescribed fines for a crime that required the near-impossible corroboration of four eyewitnesses.[83] The execution of 1680 was carried out with the support of the Kadızadeli, Vani Mehmed, though over the objections of other senior *ulema*.[84] The public stoning of a married Muslim woman for the crime of sexual intimacy (*zina*) with a Jewish tradesman – he was beheaded for the crime – is perhaps not so surprising given the empire's precarious footing in the period and Kadızadeli militancy regarding *shari'ah* rectitude and strict confessional boundaries.[85] Nonetheless, the judgment and spectacle came as an ugly

80 Abdülbaki Gölpınarlı, *Mevlânâ'dan sonra Mevlevîlik* (Istanbul, 1953), 47.

81 Bursalı Mehmed Tahir, *Osmanlı Müellifleri*, trans. A. F. Yavuz and I. Özen (Istanbul, 1972–5), 1:289; Şeyhi Mehmed, "Vekayı-i Fuzela (Zeyl-i Zeyl-i Atayı)," Istanbul, Süleymaniye Ktp., Hamidiye 939/1, fols. 233b–234b.

82 In the colonies of Massachusetts and Connecticut in the seventeenth century, capital punishment for adultery is said to have been carried out on just three occasions; Edmund S. Morgan, *The Puritan Family: Religion and Domestic Relations in Seventeenth-Century New England* (New York, 1966), 41.

83 Ronald C. Jennings, "Women in Early 17th-Century Ottoman Judicial Records – The Sharia Court of Anatolian Kayseri," *JESHO* 18 (1975): 53–114; Leslie P. Peirce, *Morality Tales: Law and Gender in the Ottoman Court of Aintab* (Berkeley, Calif., 2003), 103–5, 232, 331–3. The sultans' *kanun*s showed a preference for monetary fines in place of the severe physical penalties prescribed under Islamic law for such crimes as theft and adultery; see Mumcu, *Osmanlı Devletinde Siyaseten*, 179; Hadiye Tuncer, ed., *Yavuz Sultan Selim Han Kanunnamesi* (Ankara, 1987), 11–12. See Judith E. Tucker, *In the House of the Law: Gender and Islamic Law in Ottoman Syria and Palestine* (Berkeley, Calif., 1998), 175–8, for the way private solutions reinforced family power.

84 Raşid, *Tarih*, 1:362–3; Silahdar Fındıklılı Mehmed Ağa, *Silahdar Tarihi* (Istanbul, 1928), 1:731–2; Defterdar Sarı Mehmed, *Zübde*, 123–4; von Hammer, *Geschichte* 6:363–4, 464–5; Heyd, *Criminal Law*, 262, 340; Colin Imber, "Zinā' in Ottoman Law," in *Studies in Ottoman History and Law, Analecta Isisiana 20* (Istanbul, 1996), 175–206; Zilfi, *Politics of Piety*, 202–4.

85 Zilfi, *Politics of Piety*, 156–7. Marc Baer emphasizes the importance of Ottoman confessionalist policies in the period, especially Vani's and his patrons' efforts at mass conversion of the non-Muslim population and the Islamization of Christian and Jewish areas of the city; Baer, *Honored by the Glory*, 81–119.

surprise to many in Istanbul. Especially affronted were those who questioned whether the canonical requirement of four upright and irrefutable eyewitnesses had actually been met. According to contemporaneous accounts, Beyazizade's "new decisions on the subject of stoning shocked everyone." As a consequence, he was "loathed by all . . . among the *ulema* and the people."[86] Obviously not everyone was so shocked, as Beyazizade remained another three years as a chief justice, not to mention the fact that members of the public participated in stoning the woman to death.[87] Nonetheless, disagreement with the decision and the rarity of the event are evidence of divergent views about justice and judicial practice.[88]

Vani's motivations and probably Beyazizade's as well may have lain less in the punishment of adultery as in an effort – long standing in Vani's case – to capture Islam for the bounded and uncompromising partisanship that they themselves espoused. In overriding fellow *ulema* and the inclinations of many in the population, they asserted that claim. It was a sign of the social storms to come, though, that the episode's social and ideational fissures opened up over claims to a woman's body and an adultery conviction against a man who was not only a non-Muslim but one who made his living in a fabric shop. In the eighteenth century, sumptuary laws would become a key textual site for conflicts over just such elements. Nakşbendi adherents, including advisers to the most regulation-minded sovereigns, were important shapers of sumptuary policy, but *shari'ah*-minded social conservatism and the commitment to confessional hierarchy had wide as well as deep roots. Such views flourished because they made sense to many people without reference to any single institution or movement.

Struggles over the fundamental nature of Islamic society were bound to recur regardless of the event or era, and regardless of the seeming victory or defeat of one of the sides in these religious and political confrontations. The pursuit of righteousness and of the best society was a perennial preoccupation. It was guaranteed to remain fraught and contested as the painful developments of the eighteenth and nineteenth centuries put new strains on the existing grid of conflict and accommodation. Even if the deeper implications of the changes were barely understood, their felt symptoms sparked the eighteenth century's calls for order and restoration, this time in the lexical frame of commerce and Western encroachment.

86 Defterdar Sarı Mehmed, *Zübde*, 123–4; Raşid, *Tarih* 1:362–3; Ali Uğur, *The Ottoman 'Ulemā in the Mid-17th Century: An Analysis of the Vakā'i'u'l-Fuzalā of Mehmed Şeyhī Ef* (Berlin, 1986), 578–82. See also Imber, "Zinā," 176–8.

87 Beyazizade's tenure as Rumelia chief justice (*kadıasker*), lasting until 1683, coincided with the ascendancy of the Kadızadelis and the war party led by Grand Vizier Kara Mustafa Pasha (executed 1683).

88 Beyazizade's father, Beyazi Hasan, as *kadı* of Istanbul in 1651–2, was involved in a judicial controversy of his own, even trading blows with a *kadıasker*; Naima, *Tarih*, 5:201; Uğur, *Ottoman 'Ulemā*, 145–6; Mehmed Süreyya, *Sicill-i Osmani* (Istanbul, 1308–15/1891–7), 2:135.

In the eighteenth century, Osman III's three-year reign stands out for its blatant and often bizarre misogyny.[89] In contrast to the more family-friendly sultans who succeeded him, he is said to have ordered the women of Topkapı Palace – five or six hundred at the time – to stay out of sight when he came their way. To prevent accidental encounters, he reportedly had taps attached to his footwear to signal his approach. Apart from his single-mindedness, his view of consumption was typical of the era and of the outlook of his brother sultans. His decree of 1757, a "prohibition on women in the markets and bazaars," was briefer than some. Its sentiments about women and the masculine gendering of public space, however, were unambiguous:

> Women [*taife-i nisvan*] have been seen going about the markets and bazaars dressed in unsuitable colors [*bed renk*], with dustcoats [*ferace*s] made of fine wool [*şalı*], and huge headdresses [*bűyűk başlar*], and locks of hair protruding from their veils [*yaşmak*s]. They are not to go about in close-fitting dustcoats but in the manner of upright and virtuous folk. This imperial decree strictly commands once again that women not leave their residences, but in accordance with holy writ [*medlul-i şerif űzere*] remain in their own houses except out of needs sanctioned by holy law [*hacet-i şer'iye*] This command is issued to the representatives of each and every precinct [*mahalle*].[90]

With its Qur'anic and *shari'ah* allusions, Osman's decree was directed at Muslim women, who were sure to feel its religious weight. However, the reference to women (*taife-i nisvan*) without a further qualifier encompasses women generally and, in context, suggests repugnance toward women's bodies.[91] Physical womanliness was to be draped and veiled so as to be both desexualized as female and anonymous as to individual identity.

For Osman and those of like mind, misogyny and zealous enforcement of female propriety were two sides of the same coin. From that perspective, even properly clad women were unacceptably visible, the very coverage of their bodies and faces marking them as female. Urban space was ideally conceived as masculine, but that notion was no more stable than were other gender norms. Masculine right in the urban milieu had to be reinforced by fiat and force, lest reality completely overtake it. There were always relatively few women in the markets and bazaars, but they were far from absent as buyers and, on certain days of the week, as sellers. In addition to errands and vocational labors, women visited relatives, made pilgrimages to shrines, and took cases to court, many of them complaints against men. Still, the sovereign masculinity

[89] On the oddities of Osman's reign, see Rasim, *Resimli ve Haritalı*, 2:891–7; von Hammer, *Geschichte*, 8:177; Mouradgea D'Ohsson, *Tableau général de l'Empire Othoman* (Paris, 1788–1824), 7:74.

[90] Hâkim, "Hâkim Tarihi," B231, fol. 234b, Receb 1170/1757.

[91] In the polyglot Ottoman lexicon, the Arabic-Ottoman plural for women, *nisvan* (Ar., *niswān*; sing., *nisa'*), the preferred term for women in the Qur'an, was common parlance for women generally in period ordinances. The Persian-derived *zenan*, the Turkish *hatunlar*, and the Arabic-Turkish compound *avretler* also occur, with the last, *avretler*, "women" or "wives," having a more generic and common ring.

propounded by official rhetoric made the street scene uncomfortable for every woman and treacherous for those unaccompanied or in marginal occupations. Moreover, ill-intentioned relatives and neighbors could use the law to discredit women for personal advantage; moral ordinances had private as well as public utility.

On the streets, women were challenged not only by officers of the law but also by loutish males who relished the chance to do the sultan's and, they might say, God's will. Women themselves were watchdogs of their sisters' morality, and although their opportunities for policing others were limited by their own limited mobility, they were the eyes and ears of the neighborhoods. As for the police, they were not known for delicacy when apprised of wrongdoing. In Ottoman Turkish, as in English, it is remarkable how many words denote beating implements – *stick*, *staff*, *rod*, *cane*, *pole*, *pike*, *truncheon*, *club*, *bat*, *paddle*, *cudgel*, and *bludgeon*, among others (*asa*, *çub*, *dayak*, *değnek*, *sopa*, *sırık*, *falaka*, *çubuk*, *çomak*, *matrak*, *tomak*, *topuz*[92]). Ottoman officials who patrolled the streets did so with sticks to administer thrashings when a simple fine would not do. It was in the interests of the policing authorities to be seen as pursuing malefactors so long as the policy had the attention of the sultan or his senior officers. And as first-line enforcers, they had ample opportunity to extract bribes in return for turning a blind eye. The chronicles are not forthcoming about the number of fines, beatings, and deaths that ensued from sumptuary issuances. Because simple people were the usual victims of regulatory assaults, their discomforts were seldom tabulated. The punishment of women was even less noteworthy, but women as well as men are known to have been beaten and killed for infractions of various kinds throughout the period.[93]

Given Sultan Osman's behavior at home, it is not surprising that his aversions affected women at large. He extended his fantasy of an all-male world by ordering Istanbul's women off the streets on the three days of the week that he himself would be moving about the city.[94] Having spent fifty-some years of princely life under virtual house arrest in the inner precincts of the palace, he had perhaps already seen too many women for his own homosocial or homosexual tastes. Osman had fewer scruples about seeing or being seen by men masquerading as women, however. Although transvestite dancing boys (*köçek*) were occasionally banned from the palace in moments of imperial self-awareness, their performances apparently remained a staple entertainment of the palace even in Osman's day. A frequent subject for the painters of the period, boy-girl dancers, some known as rabbits or bunnies (*tavşan*),

92 The "stick" meaning of some of these has not survived into modern Turkish.

93 Rasim, *Resimli ve Haritalı*, 2:896; de Tott, *Memoirs*, 1, pt. 1:125–6, 162; von Hammer, *Geschichte*, 4:262; M. Turhan Tan, *Tarihî Fıkralar* (Istanbul, 1962), 33; Köse, "XVIII. Yüzyıl Sonları," 115. Indeed, the ordinances of the eighteenth and nineteenth centuries called for brutality.

94 Von Hammer, *Geschichte*, 8:177; D'Ohsson, *Tableau*, 7:74.

were immensely popular in elite circles and remained so into the nineteenth century.[95] Female impersonators enlivened royal courts throughout Europe and were perfectly at home – with attendant sexual ambiguities – wherever ideologies of male priority and exclusivism found favor.

The sumptuary frame of the eighteenth-century legislation reflects, among other things, the dynasty's reimagined imperial role. In contrast to *gazi*-warrior ancestors who had led vast armies on foreign ground, the sultans of the eighteenth century were more disposed to exercise domestic leadership. They dispatched armies but only for the command of their vizierial deputies. The monarch stayed home, a social warrior among his own people.[96] The Janissaries were central to both projects. The sultans remained rulers of their empire, but it was their Janissary police whom they most directly commanded. In this regard, too, the sultan was often, and sometimes mainly, the mayor of Istanbul.

Mustafa III and his brother Abdülhamid I were more at ease with the women in their lives than was their cousin Osman, but affection for one's own intimates is no predictor of public policy. Mustafa's and Abdülhamid's indulgence of sundry sisters, nieces, aunts, and daughters did not translate into generosity toward lesser women. Mustafa began his reign by seconding Osman's harsh initiatives.[97] One of his inaugural ordinances addressed Muslim women (*taife-i nisvan-i Müslüman, Müslüman hatunları*) and non-Muslim women. The latter specifically included both Jews and Christians (*ehl-i zimmet taifesi nisvanı, kefere nisvanı, zenan-i erbab-i zimmet ez Yahud ve Nasrani)*, although there would have been little doubt that both were intended. The dos and don'ts of the text were straightforward: Muslim women were not to wear fine wool (*şali*) or dustcoats in nontraditional colors (*rengâmiz*) or large headdresses or face-revealing veils. Christian and Jewish women's outdoor attire was to consist of black or blue dustcoats and red boots. Red and green *ferace*s and yellow leather boots were reserved for Muslim women.[98] Abdülhamid took his turn at sartorial control in 1776 with a comprehensive code – of protectionist

95 Metin And, *Osmanlı Şenliklerinde Türk Sanatları* (Ankara, 1982), 175–91; Mehmet Zeki Pakalın, *Osmanlı Tarih Deyimleri ve Terimleri Sözlüğü* (Istanbul, 1946–54), s.v.v. "çengi," "köçek," "rakkas," and "tavşan." According to Rasim, *Resimli ve Haritalı*, 2:896, Osman banned the troupes only briefly at the outset of his reign. See also Andrews and Kalpaklı, *Age of Beloveds*, 178, on the larger context of homosociability and the role of female impersonators.

96 Zilfi, "A Medrese for the Palace," 189–91.

97 Mustafa's fixation on sumptuary control is said to have been encouraged by Koca Ragıb Pasha, Osman III's last grand vizier, who until his death in 1763 served Mustafa III in the same role; Ragıb, a poet and man of letters, was a strong Nakşbendi affiliate. See Rasim, *Resimli ve Haritalı*, 2:912–13, and de Tott, *Memoirs*, 1, pt. 1:125–6, for negative assessments of Ragıb's role, although de Tott seldom has anything positive to say about persons and things Ottoman or Turkish. Itzkowitz, "Mehmed Raghib Pasha," 135–6, notes that Ragıb was regarded as liberal-minded by the foreign consuls residing in Aleppo when he served as governor, but they very likely had in mind his policies regarding trade rather than gender relations.

98 Hâkim, "Hâkim Tarihi," B233, fol. 10b, 1173 Safer/1759; see also Melek Sevüktekin Apak, Filiz Onat Gündüz, and Fatma Öztürk Eray, *Osmanlı Dönemi Kadın Giyimleri* (Ankara, 1997), 101.

inspiration – for male subjects particularly.[99] He was bent on reinstating usages from thirty years earlier to put a stop to "the lower orders hankering to emulate the middle, and the middle seeking to be the high." Aimed at public servants of every rank and degree, the regulation acknowledged that government officers were egregious transgressors against the rules they were supposed to enforce.[100]

Clothing improprieties usually took place in or close to one's own neighborhood, where the local eminences were often coreligionists. Nenad Filipovic's research offers an eye-opening perspective on the deep anxieties and complex concerns of minority leaders faced with menacing regulations. In June 1794, in response to harsh strictures during the reign of Selim III, a clearly nervous Serbian Orthodox priest admonished his flock about disobeying "the order of our masters the Ottomans." With regard to women not veiling and adults wearing gold ornaments outside the home: "first of all, God does not like it, and when he does not like it, how can the Ottomans like it?" As for young men who had taken to wearing vests (*çepken*) in imitation of Janissary garb: "We said many times earlier that because it is the costume of the Ottomans and [their] pashas, you must not wear it. . . . Really, do not say that we did not tell you. . . . The one who is good will listen and obey, and the one who does not listen, that one lacks even fear of God. . . . Let the Lord extend His grace to those who obey, and let the Lord punish those who do not obey."[101] Fear of God was common to sermonizing in all religious communities and, not incidentally, endorsed by the authoritarian state. Yet it was clearly not enough to deter everyone who thought to try out an unaccustomed fashion.

Muslim and Muslim-dominant neighborhoods, and especially their female inhabitants, were arguably subject to the strictest supervision. Muslim men and women were enjoined to abide by communal custom and religious and imperial law and thereby live up to the high standard of true belief. Members of the minorities residing in their own homogeneous communities operated at a certain remove from state officialdom. They were buffered by coreligionist neighbors and by the direct administration of their own confessional leadership. For Muslims, Islamic religious leaders from the *şeyhülislam* down to *mahalle* imams were effectively government employees. Imperial authority of every variety saturated many Muslim residential areas. Although many neighborhoods in major cities were mixed, Janissaries, Bostancıs, and other police-soldiers who were assigned to duties all over the capital tended to live in quarters with high Muslim concentrations. Senior and junior Muslim religious functionaries, in office or awaiting posts, were apt to reside near the Old City's

99 Rasim, *Resimli ve Haritalı*, 907, 1035–53; Cevdet, *Tarih-i Cevdet*, 2:50–1.

100 Cevdet, *Tarih-i Cevdet*, 2:50.

101 Personal typescript, 1–4. I thank Professor Filipovic for alerting me to this valuable text and for providing a translation and explication. According to Filipovic, the original document was uncovered in 1902 by the Bosnian Ottomanist Vladislav Skaric.

concentration of schools, mosques, and libraries, and thus in largely Muslim neighborhoods.

In the decrees of the eighteenth century, a glaring impropriety in Muslim women's dress was often held to be its revealing character. Sleeker, more tailored dustcoats were expressly forbidden in Osman III's ordinance, as they had been in edicts issued in the early eighteenth century. Inadequate veiling – diminutive or diaphanous – was always a concern, though one of many. Mustafa's decree picked up where Osman's left off, condemning transparent veils as well as the use of delicate, clinging wool (*şali*) for the prescriptively loose and opaque *ferace* dustcoat.[102] Although the sturdy *ferace* protected indoor clothing from the dirt of the street, its mandated purpose was to disguise the sight and the suggestion of female curves. As a decree of Selim III in the 1790s put it, "[I]nasmuch as Ankara *şali* is thin and delicate, there is no difference between going about in a *ferace* made of Ankara wool and wearing no coat at all." Women's home attire, their intimate garments as it were, could easily be discerned beneath flimsy coats. "This practice," the decree proclaims in something of an understatement, "has been prohibited by *ferman* many times in the past."[103]

The second impropriety, unequivocal in the decree from Mustafa's reign, was laid at the door of Muslim, Christian, and Jewish women alike. The attempt at changeable, individualized fashion on the part of some women in the city was not to be tolerated. The ostensible complaint had to do with violations of designated confessional colors, but fashion as extravagance also underlay the charge. In fact, there had already been boundary erosion on the female clothing front. Sixteenth-century legislation had stipulated that only Muslim women, not Christians or Jews, might wear the outer garment known as the *ferace*, but efforts to make it exclusively Muslim had little permanent effect.[104] By the mid-eighteenth century, the collarless or small-collared *ferace* was the baseline garb for all women, with color as an essential communal marker.[105]

Like other Ottoman clothing practices, female outer garments conveyed important cues to social exchange in a complex urban setting. Clothing took much of the guesswork out of the demands of etiquette. Muslims, Christians, and Jews approached their own coreligionists with marks of recognition and affirmation. As a seventeenth-century author put it, in a sartorially untidy

[102] *Şali* can refer to alpaca, cashmere, mohair, camlet, or other fine, expensive wool.

[103] Altınay, *Hicrî On Üçüncü*, 4.

[104] Ahmed Refik [Altınay], *On Altıncı Asırda İstanbul Hayatı (1553–1591)* (Istanbul, 1935), 47–8.

[105] D'Ohsson, *Tableau*, 4, pt. 1:149–55; also Apak et al., *Osmanlı Dönemi*, 101. See esp. Donald Quataert, "Clothing Laws, State and Society in the Ottoman Empire, 1720–1829," *IJMES* 29 (1997): 403–25, regarding Ottoman "colors of rule" in the eighteenth and nineteenth centuries.

world, "Muslims do not know who is a Muslim and who is an unbeliever, so they [mistakenly] render Islamic greetings and other respects."[106] Failure to abide by clothing rules hindered recognition of who was subject to the full weight of Islamic law and privy to its politesse and who was not. During his sojourn in Ottoman Turkey, Aaron Hill also noted clothing's class connotations, which were such that one may "pay the nice punctilios of respect, which are required from every quality to those above 'em and those below them," even if all are strangers.[107] The frame of reference in these regards was male, as males' showing of respect to appropriately attired Muslim women meant not recognizing and thus not greeting them.

Muslims had greater choice than non-Muslims – Muslim women less so than Muslim men – in outdoor colors and fabrics. Muslims of both sexes had exclusive right to the public use of the finer leather from which yellow boots and slippers were made. Until the clothing reforms of Mahmud II and his successors in the nineteenth century, yellow leather footwear (*sarı çizme*, *sarı çedik*) was fetishized as a Muslim prerogative and badge. Until that change, more than one unlucky non-Muslim male may have met his death just for putting his foot into the wrong kind of shoe.[108] Yellow boots – soft Moroccan or Moroccan-style leather – were a regulatory constant during the Ottoman centuries. Even after the fashion and the empire itself had passed into history, "the wearer of yellow boots" continued to mean "a person of importance."[109]

The fabrics used for robes and headgear had a more complicated history. The precise textiles subject to regulation varied over time, in response to innovations in production and shifts in tastes.[110] In the sixteenth and seventeenth centuries, silk and velvet brocades, satins, compound silks, and fine muslin (*kemha*, *diba*, *seraser*, *atlas*, *kütni*, and *dülbend*) along with ermine, sable, and black-fox fur were the power fabrics of the day, high-priced, scarce, and jealously regulated.[111] They symbolized imperial authority and were palpable marks of favor in the Ottoman gift economy. Their possession was supposed to be decided by patronage politics and office holding rather than markets and money. The regulation of even these rarities was not foolproof, not even when

[106] Yücel, *Osmanlı Devlet Teşkilâtına*, 117. Quataert, "Clothing Laws," 403–25.

[107] Hill, *A Full and Just Account*, chap. 12.

[108] Zilfi, "Goods in the Mahalle," 300–1; de Tott, *Memoirs*, 1:125–6; Altınay, *Hicrî On İkinci*, 84; Hâkim, "Hâkim Tarihi," B233, fol. 33b; von Hammer, *Geschichte*, 7:54–5; Defterdar Sarı Mehmed, 742; Hill, *A Full and Just Account*, chap. 12; Eldem, *French Trade*, 234. Several of the sources have reference to the same incident, however.

[109] Redhouse Press, *Yeni Türkçe-İngilizce Sözlük* (1968; repr., Istanbul, 1979), 985–6.

[110] See Suraiya N. Faroqhi, "Declines and Revivals in Textile Production," in Faroqhi, ed., *Cambridge History*, 356–75.

[111] Şevki Nezihi Aykut, ed., *Şer'iyye Sicillerine göre İstanbul Tarihi: İstanbul Mahkemesi 121 Numaralı Şer'iyye Sicili* (Istanbul, 2006), 147; Fritz Klebe, "Kleidervorschriften für Nichtmuslimische Untertanen des Turkischen Reiches im 16. Jahrhundert," *Der Neue Orient* 7, no. 4 (1920): 169–71; Altınay, *On Altıncı*, 47, 51. *EI2*, s.v.v. "Kutn: The Ottoman Empire" and "Harīr: The Ottoman Empire," by Halil İnalcık.

imperial authority was at its height, but the cost and laborious manufacture of high-end silk fabrics helped limit their circulation to mandated wearers.

In the eighteenth century, the sumptuary regime had a different bundle of fabrics to worry about. Fine wools and patterned cottons produced in France, England, and India, among other places, were entering Ottoman markets by the shipload.[112] As substitutes for elite-wear silks and brocades, they presented a host of problems. They were almost exclusively imports, with all that that portended for the balance of trade and the prosperity of indigenous producers and products. In addition, they were popular. Their appearance was appealing, and their pricing and availability dovetailed with upper- and middle-class aspirations more than had been possible with silvered brocades and satins. Given European manufacturing techniques and access to Ottoman markets as of the late eighteenth century, consumption could not be sufficiently curtailed, nor could the prestige value of the better cottons and wools be confined to just the elite orders. In attire and liquidity, consumers and the merchants and retailers who dealt in such goods were a growing affront to the crumbling Ottoman order. That so many goods were of European provenance and that so many consumers and suppliers were Christians, when the enemy on the outside was Christian as well, fueled the impulse to regulate and constrain.

Even more than feet and boots, the Ottoman head, real and symbolic, answered to a dense set of expectations. It is no accident that senior civil and military officials were so often called head (*baş*, *reis*, *ser*) this or that – *başdefterdar*, *başçavuş*, *müneccimbaşı*, *hekimbaşı*, *odabaşı*, *kapıcıbaşı*, *reisülkuttab*, *serasker*, *serdar*. Male Muslim tombstones, topped by stone versions of official Ottoman headgear, carried the symbolics of status and seniority to the grave.[113] Female grave markers, sometimes with sculpted veils and garlands, represented women's purity perhaps but also suggested their limited social identity. As for the living female head, it could convey class location through the quality and amplitude of fabric, although in the seventeenth and eighteenth centuries, non-Muslim women of the wealthier classes – like non-Muslim men – were more experimental about head coverings, as they were about outdoor clothing in general.

In life, the masculine head's adornments could denote social rank, vocation, and religious affiliation. Christian and Jewish males of the upper and middle classes had their hats or bonnets (*şapka*, *kalpak*). The turban, meanwhile, was marked as a true "Islamic symbol" (*alamet-i İslamiye*).[114] Indeed, donning the turban was synonymous with converting to Islam. As in earlier Islamic states,

[112] Faroqhi, "Declines and Revivals." Although Eldem's *French Trade* is mainly concerned with the history of French commercial activity, it also deals with the economics of taste and the role of commodities in Ottoman-European relations; on imported cloth and European competition for the Ottoman market, see 34–67.

[113] James E. P. Boulden, *An American among the Orientals, including an Audience with the Sultan and a Visit to the Interior of a Turkish Harem* (Philadelphia, 1855), 144–5.

[114] Altınay, *Hicrî On Üçüncü*, 11.

turbans were a masculine Muslim preserve, or so it was said.[115] In fact, there is ample room for debate as to what made a turban a turban – what quality of fabric, exactly how much winding, and with what final shape and size. The uniform hats of the various military orders were peculiar to those units alone. Certain monumental head toppings, the majestic *kallavi* and *örf*, and the tall, pleated *mücevveze*, were off-limits to all but a handful of high officeholders. And even those showy forms were worn only on official, usually ceremonial, occasions.[116]

Other types of wrapped or wadded dressings were a different matter. For men in official positions, not only the shape and size of a head dressing but also the quality and color of winding fabrics and the presence or absence of decorative folds, embroidery, plumes, and crests constituted an inventory of male ranks and vocations. Given the supply-and-demand woes of the time and the regime's insistence on visualized power, it is hardly accidental that Sultan Mustafa III added extra yards and plumage to his own turban, by all accounts, a unique concoction. In a similar manner, the vizier and dandy Kalaylıkoz ("Burnished Walnut") Ahmed (d. 1715) had more gold added to his already grand *kallavi* even while he brutally restricted non-Muslim and female costume.[117] The energy the two men expended to raise their own sartorial profile and beat down others' says a great deal about the regime's obsession with the appearance of things, most especially the appearance of power.

Reporting on male head dressings in the early eighteenth century, Aaron Hill commented that their "various colours, forms, and magnitudes . . . contain the marks of splendor and subjection," with "spotless white" the most desirable color, whereas "speckled" turbans were "a mark whereby they know a Christian, who must never wear one of a pure and single colour."[118] Hill's certitude notwithstanding, all that one can say about Ottoman practice is that the finished product for non-Muslim – and female – heads was not to resemble

[115] Mounira Chapoutot-Remadi, "Femmes dans la ville mamluke, *JESHO* 38, no. 2 (1995): 151–3, which also refers to Ibn Taymiyya's and other jurists' *fetva*s against "turbans" on women. Similarly, the wearing of a hat by Muslims was seen as tantamount to apostasy in the eyes of many religious thinkers.

[116] On monumentality in Ottoman headgear, see Zdzisław Żygulski, *Ottoman Art in the Service of the Empire* (New York, 1992), 107; see also Sevin, *On Üç Asırlık*, 96–7.

[117] Although Kalaylıkoz is said to have had family ties to the tinning trade (*kalay*, *kalaylı*), the "burnished walnut" meaning of his name fits his reputation for sartorial excess and vanity. See Danişmend, *İzahlı Osmanlı Tarihi*, 5:51–2; von Hammer, *Geschichte* 7:107–8; D'Ohsson, *Tableau*, 4, pt. 1:116; *DBİA*, s.v. "II. Ahmed," by Necdet Sakaoğlu, 110. On the *kallavi* and other turbans, see Sevin, *On Üç Asırlık*, 109, and the illustrations in Esin Atıl, *Levni and the Surname: The Story of an Eighteenth-Century Ottoman Festival* (Istanbul, 1999). Christoph K. Neumann, "How Did a Vizier Dress in the Eighteenth Century?" in Faroqhi, *Ottoman Costumes*, 181–217, provides a comprehensive discussion of vizierial garb, including detailed clothing inventories of two dispossessed officials.

[118] Hill, *A Full and Just Account*, chap. 12. See also C.-F. Volney, *Voyage en Syrie et en Égypte* (Paris, 1799), 2:239–40, who reports that Christians in Egypt had had to revert to "their old form of turban."

Fig. 6. Ornate head dressing of imperial women, seventeenth to eighteenth centuries. Cornelis de Bruyn, *A Voyage to the Levant* (London, 1702).

then-current Muslim male headgear as designated for civil, religious, or military officialdom. Nor should Christians and Jews make use of the colors – principally pure white, though also green or black – or the rarer gauzes out of which upper-class Muslim turbans were constructed. According to innumerable decrees, in Ottoman times and before, women and minority men were both denied the fabrics and shapes associated with elite male turbans.[119] Lower-class men also fell into the denied category, but whether Muslim or not, they lacked the means for extravagance.

On the lowest rungs of the social ladder, headgear and garments were more homogeneous across the religious confessions, especially among the urban laboring classes and among men in similar occupations.[120] It was in the middle and upper classes that sartorial minutiae could be employed as measurements

[119] See, however, Sevin, *On Üç Asırlık*, 64, 96–7, 103. Elliot, "Dress Codes," 103–23, traces legal exceptions among resident foreigners in Istanbul and elsewhere in the empire.

[120] Red wool caps imported from Marseille in the seventeenth century were said to have been popular with minority men as well as with the "poorer classes of Turk [Muslim]"; Sonia P. Anderson, *An English Consul in Turkey: Paul Rycaut at Smyrna, 1667–1678* (Oxford, 1989), 58–9. See also the illustrations of working-class garb in Quataert, "Clothing Laws," 415–19, and Ahmet Kal'a et al., eds., *İstanbul Külliyâtı, İstanbul Esnaf Birlikleri ve Nizamları 1* (Istanbul, 1998).

of worth and power. Disposable wealth and the desire to appear in prestigious garments accounted for most of the handsomely clad merchants and tradesmen, Muslim and non-Muslim, whom the official classes saw as unworthy competitors. Europeans conversant with upwardly mobile local Christians remind us that defiance and disdain were also part of the clothing competition. As the empire's military power waned, respect for the swaggering prerogatives of its officials – most especially its overbearing and underperforming military – waned along with it.[121] The negative sentiments were shared by segments of the Muslim population – hence the constant talk about reforming the military – but a groundswell occurred only in the 1820s, when Mahmud set about to rid the empire of the Janissaries. In the meantime, some of the clothing trespasses from Muslims below as well as on the part of Christians and Jews can be ascribed to disrespect for the system rather than to admiring emulation.

The politics of emanation, the halo effect of elite patronage, was equally important in the ability of *reaya* of various religions and vocations to take advantage of reserved garb. Christians, Jews, and Muslims who were employed by the Ottoman dynasty or by others of the governing elites as personal bankers, physicians, furriers, translators, and concessionaires had a share in their patron's status and prerogatives. In contrast to their patron's slaves, who literally embodied their master's status, clients could invoke the protective cover of a patron's social place. Non-Muslims who performed these elite *reaya* roles also escaped many of the rules that bound their coreligionists. They could dress in special fabrics and trimmings that their patrons conferred on them or that they purchased for themselves.

The privileges of privileged *reaya*, however, could come at a price. Access to power brought risks like those faced by the aghas, viziers, governors, and dynasts whom they served. Along with the omnipresent danger of estate confiscation, privileged *reaya* had to contend with popular jealousies. The Christian furrier, banker, and intimate of the Tulip Era's Grand Vizier Nevşehirli İbrahim Pasha (d. 1730) was high on the list of victims of the bloody uprising that toppled Ahmed III and secured the execution of İbrahim.[122] Some decades later, a palace physician on horseback in the capital was viciously beaten by a navy commander when the man did not make way fast enough. Riding on horseback, especially in the city, was a jealously guarded prerogative. Prior to the seventeenth century, even Muslim officials below the topmost ranks had been denied the right, although thereafter the ban was

[121] David Porter, *Constantinople and Its Environs in a Series of Letters from Constantinople* (New York, 1835), 2:153–8. Bernard Lewis, "Slade on Turkey," in Osman Okyar and Halil İnalcık, eds., *Türkiye'nin Sosyal ve Ekonomik Tarihi* (1071–1920) (Ankara, 1980), 215–25, sees a similar psychology of disdain on the part of Greeks in rebellion against Ottoman rule in the 1820s.

[122] Aktepe, *Patrona İsyanı*, 151–2.

softened.[123] According to the historian Cevdet, around 1817, the fact that most Muslim government officials were denied the right while non-Muslims in the service of state dignitaries could go about on horseback led to so much hostility on the part of Muslim police and other state functionaries that permissions for non-Muslims were restricted to only the disabled and infirm among them. For commoners and officials, Muslims and non-Muslims, the city remained an essentially pedestrian environment.[124]

Physicians' service to the dynasty and community at large gained them legal entitlement to clothing and transport privileges, but official patents did not afford them complete protection. Although the offending naval officer in the foregoing incident was dismissed from office and banished from the capital, it is doubtful that he was alone in thinking the physician's comeuppance well deserved. Nor was the battered physician the first or last Christian or Jewish protégé to fall victim to street aggression. The attacker was higher placed but not untypical of the sort of men who often figured in such violence. The assailants of privileged *reaya* in the heart of official Istanbul were unlikely to be everyday commoners but men affiliated with the military or having such connections. Indeed, the solidarity of the barracks often played a role in such events, with unruly individuals acting in the confidence that they would have instant defenders among nearby comrades. In the middle decades of the nineteenth century, after the destruction of the Janissaries and the reorganization of the army, European visitors who remembered the bad, old days marveled at their ability to move about Istanbul unchallenged by slurs and threats.

Breaking with history

Whatever the motives of individual consumers, by the mid-eighteenth century, clothing assertions were penetrating into the middle classes, most especially into the higher echelons of the commercial classes. Dressmaking elaborations in women's clothing routinely triggered legislation restricting buyers and sellers alike. Dressing up the *ferace* with nontraditional collars, oversized and capelike to reach the waist or scraping the ground like a long cloak, or with embroidery, braiding, or other edging, or cut from Moroccan leather, with ever deeper V-shaped necks to expose the garment beneath, made for fashion and

123 D'Ohsson, *Tableau*, 4, pt. 1:189; Koçu, *Osmanlı Tarihinde*, 33; Şanizade Mehmed Ataullah, *Tarih-i Şanizade* (Istanbul, 1290/1873), 2:249–50; Kemal Çiçek, "Osmanlılar ve Zimmiler: Papa Pavlos'nun İslâm'a Hakareti ya da Renklere İsyanı," in Çiçek and Saydam, *Kıbrıs'tan Kafkasya'ya*, 140–1. See also Altınay, *Hicrî On İkinci*, 20, and Kal'a et al., *İstanbul Esnaf Tarihi 1*, 94, for official confirmation of physicians' entitlements regarding riding on horseback and wearing elite garb.

124 Cevdet, *Tarih-i Cevdet*, 10:186. Until the loosened sumptuary laws of the nineteenth century, carriages were as restricted as horses, with strict rules as to who might use them and where.

Fig. 7. "Musicians at the Asian Valley of Sweet Waters." Women's entertainment at Göksu on the Asian coast of the Bosphorus. Pardoe, *Beauties of the Bosphorus*.

expense.[125] In periods when police were putting knives or scissors to female collars, women and the dressmakers who accommodated them turned to billowy sleeves, ornamental buttons, embroidery, frogging, pleats, and gores. When those, too, were banned, women tried voluminous collars again, and again they faced knife-bearing enforcers: "They're wearing tall headdresses and long collars and very light colors. . . . It's forbidden. . . . Wherever you see these things, cut off these collars . . . and hats."[126]

We do not know how many women, especially Muslim women, took a chance on the new styles and imported fabrics. Clearly more and more of them did, especially in bustling commercial areas, in mixed neighborhoods like those of Pera and Galata, and in the more remote suburbs of the Golden Horn and Bosphorus. Ottoman women's behavior reflected a pattern of experimentation and assertion common to women in other parts of Europe as well.[127] Responses on the part of the Ottoman authorities, however, were sharply confrontational

125 The word *collar* (*yaka*) was used for almost any extra fabric attached to the neckline of the *ferace*; see illustrations in Sevin, *On Üç Asırlık*, and Apak et al., *Osmanlı Dönemi*.

126 Karal, *Selim III'ün Hat-tı Hümayunları*, 102. Abdülhamid II (1878–1908) ordered scissors-bearing police to apprehend women wearing the *çarşaf*, the new outer garb of the late nineteenth century. One woman had her *çarşaf* cut off three times in two years; Sevin, *On Üç Asırlık*, 131. Among his many fears, Abdülhamid had cause to worry about male dissidents disguising themselves by wearing the capacious *çarşaf*. In fourteenth-century Cairo, Mamluk knives were used on women's voluminous sleeves; see Chapoutot-Remadi, "Femmes dans la ville mamluke," 150.

127 Hughes, "Sumptuary Law," 69–99.

with no sign of abatement between the 1770s and 1820s. Despite state concerns about fashion and imports as a threat to the fisc, if the regime's principal intent had been to curb costly imports, it could have looked more seriously at the dynasty's own appetites, especially at the fabrics, furnishings, and outfitted entourages required for the new royal residences sprouting up all around Istanbul.[128] Instead, the overlap between economic protectionism and status anxiety gave Ottoman regulation its aggressive and slightly desperate air in the late eighteenth century and early nineteenth century.

Edicts having to do with Muslim women's clothing faulted overdressing, underdressing, and imitation. Whatever the specific offense, the legislation usually drew on one of two damning analogies to make its point, either condemning women's attire as un-Islamic in its likeness to Christian and/or Jewish women's clothing or, in the case of large head dressings, deploring the trespass against male Muslim prerogatives. When women were warned against using many squares of cloth for their heads rather than a modest three, their double crime was profligacy and presumption. Large millinery styles were unnecessarily expensive and too much like those reserved for state eminences (*serefraz-i ricala mahsus*), it was said. An edict from 1734 refers to "big-head styles like those of European and native Greek women" (*nisvan-i Rum ve Frenge mümasıl büyük başlar*).[129] Sultans Osman, Mustafa, and Abdülhamid in later decrees made similar pronouncements, although theirs were almost lost amid their other bans and strictures.[130] Women's perceived deviations from custom were condemnable for their damage to the budgets of both household and society.[131] Whatever the truth of that criticism, history did not support the authorities on the matter of imitation.

State policies along with a formidable line of earlier Islamic dictates denounced female fashion that smacked of non-Muslimness, the foreign, the masculine, and the innovative or new.[132] The actual clothing of Muslims in the Ottoman Empire over the centuries, however, gives the lie to the notion of sartorial authenticity or unambiguous gendering. For one thing, the *ferace* itself was unisex garb. So, too, were the all-purpose shawls and sashes that both men and women wrapped, draped, and wound about themselves from

128 Şemdanizade, *Mür'i't-Tevârih*, 1:133, 162. See Quataert, "Clothing Laws," 408, regarding the court's spendthrift ways. See also Eldem, *French Trade*, 242–4, regarding European merchants' displeasure at Ottoman restrictions on luxury consumption.

129 Sami, Şakır, Subhi, *Tarih*, 34; Altınay, *Hicrî On İkinci*, 86–8; Suha Umur, "Kadınlara Buyruklar," *Tarih ve Toplum* 10, no. 58 (1988): 14/206. Compare a decree from the reign of Ahmed III warning against women's "monstrous" and "abominable and wicked" styles (*u'cube hey'etler, hey'et-i senia ve kıyafet-i faziha*) that supposedly copied non-Muslims; Altınay, *Hicrî On İkinci*, 87; İstM, 1/24, fol. 12a, for 1138/1726.

130 Hâkim, "Hâkim Tarihi," TKS B231, fol. 234b; and B233, fol. 10b.

131 See, e.g., İstM 1/24, fol. 12a.

132 Chapoutot-Remadi, "Femmes dans la ville mamluke," 145–64; *EI2*, s.v. "Dhimma," by Claude Cahen; Ahmed, *Women and Gender in Islam*, 117–18; Michael Chamberlain, *Knowledge and Social Practice in Medieval Damascus, 1190–1350* (Cambridge, U.K., 1994), 104.

head to toe. The tall cloth and leather crowns (*tac*, *hotoz*) and caps worn by both men and women in the sixteenth century were precursors of the big fashions that were the subject of complaints early in the eighteenth century.[133] The charge that Muslim women's headdresses merely copied non-Muslim wear is also facile given the interdependence and circularity of fashion flows.[134] Even apart from periodic Turkomania in France and England, European women looked to Ottoman turbans for some of their own big-headed styles.[135] The fact that female head wrappings have historically been called turbans in the West – including an overdone bejeweled and feathered creation made in England in 1794 and known to English ladies as "the Turk" – suggests an endless loop of inspiration and synthesis rather than dead-end borrowings.[136]

Like their European contemporaries, Ottoman women had an indigenous vestmental past as well as outside models for the change or stylishness they sought. Certainly they were not immune to the allure of male grandee attire. Even if that had been the case, the apparel worn by women of the palace was often as splendid and as sumptuous as any male's, give or take an outsized turban. Palace women's attire, especially in the eighteenth and nineteenth centuries when numerous princesses presided over their own households and budgets, was a source of imitation for the wives, daughters, and attendants of Istanbul's haut monde. As Lady Mary Wortley Montagu and other European travelers discovered, clothing and fashion were an absorbing object of study – for all parties – in women's harem visiting.[137]

Selim, Mahmud, and the social face of reform

Perhaps the most striking feature of sumptuary legislation was its enthusiastic endorsement by the reformers Selim III and Mahmud II.[138] Their use of the regulatory weapon had much in common with the supposedly more traditional rule of Selim's father Mustafa III and Mahmud's father Abdülhamid I, not to mention of Osman III. Both Selim and Mahmud deployed the protectionist and hierarchical discourses to which their fathers were

133 Sevin, *On Üç Asırlık*; Apak et al., *Osmanlı Dönemi*; Danişmend, *İzahlı Osmanlı Tarihi*, 3:360.

134 *EI2*, s.v. "Libās," by Y. K. Stillman and N. A. Stillman.

135 Jirousek, "Ottoman Influences," 244–9.

136 See fig. 1 in *Gallery of Fashion* for April 1794, fig. 5 in *Gallery of Fashion* for May 1794, and fig. 2 in *La Belle Assemblée* for March 1812, all as cited and posted online by Catherine H. Decker (http://regencyfashion.org), accessed November 6, 2009.

137 Mary Wortley Montagu, *Letters from the Levant during the Embassy to Constantinople, 1716–1718* (New York, 1971). Billie Melman, *Women's Orients: English Women and the Middle East, 1718–1918* (1992; repr., Ann Arbor, Mich., 1995), 119–20, discusses the mutual fascination with one another's attire during such encounters. See also the special issue "Fashion at the Ottoman Court," *P Art and Culture Magazine*, no. 3, esp. the contributions by Hülya Tezcan and Banu Mahir.

138 I omit Mustafa IV (1807–8) from these discussions because of the brevity of his reign, although he pursued similar sumptuary policies.

Fig. 8. "A Turkish [Muslim] Woman in the Dress Worn at Constantinople." The *ferace*, standard outdoor dress for Muslim women until the late nineteenth century. Dalvimart, *Costume of Turkey*.

committed.[139] The sons' social targets also remained constant. Women and non-Muslims continued to be the twin pillars of elite "othering." Indeed, along with the perennial attention to women, apprehensions about non-Muslim men can be described as feverish in the late eighteenth century and into Mahmud II's reign. Mouradgea d'Ohsson (d. 1807), a firsthand observer, contended that non-Muslim men in his day were victims of more severe treatment than women, Muslim or non-Muslim.[140] D'Ohsson's surmise is highly questionable, though, given the exhibitory nature of many male punishments in these years. The hanging of tradesmen at their storefronts was not uncommon. Far less visible were the beatings, jailings, expulsions, and drownings associated

[139] For a taxonomy of sumptuary measures, see Hunt, *Governance*, 28–35.
[140] D'Ohsson, *Tableau*, 4, pt. 1:158.

Fig. 9. Greek Islands dress, Isle of Symi. Dalvimart, *Costume of Turkey.*

with female lawbreaking.[141] For both groups, though, the legislative climate was unremitting and vindictive.

Notwithstanding the carryovers from earlier reigns, Selim's and Mahmud's departures from the past are revealing. Regulations throughout Selim's reign

[141] However, see Chapter 5 in this volume, for the public hanging of female slaves convicted of murder, and Ahmed Lûtfî Efendi, *Vak'anüvîs Ahmed Lûtfî Efendi Tarihi*, ed. Yücel Demirel (Istanbul, 1999), 3:438, for the hanging of a female burglar-arsonist. Şemdanizade, *Mür'i't-Tevârih*, 1:26, writes approvingly of the public strangling of an alleged prostitute in the 1730s. I use the term *alleged* not out of legalistic delicacy but because Şemdanizade – who was not alone in this kind of labeling – does not distinguish between women wearing inappropriate clothing and women engaging in paid sexual intercourse; the word *whore* (*fahişe*) was used loosely in moralist outpourings. The study of crime in the eighteenth century by Fariba Zarinebaf-Shahr was not available at the time of this writing.

Fig. 10. "A Sultana or Odalisk." In indoor dress. Dalvimart, *Costume of Turkey.*

and during Mahmud's first decades reveal a more potent mix of vehemence, ire, and retribution than was the case with their predecessors, although their fathers came close. Among other emphases, the two successors reinforced the statutory parallelism between women and non-Muslim men – the males normatively addressed as "Jews and Christians" (*Yahud ve Nasara taifeleri*) or "unbelievers and Jews" (*kefere ve Yahudi taifesi*).[142] The chastising of the

[142] İstM, 1/25, fol. 28a, 1179 /1766 for the latter expression; the juxtaposition of Christians as unbelievers and Jews simply as Jews (*Yahudi*, sing.; *Yahudiler*, pl.) was common in the period although inconsistent. Bernard Lewis, *The Jews of Islam* (Princeton, N.J., 1984), 22, notes the Ottoman use of the expression "the infidel's Jew" (*kâfir Yahudisi*) for Jewish subjects of a foreign Christian state.

two targets during the better part of the reform reigns' fifty years hammered home the notion of women's and minority Christians' and Jews' deleterious impact on society. More important in terms of all of these distinctive marks of the period, deadly measures became a new legislative norm.[143]

With occasional exceptions, decrees from earlier periods had signaled fines and beatings in their vaguely worded emphatic commands and dire warnings (*azim tenbih ve tekid, tehdid ve tahzir*). Capital punishment was exceptional, usually tied to overzealous individuals like Kalaylıkoz Ahmed[144] or to precipitating "panic" events.[145] Even severe beatings "not to the point of death" did not satisfy the most adamant regulators and vigilant keepers of boundaries. The vitriolic chronicler Şemdanizade (d. 1779), bristling with indignation at permissiveness, bemoans the neglect of executions for female errancy and other wrongdoing. "There can be no order without force," he declared. More than once he invoked the call to action of the ultraorthodox, to "enjoin right and prohibit wrong."[146] In the last decades of the eighteenth century, although Şemdanizade did not live to see it, the frequency of extreme penalties began to coincide with his hard-line views. Clothing offenses that used to prescribe fines and beatings increasingly called for death or banishment. When a number of women were killed outright, like many before them their bodies were cast into the Bosphorus, "in the way of the wicked," as Şemdanizade put it, or in the way of the "disappeared," as one might say in our own day.[147]

As if these measures were not harsh enough, the circle of direct culpability tightened even more around households and other alleged accomplices: "Whosoever's wife or daughter or relation she is, her husband, father, and relatives shall be punished as well."[148] Men, women, and children were to be banished from their neighborhood and city if a female relative was caught wearing a too-big collar or too-slight veil. Even without the inevitable flogging, bastinado, or ear twisting, expulsion from the city – from home – was a terrible prospect. Moreover, male relatives could be separated from their kin and livelihood and bound over to galley servitude.[149] For the tailors who

[143] The same might be said of all social regulation during the reigns of Selim and Mahmud; that is, legislation regarding social wrongdoing from prostitution and gambling to unlawful migration and clothing violations had become more regularized and punitive under these early reformist regimes.

[144] Kalaylıkoz's measures against non-Muslims when he served as stand-in (*kaimakam*) for the grand vizier in Istanbul and when he was governor of Crete were so extreme that he was banished; Raşid, *Tarih*, 3:354–5; *DBİA*, s.v. "II. Ahmed," by Necdet Sakaoğlu; von Hammer, *Geschichte* 7:107–9, 154.

[145] See, e.g., the reference to wartime conditions in the decree of 1726 during Ahmed III's reign; Altınay, *Hicrî On İkinci*, 86–8.

[146] Şemdanizade, *Mür'i' t-Tevârih*, 1:3, 26, 179; 2a:25, 28, 36; Chapter 2 in this volume; and Zilfi, "Goods in the Mahalle," 301–2.

[147] Şemdanizade, *Mür'i' t-Tevârih*, 1:26; Rasim, *Resimli ve Haritalı*, 2:896. The Bosphorus was a perennial dumping ground for official and unofficial killings of males and females.

[148] Osman Nuri Ergin, *Mecelle-i Umur-i Belediye* (Istanbul, 1338/1922), 1:897.

[149] Umur, "Kadınlara Buyruklar," 15/207.

made the offending garb, the risks were high, if not higher. It was not the first time that tailors faced death in the clothing wars, but by Selim's reign, deadly warnings were routine: "If after this ordinance any tailor should dare make a woman's *ferace* out of Ankara *şali*, he shall be hanged without mercy at his shop."[150] Executions of other members of the commercial classes "as an example to others" throughout the late eighteenth century were also occurring with frequency, felling provisioners who allegedly short-weighted or doctored foodstuffs, moneylenders and coin shavers who corrupted the currency, and interpreters who gave away state secrets.[151] Whenever the death sentence was not explicitly threatened in these decades of sharp rhetoric, presumably discretionary beatings increased in severity, especially when poorer or otherwise marginal people were rounded up. Because, under Selim particularly, ominous threats were leveled at the police if they failed in their duties, their own fears of punishment probably meant harsher justice for the population.

Although the incidence of executions is impossible to calculate, Douglas Hay's observations regarding law enforcement underscore the utility of mere threat. Selective punishment, he argues, serves authoritarian purposes precisely because of its unpredictability.[152] Punishments that could fall as if from the sky gave life to the paternalism and fear that underlay the Ottoman culture of rule. As Sultan Selim remarked of his own brutal policies, "Obedience has departed from the people.... [I]t's necessary to frighten these people a bit."[153] Given the levels of violence in the period – not just warfare but also the regime's treatment of its subjects' shortcomings – Selim's idea of a bit of additional fright is frightening indeed. Many of his subjects no doubt took his word for it when he promised in one of his edicts, "If I see any people [disobeying], I'll kill them."[154]

There is no denying the importance of these dark regnal currents. The interest of the nascent reform decades, however, lies in the juxtaposition of lethality with the masculine revisionism introduced into regulation by Mahmud II. In the final decade of Mahmud's thirty-one years on the throne, his regime, which had been killing or threatening to kill male and female clothing violators, decided not to kill male clothing violators after all. Or rather, Mahmud

150 Altınay, *Hicrî On Üçüncü*, 4, from a decree of 1206/1792, and Ergin, *Mecelle*, 1:894, for 1222/1807; cf. Rasim, *Resimli ve Haritalı*, 3:1037 for 1190/1776. Christians and Jews were heavily involved in the textile trades and dominated some branches, especially in the nineteenth century, but they did not have a monopoly on tailoring. As a rule, the edicts do not single out non-Muslim guildsmen as more culpable in the violations. On purchasers of European cloth in the eighteenth century and ethno-religious aspects of the clothing trades, see Eldem, *French Trade*, 45–54.

151 Şemdanizade, *Mür'i' t-Tevârih*, 2a:37; Hâkim, "Hâkim Tarihi," B231, fol. 270a, 353a–355a, and B233, 33b, 191a–b; Mumcu, *Osmanlı Devletinde Siyaseten*, 52.

152 Douglas Hay, "Property, Authority and the Criminal Law," in Douglas Hay et al., eds., *Albion's Fatal Tree: Crime and Society in Eighteenth-Century England* (London, 1975), 16–63.

153 Karal, *Selim III'ün Hat-tı Hümayunları*, 97.

154 Karal, *Selim III'ün Hat-tı Hümayunları*, 102.

and, following his lead, the men of the Tanzimat, abandoned officialdom's old sartorial forms and threw out the rule book that had gone with them.[155] After the promulgation of the clothing reforms of 1829, the official classes' caftans, furs, turbans, jewels, and feathers, previously worth their weight in gold, were ordered to be put away in favor of European-style frock coats and trousers and the unprepossessing fez. Official codes still called for distinctions between public servants and the general populace, and, as in other societies, the population was constantly chided to dress decently, but drab black was the new order of the day for fashion-setting bureaucrats. Mahmud eagerly embraced European dress for himself – usually in the form of a Hussar-like military uniform – and had his portrait painted while wearing it. He was presumably so dressed when he was spat at by one of his disgusted subjects.[156] The middle classes of the urban male populace gradually followed the new sartorial trend. Rural people and provincials were far more skeptical, not only because of the possible religious meaning of the change but also as a declaration of opposition to Mahmud's reforms in general.[157]

The exact reasoning behind the reversal of a half-century trend is beyond our scope here. European interventions on behalf of Ottoman Christians, the desire to assuage dissension in the Balkan provinces, and Mahmud's own pioneering personality played roles. So, too, did the human and material cost of trying to hold down the rising bourgeoisie in this manner. And then there was the psychology of reformism. Mahmud's break with the past called for an entirely new look for his modernized army and bureaucracy. Yet new clothes and new rules were not for everyone. Members of the *ulema* and other religious could continue to wear the "traditional" robes and turbans of their calling and rank.[158] Like the *ulema*, women also remained in traditional garb. And like employees on the government payroll and perhaps as though they were at the service of the state, women had little choice in the matter. In any case, the parallelism between women's dress and that of the *ulema* was more than just symbolic.[159]

What had been at stake in the old rules on minority men's attire, notwithstanding occasional invocations of the *shari'ah* principle of difference or differentiation (*ghiyar*), was status and social place. Women's appearance – the

155 Quataert, "Clothing Laws," 412–19.

156 Sevin, *On Üç Asırlık*, 118–20; Chapter 2 in this volume.

157 See Quataert, "Clothing Laws," 413; Lûtfî, *Lûtfî Tarihi*, 2, pt. 3:425, 439, 444, 449, 675; Bernard Lewis, *The Emergence of Modern Turkey*, 3rd ed. (Oxford, 2002), 99–102; İsmail Hakkı Uzunçarşılı, "Asâkir-i Mansûre'ye Fes Giydirilmesi hakkında Sadr-i Âzamın Takriri ve II. Mahmud'un Hatt-ı Hümayunu," *Belleten* 70 (1954): 223–30; Berkes, *Development of Secularism*, 125; Elliot, "Dress Codes," 121–2.

158 "Uniform turbans," that is, the distinctive styles and shapes that had denoted the official vocations, were banned for all others; Lûtfî, *Lûtfî Tarihi*, 2, pt. 3:449.

159 The gendered equivalent in the present day can be seen in the Islamic Republic of Iran's parliament, whose lay male members wear Western-style suit jackets and trousers, whereas *ulema* (*mollas*) appear in robes and turbans and female members in full-length cloaks or chadors and headscarves.

appearance of modesty – was always more closely identified with morality and faith.[160] Despite the secularizing face of nineteenth-century reformism, women, especially Muslim women, remained tethered to the old sartorial rules. Women by the 1830s were freer in their ability to move about the city and to experiment with clothing than had been possible in the mid-eighteenth century, although as always in social matters of this kind, numbers and percentages are indeterminable. What can be said is that regulations barring women from just such freedoms remained in place. And, like threats in general, regulatory rhetoric was likely to have been as compelling as actual enforcement.

Legislation and state directives continued to feed the view of women as subject to the control of men and family. The decoupling of minority men from the most disabling and confessionally distinguishing sartorial rules, as against the persisting regulation of women, only reified the formulation. In the plot lines laid out in Mahmud's decree of 1818, women are represented in transcendent terms of dire religious threat. Their dress, which "contravenes *shari'ah* rules" and "God Almighty's ordinance," is a sin as well as a crime. The mere presence of change in clothing styles, even when women's bodies remained quite covered, has sexual meaning. The bad colors and long capes that the regulation condemns are not just shameful but lascivious – literally lust inciting (*şehvetengiz*). Yet the lascivious *ferace*s this time around were not the shape-revealing sorts that had sparked earlier allusions to male arousal. Like sinfulness and crime, the attribution of shame shuttles between women's prodigality – in every sense – and the lack of necessary differentiation from the attire of Christian women (*Nasraniye*). The *ferace* is the centerpiece of this long text, but open veils are also high on its list of clothing "unbefitting Muslim folk." The notion of shamefulness here suggests a miasmic danger as well as individual sin: women's clothing infractions are "loathsome and abominable in the view of all people of the Islamic faith."[161] Or, as one of Mahmud's earlier edicts put it, "Women . . . are the cause of all manner of mischief. . . . All women are snares of the devil."[162]

The edicts' charges are not new in and of themselves. What is distinctive about them and those that would follow is their distillation down to women and the *shari'ah* saturation of the text. The insistence that Muslim women be distinguishable from "the women of the three *millet*s," Greek Orthodox, Armenian, and Jewish, reflects the long-standing *ghiyar* principle. The emphasis on

160 This point and its ramifications have been the subject of countless studies about historical and contemporary Muslim women. The present study has particularly benefited from Leila Ahmed's *Women and Gender in Islam* (New Haven, Conn., 1992); the various writings of Deniz Kandiyoti and Fatima Mernissi, which are cited throughout this volume; and Stowasser, *Women in the Qur'an*. Although the study here departs from some of the chronology and emphases of Ahmed's thesis of the conflation of women and Islamic culture, her insights were the starting point for my own thinking about women in this earlier, Ottoman context.

161 Ergin, *Mecelle*, 1:896–8.

162 Umur, "Kadınlara Buyruklar," 15/207. The language echoes the edict of 1726; Altınay, *Hicrî On İkinci*, 86–8.

females at this particular moment, in sight of male clothing reforms, points to a special salience for gender in the emerging reform era. As Kemal Çiçek has observed about the Tanzimat itself, the *shari'ah* component of that "secularizing" era has been underestimated.[163] The same can be said about the gender component of *shari'ah* concerns and moral regulation in the reform context. The fact that, relatively speaking, the *ghiyar* of masculine dress was virtually disavowed while that of women's attire remained says a great deal about the cultural autonomy of Muslim masculinity and the structured dependency of Muslim women.

Selim and Mahmud were grandchildren of the ill-fated Tulip Era sultan Ahmed III. They were acutely aware, as their fathers had been, of the need to secure their regimes' religious and moral credentials.[164] Both men pursued an orthodox strategy, a very public and publicizing part of which was sumptuary regulation – with women and, most of the time, the religious minorities as favorite soft targets.[165] The sumptuary regulation of women served the additional purpose of reaffirming male Muslim solidarity in the face of growing economic stratification and cultural divisiveness. Moral regulation, as Hunt argues, operates not just in the negative sense of fending off trespass but also as a positive force by "constituting" communities and identities. Regulation, then, is "externally regulative and internally constitutive."[166] The target audiences of regulation are not just wrongdoers and enforcers but also the entire collectivity of the wronged. As the behavior of women and the minorities was denounced, it was Muslim males of all social ranks and orders who were being particularly addressed, identified, and morally constituted.

It was in this discursive and legal context that Ottoman society awakened to the notion of slavery, its own slavery, as a problem. That is, in the years following Great Britain's resolution of 1807 to end the African slave trade, sultans, statesmen, and the ordinary public came to realize that a growing number of European abolitionists regarded all slave trading and slave systems as evils to

163 Kemal Çiçek, "Tanzimat ve Şer'iat: Namaz Kılmayan ve İçki İçenlerin Takip ve Cezalandırılması hakkında Kıbrıs Muhassılı Mehmet Tal'at Efendi'nin İki Buyuruldusu," *Toplumsal Tarih* 3, no. 15 (1995): 22–7.

164 The reasons behind Ahmed's fall were worldly, but the role of certain *ulema* and the rebels' appeal to religious values helped consolidate opposition; see Aktepe, *Patrona İsyanı*.

165 Both sultans courted members of the *ulema* and student population by hastening entry-level promotions; adding to the honorary ranks available to *ulema* hierarchs; lavishing gifts on *medrese* professors; and in Mahmud's case, launching a religious building program. See Heyd, "The Ottoman 'Ulemā," 63–96; Shaw, *Between Old and New*, 60; Zilfi, "A Medrese for the Palace" and "Elite Circulation."

166 Hunt, *Governing Morals*, 14–15; Hunt's thesis is informed by Philip Corrigan, "On Moral Regulation," *Sociological Review* 29 (1981): 313–37. See also Şerif Mardin, "Center-Periphery Relations: A Key to Turkish Politics?" *Daedalus* 102 (1973): 175. Cf. Tamer El-Leithy's discussion of historical processes in moral regulation in medieval Egypt: "Coptic Culture and Conversion in Medieval Cairo, 1293–1524," Ph.D. diss., Princeton University, 2005.

be eradicated. The institution of slavery in the Ottoman Empire, though seemingly removed from the world of goods and its privileges and restrictions, cannot be understood without reference to the norms of male dominion, the gendered hierarchy of entitlements and subordinations, which were revealed and exhaustively reaffirmed decade after decade. The prolonged Ottoman opposition to abolition is the offspring of the gender politics projected and protected in regulatory legislation of the late eighteenth and early nineteenth centuries.

Regardless of the goods, behaviors, relationships, and venues that were the ostensible triggers of social tension in the eighteenth and nineteenth centuries, the disposition of women's bodies was increasingly, albeit sometimes unconsciously, at issue. Nowhere is this more apparent than in the practice of slavery in the Ottoman Empire, especially as it had developed by the eighteenth and nineteenth centuries, and as its defenders represented it in the face of European abolitionism.

CHAPTER 4

Telling the Ottoman slave story

> The Prophet has said concerning them, "[T]hey are your brethren, whom God has placed in your hands, wherefore give them such food as ye yourselves eat, and such raiment as ye yourselves are clothed with, and afflict not the servants of your God."
>
> – al-Marghinani, *The Hedaya or Guide*[1]

> Slaves, generally speaking, are more happy, better treated, and less subject to the vicissitudes of life, than free servants in Turkey [the Ottoman Empire], and superior in these respects to the general class of menials in Europe. Under every circumstance, their condition may be considered as consummate felicity, when compared with that of the vast majority of slaves in Christian colonies and in the United States.
>
> – White, *Three Years in Constantinople*[2]

Slavery debates

The notion that slaves and other oppressed groups, despite overwhelming odds, sometimes managed to mitigate their plight, even gain advantage, has given rise to polarity in the characterization of repressive systems. In effect, the scars of victimization are weighed against evidences of indomitability and assertions of agency. If, in spite of their circumstances, some of the oppressed succeeded in creating a sphere of independence, "a resistant subculture of dignity,"[3] the system might be seen as not so vicious after all. It could even be argued that, in some instances and for some individuals, it was benign, even beneficial. On the other hand, given the irrefutable horrors of chattel slavery, it is hard to argue that social and cultural resiliency, or the triumphs of a singular

1 'Ali ibn Abi Bakr al-Marghinani, *The Hedaya or Guide: A Commentary on the Mussulman Laws*, trans. Charles Hamilton (London, 1791), 1, bk.5, 418. Subsequent references to al-Marghinani are to the 2nd ed., ed. Standish Grove, trans. Charles Hamilton (1870; repr., Lahore, 1957); Abdul Ali Hamid, ed., *Moral Teachings of Islam: Prophetic Traditions from "al-Adab al-Mufrad" by Imam al-Bukhari* (Walnut Creek, Calif., 2003), 33. On the importance of al-Marghinani in Ottoman *medrese* education and judicial practice, see Ahmet Yaşar Ocak, *Osmanlı Toplumunda Zındıklar ve Mülhidler (15.-17. Yüzyıllar)* (Istanbul, 1998), 118–19.

2 White, *Three Years*, 2:304–5.

3 James C. Scott, "Domination and the Arts of Resistance," in Stanley Engerman, Seymour Drescher, and Robert Paquette, eds., *Slavery* (Oxford, 2001), 369.

few, offset the perniciousness of the system as a whole. Slavery may have been of benefit to fortunate individuals, most especially in its Mediterranean manifestations, but the notion of systemic neutrality, much less advantage, is insupportable.

The brutalities and humane niches of slavery in the Ottoman Empire and of Old World slavery have customarily been framed in binary terms. In the Western imagination, the antipodes are represented by the – on the whole – generous accounts by European travelers to Ottoman lands over the centuries juxtaposed against the often hair-raising memoirs of former captives of the Barbary corsairs. Admittedly, the Ottoman case has not had the benefit of a large scholarly literature to take the measure of popular perceptions. By contrast, the Americas' lasting slavery debate continues to generate fruitful discussion about the nature and legacy of Atlantic slave systems. One strand of the Atlantic debate has grappled with the agency question; that is, whether or to what degree American slaves found a modicum of autonomous existence apart from the cradle-to-grave inhumanity of plantation capitalism.[4] In the judgment of some, slaves' own exertions enabled them to limit the appropriative claims of the slave condition. Slaves' art, music, worship, and community give evidence of autonomous realms beyond the system's grip. A more pessimistic view discounts slaves' resistance and ingenuity to focus on slavery's damaging legacy to individuals and society. In both conceptualizations, disagreement has turned on the character and potency of "the world the slaves made" and the slave system's larger social and psychological resonances. In the end it is slavery's historical legacy that is at issue.

The Middle East's own consideration of victimization versus agency in the experience of slaves in the Middle East – whether on its Mediterranean, Black Sea, or Indian Ocean shores – has produced a more limited scholarly conversation. Until recently, it has been a stalled debate. The historical course of the slavery discussion in and about the Middle East has been inseparable – and sometimes indistinguishable – from the wider, defensive response to the Western critique of the Ottomans, Islam, and Muslim societies generally.[5] European-directed abolitionism of the nineteenth century was commonly understood by Middle Easterners, especially Muslims, to misapprehend Middle Eastern realities. Because abolitionism coincided with Europe's expansion into the Middle East and North Africa, it was also perceived as another, barely camouflaged thrust of European imperialism.

4 See, e.g., John W. Blassingame, *The Slave Community: Plantation Life in the Antebellum South* (New York, 1972); Stanley M. Elkins, "The Slavery Debate," *Commentary* 60 (1975): 40–54; Robert W. Fogel and Stanley L. Engerman, *Time on the Cross: The Economics of American Negro Slavery* (Boston, 1974); Eugene D. Genovese, *Roll, Jordan, Roll: The World the Slaves Made* (New York, 1974); Herbert G. Gutman, *The Black Family in Slavery and Freedom, 1750–1925* (New York, 1976).

5 This observation was first put forward by Toledano, *Slavery and Abolition*, in an overall argument that implicates Western scholars in the apologist discourse (see esp. ix–xii and 134–68).

A formal, state-led defense of the empire's slavery and slave trade had become unavoidable by the 1830s. Although the British Parliament had voted to abolish the African slave trade in 1807, the pressure on the Ottoman government to end the importation of Africans began to be felt only with the rise of British influence in the 1830s.[6] In virtually every decade of the nineteenth century, and most certainly in the 1830s, the Ottomans were engaged in perilous regional and international conflicts. The regime and particularly the reform factions were anxious to present the country and their governing project in a favorable light to secure foreign assistance (usually British, intermittently French, and once or twice Russian) against European foes (usually Russian, intermittently French, and once or twice British) and the latter three's regional surrogates. The Ottoman response to abolitionism, tempered by skepticism at the movement's foreign provenance, took the form of denial.[7] The existence of slavery was readily admitted, but its comparability with New World slavery was firmly denied. The rejectionist line of reasoning continued to be endorsed by succeeding generations. In arguing for difference, Ottoman apologists endowed the slavery practiced in the empire with a forgiving gloss of paternalism. The Ottoman discourse on slavery was more self-conscious in the age of abolition than it had been when the system was unchallenged. Its substance, however, was ages old. It focused not on the brutalities of human merchandising or on the character of slavery's legacy but on the Ottoman Islamic institution's purported mildness, even kindliness, at least insofar as its dominant variant, domestic slavery, was concerned and always in contrast to New World systems.

In its outlines, the story of Ottoman slavery parallels the historical course of Islamic Middle Eastern slavery. Islamic regimes like the Ottoman Empire defined liability to enslavement not in terms of race, color, or ethnicity but in accordance with the conjoined attributes of geography and religion. Non-Muslims of every stripe – Christians, Jews, Zoroastrians, or animists – who resided outside the Islamic domain or outside its treaty states were legitimate prey. In contrast, non-Muslim subjects of the empire were so-called covenanted people (Ar., *dhimmis*; T., *zimmis*). By law, they were exempt from slavery, except for the periodic conscription of young males for the *devşirme* levy. Tens of thousands of foreign non-Muslims – men, women, and children, irrespective of race or ethnic origin – were enslaved over the centuries. Once

[6] On British abolitionism, see Howard Temperley, *British Antislavery, 1833–1870* (Columbia, S.C., [1972]). British-Ottoman relations in the nineteenth century are treated in Allan Cunningham, *Collected Essays*, ed. Edward Ingram (London, 1993); Harold Temperley, *England and the Near East: The Crimea* (Hamden, Conn., 1964); Frank Edgar Bailey, *British Policy and the Turkish Reform Movement: A Study in Anglo-Turkish Relations, 1826–1853* (Cambridge, Mass., 1942).

[7] Ehud R. Toledano, *The Ottoman Slave Trade and Its Suppression, 1840–1890* (Princeton, N.J., 1982), 91–147; Y. Hakan Erdem, *Slavery in the Ottoman Empire and Its Demise, 1800–1909* (London, 1996), 85–93.

within the empire, they became the property of Ottoman owners, male and female, Muslim and non-Muslim.

Slaves labored in every capacity, skilled and unskilled, intimate and remote, esteemed and degraded. They served as guards and lackeys, porters and field hands, miners and masons, scribes and musicians. Most of all, they were household workers, everything from house stewards, gardeners, eunuchs, and wet nurses to laundresses, maids, cooks, and bedmates. Manumission was encouraged by law and commonly practiced. The pool of enslaved persons was thus not strikingly different from the freed and free men and women who inhabited the major cities. Resistance in the form of collective rebellion was rare, and significant numbers of manumitted slaves not only inherited from their former masters and mistresses but also outdistanced many freeborn contemporaries in social status and material condition. This was the Islamic adaptation of the region's Near Eastern and Mediterranean heritage. It was an open slave system. It was not built on the kind of "we-they dichotomy" that characterized the Western hemisphere's "closed" system of racialized chattel bondage and social immobility from generation to generation.[8]

In constructing the prevailing narrative, modern historiographical interest has taken a formalist approach. Research has most often been concerned with quantification and legal taxonomy. Thus, something is known about the number, ethnicity, and gender of slaves traded in specific locales; the legal categories and dimensions of slave bondage; the recruitment of slaves; important trade routes and markets; and labor specialization, including concubinage and slave soldiery.[9] Unlike the victim-agency debate in Atlantic studies, the

[8] Peter Kolchin, *American Slavery, 1619–1877* (New York, 1993), 4; James L. Watson, ed., *Asian and African Systems of Slavery* (Oxford, 1980), 12.

[9] Works on Ottoman slavery, especially of the northern-tier provinces, include Gabriel Baer, "Slavery and Its Abolition," *Studies in the Social History of Modern Egypt* (Chicago, 1969), 161–89; Alan Fisher, "The Sale of Slaves in the Ottoman Empire: Markets and State Taxes on Slave Sales," *Boğaziçi Üniversitesi Hümaniter Bilimler Dergisi* 6 (1978): 149–74, "Chattel Slavery in the Ottoman Empire," *Slavery and Abolition* 1 (1985): 25–45; Fisher, "Studies in Ottoman Slavery and Slave Trade, II: Manumission," *JTS* 4 (1980): 49–56; Halil İnalcık, "Servile Labor in the Ottoman Empire," in A. Ascher et al., eds., *The Mutual Effects of the Islamic and Judeo-Christian Worlds: The East European Pattern* (New York, 1979); Toledano, *The Ottoman Slave Trade*; Toledano, *Slavery and Abolition in the Ottoman Middle East* (Seattle, 1998); Toledano, *As If Silent and Absent: Bonds of Enslavement in the Islamic Middle East* (New Haven, Conn., 2007); Ronald C. Jennings, "Black Slaves and Free Blacks in Ottoman Cyprus, 1590–1640," *JESHO* 30 (1987): 286–302, in Ronald C. Jennings, *Studies on Ottoman Social History in the Sixteenth and Seventeenth Centuries: Women, Zimmis and Shariah Courts in Kayseri, Cyprus and Trabzon*, ed. Suraiya Faroqhi (Istanbul, 1999); Gülnihal Bozkurt, "Köle Ticaretinin Sona Erdirilmesi Konusunda Osmanlı Devletinin Taraf Olduğu İki Devletlerarası Anlaşma," *OTAM* 1, no. 1(1990): 45–77; Erdem, *Slavery in the Ottoman Empire*; İzzet Sak, "Konya'da Köleler," *OA* 9 (1989): 159–97; Abdullah Martal, "19. Yüzyılda Kölelik ve Köle Ticareti," *TveT* 121 (Ocak 1994): 13–22; Ahmed Akgündüz, *İslâm Hukukunda Kölelik-Câriyelik Müessesesi ve Osmanlı'da Harem* (Istanbul, 1995); Colin Imber, "The Hanafi Law of Manumission: A Problem in the *Fatwa*s of Dürrizade Mehmed 'Arif," typescript, personal copy; Karl Jahn, *Türkische Freilassungserklärungen des 18. Jahrhunderts (1702–1776)* (Naples, 1963); Hasan Tahsin Fendoğlu, *İslâm ve Osmanlı Hukukunda*

Ottoman story has had little to say about the impact of slavery on the lives of freed slaves, much less on society at large, and less still on consequences to the postabolition era or modern successor states.[10] Yet slavery was not a freestanding institution lacking moral and material attachment to the rest of society. It was culturally and institutionally integral to both state and society. As in North America of the eighteenth and nineteenth centuries, ruling elements, who enforced the law and bent it to their own ends, were the country's chief slaveholders. And as in America, the Ottoman state enlisted slave labor to erect its capitals and monuments. The history of Ottoman slavery coincides with the rise, if not the birth, of the empire. Its legitimacy was defended and its demise resisted, at least in some quarters, until the empire's end. An introduction to the history and problematics of slavery among the Ottomans is the subject of this chapter.

Slavery in the Ottoman Islamic world

Until recently, the received wisdom regarding Ottoman slavery put forward an institutional story. It privileged in particular the state's largely successful project of training young male captives for service as imperial soldiers and administrators. Indeed, the decline paradigm, which had long served as the bedrock of much of the historiography of the Ottoman Empire, was itself predicated on the rise and decline of Ottoman military prowess.[11] The decline theory identifies the empire's greatest power with the achievements of the slave-dominated military and situates both in the period from 1400 to 1600. The ensuing centuries are treated as a fall from that peak. They are measured

Kölelik ve Câriyelik (Istanbul, 1996); Yvonne J. Seng, "Fugitives and Factotums: Slaves in Early Sixteenth-Century Istanbul," *JESHO* 39 (1996): 136–69; Seng, "A Liminal State: Slavery in Sixteenth-Century Istanbul," in Shaun E. Marmon, ed., *Slavery in the Islamic Middle East* (Princeton, N.J., 1999), 25–42; Halil Sahillioğlu, "Slaves in the Social and Economic Life of Bursa in the Late 15th and Early 16th Centuries," *Turcica* 17 (1985): 43–112; Nihat Engin, *Osmanlı Devletinde Kölelik* (Istanbul, 1998); Suraiya Faroqhi, "From the Slave Market to Arafat: Biographies of Bursa Women in the Late Fifteenth Century," *TSAB* 24, no. 1 (2000): 3–20; Faroqhi, "Black Slaves and Freedmen Celebrating, Aydın, 1576," *Turcica* 21–23 (1991):205–15; Zilfi, "Servants, Slaves," 1–33; Zilfi, "Thoughts on Women and Slavery in the Ottoman Era and Historical Sources," in Amira El-Azhary Sonbol, ed., *Beyond the Exotic: Women's Histories in Islamic Societies* (Syracuse, N.Y., 2005), 131–8; Baki Tezcan, "Dispelling the Darkness: The Politics of 'Race' in the Early Seventeenth-Century Ottoman Empire in the Light of the Life and Work of Mullah Ali," in Tezcan and Barbir, *Identity and Identity Formation*, 73–95; Géza Dávid and Pál Fodor, eds., *Ransom Slavery along the Ottoman Borders: Early Fifteenth–Early Eighteenth Centuries* (Leiden, 2007).

10 However, for the impact of slavery in Morocco, an important slaveholding state outside the Ottoman Empire, see Mohammed Ennaji, *Serving the Master: Slavery and Society in Nineteenth-Century Morocco* (New York, 1999); Daniel J. Schroeter, "Slave Markets and Slavery in Moroccan Urban Society," *Slavery and Abolition* 13 (1993): 185–213. The invaluable studies by Toledano and Erdem treat some of these themes and interrogate the Ottoman narrative, but they do not fundamentally alter the historiographical terrain.

11 For the implications of the decline theory, see Christoph K. Neumann, "Political and Diplomatic Developments," in Faroqhi, *Cambridge History of Turkey*, 44–62; see also Kafadar, "Janissaries and Other Riffraff," 113–19.

chiefly in military and territorial terms – high politics, if you will – with both the imperial regime and its once fearsome and loyal slave military disintegrating and doomed. In the received narrative, the slave system stands against an asocial background with scant reference to nonmilitary slaveholding.

Some years after the establishment of the Ottoman dynasty in Anatolia and the Balkans, non-Muslim youths began to be taken captive – outside the Ottoman domain and, increasingly in contravention of Islamic law, inside it – to be trained as the sultan's own slaves (*gulam*s, *kul*s, or *kapı kulu*s). The boy captives were converted to Islam as part of their general indoctrination. Those more or less aggressive, the comely, and the quick witted were channeled into one of several imperial vocations. Some of those sons of Christian peasants and shepherds became courtiers and palace hierarchs. They could rise as far as their talents and ability to attract favor could carry them. Indeed, the roster of Ottoman grand viziers and admirals is filled with these slaves turned potentates.

Most male slave recruits of the early Ottoman centuries, however, lived out their employment where it commenced and where the state most required them, in the rank and file of the standing infantry (Janissaries) and standing cavalry (*sipahi*s of the Porte). Some were attached to the militarized households of the commanders, governors, and notables of the realm. The youths conscripted for these roles – the youths of the levy (*devşirme*), as they were known – and other slave recruits who earned a place among them belonged to a select category of captive.[12] In nomenclature, legal status, garb, and functions, they were distinct from ordinary slaves (*abd*, *esir*, *rıkk*, *köle*), who were destined for more common owners and common pursuits. Although *kul* captives were privy to lofty distinctions, their relationship to the honors and prerogatives of royal slave status was conditioned on the sultan's will.

As extensions of the sultan's authority, *kapı kulu* or *gulam* (Ar., *ghulām*) slaves were entitled to wield the powers of their imperial attachment over ordinary subjects (*reaya*) of whatever religion. When called on, they also wielded the powers of their office, whatever it might be, over dismissed or disgraced *askeri* superiors, subordinates, or comrades. Notwithstanding their empowerment and signifying attire, *kul*s were human property. No part of the houses, gems, robes, and slaves that they might acquire on graduation into paid officialdom was theirs to bequeath if the sultan, for his own reasons, decided otherwise. As was true of ordinary slaves unless manumitted, any wealth or property held by *kul* slaves – even if graduated – could revert to their

[12] For the shades of disagreement regarding the legality of internal slavery and the legal status of *kul* slaves, see *EI2*, s.v. "Ghulām, Ottoman Empire," by Halil İnalcık; also İnalcık, *Ottoman Empire*, 87–8; Mumcu, *Osmanli Devletinde Siyaseten*, 63–7; Erdem, *Slavery in the Ottoman Empire*, 1–11; Colin Imber, *Ottoman Empire, 1300–1650: The Structure of Power* (Basingstoke, U.K., 2002), 128–42; Gibb and Bowen, *Islamic Society and the West*, 1, pt. 1:43–4; İsmail Hakkı Uzunçarşılı, *Osmanlı Devleti Teşkilâtından Kapukulu Ocakları I* (1943; repr., Ankara, 1988); Dror Ze'evi, "Kul and Getting Cooler: The Dissolution of Elite Collective Identity and the Formation of Official Nationalism in the Ottoman Empire" *Mediterranean Historical Review* 11, no. 2 (1996): 177–95; Ercan, *Osmanlı Yönteminde*, 163–6.

master. The master of *kul* slaves, the sultan, could seize from them whatever property he wished, without reference to the courts and without the evidentiary strictures of Islamic law.

In acting against their most prominent officials, whether slave or free in origin, the sultans often sought judicial sanction in the form of the *şeyhülislam*'s *fetva*. Formal legality was thereby observed, but rulers were not obliged to pursue the *shari'ah* route with their *kul* servitors. The sultan's discretionary authority with regard to the punishment of his subjects was, for all intents and purposes, absolute, although he tended to reserve its full weight for his own officials and for the *askeri* class generally. In a study of political executions, Mumcu counts more than 40 incumbent and ex–grand viziers executed by imperial order out of a total of 182 who served between the fourteenth and the mid-nineteenth centuries. Most of the executed met their end in the sixteenth and seventeenth centuries, and most, though not all, were of slave origin.[13] Mahmud II, who said good-bye to many things in his reign, apparently dispatched the last of the grand vizierial sacrifices in 1821, some five years before ridding himself of the Janissaries and embarking on his reforms.[14]

The encumbrances and disabilities of the slave condition pervaded the military, administrative, and palace branches of officialdom despite the fact that the free and freeborn always outnumbered the slave soldiery and slave-origin bureaucrats and administrators. The *ulema*, traditionally the preserve of the free, were not affected by such ambiguities. In contrast, the domination of high administrative and military posts by slave servitors particularly in the sixteenth and seventeenth centuries imbued those branches with the slave ethic. Servility had its attractions as a prerequisite for prestigious office. As Andrews and Kalpaklı point out, being mastered – having a master – was a positive, even a necessary, social value for subordinates in the period.[15] It is not surprising that freeborn Muslims were eager to share in the perquisites of the standing army. In exchange for entry into what was in origin a slave soldiery, even the freeborn had to submit to the traditions of *kul* servitude and adapt to the *kul* ethic.

13 Mumcu, *Osmanlı Devletinde Siyaseten*, 73–5. Mumcu lists twenty-three grand viziers killed while technically still in office; those killed following dismissal add up to twenty-one rather than the twenty that he counts. Circumvention of public opinion was accomplished by the convenient death of a banished official, either on the road or in a distant province. Danişmend, *İzahlı Osmanlı Tarihi*, 5:106, gives a figure of 215 for the total of grand viziers from the origin of the empire until 1922.

14 Mahmud's victim was Benderli Ali Pasha, who was accused of treason in connection with the Greek rebellion; Mumcu, *Osmanlı Devletinde Siyaseten*, 92; Danişmend, *İzahlı Osmanlı Tarihi*, 5:72. Ahmed Midhat Pasha, who was twice grand vizier in the 1870s when he ran afoul of Abdülhamid II (1876–1909), served in interim posts before being imprisoned in Ottoman Arabia and murdered there on Abdülhamid's orders. On Midhat Pasha's trial, imprisonment, and death, see Ali Haydar Mithat, *The Life of Midhat Pasha* (1903; repr., New York, 1973), 207–41, and Chapter 5 in this volume.

15 Andrews and Kalpaklı, *Age of Beloveds*, 233.

Between the fifteenth and mid-seventeenth centuries, most *kapı kulu* conscripts were gathered in the Balkans from the rural Christian subjects of the empire, although even in the earliest centuries, freeborn Bosnian Muslims were entitled to enroll in what was, for its time, the most prestigious and feared military organization in Europe and western Asia. The Ottoman Empire's military triumphs, from the capture of Constantinople in 1453 until the great losses against the Holy League, the Habsburg Empire, and Russia in the late seventeenth century, were credited to its courageous and disciplined slave corps, particularly the famous Janissaries. In fact, the Janissaries themselves were not shy about putting forward the same grandiose claim.[16] Perhaps inevitably, Ottoman defeats came to be laid at the door of the Janissaries. They and the entire *kapı kulu* class of military-administrative officials were viewed as performing less like loyal soldiers and servitors and more like political infighters and urban tradesmen. Indeed, the thematic touchstones of the Ottoman imperial and slavery narratives have also figured in *kapı kulu* or Janissary history: the changing role of the *kapı kulu* class, both as an armed force and as deputized and undeputized lords of the realm for some three hundred years; social and political tensions among empowered converts, represented by the *kapı kulu*s on the one hand, and freeborn Muslims, especially Anatolian Turks and Kurds, on the other hand;[17] and the eventual replacement of slave soldiery and slave-dominated households by new forms of military recruitment and organization in the eighteenth and nineteenth centuries.

The personal relationship of *kul* slaves to the sultan – a relationship that was more implied than real, given *kul* numbers in the seventeenth and eighteenth centuries – assured them of a certain collective standing. The darker side of privilege and access, though, was the increase in individual vulnerability. The historiographical debate over whether *kul* slaves can be regarded as slaves in the "true" sense ought to turn not on superior power and status but on their ultimate disposability as human beings. It is true that they differed from ordinary slaves in not being subject to the debasement of auction and sale. Yet precisely because they were not slaves in the traditional sense – that is, they were not shielded by the ameliorating code of *shari'ah* law – their personal vulnerability was arguably greater than that of ordinary slaves. As the sultan's property, their very persons were at the disposal of their royal master. They were subject to capital punishment for reasons of politics (*siyaset*), in accordance with the sultan's absolute will.[18] While ordinary masters' treatment

[16] Antoine Galland, *Journal d'Antoine Galland pendant son séjour à Constantinople, 1672–1673*, ed. C. Schefer (Paris, 1881), 1:159–61. See also Mustafa Akdağ, *Türkiye'nin İktisadî ve İctimaî Tarihi* (Istanbul, 1974), 2:158, regarding tensions and animosities arising from *kuls* as converts in positions of power. For the classic identification of the *kul* system with Ottoman successes and failures, see Albert C. Lybyer, *The Government of the Ottoman Empire in the Time of Suleiman the Magnificent* (1913; repr., New York, 1966).

[17] *EI2*, s.v. "Ghulām, Ottoman Empire" by Halil İnalcık, 1086; Akdağ, *Türkiye'nin İktisadî*, 2:158.

[18] Mumcu, *Osmanlı Devletinde Siyaseten*, 63–7.

of their slaves was limited by the strictures and enjoinments of *shari'ah* law, the sultan's own slaves, elite in other ways, had no legal recourse from his wrath. As a practical matter, however, the collective power of the *kapı kulu*s, especially those who were Janissaries, helped ensure the privileges and status of the majority. Exemplary executions of Janissaries and other officers of the state, when they occurred, usually affected men in the topmost, more politicized ranks.

With regard to the demography of slavery, the Ottoman narrative centers on the male slave experience and the shifting ethnicity of slave recruitment. The map of large-scale enslavements over the centuries generally follows the historical course of the empire's military raids and conquests. Like Ottoman territorial incursions, slavery's ethnic trajectory moved from southern Slavs and Greeks in the fourteenth and fifteenth centuries to Austro-Germans, Hungarians, northern Slavs, Iranians, and sub-Saharan Africans in the sixteenth and seventeenth, to Abkhazes (*Abaza*s), Circassians (*Çerkes*), Georgians, and other Caucasus populations in the eighteenth and nineteenth centuries. Alongside all of these was an irregular flow of Africans. For Istanbul and the northern-tier provinces, the rising proportion of African slaves relative to "white" slaves climaxed in the nineteenth century.

Meantime, the significance of gender in the history of Ottoman slavery has been seriously neglected. The received narrative has treated female slavery as a minor addendum to the elite male and ethnic story. The scholarly interest in women's experience of slavery has, for the most part, been confined to polygyny and concubinage and quantitative speculation at that: How many men were polygynous? How many wives or concubines did men have? What percentage of men had large harems? As for the matter of coerced female sexual usage, it has generally been unproblematized and severed from other social issues and processes. Recent historiography has produced important exceptions to that untold and undertold story, notably Peirce's study of the Ottoman dynastic household of Topkapı Palace as well as pathbreaking contributions by Toledano.[19] The core Ottoman narrative nonetheless remains tied to a masculine and institutional logic, with slave women and female sexuality incidental to its structure and exposition.

[19] Peirce, *Imperial Harem*; Ehud R. Toledano, "Shemsigul: A Circassian Slave in Mid-Nineteenth-Century Cairo," in Edmund Burke, ed., *Struggle and Survival in the Modern Middle East* (Berkeley, Calif., 1993), 59–74; Toledano, *Slavery and Abolition*, 20–80; and see the interesting study by Hedda Reindl-Kiel, "Mord an einer Haremsdame," *Münchner Zeitschrift für Balkankunde* 7–8 (1991): 167–89; see also Zilfi, "Muslim Women," 233–6, 252–53. See also the important literature on Egypt: Jane Hathaway, "Marriage Alliances among the Military Households of Ottoman Egypt," *Annales Islamologiques* 29 (1995): 133–49; Mary Ann Fay, "Women and Households: Gender, Power, and Culture in Eighteenth-Century Egypt," Ph.D. diss., Georgetown University, 1993, and; Fay, "Women and *Waqf*: Property, Power, and the Domain of Gender in Eighteenth-Century Egypt," in Zilfi, *Women in the Ottoman Empire*, 28–47; Afaf Lutfi Al-Sayyid Marsot, "Marriage in Late Eighteenth-Century Egypt," in Philipp and Haarmann, *Mamluks in Egyptian Politics*, 282–9.

Fig. 11. "Sultan Osman II (1618–1622) with His Vezir Davud Pasha." With Janissaries and slave captives. Photo © 2009 Museum Associates/LACMA/Art Resource, New York.

The Ottoman slave system was descended from pre-Islamic, Islamic Near Eastern, and Mediterranean heritages. As Old World practice, it was distinguishable on several counts from the Western hemisphere's closed, single-race system.[20] As in other Old World systems, slaves were sometimes deputized

[20] On typologies of slavery and Old World versus New World characterizations, see esp. Moses I. Finley, *Ancient Slavery and Modern Ideology*, ed. Brent D. Shaw (Princeton, N.J., 1998); Moses I. Finley, ed., *Classical Slavery* (1987; repr., London, 2003); Robin W. Winks, ed.,

to exercise authority over free persons – an unpardonable breach in most Atlantic slaveries. Moreover, many former slaves, some getting their start while still the property of others, rose to authority on their own account. Like free-origin members of the Ottoman military, the military's slave contingents were *askeri*. In a society that taxed material production, *askeri* groups – military, civil, and religious – were nonproducers in the tax-generating sense and so exempt from the taxes levied on the largely agrarian population.[21] The Janissaries, despite their slave origins and slave status, were in a position of authority over freeborn Muslims and non-Muslims, including those possessing wealth and position. In the nineteenth century, black slave soldiers sometimes operated under separate or less equal conditions while serving in the Egyptian, Moroccan, and central Ottoman armies, but garbed in the transformative mantle of the state, they exercised authority over free white and black civilians.

Slave ethnicities and races were subject to broad but highly fluid, historically contingent, and regionally variable social hierarchies. Customarily, lighter-skinned people (by Middle Eastern, Asian, and Mediterranean standards) were more socially advantaged than the darkest-skinned sub-Saharans in most but not all circumstances. And often one or another ethnic group or phenotype came to be preferred for certain occupations. Islamic law, however, made no such distinctions. No race or ethnicity was excluded by *shari'ah* law from the possibility of enslavement, and none was excluded from the opportunities of manumission and social achievement. Interracial as well as interethnic mixing was common and legal, although white- and light-skinned male access to African females rather than African male access to white females was the preferred mode of mixing. There were always exceptions to these generalities, however. In the late nineteenth century, with racial attitudes apparently hardening, when emancipated black female slaves married, it was usually to another black "but sometimes to a white person."[22] And in the period of this study, there was no law or imperial custom stopping black officials or free civilians from purchasing or owning white as well as African women for marriage or concubinage. Many did so.

Slavery: A Comparative Perspective: Readings on Slavery from Ancient Times to the Present (New York, 1972); Watson, *Asian and African Systems*; David Brion Davis, *The Problem of Slavery in Western Culture* (Ithaca, N.Y., 1966); Davis, *Slavery and Human Progress* (1984; repr., New York, 1986).

21 İnalcık, *Ottoman Empire*, 67–9; İnalcık with Quataert, *An Economic and Social History*, 16–17.

22 Leyla (Saz) [Leyla Hanım], *The Imperial Harem of the Sultans: Daily Life at the Çırağan Palace during the 19th Century*, trans. Landon Thomas (Istanbul, 1994), 71; Judith E. Tucker, *Women in Nineteenth-Century Egypt* (Cambridge, U.K., 1985), 190. For examples of such marriages in the late nineteenth century, see Börte Sagaster, *"Herren" und "Sklaven": Der Wandel im Sklavenbild türkischer Literaten in der Spätzeit des Osmanischen Reiches* (Wiesbaden, 1997), 16.

Boundaries and limits

Wherever slaves were owned, economic considerations moderated owners' behavior. As consumers of slaves and investors in their usefulness and longevity, Ottoman slaveholders were no different in their desire to maximize the utility of their property. The purchase and maintenance of slaves required appreciable outlays of capital under ordinary market conditions. Prudent owners and commercial dealers sought to maintain the value of their human assets by minimizing their exposure to physical injury and undue psychological distress. In contrast to the thoroughgoing sovereignty of slaveholders elsewhere, Muslim owners were also constrained toward benevolence by religious law (*shari'ah*), sultanic decree (*kanun*), and custom. In the realm of formal constraints, Islamic law is at pains to safeguard the property rights of owners, but it interposes itself between owner and owned in the matter of human property.

Among the Ottomans, as in other premodern Islamic systems, recognition of the slave's human character took many forms. The law and public opinion offered protections against maiming and other acts of extreme physical cruelty. Slaves had the right to request their own resale if they were unhappy with their current owner. How many were able to make that right a reality is open to question, as master-slave compatibility belonged to the unrecorded realm of informal solutions rather than the law. One finds anecdotal evidence of greater assertiveness on the part of slaves as of the mid-nineteenth century, but the behavior has to be placed in context. The period after 1840 was anomalous because of regular foreign intervention, everything from asylum for slave fugitives and diplomatic arm twisting to ship interdictions in the Indian Ocean and the Mediterranean. These pressures, together with a growing discourse of rights in the empire and greater observance of shortened slave tenures, led urban owners to comply with the spirit of the law.[23] Under most circumstances, and certainly before such pressures began to be felt, the very foreignness of slave captives blocked the path to courtroom solutions. Slaves' ignorance of both the language and the law argues against any consistency in legal recourse.

Instances of physical abuse, which were subject to the courts, confirm some amount of slaves' access to legal remedies. They may also be evidence of community outrage at slave owners' undue violence. The preeminent jurists of their day, the *şeyhülislams* or grand muftis of the empire, responded to a variety of queries regarding the penalties to be imposed on owners who willfully blinded their own male slave ("terrible torment in the hereafter and

[23] On these conditions, particularly the role of foreign intervention and fugitives in the late nineteenth century in the Istanbul region and elsewhere in the empire, see Erdem, *Slavery in the Ottoman Empire*, 160–73. Both Toledano, *Ottoman Slave Trade*, and Erdem, *Slavery in the Ottoman Empire*, focus on the late nineteenth century in considering the forms of foreign pressure. On Ottoman abolitionist thought and the lack of it, see Toledano, *Ottoman Slave Trade*, 272–8; Erdem, *Slavery in the Ottoman Empire*, 125–32.

severe punishment – flogging – in this world"), murdered on the spot an inebriated slave who insensibly entered his master's harem ("apart from sin, he incurs no worldly blame"), pressed his foot against his male slave ("if with force, it is not [permitted]"), or castrated his slave to make him a eunuch ("he is a criminal").[24]

Islamic law also opens the way for slaves to bargain with slavery to cut short their servitude. Chief among these master-slave bargains was the conditional emancipation contract known as *mükatebe*. The contract was an agreement between master and slave, witnessed and registered with the court. The slave promised to pay the willing owner a specified amount of cash or other compensation, usually within a set number of years, as the purchase price of freedom. Like indentured servitude, *mükatebe* arrangements transformed absolute slavery into a limited, contractual status. Owners consented to provide wage opportunities in direct employment under their own supervision or in released time for employment elsewhere. Slaves earned the agreed-on sum and were thus enabled to "ransom themselves."[25] Payments could be made in installments or in a final settlement in cash or in kind.

Conditional contracts were most common in urban settings, although money could be made wherever labor was needed for construction, repair work, and craft production. İnalcık notes the widespread use of conditional contracts among Bursa silk weavers in the fifteenth and sixteenth centuries. Skilled slaves variously earned their freedom "upon the completion of one hundred pieces of taffeta," or "ten brocades."[26] One male slave even contracted to deliver two female slaves (*cariye*) in exchange for his freedom.[27] More often over the centuries, the *mükatebe* exchange took the form of cash compensation or years of employment, although as with Ottoman slavery as a whole, local conditions created variations on the dominant theme. Öztürk, for example, did not find the cash-compensated *mükatebe* to be the prevailing form in his study of seventeenth-century Istanbul records. Still, sums of cash or years of service are the normative modes in the legal literature.[28]

Conditional contracts held certain advantages for owners. In an emancipatory climate such as that which existed in the fifteenth century, Sultan Mehmed II, the conqueror of Constantinople/Istanbul, gave captive Byzantines the chance to earn their freedom in five years. Short-term enslavement

[24] Düzdağ, *Şeyhülislâm Ebussuûd*, 120; also [Çatalcalı] Ali Efendi, *Şeyhülislam Fetvaları*, trans. İbrahim Ural (n.p., 1995), 121.

[25] İnalcık, "Servile Labor," 28; Yenişehirli Abdullah, *Behcet*, 137.

[26] İnalcık, "Servile Labor," 27–9; also Suraiya Faroqhi, "Labor Recruitment and Control in the Ottoman Empire (Sixteenth and Seventeenth Centuries)," in Quataert, *Manufacturing in the Ottoman Empire*, 19–24; Suraiya Faroqhi, *Making a Living in the Ottoman Lands, 1480–1820* (Istanbul, 1995), 125–6.

[27] Yenişehirli Abdullah, *Behcet*, 131.

[28] Said Öztürk, *Askeri Kassama ait Onyedinci Asır İstanbul Tereke Defterleri* (Istanbul, 1995), 197; Yenişehirli Abdullah, *Behcet*, 131–2, 137; Çatalcalı Ali, *Fetava-i Ali Efendi* (Istanbul, 1305/1887), 1:175–7; Düzdağ, *Şeyhülislâm Ebussuûd*, 125–6.

was then common and perhaps in some quarters expected.[29] At any time, contracts promised a consistent level of productivity. They also enhanced the owner's reputation for generosity without entailing the capital loss associated with immediate manumission. As for *mükatebe* slaves themselves, with freedom in sight and the impossibility of being sold while under the contract, they would be inclined to apply themselves more diligently. Certainly, their owners hoped they would give up disruptive behavior and thoughts of fleeing. Although the *mükatebe* was not so magnanimous as unconditional manumission, it was a far cry from selling off slaves or keeping them indefinitely so as to pass them on to heirs. The frequency of these contracts, along with other emancipatory promises, reflects an Islamic view of slavery as a mutable and impermanent condition.

In Old World slaveries, the incidence of sexual relations between male owners and female captives fell somewhere between customary and expected. Leaving aside for the moment the issue of slaves' sexual vulnerability, proximity to any superior increased opportunities for gaining favor. Sexual appeal was one of the few potential weapons female slaves possessed as individuals. In Ottoman society, sexual relations between masters and female slaves, with resultant offspring, were commonplace. The high incidence of these relationships and of the legal muddles they occasioned – most having to do with paternity and/or inheritance – is suggested by the many *fetva*s and commentaries that the legal minds of the time devoted to such entanglements.[30] The incidence of complications did not deter male owners. The law itself supported their right to sexual access. The scriptural authority on which the law was based inhered in the Qur'anic recognition of a master's sexual entitlement to "all that his right hand possesses," that is, to the female slave property in his absolute possession.[31] The Qur'anic allowance was a compelling recognition of a problematical practice. The reckoning of *shari'ah* law with the Qur'anic provision and with relevant *hadith*s of the Prophet Muhammad underscored that recognition.[32]

Male acknowledgment of paternity was as socially defining for a slave mother and child as it was for a free wife and her offspring, so long as the father of the child was also the slave mother's owner. If the owner–father acknowledged paternity, the offspring of a slave mother and her master

[29] Halil İnalcık, "The Policy of Mehmed II toward the Greek Population of Istanbul and the Byzantine Buildings of the City," *Dumbarton Oaks Papers*, nos. 23–4 (1969–70): 231–49.

[30] Çatalcali Ali, *Şeyhülislam Fetvaları*, 84–8, 109; Çatalcalı Ali, *Fetava*, 1:57, 128–32; Yenişehirli Abdullah, *Behcet*, 133–5; cf. Düzdağ, *Şeyhülislâm Ebussuûd*, 121–4, for the sixteenth century.

[31] Abdullah Yusuf Ali, trans., *The Holy Qur'an: Text, Translation and Commentary* (New York, 1988), iv:3.

[32] Colin Imber, "Eleven Fetvas of the Ottoman Sheikh ul-Islam 'Abdurrahim," in Muhammad Khalid Masud, Brinkley Messick, and David S. Powers, eds., *Islamic Legal Interpretation: Muftis and Their Fatwas* (Cambridge, Mass., 1996), 141–9; Baber Johansen, "The Valorization of the Human Body in Muslim Sunni Law," *Princeton Papers* 4 (Spring 1996): 70–112.

Fig. 12. "The Aurut [Avrat] Bazaar, or Slave Market." Mistakenly labeled "Women's Market." Robert Walsh and Thomas Allom, *Constantinople and the Scenery of the Seven Churches of Asia Minor* (London, n.d.).

effectively took his or her status from the paternal line and became free.[33] If the father was someone other than the owner, however, the child took its status from the mother. In that case, both mother and child remained slaves unless emancipated. This latter consequence resulted when an owner permitted or obliged his female slave to marry a free man or another slave. Thus, even with an owner's approval and permission, a non-owning father's free status and acknowledgment of paternity counted for nothing against the slave owner's continuing rights of possession. In permitting his slave woman to marry, the owner relinquished his sexual rights to the woman, but that is all. The woman's children were the owner's property, as their mother was.

The close monitoring of all male-female mixing in stable household and neighborhood settings made it difficult, but far from impossible, for masters to disavow paternity. The high premium that Ottoman society placed on fertility and procreation and the fact that children born outside of legal marriage did not suffer the stigma of illegitimacy meant that owners were less likely to deny or escape paternity than would be the case in monogamous or nonslaveholding societies. Nonetheless, outright denials or the quick sale or forced marriage

[33] İstM, 1/25, for 1179/1765–6; Sak, "Konya'da," 189–90. For controversies surrounding paternity, see Uri Rubin, "'Al-Walad li-l-firash': On the Islamic Campaign against 'Zina,'" *SI* 78 (1993): 5–26; Imber, "The Hanafi Law of Manumission," typescript, 6.

of a female slave to another male could be used to evade responsibility.[34] Numerous *fetva* opinions grapple with just such contingencies, as paternity and the child's inheritance status were so often at issue. An opinion rendered by the eighteenth-century *Şeyhülislam* Yenişehirli Abdullah determines the child to be the offspring of the previous owner "if slave woman X is sold to another and then gives birth in less than six months from the date of her sale."[35] The mother could take comfort in her child's protected status or coming freedom. However, she had no guarantee of being able to fulfill a mothering role or remain close to her child. In this kind of case, she could be resold or married out of the picture entirely.[36]

When the owner himself acknowledged paternity, even if the child was stillborn or if the child was born after the master's death (so long as he acknowledged the pregnancy as his doing), the status of the slave mother rose on the demonstration of having carried a child.[37] According to an often cited *hadith* of the Prophet, "'her child has set her free,'"[38] the mother (or almost mother or expectant mother) was not to be sold away from her owner-consort and child. She was also to gain her freedom on the owner's death, if he had not freed her before then.[39] However, even when recognized by the father, the *ümm-i veled*, as she was known in Ottoman Turkish (Ar., *umm walad*), literally, a "[slave] mother of a [master's] child," did not occupy the same position with respect to her child as did a childbearing free woman. Unless freed, the slave mother could not invoke *shari'ah*-stipulated mothering rights (*hızanet hakkı*) to remain with her child during his or her early years.[40] Separation from her child might be her lot. In contrast, according to *hızanet* stipulations, free women – whether still married, separated, or divorced – were entitled to be the primary caregivers for their offspring during the child's early years. In consequence of that role, they were also entitled to a maintenance allowance (*nafaka-i hızanet*) from the father until the children reached puberty, customarily seven years old for boys and nine for girls.[41]

34 See Chapter 5 in this volume.

35 Yenişehirli Abdullah, *Behcet*, 133–5. See also Ömer Nasuhi Bilmen, *Hukukı İslâmiyye ve Istılahatı Fıkhiyye Kamusu* (Istanbul, n.d.), 2:415.

36 The different kinds of paternal recognition and when they confer only a protected status rather than inheritance rights according to the four schools of Sunni Islamic jurisprudence are discussed in Jonathan E. Brockopp, *Early Mālikī Law: Ibn 'Abd al-Hakam and His Major Compendium of Jurisprudence* (Leiden, 2000), 201–4.

37 Jurists dispute whether a miscarriage warrants the entitlement; see *EI2*, s.v. "Umm al-Walad," by Joseph Schacht.

38 Al-Marghinani, *Hedaya*, 267.

39 Sak, "Konya'da,' 189–90, 199–200; İstM 1/25, Şevval 17, 1179/March 8, 1766. See also the discussion of the *ümm-i veled/umm al-walad* especially according to the Maliki school, in Brockopp, *Early Mālikī Law*, 192–205.

40 Al-Marghinani, *Hedaya*, 139 (bk. 4, ch. 14); *EI2*, s.v. "'Abd,'' by R. Brunschvig, makes a contrary assertion.

41 Remarriage and other circumstances, however, could lead to the loss of a free mother's entitlement and stipend; al-Marghinani, *Hedaya*, 138–40, 146; Judith E. Tucker, "The Fullness

Although the recognized slave mother could not be sold away from her child, the notion that she occupied a status approaching that of a legal wife is untenable. Her owner might not be able to sell her, but as owner, he could marry her off to whomever he pleased, and her new husband might live at a distance from her owner's domicile and her child. An *ümm-i veled* remained at her owner's disposal, her primary occupation still slave to her master, not mother to her child.[42] This reality is borne out by the difference between female slaves and free women with respect to the practice of coitus interruptus (T., *azil*; Ar., *'azl*). By law, a married woman was entitled not only to sexual relations with her husband and sexual satisfaction from him but also to sexual relations with the prospect of childbearing. Although coitus interruptus was permissible under the law, it could be practiced only if a wife agreed to it. Slave women had no such right; thus, their hopes for *ümm-i veled* status and emancipation might have been thwarted from the outset.[43]

Islamic laws of inheritance could also wreak havoc with the *ümm-i veled*'s emancipation prospects. Her manumission was not an unambiguous mandate. Rather than being automatic on the owner-consort's recognition, as it is usually represented,[44] emancipation could be impeded by claims on the owner's estate and the personal inclinations of legal heirs. Reluctant heirs and the legal niceties of inheritance law could override an owner's most heartfelt intentions. A slave woman could have her hopes dashed when, on the owner's demise and in the absence of other witnesses to corroborate her status, heirs disavowed the legator's declaration of paternity. This sort of survivors' ploy, to limit the number of legal heirs and/or to hold on to all estate assets, is a commonplace in modern courts as well. In the Ottoman context, paternity denials by survivors were more likely to occur, and to be believed, when the child of the presumptive *ümm-i veled* was still in utero, when the baby was stillborn or predeceased the father, or when the child was just an infant. The law could say what it liked, but the near sanctity of the home and household limited the law's reach without the active and honest cooperation of the household's members.

The dilemma of an insufficient estate affected all claimants and heirs but fell hardest on slaves who had hoped for emancipation or for continued residence in the deceased master's household. Even slaves who had been promised freedom upon a master's death were at risk if the deceased's estate, by debiting the market value of a promised slave (*müdebber*), could not meet outstanding debts and heirs' mandated shares. Like any free adult Muslim, an owner-consort

of Affection: Mothering in the Islamic Law of Ottoman Syria and Palestine," in Zilfi, *Women in the Ottoman Empire*, 232–52.

42 Al-Marghinani, *Hedaya*, 139 (bk. 4, chap. 14).

43 For differences between the various schools of jurisprudence on this issue, see Donna Lee Bowen, "Muslim Juridical Opinions concerning the Status of Women as Demonstrated by the Case of *'Azl*," *JNES* 40, no. 4 (1981): 323–8; Shatzmiller, *Her Day in Court*, 98.

44 Düzdağ, *Şeyhülislâm Ebussuûd*, 31; see, e.g., Edward William Lane, *An Account of the Manners and Customs of the Modern Egyptians: The Definitive 1860 Edition* (Cairo, 2003), 102, 185; Davis, *Ottoman Lady*, 109; Fendoğlu, *İslam ve Osmanlı*, 226–33.

had the right to execute a written testament (*vasiyetname*) bequeathing cash, goods, or immovables to chosen beneficiaries. The value of the bequests could not exceed one-third of the estate's net value as determined by the courts.[45] Because the inheritance rights of various relatives are spelled out in the Qur'an and are thus mandatory successions, the rights of Qur'anic heirs to individual shares of the two-thirds portion must be fulfilled before a decedent's bequests can be awarded. A deathbed declaration of emancipation, for example, constituted a bequest in the amount of the slave's value. Uncontested *ümm-i veled*s, but not ordinary promised slaves, had a prior-claim right to freedom, thus their original purchase price was not to be held against the discretionary third. However, the *ümm-i veled*'s rights sometimes faltered depending on the state of the estate at the time she attained her status. If the deceased had incurred excessive debts prior to the *ümm-i veled*'s pregnancy or childbirth and his acknowledgment of paternity, his heirs claimed the right to sell her, as they did almost every category of slave caught in an estate shortfall.

A paternally acknowledged child of an owner and his *ümm-i veled* was free. He or she stood to inherit a son's or daughter's share of the father's estate. When a slave woman was not recognized as an *ümm-i veled*, however, her child might remain as a slave with the owner's family while the slave mother was dispatched elsewhere, to another master or mistress or to a forced marriage.[46] Islamic manuals of slave-owning ethics advise owners to refrain from even threatening to sell their slaves, lest loyalty be undermined.[47] But until an estate's solvency, in Qur'anic terms, was established, a promise was only a promise. The possibility of yet another deracination, even if unspoken, was always present for every slave. Given the rivalrous business of estate dissolution and the problem of oral evidence, no pending manumission was ironclad.

The fact that slaves as human beings had a certain legal standing enabled them to participate in charges brought against masters or mistresses who failed to provide adequate nourishment or otherwise abused them. Owners' rights were also tempered by the laws governing unintended emancipation. Just as with husbands who regretted blurting out the "I divorce thee" Islamic divorce

[45] Yusuf Ali, *Holy Qur'an*, s.ii:180–2, 240; s.iv:7–12, 176, and the translator's notes, 71, 96, 235. Also Mahomed Ullah ibn S. Jung, ed., *The Muslim Law of Inheritance, Compiled from Original Arabic Authorities with Arabic Text. . . and Their English Translation* (Lahore, n.d.); N[oel] J[ames] Coulson, *Succession in the Muslim Family* (Cambridge, U.K., 1971), 213–58, for additional restrictions on testamentary bequests.

[46] On testaments and mandatory heirs, see al-Marghinani, *Hedaya*, 670–703; Coulson, *Succession in the Muslim Family*, 29–75; also Fisher, "Studies in Ottoman Slavery," 52, for unemancipated *ümm-i veled*s; and Kal'a et al., *İstanbul Külliyâtı, İstanbul Ahkâm Defterleri: İstanbul'da Sosyal Hayat 1* (Istanbul, 1997), 46–8, 215–16; Çatalcalı Ali, *Fetava*, 1:38–40, 128–32, 163–4, 168–73; Çatalcalı Ali, *Şeyhülislam Fetvaları*, 88; Yenişehirli Abdullah, *Behcet*, 62–3, 129–35, for slave mothers and disputed status.

[47] Nasir al-Din Tusi, "Ahlāq-i Nāsirī," qtd. in Hans Müller, *Die Kunst des Sklavenkaufs nach arabischen, persischen und türkischen Ratgebern vom 10. bis 18. Jahrhundert* (Freiburg im Breisgau, 1980), 168.

formula, slave owners' utterances had legal force. Masters and mistresses who, while drunk, angry, or joking, or through careless syntax, uttered a formula of manumission – "be free," "you are free" – could not take back the pronouncement once spoken.[48] Some slave owners and many husbands woke up to an empty house as a result of the laws on unintended release, though only if there had been witnesses to the declaratory act or if owner or husband admitted to it.

More often when words were at issue, the *şeyhülislam* or, in the provinces, a local mufti, was asked to decide whether a particular combination of words constituted a valid manumission. Surviving *fetva*s testify to the high stakes involved in such disputes. They also suggest that membership in the master class did not guarantee a firm grip on the law, much less on their own habits of speech: "If Zeyd [as the anonymous subject was called], an owner of male and female slaves, says 'All of these are not slaves, they are free,' are the slaves in his possession free?" The *şeyhülislam*'s answer was yes. Freedom was also immediate for a slave whose owner had said to him, "You are my son." However, the use of comparative or allusive expressions – "She is like a wife to me," "You are like a son to me," "Come here, my son" – did not result in liberation for the slaves who were so described, according to Ottoman jurisconsults.[49] One can imagine the hopefulness of slaves and sympathetic (or mischievous) onlookers who thought they had caught the master or mistress in a costly slip of the tongue.

An Islamic communal ethic based on Qur'anic principles, *hadith*s, and popular maxims encouraged magnanimity in the master class: "One should feed them with the like of what one eats and clothe them with the like of what one wears. You should not overburden them with what they cannot bear, and if you do so, help them."[50] And, "'God has given you the right of ownership over them; He could have given them the right of ownership of you.'"[51] The Ottoman Islamic discourse on slaveholding was built on these humane expectations. It also resonated with the practical applications of court verdicts and the opinions of muftis who constantly had to pronounce on master-slave conundrums. Nonetheless, a voluntary ethic and occasional juristic rulings were merely checks on brutality, not guarantees against them. In settled communities and in urban neighborhoods, slave owners were more likely to be

48 Çatalcalı Ali, *Fetava*, 1:160–2; Imber, "Hanafi Law of Manumission," typescript, 2, and his "'Involuntary' Annulment of Marriage and Its Solution in Ottoman Law," in Colin Imber, *Studies in Ottoman History and Law* (Istanbul, 1996), 217–51. For disputes and court claims, see İstM 2/178, fol. 20a; Ahmet Kal'a et al., eds., *İstanbul Külliyâtı: İstanbul Ahkâm Defterleri, İstanbul'da Sosyal Hayat 2, 1755–1765* (Istanbul, 1998), 182.

49 Yenişehirli Abdullah, *Behcet*, 128–30; Çatalcalı Ali, *Fetava*, 1:160–2, 166; al-Marghinani, *Hedaya*, 166–9. Depending on context, the word *oğul* can mean either "son" or "boy," while *kız* is either "daughter" or "girl."

50 Muhammad ibn Ismail Bukhari, *Al-Sahih*, vol. 3, bk. 46, no. 721, http://www.usc.edu/schools/college/crcc/engagement/resources/texts/muslim/search.html.

51 *EI2*, s.v. "'Abd," by R. Brunschvig, 25.

concerned about their reputations. And in such environments, law courts were known entities, regularly staffed and ready to hear complaints, to which the ten thousand or more extant Ottoman court registers bear witness. Under conditions of demographic stability and peacetime administration, slaves were more apt to find humane practice the norm. In wartime, and perennially along the empire's many troubled borders as well as in regions prone to banditry, humane practice was ephemeral, at best.

The relative mildness of domestic or household forms of slavery, especially in upper-class settings, and wishful thinking about the congruence between ideals and reality, sanitized the popular image of slave practices. The regional, episodic, and often out-of-sight character of the most death-dealing employment – Anatolian and Saharan quarrying, Iraqi and North African dredging operations, and Mediterranean galley slavery – enabled the benign view to flourish. Moreover, the hardships endured by slaves in such occupations were not substantially different from the backbreaking exertions of corvée laborers and other technically free workers throughout the early modern world. Even the Ottomans' dreaded galleys were considered by many Europeans to be more humane – by early modern standards – than the galleys and maritime prisons of France and Spain. Assertions like Slade's that slaves and convicts in France's infamous Toulon prison were "one hundred times worse off" than were Christian captives at Istanbul are overstatements. They are all the more hyperbolic if they are presumed to apply to all eras or to every port and harbor on the empire's shores.[52] However historians might assess the treatment of Ottoman and Ottoman-Barbary galleys and maritime work gangs, the dead, the dying, and the starving among them tended to be outside the view and even the consciousness of household slave owners and the system's eventual apologists.

Closer to the domestic heartland of the slave system, the training of palace concubines or odalisques (T., *odalık*) and *devşirme* boys made for another kind of blind spot for those who would compare Mediterranean slavery

[52] Adolphus Slade, *Records of Travels in Turkey, Greece, etc., and of a Cruise in the Black Sea, with the Capitan Pasha, in the Years 1829, 1830, and 1831* (London, 1833), 1:104; Mehmet İpşirli, "XVI. Asrın İkinci Yarısında Kürek Cezası ile ilgili Hükümler," *İ.Ü.E.F. Tarih Enstitüsü Dergisi*, no. 12 (1982): 206. See also the discussions of semiautonomous North Africa and galley slavery by Linda Colley, *Captives* (New York, 2002), 82–98, 113–19, 122–34; Lucette Valensi, "Esclaves chrétiens et esclaves noirs à Tunis au xviiie siècle," *Annales* 22 (1967): 1267–88; Ellen G. Friedman, *Spanish Captives in North Africa in the Early Modern Age* (Madison, Wis., 1983), 59–89; Gillian Lee Weiss, "Back from Barbary: Captivity, Redemption and French Identity in the Seventeenth- and Eighteenth-Century Mediterranean," Ph.D. diss., Stanford University, 2002. Robert C. Davis's *Christian Slaves, Muslim Masters: White Slavery in the Mediterranean, the Barbary Coast, and Italy, 1500–1800* (New York, 2003), tends more toward selective anecdotalism but is valuable nonetheless. Colley's *Captives* and *The Ordeal of Elizabeth Marsh: A Woman in World History* (New York, 2007), eschew the paradigm of European victimization by situating Barbary piracy in the context of international competition, the roles of ordinary male and female captives, and the domestic politics of captive narratives.

favorably with practice in the Atlantic. For the most part, the courtiers and harem denizens who were the finished products of palace instruction came to their graceful and self-effacing mien in consequence of the hard knocks of slave recruitment and vetting. This was especially true of the period when the *kul* system was at its height, prior to the eighteenth century. Although the instruction of imperial slaves took place behind the barricade-like walls of Topkapı Palace, contemporaries testified to the harsh treatment meted out to young captives. In the early seventeenth century, the Venetian Ottaviano Bon claimed that harem women whose behavior was found wanting were "extreamly [*sic*] beaten by their overseers," while the boys of the levy, the "embryo grandees of the empire,"[53] were likewise beaten severely and often by their instructors.[54] It is presumably these latter rigors that produced the disciplined troops so admired by the Habsburg ambassador Busbecq on his visit to the court of Süleyman in the late sixteenth century: "The most remarkable body of men were several thousand Janissaries, who stood . . . so motionless that, as they were at some distance from me, I was for a while doubtful whether they were living men or statues."[55] A French envoy in 1573 similarly wondered at the "palisade of statues" as thousands of Ottoman soldiers and courtiers "remained immobile in that way more than seven hours, without talking or moving. Certainly it is almost impossible to comprehend this discipline and this obedience."[56] The modes of training and inculcation that produced "this discipline and this obedience" are explored in the course of the present study. It can be said here, though, that of all the surviving images of the sultan's servitors, the most revealing of imperial slaves' legal condition and of the route that they had traveled is a colorful miniature of cowering young boys of the levy flanked by adult males with sticks.[57] Lest we get carried away with the idea of Oriental difference, however, it is well to remember that, until recently, the education of children and dependents the world over was usually a matter of adults with sticks.

The organizational demeanor of nonroyal slave-owning households could be almost as opaque and misleading as that of the palace. Although the homes of society's wealthier members were opened to neighbors and friends in celebration of Muslim holidays and consequential family celebrations, most household life and family interaction took place in the home, and often in its innermost precincts. The demographic density of the popular urban quarters did not allow the poor much privacy. The town houses and villas of the

[53] Slade, *Records of Travels*, 1:135.

[54] Ottaviano Bon, *The Sultan's Seraglio: An Intimate Portrait of Life at the Ottoman Court*, ed. Godfrey Goodwin (London, 1996), 68.

[55] Busbecq, *Turkish Letters*, 41.

[56] Qtd. in Gülru Necipoğlu, *Architecture, Ceremonial, and Power: The Topkapı Palace in the Fifteenth and Sixteenth Centuries* (Cambridge, Mass., 1991), 64, 66.

[57] Esin Atıl, *Süleymanname: The Illustrated History of Süleyman the Magnificent* (New York, 1986), 95, "Recruitment of Tribute Children."

middle and upper classes were a different matter. The disciplining of household slaves – and the justice or injustice of their punishments – could be as remote from public view as galley slaves at their oars or as *kapı kulu* youths on the road to Ottoman manhood.

Frontiers of enslavement

One of the least publicized mechanisms of slavery was the act of enslavement itself. Brute force was the lubricant of enslavement and transport. At the very least, captives on route suffered forced marches, scant food, bad water, exposure, filth, disease, and raw fear. Outsiders who had occasion to view Black Sea captives in transit were struck by their deplorable state. In the seventeenth century, Sir John Chardin described a shipment "of women and children, half-naked, or covered with rags and filth" loaded onto a vessel for the voyage south. A nineteenth-century account of a debarkation tells a similar story, as hundreds of females who survived their "middle passage" across the Black Sea arrived dirty, ragged, and seemingly famished.[58]

The two reports, separated by two hundred years, hasten past the girls' health to ponder whether they measured up to the image of harem beauties. Chardin thought the women "resplendent with beauty," whereas the nineteenth-century observer confessed disappointment at their appearance. Before the mid-nineteenth century, the Western male gaze with respect to women in the Islamic East need not be thought of as substantially different from that of indigenous, primarily male observers and consumers. It was overwhelmingly the Ottoman, Middle Eastern, African, and Eurasian male gaze that determined how female bodies were to be distributed.[59] The convergence between the view of insider and outsider suggests a common proprietary standpoint, the one more real and the other purely aspirational. With regard to Ottoman realities, the maltreated cargoes of white female captives – supposedly the most prized and preferred of female slaves – exposes the underside of metropolitan slavery and the rationales that fed imperial apologetics and self-perceptions. As an Egyptian lawyer put it some years later in defense of a slave-owning client in Cairo, "What guilt is there for the man who takes the kidnapped from misery to happiness, from hunger to ease of life, replacing their ragged clothes with beautiful robes, supporting them with money, treating them with the kindness that both his religion and his sense of humanity dictate to him?" After all, he argued, "[H]e does not buy them for trade or for profit."[60] The linkage between disrepute and capitalism accords with the rhetoric of denial

58 Sir John Chardin, qtd. in James E. DeKay, *Sketches of Turkey in 1831 and 1832* (New York, 1833), 279; Davis, *Ottoman Lady*, 116.
59 Zilfi, "Muslim Women," 226–32.
60 Qtd. in Eve M. Troutt Powell, *A Different Shade of Colonialism: Egypt, Great Britain, and the Mastery of the Sudan* (Berkeley, Calif., 2003), 154.

and the insistence on the moral superiority of Islamic culture.[61] A British travel guide of 1871 reflects Britain's own colonial position of the time. Advising its readers of what was in store for newly captured white females, it casually endorses the better-off argument employed by Middle Easterners themselves: "Their complexions are sallow, and none of them are [*sic*] even good looking. But the daily Turkish bath, protection from the sun, and a wholesome diet, working upon an excellent constitution, accomplish wonders in a short space of time."[62]

The passage out of Africa into the Mediterranean world has lately come to be understood as possessing virtually the same lethality as the treks and voyages of the Atlantic trade.[63] A growing literature on the trans-Saharan and Indian Ocean trades puts to rest any comforting myth of the system's benignity. The major trans-Saharan routes to the main North African outlets in Egypt, Libya (Tripoli), and Morocco[64] combined arduous length and brutal discipline with countless natural and man-made perils, not the least of which was the susceptibility of sub-Saharan Africans to sickness in their new environment.[65] Slave traders' despicable treatment of captives being driven north from the Sudan and West Africa seems not to have been much different from the overland horrors inflicted by the Atlantic-bound trade. There is also the incalculability of deaths and injuries at the point of capture. In any case, the

[61] Powell, *A Different Shade*, 154.

[62] John Murray, *Handbook for Travellers in Turkey in Asia, including Constantinople, the Bosphorus, Dardanelles, Brousa and Plain of Troy*, rev. ed. (London, [1871]), 115; cf. Toledano, *Slavery and Abolition*, 37.

[63] John Wright, *The Trans-Saharan Slave Trade* (London, 2007), provides a judicious yet devastating review of trans-Saharan slave traffic into North Africa – the Maghreb – from the medieval period through the nineteenth century.

[64] Algiers and Tunis, though important, did not handle the traffic of the other trans-Saharan entrepôts; Wright, *Trans-Saharan Slave Trade*, 47.

[65] Michel Le Gall, trans., "Translation of Louis Frank's *Mémoire sur le commerce des nègres au Kaire, et sur les maladies auxquelles ils sont sujets en y arrivant* (1802)," in Marmon, *Slavery in the Islamic Middle East*, 69–88; Terence Walz, "Black Slavery in Egypt during the Nineteenth Century as Reflected in the Mahkama Archives of Cairo," in John Ralph Willis, ed., *Slaves and Slavery in Muslim Africa* (London, 1984–5), 2:142–3; Leyla Saz, *Imperial Harem of the Sultans*, 70–90; George Michael La Rue, "The Frontiers of Enslavement: Bagirmi and the Trans-Saharan Slave Routes," in Paul E. Lovejoy, ed., *Slavery on the Frontiers of Islam* (Princeton, N.J., 2004), 41–2; *Anti-Slavery Reporter*, November 29, 1843, 221–2; Lane, *An Account*, 186. On the trans-Saharan debates, see Seymour Drescher and Stanley L. Engerman, eds., *A Historical Guide to World Slavery* (Oxford, 1998), 34, 42–4; Toledano, *Slavery and Abolition*, 6–9; J. E. Inikori, "The Origin of the Diaspora: The Slave Trade from Africa," *Tarikh* 5 (1978): 1–19; Mordechai Abir, "The Ethiopian Slave Trade and Its Relation to the Islamic World," in Willis, *Slaves and Slavery*, 2:123–36; Ralph A. Austen, "The Mediterranean Islamic Slave Trade Out of Africa: A Tentative Census," *Slavery and Abolition* 13 (1993): 214–48; Thomas M. Ricks, "Slaves and Slave Traders in the Persian Gulf, 18th and 19th Centuries: An Assessment," in Patrick Manning, ed., *Slave Trades, 1500–1800: Globalization of Forced Labour* (Brookfield, Vt., 1996), 286–7; John Hunwick and Eve Troutt Powell, eds., *The African Diaspora in the Mediterranean Lands of Islam* (Princeton, N.J., 2002); Wright, *Trans-Saharan Slave Trade*, 82–6.

heavy mortality of "successfully" transported black Africans is itself an object lesson in moral obtuseness. African deaths by more or less natural causes, even when slaves had arrived at their destination and were being fed and cared for much as free laborers, were extraordinarily high. Most of the evidence comes from eighteenth- and nineteenth-century reports, but there is no reason to think that slaves fared better in earlier centuries. Medieval sources, in fact, tell a similar miserable story.

The causes of premature (natural-death) slave mortality among Africans remained a puzzle for the medical minds of nineteenth-century Egypt and North Africa, where the incidence was apparently highest. The fact that black slaves, including lighter-skinned "Abyssinians," died at alarming rates should have come as no surprise, however. It had been well attested since the caliphs ruled from Baghdad. Seven hundred years of buyers' guides for Middle Easterners engaged in the slave trade – written in Arabic, Persian, and Turkish in iterative versions down to the nineteenth century – repeated the warning that Africans from the Sudanic regions were prone to illness "when far from their homelands." The manuals also cautioned that Abyssinian captives, though desirable as house servants and, if female, as concubines, "were weak of body and did not live long" in their new environments.[66] Leyla Saz's warm reminiscences of the late nineteenth century about the brief lives of two African slave girls – her and her sister's gifts from their father – testify to the fragility of captives' lives even under the best of circumstances. Little Yekta and Yasemin survived their Mediterranean voyage but not for long the chill of Istanbul and Ottoman Rusçuk (Ruse in Bulgaria).[67] Melek Hanım writes of a similar death toll for her African slaves in the mid-nineteenth century. Their ailments may not have been peculiar to them, however. Melek's own young son succumbed to illness at the same time.[68] In the 1830s, staggering death rates among black conscripts for the new Egyptian army of Mehmed Ali Pasha (1805–48) led to the abandonment of that project, though the importation of black slaves continued.[69]

In the face of what should have been sobering realities, buyers and other receivers at the slaves' urban destinations persuaded themselves – if they thought about it at all – that rough handling and adverse consequences to the enslaved occurred incidentally or by the will of God. The upper-class consumers of slave labor, whether in the Ottoman Empire, Egypt, Morocco, or

[66] Müller, *Die Kunst*, 136, 187; cf. Lane, *An Account*, 184. [67] Leyla Saz, 78–80, 85–9.

[68] Melek Hanım [Melek-Hanum], *Thirty Years in the Harem, or, the Autobiography of Melek-Hanum, Wife of H. H. Kıbrızlı-Mehemet-Pasha* (New York, 1872), 51.

[69] Khaled Fahmy, *All the Pasha's Men: Mehmet Ali, His Army, and the Making of Modern Egypt* (Cambridge, U.K., 1997), 88–94; Ahmad Alawad Sikainga, "Comrades in Arms or Captives in Bondage: Sudanese Slaves in the Turco-Egyptian Army, 1821–1865," in Miura Toru and John Edward Philips, eds., *Slave Elites in the Middle East and Africa: A Comparative Study* (London, 2000), 202.

Iran, could claim that those among them who mistreated slaves and subordinates were of a different social order. Upper-class Ottomans, especially those connected to the central government and invested in the mores of Istanbul, could add that those responsible were not really *Ottoman* as they would apply the term, in its limited sense of the refined, upper-class Muslim, and Ottoman Turkish-speaking leadership of the empire. They were mistaken.

In response to nineteenth-century critics, British abolitionists in the main, the Ottomans as well as Egyptians, Moroccans, and Iranians, representing the major Middle Eastern and North African political entities of the day, adhered to the position that slaveholding under Muslim auspices was a thing apart from other slaveries inasmuch as it was governed by Islamic and customary constraints.[70] Nineteenth-century apologists – followed by a fair amount of present-day commentary – acknowledged that Ottoman slaveholding was a "system of many systems," to use Parish's phrasing,[71] but they rightly singled out domestic slavery as its signature form. Most took the position that the repellent features of nondomestic variants like agricultural slavery were outweighed by the relative mildness of the dominant mode.

The bulk of the historiographical literature in fact concurs with the premise that slavery, understood as household slavery, was generally moderate and temporary.[72] European observers, many of whom were no friends of Islam or the Ottomans, attested to slavery's mild character in regions and situations open to their view. Slavery in Ottoman hands may not have been the "consummate felicity" suggested by Charles White, but for most firsthand observers, domestic slaveholding in the Ottoman-era East possessed too many moderate features to deserve likening to the Americas' "lords of the lash." Toledano has challenged the premises and standpoints of the benign school, but the nineteenth century's generalized verdict has been difficult to overturn with regard to the Ottoman Empire's central provinces.[73]

[70] Ahmet [Ahmed] Midhat Efendi, *Üss-i İnkılap: Kırım Muharebesinden II. Abdülhamid Han'ın Cülûsuna kadar*, ed. Tahir Galip Seratlı (Istanbul, 2004), 2:149–50; but see Berkes, *Development of Secularism*, 282–4, regarding Ahmed Midhat Efendi's more progressive views on slavery in other works; see also Erdem, *Ottoman Slavery*, 85–7, 104–5, 126–32; Toledano, *Slavery and Abolition*, 122–34, and *Ottoman Slave Trade*, 72–83; Eve Troutt Powell, "Slaves or Siblings? 'Abdullah al-Nadim's Dialogues about the Family," in Israel Gershoni, Y. Hakan Erdem, and Ursula Wocöck, eds., *Histories of the Modern Middle East: New Directions* (Boulder, Colo., 2002), 155–65.

[71] Peter J. Parish, *Slavery: History and Historians* (New York, 1989), 5.

[72] For Toledano's discussion of this point, see *Ottoman Slave Trade*, 272. Dissenting voices in recent years have come from inside and outside the field, although most negative generalizations regarding Mediterranean or Islamic slavery draw chronologically from the middle to late nineteenth century and geographically from Egypt, North Africa (particularly Morocco), and bits and pieces from the Indian Ocean. See Austen, "Mediterranean Islamic Slave Trade"; W. G. Clarence-Smith, ed., *The Economics of the Indian Ocean Slave Trade in the Nineteenth Century* (London, 1989); Janet J. Ewald, "Slavery in Africa and the Slave Trades from Africa," *AHR* 97 (April 1992): 465–85.

[73] Toledano, *Slavery and Abolition*, 3–19; see also Ennaji, *Serving the Master*, 26–85, regarding Morocco.

Fig. 13. Town scene in Larisa, Ottoman Thessaly, with African free man of middling class. J. L. S. Bartholdy, *Voyage en Grèce* (Paris, 1807).

Emancipation and manumission

In contrast to the perpetual bondage of the New World, the status of slaves in the Ottoman world was dynamic and in many respects historically contingent. On wartime peripheries to the east and west in the seventeenth and eighteenth centuries, whole populations were captured one year and freed the next. Mass emancipation for captives of the warring combatants was usually built into treaties between the Ottomans and their adversary of the moment. Prisoner exchanges with Austria, Venice, Russia, and Iran were periodically heralded throughout the empire.[74] Although slaveholders on both sides were ordered to surrender the affected captives at designated collection points, many slaves

[74] İstM 2/184, fol. 142b; İstM 14/286, fols. 15b–16a; Reşat Ekrem [Koçu], *Osmanlı Muahedeleri Kapitülâsiyonlar, 1300–1920, ve Lozan Muahedesi, 24 Temmuz 1923* (Istanbul, 1934), 70, 79–80, 82, 103, 111–13, 407–8; Karl Jahn, "Zum Loskauf christlicher und türkischer Gefangener und Sklaven im 18. Jahrhundert," *ZDMG* 111, no. 1(1961): 63–85; Erdem, *Slavery in the Ottoman Empire*, 21, 31–3; "Mühimme Defteri," Chicago, Regenstein Library, vol. 44, no. 111, 733–44, for the ransoming of Christian captives by the Austrian envoy ; Géza Dávid, "Manumissioned Female Slaves at Galata and Istanbul around 1700," in Sabine Prätor and Christoph K. Neumann, eds., *Frauen, Bilder und Gelehrte: Studien zu Gesellschaft und Künsten im Osmanischen Reich–Festschrift Hans Georg Majer* (Istanbul, 2002), 1:229–36; see also Zsuzsanna J. Újvary, "A Muslim Captive's Vicissitudes in Ottoman Hungary (Mid-Seventeenth Century)," 141–3; Géza Dávid, "Manumitted Male Slaves at Galata and Istanbul around 1700," in Dávid and Fodor, *Ransom Slavery*, 183–4.

remained in bondage years after their technical emancipation.[75] On the western front, on the European side of the border, Osman Ağa from Ottoman Temesvar (Timisoara in Romania), a seventeen-year-old Ottoman official captured by the Austrians at Lipova in 1688, was denied release for eleven years, even though his ransom had been paid almost immediately. The Treaty of Karlowitz (1699) stipulated that war captives be exchanged expeditiously, but there was foot-dragging all around. Osman's memoir makes it clear that many Ottoman Muslims were being held illegally. Nonetheless, there, as on every front, not all captives were eager to return home.[76]

Legal exceptions built into the rules of exchange concerned Christians who had converted to Islam while among the Ottomans and Muslim converts to Christianity who chose to stay among their new coreligionists. Although converts on both sides often refused repatriation, in the long history of Ottoman-European confrontation, the Ottomans usually prevailed in the competition for war prisoners' hearts and minds. Well after the heady days of Ottoman victories, as late as 1690, Europeans were embarrassed to find that "there might be several complete French Regiments in the Ottoman Army."[77] On the seas, many of the Barbary corsairs who preyed on Christian shipping were Christian converts to Islam, or "renegades," as they are disparagingly styled in European literature.[78] In 1675, some three thousand liberated Slavic slaves preferred to return to their Muslim captors, although when they tried to do so, all were massacred by the infuriated Cossacks who had liberated them.[79] In 1812, when 1,000 Russian soldiers were released from captivity, 116 of their number converted to Islam and stayed behind in Istanbul.[80] As late as the

[75] İstM, 2/183, fols. 42b–43a, and 14/286, fols. 15b–16a; see also Chapter 5 in this volume.

[76] Osmân Agha de Temechvar, *Prisonnier des infidels: Un soldat ottoman dans l'empire des Habsbourg*, ed. Frédéric Hitzel ([Paris], 1998), 138–44. A number of important articles on Muslim and Christian captives appear in *Turcica* 33 (2001), including Eyal Ginio, "Piracy and Redemption in the Aegean Sea during the First Half of the Eighteenth Century" (135–47); Pál Fodor, "Piracy, Ransom Slavery and Trade: French Participation in the Liberation of Ottoman Slaves from Malta during the 1620s" (119–34); and Maurits H. van den Boogert, "Redress for Ottoman Victims of European Privateering: A Case against the Dutch in the Divan-i Hümayun (1708–15)" (91–118). See also Rosita D'Amora, "Some Documents concerning the Manumission of Slaves by the Pio Monte della Misericordia in Naples (1681–1682), *Eurasian Studies* 1, no. 1 (2002): 37–76.

[77] Zilfi, *Politics of Piety*, 154.

[78] Weiss, "Back from Barbary," 335; Friedman, *Spanish Captives in North Africa*, 73. A "renegade legion" made up of former Spanish subjects was part of the Moroccan military; see Fatima Harrak, "Mawlay Isma'il's *Jaysh al-'Abīd*: Reassessment of a Military Experience," in Toru and Philips, *Slave Elites*, 181. See also Tal Shuval, "Households in Ottoman Algeria," *TSAB* 24, no. 1(2000): 45–7, regarding converts holding important positions in Algeria and as beneficiaries of their masters' *vakfs*.

[79] Mikail Kizilov, "The Black Sea and the Slave Trade: The Role of Crimean Maritime Towns in the Trade in Slaves and Captives in the Fifteenth to Eighteenth Centuries," *International Journal of Maritime History* 17, no. 1(2005): 230.

[80] Câbî Ömer, *Câbî Târihi*, 2:872–3.

1830s, a number of Greek women seized in the course of the Greek struggle for independence were refusing repatriation from Egypt, to which they had been taken by the Ottomans' Egyptian vassals.[81]

Males in every century could achieve self-emancipation through valorous conduct on the battlefield. In 1810, a black slave was freed after showing exemplary courage in a volunteer mission behind enemy lines.[82] A kind of categorical emancipation was also a possibility, even before abolition began to take hold in the later nineteenth century. Charles White took note of Sultan Abdülmecid's (1839–61) palace lancers. One squadron, all mounted on gray horses, was "entirely composed of negroes, principally deserters from Mehemet Ali's [slave] army."[83]

Individual manumission, a more everyday event, was set in motion on the initiative of the slave owner. To emancipate one's slave was a much-lauded, pious act encouraged by centuries of Muslim practice and often accompanied by celebration and gift giving. Manumissions were especially common in dying testaments, when thoughts turned to eternal balance sheets. Contrary to Meillassoux's dark generalization, however, countless acts of manumission by Ottoman Muslims, Christians, and Jews occurred in the fullness of owners' lives and for quite able-bodied slaves, where the self-interest of manumitters is far from self-evident.[84] In the formula of a typical manumission declaration (*itâkname*) in 1742, the lady Saliha, resident of Istanbul and daughter (*bint*) of a certain İshak Efendi, "for the love of God Almighty," freed her slave Ruhsar, "an open-browed, dark-eyed female of Georgian origin, who hereinafter shall be as other true free women (*harair-i asliyat gibi*)."[85] Many slaves were registered in the *kadı* courts as *müdebber*. In the absolute arrangement (*tedbir-i mutlak*) that sealed the promise of their manumission, *müdebber* slaves were to be awarded freedom on their master's or mistress's death. It should be said, though, that a fair number of court cases and muftis' *fetva*s regarding this status appear in the literature because of dispute, not agreement.[86] When the promise held, the slave could not be sold – even when an owner had reason to regret the arrangement. A relevant *fetva* in the aftermath of a *müdebber* slave's assault on his owner denied the owner's authority to sell his assailant even

[81] Slade, *Records of Travels*, 1:57–8; Tucker, *Women in Nineteenth-Century Egypt*, 169–70; Lane, *An Account*, 184–5. On the conflict and its victims, see [Y.] Hakan Erdem, "'Do Not Think of the Greeks as Agricultural Labourers': Ottoman Responses to the Greek War of Independence," in Faruk Birtek and Thalia Dragonas, eds., *Citizenship and the Nation-State in Greece and Turkey* (London, 2005), 67–84; Erdem, *Slavery in the Ottoman Empire*, 26, on the enslavement of Greek *zimmi* subjects of the empire.

[82] Câbî Ömer, *Câbî Târihi*, 1:664–5. [83] White, *Three Years*, 1:299.

[84] Claude Meillassoux, *The Anthropology of Slavery* (Chicago, 1991), 120–1.

[85] İstM, 2/178, fol. 1b; cf. İstM 2/183, fol. 16a; 6/404, fol. 10; 14/286, fol. 20b; see also Ahmet Akgündüz, ed., *Şer'iye Sicilleri Mahiyeti, Toplu Kataloğu ve Seçme Hükümler* (Istanbul, 1988–9), 1:225–6.

[86] Erdem, *Slavery in the Ottoman Empire*, 7; *EI2*, s.v. "'Abd."

though the slave had obviously tried to speed up the emancipation process by killing the person who stood in his way.[87]

Along with freedom itself, slave owners often conferred a further Islamic benefaction by providing the newly emancipated with gifts and goods to ease the transition to freedom.[88] A contemporary of Saliha bint Ishak, a certain Hajja Zeyneb, daughter of Abdi Efendi, son of Ebubekr, a woman of wealth and pious reputation (she had made the pilgrimage to Mecca, hence the title *Hajja*), made generous provision for her several freed slaves in the late summer of 1743: "And when, by Almighty God's decree, I die, let my . . . freed slave Emine, an Abaza by origin, be given 50 silver pieces (*guruş*), 3 cushions, 6 bolsters, 2 quilts, a mattress, 4 saucepans with lids, a tray table, a frying pan, 10 copper dishes, a basin and ewer, and a candlestick." Fifty *guruş*es in the mid-eighteenth century was about a year's salary for a low-wage worker, enough to purchase a simple dwelling or even a half share in an able-bodied slave.[89] These emancipation trousseaus in fact could take any number of forms. In Konya, in the seventeenth century, a newly emancipated woman received five sheep to help her make her way in freedom.[90]

Hajja Zeyneb, the benefactress of Emine, bequeathed equally generous emancipation trousseaus to three other female ex-slaves, all Georgians by birth, as well as to her freed male slave Ahmed. The five slaves, all bearing Muslim names, including the patronymic of the converted, son or daughter of Abdullah, had apparently become Muslim, although we do not know how their conversions came about. It is entirely likely that Zeyneb had acquired these slaves, obviously favorites, as children. If the five had entered the empire as parentless minors, they would have been treated as Muslims, as the law regarded orphaned slaves as presumptive Muslims.[91] Although Muslims could not legally be enslaved, Iranian Shiites in the heat of the many Ottoman-Safavid conflicts between the sixteenth and eighteenth centuries sometimes found themselves defined out of Islam and into slavery.[92] The Safavids routinely killed Sunnis rather than take them prisoner, but neither side could take pride in the behavior of its armies; there was plenty of random and revengeful slaughtering along with enslavement on the part of the Ottomans as well.[93] False enslavement was also endemic in Africa, as were debates about who

[87] Çatalcalı Ali, *Şeyhülislam Fetvaları*, 113–14; Düzdağ, *Şeyhülislâm Ebussuud*, 125.

[88] Sak, "Konya'da," 182–3. [89] İstM, 2/184, 12a–13b; cf. Öztürk, *Askeri Kassama*, 198.

[90] Sak, "Konya'da," 183. [91] Düzdağ, *Şeyhülislâm Ebussuûd*, 119.

[92] For various rulings, see Düzdağ, *Şeyhülislâm Ebussuûd*, 109–12; see also Elke Eberhard [Niewöhner], *Osmanische Polemik gegen die Safawiden im 16. Jahrhundert nach arabischen Handschriften* (Freiburg im Breisgau, 1970), 48ff.; Hans Dernschwam, *Hans Dernschwam's Tagebuch einer Reise nach Konstantinopel und Kleinasien (1553/55)*, ed. Franz Babinger (Munich, 1923), 89; Erdem, *Slavery in the Ottoman Empire*, 21–2; and Chapter 5 in this volume.

[93] Erdem, *Slavery in the Ottoman Empire*, 21.

was or was not really Muslim and thus who could legally be deprived of freedom. Simply put, enslavement at the point of capture was a crude and vicious operation.[94]

It should be noted that conversion to Islam by persons already enslaved did not result in automatic emancipation. Slaves were under varying amounts of pressure to convert. Many did so for practical reasons, to please their owners in the hope of emancipation or simply to gain better treatment. Zeyneb's slave Ahmed, who bore the pilgrim's title *el-Hajj*, had perhaps shown a special commitment to his new faith and earned his honorific by accompanying his mistress on her pilgrimage to Mecca. Slaves who chose to convert to Islam no doubt found it difficult to resist the overtures and enticements that many householders would have offered. In a *fetva* of the late seventeenth century, for example, a slave earned his freedom after fulfilling his master's wish that he recite the Qur'an twenty times.[95]

Much of the defense of Middle Eastern slavery goes beyond rationales of "benevolent stewardship"[96] to single out social mobility as the distinguishing feature of household slavery, if not of all Ottoman and Islamic slaveries. Many of the enslaved, the argument goes, would have succumbed to the Hobbesian agonies of Africa and the Eurasian steppe had they not been taken into Ottoman households. Like the assertion of a salubrious relationship between Southern planters and their slaves in the American South, Ottoman defenders saw in domestic slavery benevolent paternalism as well as a route to status and security. Both of the latter were admittedly in short supply in the slaves' native lands. The notion that the reservoir peripheries of Eurasia and Africa were rendered unstable because of the slavery system of the imperial center does not seem to have crossed slaveholders' minds. Yet the empire's appetite for slave labor reinforced, if not created, the decentralization and pauperization that eased the slave raider's task.[97] For apologists in the metropolitan center, the existence of these wretched borderlands rendered slave recruitment all the more defensible. Mehmed Ali Pasha, the autonomous viceroy of Ottoman Egypt, offered this kind of meliorist argument to fend off British abolitionists. "In their own country they live on almost nothing. There is no peace amongst them," he told an abolitionist interlocutor in 1840. Although acknowledging the terrible mortality rates that prevailed among Africans transported north, his defense of slavery as a practice sounded the usual exculpatory note: "'[S]lavery . . . is a very different thing with us to what it is in

[94] See Chapter 5 in this volume. [95] Çatalcalı Ali, *Fetava*, 1:162.

[96] Kolchin, *American Slavery*, 89.

[97] Historians of Africa and the Atlantic trade stress the distortive impact of slaver states on decentralized neighbors; see, e.g., Jack Goody, "Slavery in Time and Space," in James L. Watson, ed., *Asian and African Systems of Slavery* (Berkeley, Calif., 1980), 41; Martin A. Klein, "State of the Field: Slavery," paper presented to the Annual Meeting of the Organization of American Historians, Boston, 2004.

the other countries.'"[98] Self-serving logic in large measure accounts for the propensity – even of those who had witnessed the lethality of capture and transport – to turn a blind eye to enslaving other human beings.

In the eighteenth and nineteenth centuries, the Russian Empire, equipped with its own systems of bondage and murderous expansionism, advanced to the shores of the Black and Caspian seas. Suppliers for the Ottoman slave market were gradually shut out of their traditional hunting grounds. Ottoman demand for white slaves, the preferred and – taking into account the spoils of war and refugee flows – most common form of captive flesh in the northern-tier provinces of the empire, was increasingly met by raids, purchases, and self-enslavements in the northern Caucasus. The largest identifiable group – whether they can be called an ethnic group is debatable – among the slave recruits of these later centuries was that of the Circassians. The term referred specifically to the Adyghe and Abkhaz (in Turkish, *Abaza*) groups. Like the broad reach of the term *Abyssinia* for Ethiopia and the Sudanic lands, however, *Circassian* often applied to northern Caucasus populations generally.[99] Circassians became increasingly more available as their own homelands were wracked by warfare and insecurity, both of which were on the rise with the changing configuration of empires and allies on the Eurasian steppe. Conditions turned even more lethal in the mid-nineteenth century, when Russia's conquest of the region brought with it the sort of forced removals and deportations that, Toledano reminds us, are today called "ethnic cleansing."[100] Most of the displaced – estimated at a half million or more between 1856 and 1865 – found refuge in the Ottoman Empire.[101]

Slaves in society

Of the Circassians who entered the Ottoman Empire as slaves in the eighteenth and nineteenth centuries, many had at best been hereditary serfs – the property of Circassian lords – in their native villages.[102] In the Ottoman environment, these serfs-turned-slaves could increasingly look forward to freedom in as

[98] Report of Dr. R. R. Madden on his visit with Mehmed Ali Pasha in Alexandria, in *Anti-Slavery Reporter*, September 9, 1840, 231–2; cf. the abolitionist Thomas Clarkson, excerpted in Hunwick and Powell, *African Diaspora*, 194.

[99] *İA*, s.v. "Çerkesler," by Halil İnalcık; *EI2*, s.v. "Čerkes," by the same author; also Raoul Motika and Michael Ursinus, eds., *Caucasia between the Ottoman Empire and Iran, 1555–1914* (Wiesbaden, 2000); David Cameron Cuthell, "The Muhacirin Komisyonu: An Agent in the Transformation of Ottoman Anatolia, 1860–1866," Ph.D. diss., Columbia University, 2005; W. E. D. Allen and Paul Muratoff, eds., *Caucasian Battlefields: A History of the Wars on the Turco-Caucasian Border, 1821–1921* (Cambridge, U.K., 1953).

[100] Toledano, *Slavery and Abolition*, 83; Cuthell, "Muhacirin," 39–40, 191–5.

[101] *EI2*, s.v. "Čerkes," by Halil İnalcık; Cuthell, "Muhacirin," 251–2; Toledano, *Ottoman Slave Trade*, 149–51; Toledano, *Slavery and Abolition*, 81–5; Justin McCarthy, *Ottoman Peoples and the End of Empire* (London, 2001), 21.

[102] Toledano, *Ottoman Slave Trade*, 148–84; Toledano, *Slavery and Abolition*, 81–107, 117–34; Erdem, *Slavery in the Ottoman Empire*, 26.

few as seven years and surely before old age. This was especially the case in the nineteenth century, when seven- to ten-year maxima were becoming the custom, a substitute for forthright abolition.[103] Given imperial demand- and supply-side pauperization, Circassian parents and other kin had been notorious for their willingness to sell or otherwise arrange the enslavement of their minor children. The practice was so common in the case of young girls that it is said to have been regarded as not much different from an apprenticeship, in this case, for the Ottoman marriage market. In the 1830s, Julia Pardoe had unusual access and several years' residence in Istanbul. She was one of many visitors surprised by the grassroots integration between the Ottoman slave system – specifically its ruling-class harems – and Circassian society. According to Pardoe, "[A]lmost all the youth of both sexes in Circassia insist upon being conveyed by their parents to Constantinople [Istanbul] where the road to honour and advancement is open to every one."[104]

The road to advancement was hardly open to everyone, but belief in the empire's magic was pervasive. The life chances of young girls in Circassia were at best grim. Girls from impoverished backgrounds – or perhaps one should say the relatives who had charge of young girls – were especially susceptible to the lure of Istanbul. The commoditization of young women and their export to surrounding empires long predated the Ottoman Empire. The Roman Empire, the Italian city-states, the Mamluk sultanate of Egypt – both of the latter for a time competing with the Ottomans – had regularly and successfully traded in slaves from the Caucasus region. However, through Circassian and other Caucasian intermediaries, the Ottomans virtually colonized the north Caucasus for slaving purposes.

Meillassoux portrays the heinous imbalance between enslavement zones and slave-consuming metropoles as "a permanent relation of extortion" whereby "the pillaging and pillaged populations" belong to separate political universes.[105] The dichotomy between victim societies and predatory central states, however, exaggerates the incongruity between the Ottoman Empire and the empire's northern periphery. Although the dichotomy identifies the transnational economics of the relationship between the two, it discounts the social linkages that made the Caucasian trade viable for so long. The major slave providers on site in the Caucasus were indigenous tribal leaders, landlords, and other local opportunists whose wealth and standing were secured by slavery and the slave trade. Their continued success depended on the ability to

[103] By the late nineteenth century, the government's accretional abolitionism effectively converted Circassian slavery into fixed-term bondage (*mükatebe*); see Erdem, *Slavery in the Ottoman Empire*, 9–10, 154–60; Toledano, *Slavery and Abolition*, 95–9; Leyla Saz, *Imperial Harem of the Sultans*, 66, 71.

[104] Julia Pardoe, *The City of the Sultan, and Domestic Manners of the Turks, in 1836*, 2nd ed. (London, 1838), 1:90, 108–9, 112–13; White, *Three Years*, 2:289–91; Toledano, *Slavery and Abolition*, 34, 37–8, 59, and *Ottoman Slave Trade*, 118; Davis, *Ottoman Lady*, 100–1; Erdem, *Slavery in the Ottoman Empire*, 48–51.

[105] Meillassoux, *Anthropology of Slavery*, 75–6.

master the local landscape through the use of enslaved kin, compatriots, and foreigners. It also depended on their reading of the Ottoman market and the lucrative export of some of their captives to imperial brokers. The slave trade with the Ottoman Empire created enduring interdependencies with Circassia, eventually including religious and cultural identification with the powerful Muslim empire to the south. The smoothing out of difference between the societies' dominant classes bolstered the ruling position of elites on both sides of the frontier. *Symbiosis* rather than *dichotomy* better describes relations between the owning classes of center and periphery.

More than one seasoned traveler remarked on an atmosphere of nonchalance and jollity among Circassian girls awaiting purchase in the slave market. Black female slaves were also seen laughing and joking, but the notion of their being "content with their lot" disappears against the many reports of their hardships relative to Circassians and Georgians.[106] Good humor is a useful and usually necessary strategy for underlings of every sort. The job of slaves was to be pleasing or, at the very least, to give the appearance of docility. Slaves in the marketplace hoped to appeal to potential buyers, especially those representing stable and affluent households. Incorporation into almost any household in which paternalism reigned was regarded as preferable to the zoo-like incarceration of the market. And because dealers wanted to make a sale, they surely encouraged their charges to put aside scowls and frowns.

In the northern provinces, sub-Saharan Africans were more deracinated than Black Sea slaves. Separated from their homelands by climate as well as by distance, they also had relatively few well-placed coethnics to call on in the metropolitan environment. North African cities were apt to be more accommodating than Istanbul in that regard.[107] The sources agree that sub-Saharans also suffered from the overall tendency to assign Africans to the more laborious and menial tasks, thus, for example, the clustering of African females in the below-stairs occupations of kitchen and laundry. The vast majority of black male slaves were, like black females, employed as domestics, although many were common laborers. Sub-Saharan male slaves and freemen also served as soldiers and seamen for the empire and the provincial regencies of North Africa.[108] Non-Ottoman Morocco in the eighteenth and nineteenth centuries and semiautonomous Egypt in the nineteenth century adopted

[106] Louis Enault, *Constantinople et la Turquie* (Paris, 1855), 430; White, *Three Years*, 2:289–93; Théophile Gautier, *Constantinople* (New York, 1875), 58; Slade, *Records of Travels*, 2:29, 243; Pardoe, *Beauties of the Bosphorus*, 129; *Anti-Slavery Reporter*, April 2, 1845, 68; Richard Pankhurst, "Ethiopian and Other African Slaves in Greece during the Ottoman Occupation," *Slavery and Abolition* 1, no. 3 (1980): 341–3; Le Gall, "Translation of Louis Frank's Mémoire," 76.

[107] *Anti-Slavery Reporter*, May 1, 1844, 77, whose correspondent in Morocco reported that "all the great dignitaries of this immense empire [are] of the coloured race, some of them of the blackest Guinea dye; the emperor himself being also a fourth or fifth caste."

[108] That is, the semiautonomous provinces of Algiers (Algeria), Tunis (Tunisia), and Tripoli (Libya).

large-scale African slave recruitment for their militaries. However, the more common pattern for African slaves across the Mediterranean throughout the early modern period was as domestic and common labor with a smattering of males in military and military-support roles.

Both male and female African slaves benefited from the general curtailment of slave tenure and later of abolitionism, although responses to the prospect of emancipation varied. Black eunuchs, who presided over the gender-segregated security of the imperial harem and of the palace's upper-class imitators, saw little advantage in emancipation. As eunuchs, theirs was an anomalous existence to begin with. By the mid-nineteenth century, their lives and livelihoods were bound up with a vanishing and increasingly more impugned way of life.[109] And, having been castrated and removed from the Sudan region as young boys, their family connections were probably irretrievable.

Male and female slaves who had grown attached to their owners' families or had simply grown old in their service, had little desire to trade the security of a known middle- or upper-class existence for the sobering uncertainties of self-support.[110] If a suitable husband could not be found for female slaves, they often remained with their master or mistress as free servants, when that was an option. Because former owners remained responsible for their freed slaves, reputable owners endeavored to meet at least the letter of the law regarding their former charges' welfare. The less scrupulous, of which there were no doubt many, tried to sell off or simply manumit slaves who had outlived their usefulness as workers. And in contrast to Hajja Zeyneb and her manumission trousseaus, other owners left it to their fellow Muslims' charity and the public treasury (*beytülmal*) to tend to castoff slaves. In 1817, for example, a former slave, an African woman (*zenciye*) named Mes'ude, won freedom from her female owner, a certain Fatıma Hatun, by directly petitioning the sultan.[111] During the time of her service as an obedient slave in the possession of Fatıma, Mes'ude had become disabled. Seeking relief from her difficult labors, she begged the sultan's mercy. Sultan Mahmud responded with 650 *guruş*es to compensate Fatıma for emancipating her slave. Mes'ude, however, was not satisfied with just emancipation and followed up her petition with a visit to the *shari'ah* court to seek an order requiring Fatıma to give her the two-hundred-*guruş*es difference between the sultan's bequest and Mes'ude's original purchase price. The court found no grounds for the claim.[112] Whether Fatıma showed some generosity in other ways is not a part of the court record.

[109] Erdem, *Slavery in the Ottoman Empire*, 9–10; White, *Three Years*, 2:352–3; de Tott, *Memoirs*, 1, pt. 1:77; Leyla Saz, *Imperial Harem of the Sultans*, 71; Ehud R. Toledano, "The Imperial Eunuchs of Istanbul: From Africa to the Heart of Islam," *MES* 20, no. 3 (1984): 379–90; Toledano, *Slavery and Abolition*, 41–53.

[110] Leyla Saz, *Imperial Harem of the Sultans*, 64; White, *Three Years*, 2:341.

[111] Toledano, *Ottoman Slave Trade*, 64, mentions two later state interventions, both on behalf of African females.

[112] Aykut, *İstanbul Mahkemesi 121 Numaralı*, 130.

In Ottoman-style Old World slavery, as in ancient Greece and Rome, the success stories of a visible minority offered a compelling argument for slavery's redeeming features. Innumerable male and female former slaves in every generation surpassed the freeborn to assimilate to upper-class Ottomanism. The most striking examples of rags-to-riches mobility were the *kapı kulu*s, the sultan's cadres who monopolized the premier military-administrative posts in the classical era, and the women of the imperial harem, the enslaved foreign women who would become consorts and mothers of sultans. As Imber points out, former slaves of an *askeri* owner retained *askeri* status after manumission.[113] Notwithstanding the privileges and advantages of what Toledano calls the "*kul*-harem" elite, they were far outnumbered by the ordinary slaves of lesser households, not to mention the unfortunates assigned to work gangs and galleys.[114]

Ordinary freed male and female slaves continually replenished the urban mix and, not incidentally, helped populate the urban lower orders. In the sixteenth century, when Istanbul was the largest city in Europe and western Asia, slaves and former slaves made up about 20 percent of its population. The combined total of both slave and manumitted in Bursa, a vibrant silk-producing center in western Anatolia, may have been as high as 50 percent. However, Bursa's heavy slave presence declined – along with the city's silk industry – to less than 4 percent by the end of the seventeenth century.[115] A study of the estates of ruling-class (*askeri*) families in Edirne in the seventeenth century reveals that almost half were slave owners. It is possible, then, that Edirne's slave population, like Bursa's, came to be concentrated in the small percentage of city families belonging to the ruling elite.[116] In the nineteenth century, Aleppo was likewise not a heavy consumer of slave labor. In addition to the availability of cheap domestic labor, the difference, according to Meriwether, may have had to do with the paucity of great – officially connected – households in the city.[117] Istanbul, meanwhile, maintained its primacy as employer par excellence of domestic slave labor and as the great melting pot for the manumitted.

Over the centuries, the majority of the captive and emancipated populations of Istanbul and its environs were Europeans and Eurasian steppe dwellers.

113 Imber, *Ottoman Empire*, 246.

114 Toledano, *Slavery and Abolition*, 20–53, for his discussion of the phenomenon.

115 See Sahillioğlu, "Slaves in the Social," 43–112; Haim Gerber, *Economy and Society in an Ottoman City: Bursa, 1600–1700* (Jerusalem, 1988), 11; Suraiya Faroqhi, "Migration into Eighteenth-Century 'Greater Istanbul' as Reflected in the *Kadı* Registers of Eyüp," *Turcica* 30 (1998): 170, notes that the percentage of slaves in an important Istanbul suburb plummeted between the sixteenth and eighteenth centuries; Ronald C. Jennings, *Christians and Muslims in Ottoman Cyprus and the Mediterranean World, 1571–1640* (New York, 1993), 108, sees a similar downward trajectory on Cyprus.

116 İnalcık, "Slave Labor and the Slave Trade," typescript, 1975, 9.

117 Margaret Lee Meriwether, *The Kin Who Count: Family and Society in Ottoman Aleppo, 1770–1840* (Austin, 1999), 99; Tucker, *Women in Nineteenth-Century Egypt*, 167, suggests a similar trend for Cairo.

Vast numbers of them were seized in the military's expeditions of conquest in Europe and western Asia. Between campaigns, slaves were also procured in near-constant commercial raids by allies in the Black Sea region. Through the combination of these enormously productive means, the capital and adjacent provinces were supplied with the bulk of their slave labor, although from the mid-eighteenth century onward, war-captive slaves were a rapidly declining percentage of the whole.

African slaves were a regular part of the urban slave population in the northern provinces from the sixteenth century onward. The Ottoman conquest of Egypt in 1517 and of North Africa east of Morocco in subsequent decades opened up Africa to greater exploitation. More than likely, sub-Saharan Africans did not become a majority of the enslaved populace in Istanbul and the north until sometime in the nineteenth century, and not consistently so until the last quarter of the century. That is, their numbers must be measured against the flows of white captives, especially given the enormous numbers of the latter entering the empire even in the nineteenth century. In any case, various of the Ottoman islands of the Mediterranean and the southern provinces, which is to say Egypt and North Africa, reflected a different chronology and a different pattern of demographic change with respect to the relative proportions of African to European slaves. Ottoman estate registers, with their line-by-line inventories of the property of deceased persons, together with *kadı* court records of adjudicated and notarized cases, give a sense of urban slaveholding by private owners and support the thesis of the "whiter" demography of northern-tier slaveholding.[118] The use of slaves by the state is less clearly drawn. Galley labor, the deadly abyss for captive manpower all over the Mediterranean, swallowed thousands of Ottoman slaves and common prisoners of all races and ethnicities.[119] European representations of sixteenth- and seventeenth-century maritime warfare against the Ottomans suggest that some of the galley slaves who went down with defeated Ottoman ships were black Africans. Because the galleys were also filled with free men consigned there for what the authorities of the day regarded as crimes, the Africans among them could also have been free men.[120]

Like overall slave numbers, estimates of the ratio of European to African slaves in any region of the empire is necessarily speculative. Firmer figures for the eighteenth and nineteenth centuries, the period with which the present

[118] In addition to published and unpublished documents (*kadı* registers, *Mühimme Defterleri*) for the seventeenth and eighteenth centuries, Seng, "Fugitives," 157, notes that sixteenth-century estates for Üsküdar, reflecting the property of individuals from all over Anatolia, show few Africans among the many slaves inventoried; M. Çağatay Uluçay, *Harem II* (Ankara, 1992), 13, commenting on customs receipts for female slaves (*cariye*) in the period 1184–1250/1770–1834, finds mostly Georgians, Circassians, and Abkhazian girls and women.

[119] See İpşirli, "XVI. Asrın İkinci Yarısında Kürek," 203–48; Chapter 6 in this volume.

[120] For example, depictions of sea battles on the walls of the Church of the Knights of San Stefano in Pisa. I thank Professor Silvana Patriarca for providing this reference.

study is concerned, must await a systematic study of Ottoman customs registers and related tabulations along with household data.[121] Even then, black-market trade, illegal capture and kidnapping, the resale market and reexport, and regional variation immeasurably complicate the task. With the apparent attrition in overall slave numbers at least in the northern provinces between the sixteenth and nineteenth centuries – given the regional decline in military households and slave soldiery – Africans weighed more heavily in the demographic balance.[122]

Although scholarship on the nineteenth-century trade points to an African majority among slaves in Istanbul and the empire in the century, there is reason for caution at least for the northern provinces.[123] Wright, for example, calculates that figures for the entire trade to the Mediterranean have been exaggerated inasmuch as they rely on estimates regarding peak years to produce averages for entire centuries, if not millennia.[124] Citing the "hyperactive figures" of the slave trade, he notes wide fluctuations in slave numbers from year to year in both the eighteenth and the nineteenth centuries. He rightly points to demand-side crises in the slave-importing countries as an additional reason for skepticism.[125] A high-tide year of eight thousand souls reaching Ottoman and non-Ottoman North Africa for both settlement and export was exceptional, with three thousand or so per annum the more likely figure. In any case, the demographics of the white trade must also be taken into account. The flood of Circassian slave-migrants into Ottoman Europe, Istanbul, and Anatolia in the 1850s and 1860s produced a European-tilted racial breakdown, at least for those decades. The Circassian moment is another reminder of how slave numbers and categories could spike dramatically from one decade to the

[121] Uluçay, *Harem II*, 13; İnalcık, "Servile Labor," 47n10, 51nn46–7, regarding slave-tax (*pencik*) data and survey registers (*Tapu Defterleri*).

[122] Erdem, *Slavery in the Ottoman Empire*, 55–8.

[123] William John Sersen, "Stereotypes and Attitudes towards Slaves in Arabic Proverbs: A Preliminary View," in Willis, *Slaves and Slavery*, 1:95; Lewis, *Race and Slavery: An Historical Enquiry* (New York/Oxford, 1990), 12; Toledano, *Slavery and Abolition*, 6, 57; Toledano, *Ottoman Slave Trade*, 8.

[124] Wright, *Trans-Saharan Slave Trade*, xiv, 38–40, 52–5, 167–72; for a similar view, see Inikori, "Origin of the Diaspora," 1–19. A historical source from 1802 argues that, in his day, (presumably European) figures regarding the trade in Egypt were "absolutely exaggerated"; see Le Gall, "Translation of Louis Frank's Mémoire," 76. Cf. Ricks, "Slaves and Slave Traders," 279–89, regarding similar vagaries in slave use by Iran, Oman, and other Persian Gulf entities between the eighteenth and the nineteenth centuries. For the height of the trans-Saharan trade between the ninth and the fifteenth or sixteenth centuries, Wright calculates that, at most, five thousand African slaves arrived in North Africa annually but admits that the Mongol invasions, European occupation of Tripoli, plagues, and other calamities have yet to be taken into account. He notes that British sources put the figure for the 1840s and 1850s at eight thousand sub-Saharan Africans per annum as a maximum sum by all routes to the Mediterranean, including slaves retained in all North Africa as well as those exported to Istanbul and the Levant.

[125] Wright, *Trans-Saharan Slave Trade*, 39–40, 53.

next and of how different regions within the vast empire experienced supply and demand according to specific local conditions.[126]

Cairo, resembling Istanbul in size, social complexity, and elite density, was at various times at least its equal in the consumption of ordinary and elite slaves. Like Istanbul, Cairo's slave trafficking and rates of manumission varied over the centuries. Egypt is said to have had at least thirty thousand slaves around 1838, some three-quarters of whom were Africans.[127] Cairo itself accounted for more than half of the total. Like the country as a whole, Cairo's slave population leaned heavily toward black Africans.[128] The city's proximity to the non-Muslim populations of central and southern Sudan made it a bustling entrepôt for the eastern Mediterranean branch of the African trade. After 1750, most of Egypt's African slaves seem to have been supplied by the Darfur sultanate.[129] From markets in Cairo and its environs, black slaves from the Sudan were dispatched to Istanbul, Izmir, Salonica, and Greater Syria. Cairo was also a significant end destination for voluntary African migrants. Presumably most of the arrivals were Muslims. Many were ex-slaves. John Bowring, writing in 1840, claimed that Egypt under Mehmed Ali's regime experienced "an immense influx from Nubia of free blacks," whose numbers at the time he estimated at five thousand in Cairo alone.[130]

Slaves' experience and expectations of freedom can be considered only in the most general terms, except for the relatively few individuals for whom we have personal testimony.[131] Once enfranchised, elite and ordinary slaves had markedly different expectations and experiences of freedom. Both remained in greater or lesser relationships of dependency with respect to their old masters. If the relationship was advantageous as well as amicable, the freed could rely on continuing patronage. Unless there was a break between master or mistress and slave, manumitted elite slaves held on to their *askeri* social rank and

126 See Erdem's discussion of these peak-and-valley episodes and their effect on the slave trade, *Slavery in the Ottoman Empire*, 55–8.

127 Baer, "Slavery and Its Abolition," 167–8, suggests that the real number could be greater if slaves in transit were taken into account. Ennaji, *Serving the Master*, 3–7, noting non-Ottoman Morocco's accelerated consumption of African slave labor in the early nineteenth century, estimates its slave population to be more than 120,000.

128 John Bowring, *Report on Egypt, 1823–1838, under the Reign of Mohamed Ali*, new ed. (London, 1998), 28–9, 222–77; R. S. O'Fahey, "Slavery and Society in Dar Fur," in Willis, *Slaves and Slavery*, 2:83.

129 O'Fahey, "Slavery and Society in Dar Fur," 83; Cengiz Orhonlu, *Osmanlı İmparatorluğu'nun Habeş Eyaleti* (Istanbul, 1974), 100–2.

130 Bowring, *Report on Egypt*, 28.

131 Toledano's aptly titled *As If Silent and Absent* is a notable exception in uncovering individual slaves' stories, especially for the later nineteenth century, for which the sources are more ample. Although accounts by Barbary survivors are often overblown as individual evidence, exaggerated as generalization, and blind to brutalities against minorities, dissidents, and outsiders in the captives' homelands, the horrors of Barbary captivity were real and far too numerous to be discounted; on personal testimony, see Weiss, "Back from Barbary," 47–9, 58; Friedman, "Spanish Captives," 74–5.

privileges, including the tax exemptions that their elite-class (*askeri*) owners enjoyed.[132] In the seventeenth century, the powerful Köprülü family of viziers was renowned for placing its freed slaves and other clients in high imperial office. At least one, Abaza Siyavuş Pasha, became a grand vizier himself and married a Köprülü daughter along the way.[133] Marriages between manumitted slaves and the sons and daughters of more middle-class slave owners were also not uncommon, but their incidence is not known. By far the more usual conjugal tie in slaveholding families was that between female slaves and their masters. When owners determined to marry their own slave women, they were obliged to emancipate them first and provide the marital gift (*mehr*), which was by law a bride's own property and was required by Islamic law's conception of marriage as a contract.[134]

Islamic laws of inheritance helped shore up postmanumission social ties. Former slaves often inherited from their masters, as named beneficiaries or indirectly through appointment to a post in the former owner's charitable endowment (*vakf*).[135] Indeed, slaves are said to have been "the social group most frequently supported by founders of [*waqf*] from the sixteenth to nineteenth centuries."[136] A guarantee of a master's abiding interest in an ex-slave's welfare was provided by the so-called *vela* right (Ar., *wala'*), the *shari'ah* principle by which former slave owners conditionally inherited from their ex-slaves. Former owners became conditional heirs to their freed slaves' property, when and if there was property, in the absence of first-line heirs.[137] The right, which remained valid regardless of the state of affections between the individuals, was confirmed in the deed of manumission. The owner attested to a slave's release by renouncing any and all financial claims on the freed individual apart from rights as heir (*hakk-ı velâdan gayri*). The provision offered owners a chance to recover costs they believed they incurred in the slave's purchase or upkeep.[138] Insofar as the larger community was concerned, the inheritance position of owners, like that of extended-family members, served broad welfare interests. It encouraged manumission and other magnanimous

132 Imber, *Ottoman Empire*, 246.

133 Danişmend, *İzahlı Osmanlı Tarihi*, 3:463; Raşid, *Tarih*, 2:15.

134 Colin Imber, "Women, Marriage, and Property: *Mahr* in the *Behcetü'l-Fetāvā* of Yenişehirli Abdullah," in Zilfi, *Women in the Ottoman Empire*, 81–104.

135 Gabriel Baer, "The Waqf as a Prop for the Social System (Sixteenth-Twentieth Centuries)," *Islamic Law and Society* 4, no. 3(1997): 264–97; Hasan Yüksel, *Osmanlı Sosyal ve Ekonomik Hayatında Vakfların Rolü* (Sivas, 1998), 97; Ron Shaham, "Masters, Their Freed Slaves, and the *Waqf* in Egypt (Eighteenth-Twentieth Centuries)," *JESHO* 43, no. 2 (2000): 162–88.

136 Shaham, "Masters, Their Freed Slaves," 163, with reference to Gabriel Baer.

137 That is, they became residual agnatic heirs; H. A. R. Gibb and J. H. Kramers, eds., *Shorter Encyclopaedia of Islam* (Ithaca, N.Y., 1953), s.v. "Wilāya"; Ulrike Mitter, "Unconditional Manumission of Slaves in Early Islamic Law: A *Hadīth* Analysis," *Der Islam* 78 (2001): 35–72.

138 For estates and claims, see İstM, 2/178, fol. 20a; 2/184, fol. 12a–14a; 14/286, fols. 12a, 20b. Also Sak, "Konya'da," 190–1; see Seng's discussion of masters' rights and slaves' estates ("Fugitives and Factotums," 148–52, 168–9).

gestures, offering hope and incentives to good behavior to those still enslaved. It also reminded owners that they had a material, as well as a moral, stake in their former slave's well-being and social integration.

Although the household of a slave's captivity was the core of a former slave's social being, the network of everyday living was often made up of ethnic, linguistic, and regional comrades. Indeed, most compatriots had traveled a similarly perilous road into the community of free Ottoman subjects. As Kunt has shown for ruling-class households in the seventeenth century, ethnic and racial or blood line (*cins*) ties were the foundation of some of the most powerful patronage networks in the empire.[139] The large numbers of slaves and former slaves in the general urban population and the ethnic and linguistic diversity of the empire even apart from its captive imports, provided the social material for the creation of ethnic communities and subcultures.

Slaves who had arrived in the empire "socially dead," in Patterson's phrasing,[140] did not have to remain so on emancipation. Once free, they could marry whom they wished and settle where their resources permitted. In addition to the incorporative possibilities of marriage and clientelism, freed slaves had reason and opportunity to avail themselves of compatriot connections. That they could do so is evidenced by the ethnic clustering that characterized labor patterns in Middle Eastern cities. For Georgians and Circassians, as well as Russians, Ukrainians, Poles, and Serbs, among others, tapping into compatriot patronage was facilitated by the large representation of those communities in the general population. In the eighteenth and nineteenth centuries, Georgians and Circassians could be found everywhere on the social ladder. Their patronage networks reached into the highest echelons of state, including the imperial palace itself. Mehmed Hüsrev Pasha (d. 1855), who started as a palace-reared slave and ended as admiral of the fleet and grand vizier, brought up and placed into office some forty to fifty slaves, most of them fellow Circassians.[141] The African *kul* Sünbül Molla Ali (d. 1622), who as Rumelia's chief justice achieved the second-highest religious post in the empire, is said to have always helped those who were of his color. Indeed, he himself had benefited from African-Ottoman patronage as a client of the chief black eunuch of the palace, through whose auspices he was entered into the *ulema* ranks.[142]

139 Kunt, "Ethnic-Regional (*Cins*) Solidarity," 233–9; also Rifa'at 'Ali Abou-El-Haj, "The Ottoman Vezir and Pasha Households, 1683–1703: A Preliminary Report," *JAOS* 94 (1974): 438–47.

140 Orlando Patterson, *Slavery and Social Death: A Comparative Study* (Cambridge, Mass., 1982).

141 Ahmed Lûtfi Efendi, *Vak'a-nüvis Ahmed Lûtfî Efendi Tarihi*, ed. M. Münir Aktepe, 9:223; *İA*, s.v. "Hüsrev Paşa, by Halil İnalcık; Carter V. Findley, *Ottoman Civil Officialdom: A Social History* (Princeton, N.J., 1989), 78–9.

142 Katib Çelebi, *Fezleke-i Tarih*, 2:62–3; Atayı, *Zeyl-i Şakaik*, 684–6; Süreyya, *Sicill-i Osmani*, 3:510. Baki Tezcan's "*Dispelling the Darkness*," 73–95, explores "Sünbül" Molla Ali's life and career in the context of racial attitudes in the seventeenth century.

Race, color, ethnicity

Ethnic tensions and rivalries were a recurring reminder of the empire's remarkable heterogeneity and the delicate balancing act of intercommunal concord. Dishonoring remarks and labels were frowned on in social intercourse and were sometimes criminalized. They were nonetheless unavoidable in hard times and in the heat of competition. In the seventeenth and eighteenth centuries, the sneering deprecation of Turks, Kurds, and Gypsies in literary and official parlance was common shorthand for outsiders and rabble. It should be remembered that, until the late nineteenth century, the Ottoman elites did not identify themselves as Turks, which to them had the ring of uncultivated peasants and tribal people.[143] Nonetheless, in the cockeyed typecasting practiced by European observers even into the nineteenth century, *Turk* and *Muslim* tended to be synonymous. Black Africans could not have expected to escape racialist derogation when members of ostensibly dominant ethnicities could not. Nonetheless, race-baiting was not systematic or a matter of policy or law. And in religious terms, if the parties in question were all Muslim, regardless of their origins, such derogation was regarded as unseemly and un-Islamic.

The greater a slave's assimilation to an Ottoman and Islamic identity, the greater were his or her protections and recourse from slurs or blatant discrimination. Slaves who had an imperial connection found that their political access added a layer of insulation from slights as well as the expectation of social deference. The imperial black eunuchs, who were among the richest and most powerful figures in the realm between the sixteenth and nineteenth centuries, were treated with self-abasing courtesy by most of their fellow *askeri*s as well as by the public at large. Indeed, eunuch officers were in a position to demand it. In Medina, the traveler Burckhardt observed, "'When they pass through the Bazar [*sic*] everybody hastens to kiss their hands.'"[144] In a discussion of similar public hand kissing in Cairo, Powell notes that official station and patronage could subvert the distinctions laid out by social hierarchies.[145]

Of course, not everyone proffered their respect so easily. In addition to individuals whose day-to-day encounters led them to pigeonhole black Africans into society's lowly serving classes, there were others whose experience of empowered Ottoman Africans rendered them more racist rather than less. An anonymous Ottoman critic, describing the power of the imperial black

[143] "Mindless Turks" (*Etrak-i bi-idrak*) and "unclean Turks" (*Etrak-i na-pak*) were two favorite slurs among the literati. See Dankoff, *An Ottoman Mentality*, 64; and Câbî Ömer, *Câbî Târihi*, 2:913. Kunt, *Sultan's Servants*, 237–8, posits an east-west fault line in elite politics of the seventeenth century, with Bosnians and Albanians vying against Circassians and Georgians, among others.

[144] Cited in John O. Hunwick, "Black Africans in the Mediterranean World: Introduction to a Neglected Aspect of the African Diaspora," in Elizabeth Savage, ed., *The Human Commodity* (London, 1992), 23.

[145] Powell, *A Different Shade*, 56–8.

eunuchs at the turn of the eighteenth century, denounced the eunuchs in particular and their racial origins in general in venomous, dehumanizing terms. It is difficult to regard the author as representative of elite, much less general, Ottoman thinking, however. The target of his rage was the unrivaled wealth and favor that the eunuchs were accorded by the dynasty and its deputies.[146] Evliya Çelebi, among others of the discursive elite, praised many of the same "lords of the palace," especially those who set a standard of scholarship or put their wealth at the service of the Muslim community.[147] Given the emanation politics of Ottoman autocracy, Africans who served as officers of the realm represented the sultan and were treated accordingly. Still, the anonymous critic's diatribe discloses a depth of racial animus that was far from his alone.[148] It also indicates that the ostentatious power of the eunuchs – which was unchallenged until the mid-eighteenth century – may have been a mixed blessing for ordinary black slaves.

Race, or more precisely, skin color, was an important predictor of work lives and social expectations. A preference for lighter-skinned slaves promoted racialized labor segmentation and stereotypes but did not dictate them. Sub-Saharan males and females usually sold for less than comparable Europeans and Caucasian peoples. Black eunuchs – who were always highly valued and in limited supply – and Ethiopian (*Habeş*) women were regular exceptions.[149] The category of *Ethiopian* was fluid, more a matter of phenotype than specific geography. The classification and pricing of dark-skinned, broad-featured Africans – usually identified as *Zenc* or *Arap* – channeled them into work that was physically demanding and no friend to beauty or long life.

If the commercial terrain of slave dealing was to an important degree color-coded, it was not consistently or ideologically so. In periods prior to the nineteenth century, when European and African slaves were both plentiful, male and female slaves of all hues and physiognomies were undifferentiated objects of herding, ogling, and pawing. Nicolas de Nicolay's encounters with market mores in the mid-sixteenth century leave little doubt that "whiteness" or Europeanness was no defense against indignity and bestialization.[150] Although Dernschwam's ugly memoir is unremittingly hostile to anything Ottoman or Muslim, he notes differences in the experience of captive European males.[151]

146 Yücel Özkaya, "XVIII. Yüzyıl İkinci Yarısına ait Sosyal Yaşantıyı Ortaya Koyan bir Belge," *OTAM*, no. 2 (Ocak 1991): 303–20.

147 Dankoff, *Intimate Life*, 274; White, *Three Years*, 3:348–55.

148 Tezcan, "Dispelling the Darkness," 82–5.

149 Baer, "Slavery and Its Abolition," 168, 172; Toledano, *Ottoman Slave Trade*, 64–7; White, *Three Years*, 2:284–6; Sak, "Konya'da," 162–75; Leyla Saz, *Imperial Harem of the Sultans*, 59–62, 76; Schroeter, "Slave Markets," 194–5; Walz, "Black Slaves in Egypt," 139–41; Abir, "Ethiopian Slave Trade," 123–36.

150 Nicolas de Nicolay, *The Nauigations into Turkie* (1585; repr., Amsterdam, 1968), 62.

151 Dernschwam, *Tagebuch*, 140–2. For Dernschwam, every Muslim woman of any age or station was a "whore." One hopes that his memoir has not found its way into the library of Pope Benedict XVI or others who quote medieval polemic as unblemished truth.

Although some captives were obviously doing quite well in the mid-sixteenth century, he contends that many others of these purported slaves of choice were barely subsisting in the employ of their Balkan and Anatolian owners. Over the long run, black slaves were more consistently at a disadvantage, but their plight was relative. In the context of household labor, their exertions and extended hours would not have differed much from those of free domestics, and their food was probably more to be counted on. Still, there is no real comfort in such generalizations, especially since we have little information about racial differences in slaves'disadvantages outside the household – as castoffs or as elderly or disabled individuals – in the period prior to the 1840s.

That gender, more than race, was foundational to slave employment, however, is suggested by the way that older male and female slaves were classed by age and abilities, with scant regard for race-color grading. Older men – in contrast to children, adolescent beardless youths, and young adult males, categories associated with desirability – were more or less intermingled at the point of sale and employed according to individual physical capacities. White and African women who had been delivered to the Istanbul market (Esir Pazarı) for resale were apparently confined under the same mixed conditions and priced on evidence of special skills and compliant personality.

Charles White, visiting in 1844, identified the hovel-like cubicles on two sides of the market's courtyard as tenanted by "second-hand negresses (Arâb), or white women (beiaz [*beyaz*]) – that is . . . slaves who have been previously purchased and instructed, and are sent to be resold." The third side was "reserved for newly-imported negresses, or black and white women of low price."[152] Among the mixed group of white and nonwhite females whose reselling White witnessed, an African woman was singled out by "good recommendations as a superior cook and [seamstress]," occupations for which African women were often tracked. However, the woman had been resold multiple times "on account of incorrigible temper."[153] Perhaps because good cooks were in short supply and the (much-reduced) price was right, a buyer eventually claimed her. The price of trained and skilled slave women ordinarily rose the second or third time around in consequence of their experience and acculturation. For women who had been taken into a household with sexual purposes in mind, a return to the market was said to depreciate their value, on the assumption that "incorrigibility" had led their owners to part with them.

The life of the galley slave offers further cautions about the limits of racial specialization. Ottoman male criminals – Europeans, Turks, Kurds, and Caucasian peoples, Muslims and non-Muslims – who were sentenced to galley servitude perished along with slave hands, whatever their color, when ships went down. And in neither case was much made of their deaths.

[152] White, *Three Years*, 2:282; cf. Albert Smith, *Customs and Habits of the Turks* (Boston, 1857), 38, for a description of Izmir's main slave market around the same time.

[153] White, *Three Years*, 2:284–5.

Aside from the lower and often lowly position of sub-Saharans in the slave hierarchy, free blacks were less numerous than free whites in the societies of the northern provinces. If broad featured and dark complexioned, they had the added burden of identification with menial or slave status.[154] Unlike the situation in Morocco and other parts of North Africa in the nineteenth century, there is no evidence of systematic mistreatment in the northern provinces, but anecdotal reports, together with the snide allusions that appear in the general literature, are indicative of routine deprecation. Leyla Saz (d.1936), commenting on the discrimination experienced by female house slaves, flatly categorized the situation of all black slaves in late-nineteenth-century Istanbul and its environs as pitiable.[155]

Saz's discussion of black females' personal aptitudes and cultural practices describes the struggles of African slave women to combat slurs and disparagement from white slaves, a situation that Saz found to be commonplace in the large households of her day. The derogation surely carried into the lives of freed Africans in their search for work, places to reside, and marriage partners. A contemporaneous British report paints a sunnier picture of the African experience. However, it focuses not on the domestic hierarchy but on males and military-based socioeconomic integration. The author, the British naval officer Adolphus Slade (d. 1877), writing about the 1830s, noted that freed blacks served alongside freeborn men in the Ottoman navy in "exactly the same position with respect to pay, quarters, rations, and clothing as the Turkish marines." He insists they were treated kindly, having their training not by alien commanders, but by their own black officers, who had already risen in the imperial service. With African mortality rates elsewhere in mind, his report concludes that the black marines were "healthy and appear contented," very few having fallen ill in the northern Mediterranean winter.[156]

Saz and Slade are at cross-purposes in assessing the treatment of Africans. Other commentaries only add to the mixed picture. For the masses of Africans transported into Ottoman space, the outlook was apt to be unforgiving, especially in comparison to Europeans' and Caucasian people's chances. The majority of Africans faced discrimination or worse, although many males found freedom, comradeship, and sometimes eminence. A number of African-origin and African-descended generals (pashas) and other high officers could

[154] The literature on stereotypes and adages regarding Africans for the most part consists of ahistorical compilations. The negative characterizations, however, testify to the endurance of ethnic derogation in literature and lore; see Manfred Ullman, *Der Neger in der Bildersprache der arabischen Dichter* (Wiesbaden, 1998); Sersen, "Stereotypes and Attitudes," 92–105; Hunwick and Powell, "Perceptions of Africans in Some Arabic and Turkish Writings," *African Diaspora*, 33–50; Lewis, *Race and Slavery*. See also John Hunwick, "Islamic Law and Polemics over Race and Slavery in North and West Africa (16th-19th Century)," in Marmon, *Slavery in the Islamic Middle East*, 43–68.

[155] Leyla Saz, *Imperial Harem of the Sultans*, 70–1, 76–9.

[156] Qtd. in Lewis, *Race and Slavery*, 70.

be found in the Ottoman army in the 1830s.[157] In addition to Sünbül Molla Ali in the *ulema*, Arap Ahmed Bey (d. 1571), a commander of the fleet and governor of Rhodes, and Arap Receb Pasha (d. ca. 1689), the commander in chief of the Ottoman army on the Austrian front, reached two of the most coveted positions in the military-administrative career.[158] Like the ethnic labels that were applied to the various white ethnicities, black Africans bore the identifier *Arap*. Although *Arap* was not included as a byname for Molla Ali, Tezcan argues that *Sünbül*, literally "hyacinth," substituted for it as a marker of blackness because it was a common name for black eunuchs in palace service.[159]

Social eminence was in shorter supply for black females than for black males, but most found community, and some arrived at wealth or gained the prestige and security of patronage. African women also seem to have been able to make a virtue out of what to strict Muslim eyes would be regarded as heterodox practice. The skilled use of African spirituality helped to establish some women and men as diviners, herbalists, and keepers of African folkways. In their own communities and in harems in general, female spiritualists were sought out for active performance, fortune-telling, medicaments, and spells. In contrast to North African society, where the presence of sub-Saharan African female divines was more dense and diverse, African women's choreographic seizures and visionary rites in Istanbul and Anatolia have a distinctly commercial flavor. Whether the audiences who sought the women out were repelled or gratified, they paid for the experience.[160]

In comparison to the success of African and Afro-Turkish soldiers in the nineteenth century's Ottoman army, African slaves' prospects in civilian society were more modest but not insignificant. The verdict of native and foreign observers that black domestic slaves were better off than ordinary free servants, however, is a purely materialist judgment. It is less a paean to paternalistic slaveholding than a commentary on the hardscrabble existence of the early modern era's working poor. Whether the slaves themselves would have concurred with the bright assessment of their relative well-being is another question. The inconsistency of the information at our disposal mirrors the slaves' own unpredictable reality.

157 Pardoe, *City of the Sultan*, 2:152–7; Slade, *Reports of Travels*, 1:103–4.

158 Defterdar Sarı Mehmed Paşa, *Zübde-i Vekayiat (Olayların Özü)*, trans. Abdülkadir Özcan (Istanbul, 1977–9), 2:181–2; 3:8; Danişmend, *İzahlı Osmanı Tarihi*, 2:397.

159 Tezcan, "Dispelling the Darkness," 82–5, regarding the name Sünbül and its usage with respect to Molla Ali.

160 John O. Hunwick, "The Religious Practices of Black Slaves in the Mediterranean Islamic World," in Lovejoy, *Slavery on the Frontiers of Islam*, 149–71; "Religion and Community," in Hunwick and Powell, *African Diaspora*, 147–61; Leyla Saz, *Imperial Harem of the Sultans*, 71–6; Faroqhi, "Black Slaves and Freedmen Celebrating," 205–15; Pardoe, *City of the Sultan*, 1:276–8. Toledano's *As If Silent and Absent*, 204–54, is the fullest exploration of the limits and realities of what he calls "Ottoman cultural creolization," particularly regarding African cultural survivals among the freed and enslaved.

Although Africans could not compete for consistent high position against white insider-outsiders like Georgians and Circassians, the black eunuchs of the imperial palace presided over large entourages and dispensed enormous amounts of patronage in the way of official appointments and emoluments. Molla Ali was not the first or last recipient of their largesse, although he was one of the few to find it in the upper reaches of the *ulema*. Some of their largesse reached ordinary fellow Africans, but freed blacks also found the kind of street-level compatriot sponsorship that aided freed white slaves. Freed blacks managed to establish various kinds of communities and organizational structures in Istanbul and other Turkish-speaking regions and more widely in Ottoman North Africa and Arabia.

Travelers to the Arabian Peninsula and Greater Syria in the nineteenth century commented favorably on blacks' social integration. In Mecca, black Africans were said to "compete with the free-born on a footing of perfect equality" and to be "represented among the influential burghers and the owners of houses and business establishments." In central Arabia around Riyadh, emancipated blacks enjoyed a status "not of emancipation only, but of social equality also."[161] Given direct patronage ties to local grandees, many African slaves possessed enviable advantages relative to free inhabitants. Discrimination based on color was not unknown in these regions, but in many respects, black Africans seem not to have been worse off than free Arabs from the less pedigreed tribes. In any case, many free Arab tribesmen of long lineage were phenotypically indistinguishable from black Africans.

Social discrimination was the product of complex and finely drawn calculations not easily condensed to race or color prior to the nineteenth century and the growing entrenchment of European and American racial categories. Despite the numerous optimistic testimonies of African assimilation and acceptance, however, they are not generalizable to the whole empire, much less to non-Ottoman Indian Ocean lands and Morocco. Regional politics and practices made for radically different slave stories, irrespective of the slaves' color or origin. The variability of the sources only adds to the difficulty of recovering those stories. Most firsthand accounts of slaves' experience, apart from the large but tendentious literature on Barbary captivity, derive from

161 The travelers C. Snouck Hurgronje and William Gifford Palgrave, excerpted in Hunwick and Powell, *African Diaspora*, 166–9; see also William Ochsenwald, "Muslim-European Conflict in the Hijaz: The Slave Trade Controversy, 1840–1895," *MES* 16, no. 1 (1980): 114–26; Albertine Jwaideh and J. W. Cox, "Black Slaves of Turkish Arabia during the 19th Century," *Slavery and Abolition* 9, no. 3 (1988): 45–59. For communities elsewhere, see Kal'a et al., *İstanbul'da Sosyal Hayat 1*, 182, and Allan G. B. Fisher and Humphrey J. Fisher, "Slavery amongst the Muslims of Africa," in Winks, *Slavery: A Comparative Perspective*, 108–15. On surviving communities in the northern provinces, see Alexander Lopashich, "A Negro Community in Yugoslavia," *Man* 58 (1958): 169–73; Pankhurst, "Ethiopian and Other African Slaves," 339–44; and in modern Turkey, h-net.msu.edu, H-Turk (archive), May 9–13, 2000.

the later nineteenth century, a period whose politics, economies, and social structures considerably deviated from those of earlier times.

Captors and captives

Historically, most slaves in the Ottoman Empire began as captives of war. The numbers available through victories on the battlefield steadily dropped after the sixteenth century, but even battlefield misadventures yielded slave booty. As late as the eighteenth century, the Ottoman army, with its Crimean Tatar allies, carried off tens of thousands of captives in what were technically campaign losses. The palace official Derviş Abdullah notes in his memoir that a late-seventeenth-century campaign against Austria yielded so many captives – eighty thousand, he says – that a slave could be bought for the price of a cup of coffee. In 1650, so many slaves were seized in a single Walachian campaign that every two Ottoman soldiers were said to have taken possession of fifteen captives. Such gargantuan estimates are probably exaggerations, but the real numbers were likely in the tens of thousands, remarkable for one of the most catastrophic epochs in Ottoman history.[162] For most of the long history of the Ottoman Empire, sustained slave ownership was a prerogative of the very wealthy.[163] The campaigns that had allowed for a broader distribution of captured wealth and manpower in the fifteenth and sixteenth centuries were barely a memory by the eighteenth century. The same could be said of the once-dominant slave-soldier households of the administrative elites.[164] Such households, essentially built around a militarized male core, survived even into the nineteenth century. By then they were few and far between, and their slave manpower was apt to be acquired from commercial dealers or by voluntary enslavement rather than military campaigns. On the Black Sea steppe, the Crimean Tatars were the most famous – or notorious, depending on one's point of view – slave drovers. Even after the Russian seizure of the Crimea in the late eighteenth century, Tatar horsemen continued to mount raids and compete with Circassian and Abkhaz hunters in the Caucasus.

For elite and ordinary slaves and ex-slaves, from the moment of the conquest of Constantinople in 1453 until the end of the empire, Istanbul was the heart of the Ottoman slave system, most particularly of its white slave system. Slaves

[162] Osman Çetin, *Sicillere göre Bursa'da İhtida Hareketleri ve Sosyal Sonuçları, 1472–1909* (Ankara, 1994), 50; Cengiz Orhonlu, "Derviş Abdullah'ın Darussaade Ağaları hakkında bir Eseri: Risale-i Teberdariye fi Ahval-i Daru's-Saade," in Türk Tarih Kurumu, *İsmail Hakkı Uzunçarşılı'ya Armağan* (Ankara, 1976), 243; Erdem, *Slavery in the Ottoman Empire*, 30; but see İnalcık, "Servile Labor," 51, on battle statistics.

[163] İnalcık, "Servile Labor," 26–7; Sak, "Konya'da," 175.

[164] There were exceptions, even up to the nineteenth century, but they were far from the norm; see *İA*, s.v.v. "Gulam" "Hüsrev Paşa," and *EI2*, s.v. "Ghulām, Ottoman Empire," all by Halil İnalcık.

who crossed the free-unfree divide were conspicuous in the upper classes of the eighteenth and nineteenth centuries, as they had been in the sixteenth and seventeenth. Scores of viziers and commanders in the eighteenth and nineteenth centuries, from the pashas Gürcü İsmail, Küçük Hüseyn, Ahmed Hürşid, and Mehmed Hüsrev to Halil Rifat, İbrahim Edhem, and Tunuslu Hayreddin, had begun as slaves. Far from disguising their origins, many reveled in them, proud of the obstacles they had overcome and eager to associate themselves with the glory days of the empire and its slave soldiery.[165] This kind of spectacular ascent and the seemingly painless absorption of ex-slaves into the general population made the boundary between freed and freeborn seem invisible or irrelevant to many commentators. Ottoman statesmen and literati who argued their country's case in the nineteenth century could cite similar examples among acquaintances. They could look at their own origins and marriage partners as well as the bloodlines of the dynasty to affirm their view of slavery as a source of family and distinction.

The presence of compatriots in slave society, a seeming lifeline for the enslaved, had a darker aspect than that of comradely patronage and mutual aid. It is a commonplace that men and women of the same ethnicity, one's own people by contemporaneous measures, were deeply implicated in slave procurement. Often raiders, drovers, and dealers were little more than internal brigands, physically or ethnically indistinguishable from those whose freedom they stole for profit and position. A further irony was the ease with which former slaves shifted from captive to captor after their own freedom was secured. The most prodigious slaveholders, apart from the royal family, were members of the vizierial elite, the upper echelons of military-administrative officialdom. Because so many grand viziers and ordinary viziers had risen from the *kapı kulu* or *gulam* ranks, ex-slaves were arguably the empire's greatest slavers. Lütfi Pasha (d. 1563), an Albanian product of the boys' levy; Rüstem Pasha (d. 1561), a Croatian *kul*; and Sokollu Mehmed Pasha (d. 1579), a *kul* of Serbian origin, were exemplars of the outsized, sixteenth-century type. Each ruled a household of a thousand slaves or more. Lesser viziers of the time are said to have held between five hundred and six hundred.[166] Even under the more straitened conditions of the seventeenth century, vizierial appointees strove to meet the patriarchal expectations of their rank. Grand viziers like Melek Ahmed Pasha (d. 1662), an Abkhaz, and the freeborn Turkish Merzifonlu Kara Mustafa Pasha (d. 1683) – the latter, as the sultan's deputed servitor, was functionally a *kul* or *gulam* – counted hundreds of male and female slaves among their possessions. The ex-slave Mehmed Hüsrev Pasha (d. 1855) may have owned fewer slaves than his predecessors, but they sufficed to

[165] DeKay, *Sketches of Turkey*, 321; Slade, *Records of Travels*, 1:478–80; Yücel, *Kitâb-i Müstetâb*.

[166] Imber, *Ottoman Empire*, 168; *EI2*, s.v. "Ghulām, Ottoman Empire," by Halil İnalcık, 1090.

make him, in İnalcık's words, "[t]he last great representative of the *ghulām* system."[167]

Particularly insidious was the role of ex-slave compatriots in the mechanics of enslavement. Their own firsthand experience made them especially valuable in priming their coethnics for the path they themselves had traveled. The documentary remains of the trade do not allow for a detailed picture of those whose vocation was slavery. However, surviving records suggest the deep involvement of former slaves, whether or not compatriots, in perpetuating Ottoman slave culture. Former slaves identified vulnerable targets. Many were the small-time and big-time brokers and traders without whom there would have been no slave labor for urban customers. Probably the most notorious former slaves turned slavers were the Barbary pirates and their onshore confederates. Operating as near-autonomous Ottoman vassals from their strongholds at Tunis, Tripoli, and Algiers, many corsairs in every century commenced adult life as Ottoman captives. After converting to Islam, they devoted themselves to the profitable seizure of former compatriots and coreligionists.[168]

An Ottoman price register from the seventeenth century suggests that, in the main Istanbul market, six of seventeen slave brokers (*esirci dellalları*) had probably once been slaves.[169] In court cases involving false enslavement and similar disputes, apparent ex-slaves (bearing the usually telltale patronymics *ibn Abdullah* [son of Abdullah] or *bint Abdullah* [daughter of Abdullah][170]) make a regular, unsavory appearance as dealers (*esirci*) and defendants.[171]

The actual traffic in slaves touched an even greater number of lives than the notion of slavery as trade suggests. For one thing, the final stages of slaves' presale journeys unfolded in plain sight of the Ottoman public. Whether embarking or debarking at some port, enslaved men, women, and children were on exhibit until their incorporation into a household or labor system. Many reached their market destinations on foot. Busbecq, in the late sixteenth century, speaks of "wagon-loads of boys and girls," and young and old men "driven along in herds or . . . tied together with chains" on the road between the Hungarian front and Istanbul.[172] Once in Istanbul, captives were paraded through the streets, proving the army's prowess and justifying the sacrifices of war. Captives often changed hands several times between the point of capture and urban markets. Their arrival in a household was seldom a final

167 *EI2*, s.v. "Ghulām, Ottoman Empire," by Halil İnalcık, 1091; Findley, *Ottoman Civil Officialdom*, 77–80; von Hammer, *Geschichte*, 6:427.

168 Friedman, "Spanish Captives," 61, 73; Weiss, "Back from Barbary," 335ff.

169 Mübahat Kütükoğlu, *Osmanlılarda Narh Müessesesi ve 1640 Tarihli Narh Defteri* (Istanbul, 1983), 257; see also Özdeğer, *1463–1640 Yılları*, 40.

170 That is, son or daughter of Abdullah, with *Abdullah* being the Islamic patronymic substituting for the captive's original surname.

171 See Chapter 5 in this volume.

172 Busbecq, *Turkish Letters*, 44; cf. Imber, *Ottoman Empire*, 132.

destination but the first of several sales and resales. Even the most prized and cosseted captives were initially taken to entry-level households, often the homes of the dealers themselves, to be trained and embellished for more profitable sale.

As property, slaves were calculated into the estates of deceased owners and distributed to heirs. Given the partible character of Islamic inheritance, each of several heirs might inherit a fraction of a slave. Selling, recommoditizing the inherited slave, was often a necessity. The deceased's possibly beloved slave was thereby turned into ready cash. As intermediaries between the privileged members of the household and the business of the street, male and female domestic slaves were in any case a quotidian presence in the urban environment. Their clothing was not always distinguishable from the garb of free folk. Except in the very richest households in which girls were groomed as daughters, most slaves could be recognized by their serving roles and extreme tractability in the presence of their owners. Although the mass of subjects of the empire were not slave owners, they cannot have been unaware of the human merchandise and merchandising in their midst.

Slave ownership was concentrated within the Muslim population, and within its uppermost strata in particular. About 80 percent of owners were male, and males, in line with their greater wealth, overwhelmingly predominated among owners of multiple slaves.[173] Often and for prolonged periods, both native and nonnative Christians and Jews were forbidden to own slaves. Jennings, for example, found no evidence of Christian or Jewish owners on Cyprus in the late sixteenth century and first decades of the seventeenth century.[174] The rules, however, were apparently made to be broken. Christian and Jewish slaveholders could be found in virtually every century and locale, though never commensurately with Muslim ownership.[175] Sometimes Christians and Jews owned slaves publicly and even with some pomp. At other times, they maintained possession inconspicuously, though often in the knowledge of

[173] Öztürk, *Askeri Kassama*, 202. [174] Jennings, *Christians and Muslims in Ottoman Cyprus*.

[175] İstM 2/178, fol. 25a; Necati Aktaş, Nezihi Aykut, Mücteba İlgürel, Mehmet İpşirli et al., eds., *Dîn-i Hümâyûn Sicilleri Dizisi I: 3 Numaralı Mühimme Defteri (966–967/1558–1560)* (Ankara, 1993), 1:235, 296–7, 309, 335, 400; Ahmet Kal'a et al., eds., *İstanbul Külliyâtı, İstanbul Ahkâm Defterleri: İstanbul Ticaret Tarihi-1 (1742–1779)* (Istanbul, 1997), 18; Kal'a et al., *İstanbul'da Sosyal Hayat 1*, 42, 56; İnalcık, "Servile Labor," 43; Sahillioğlu, "Slaves in the Social," 83–6; Sak, "Konya'da," 161, 182; Abdullah Saydam, "Esir Pazarlarında Yasak Ticaret: Hür İnsanların Satılması," in Çiçek and Saydam, *Kıbrıs'tan Kafkasya'ya*, 117–20; Schroeter, "Slave Markets," 203–4; Lane, *An Account*, 104; Baer, "Slavery and Its Abolition," 167; Erdem, *Slavery in the Ottoman Empire*, 28–9; Faroqhi, *Men of Modest Substance*, 30; Friedman, "Spanish Captives," 59; *DBİA*, s.v. "Esir Ticareti," by Necdet Sakaoğlu, 201–2; Seng, "A Liminal State," 28–9; Seng, "Fugitives and Factotums," 136–69; Robert Mantran, *Histoire d'Istanbul* (Paris, 1996), 261; Kütükoğlu, *Osmanlılarda Narh*, 84; Marc David Baer, "Islamic Conversion Narratives of Women: Social Change and Gendered Religious Hierarchy in Early Modern Istanbul," *Gender and History* 16, no. 2 (2004): 425–58. See also S. D. Goitein, "Slaves and Slavegirls in the Cairo Geniza," *Arabica* 9 (1962): 5–7, for Egypt and Muslim Spain in the medieval period.

neighbors and probably of local authorities as well.[176] Muslim silent partners were known to front for non-Muslim colleagues in the Barbary trade when restrictions were in place. The repetition of prohibitions between the sixteenth and nineteenth centuries underscores the absence of a single, empire-wide position on the issue. Indeed, slaveholding protocols differed from region to region as well as over time.[177]

The softness of the slaveholding ban is evidenced not only by the persistence of Christian and Jewish ownership but also by the authoritative voice of juristic opinion. *Fetva*s from the end of the seventeenth century confirm both the fact and, in various circumstances, the permissibility of non-Muslim ownership at that time. Şeyhülislam Çatalcalı Ali, queried on whether Ottoman Jewish and Christian owners could be compelled to sell to Muslims Christian slaves whom they had purchased, responded in the negative. If there had been a general prohibition, compulsory sale should have been in order. The jurist did, however, reiterate the often cited bottom-line boundary of Islamic legal opinion. That is, non-Muslims were not allowed to purchase slaves who were already Muslim, and if any slaves in their possession opted to convert to Islam, they would have to be sold to other Muslims.[178] Yet as Ben-Naeh has found in the case of Jewish owners, that rule, too, was sometimes bypassed.[179]

The conditions placed on non-Muslim ownership stemmed from the principle of Muslim primacy and the view that a believer's bondage to a nonbeliever created an untenable inversion of the religious order. Slave ownership, like luxury attire, was supposed to identify the main players in society's story, but it sometimes failed to do so. In Egypt in the nineteenth century, Jews and Christians are said to have been quite free to trade in Muslim slaves.[180] The inconsistency of the ban was a function of its essentially political (*kanun*) as opposed to religious (*shari'ah*) foundation in law. Prohibitions and their assiduous implementation came and went as wars and other pressures fed into the policies of individual sultans and ministers. In the main, restrictions responded to shifts in supply and prices. The combination of the two generally prevented 90 percent of Muslims from emulating their wealthier coreligionists and the wealthy but less numerous non-Muslim owners. As in the case of clothing, state efforts to prevent Christians and Jews from obtaining slaves were neither consistent nor successful. As slaves became established as a high-priced item of trade, the regime, backed by Muslim public opinion, sought to make slave ownership a symbol of high status and so a Muslim preserve. The religious tincture of ownership legislation, as with clothing laws, recast economic and class differences in confessional terms. Although many Ottomans wholeheartedly believed in the religious rectitude of non-Muslim

[176] Yaron Ben-Naeh, "Blond, Tall, with Honey-Colored Eyes: Jewish Ownership of Slaves in the Ottoman Empire," *Jewish History* 20 (2006): 315–32, brings new evidence to bear on these points.

[177] Faroqhi, "Quis Custodiet," 253–4, 262; Uluçay, *Harem II*, 13.

[178] Çatalcalı Ali, *Şeyhülislam Fetvaları*, 145.

[179] Ben-Naeh, "Blond, Tall," 323.

[180] Baer, "Slavery and Its Abolition," 167.

discomfort, policy makers saw in the prohibition a prescription to relieve economic tensions and shore up Muslim unity.

The supply and price of slaves varied widely and unpredictably over the hundreds of years of Ottoman slave consumption, and even between the opening of the eighteenth century and the mid-nineteenth century. The enslavement reservoirs of Eurasia and Africa provided a fairly constant stream of captives to meet upper-class demand. The democratization of slave ownership mostly depended on the Ottoman military. Military campaigns often produced a flood of new slaves for the market. With lower prices, slaveholding drifted down to the more middle classes.[181] The costs of upkeep, however, stood in the way of sustained lower-middle-class ownership. Unless slaves were hired out for a wage or engaged in production of some kind, marginal owners were hard pressed to justify a nonproducing addition to the household. In wealthy establishments of numerous slaves, the division of labor created a hierarchy of ranks and tasks wherein some slaves did not have to labor at all. While unprivileged slaves toiled, the favored male and female ranks ministered to their masters and mistresses, their very superfluity affirming their owners' status.

The wealthiest classes were not all of a piece, however. The lavish redundancy projected by the hundreds of male and female slaves of the palace was the emulative model for the military-administrative cadres. Some members of the religious elites, both *medrese*-trained jurists (*ulema*), and sheikhs of the Sufi mystic orders (*tarikat*) also had large households with numerous slaves. For the most part, however, *ulema* and bureaucratic officers could afford to put less emphasis on slave-denoted pomp because of their access to ready-made entourages of students, apprentices, out-of-office (*mazul*) clients, and other free dependents. In other words, established *ulema* were as likely as their military peers to have slaves, but they had less need for large slave contingents that marked the public display of men of the sword. To the extent that inheritance registers (*tereke defterleri*) and other sources allow for an Ottoman collective portrait, the vast majority of households did not possess slaves. Of those that did, the great majority had only one. Duben and Behar speculate that, in the nineteenth century at least, the possession of just a single slave may have been enough for a claim to gentility.[182]

Shades of resistance

Most historians take the view that resistance in the form of violent or nonviolent struggle characterized even the most lopsided relationships of power.

[181] Suraiya Faroqhi, *Towns and Townsmen of Ottoman Anatolia: Trade, Crafts and Food Production in an Urban Setting* (Cambridge, U.K., 1984), 278. In nineteenth-century Egypt, middle-class ownership was more widespread; see Baer, "Slavery and Its Abolition," 163, 167; Lane, *An Account*, 183; see also Philippe Fargues, "Family and Household in Mid-Nineteenth-Century Cairo," in Doumani, *Family History in the Middle East*, 23–50.

[182] Duben and Behar, *Households*, 50; Özdeğer, *1463–1640 Yılları*, 128–32; Öztürk, *Askeri Kassama*, 201.

There is far less consensus regarding the component parts of resistance and the extent to which its theorization can illuminate changes and adaptations in institutionalized practices like slavery.[183] Clearly, sabotage qualifies as resistance, as does open rebellion, particularly if collectively executed. Less clear is the weight to be accorded to behaviors like feigned incapacity, theft, or strategic illness, even if the sources and methodology for uncovering such actions were at hand, which they are not. More contentious still is the distinction between resistance and accommodation. Does a slave woman's flirtation to attract the sexual interest of her master count as resistance to her initial enslaved position? Or is it an accommodation, a step up but with a substantial price attached to it? The slave is able to improve her circumstances, but only by adding to her owner's investment – providing him with offspring – and by continuing to participate in her own exploitation.

Seduction can be both accommodation and resistance, if we can be sure that the initiative or the design lay with the woman herself. The structure of larger households lent themselves to this sort of opportunity. The many slave women of large elite households, some of whom were the property of other women, vied for male favor. In so doing, they sought to gain access to the prioritized ranks and rewards that males of the household were able to dispense. In the most typical slaveholding pattern, a household possessed only one slave, a female, and her owner was male.[184] The male owner's purchase of a slave for himself – for whatever purpose – was arguably already a first step toward acquiring a sexual partner. If a sexual liaison came to pass, the initiative would seem to have been the owner's. In any case, if resistance requires that actions be disadvantageous to the owner or to the system, female seductiveness was neither. As a strategy for survival, it fortified too many of slavery's rules and premises to be resistant.

Collective rebellion among Ottoman slaves was almost unheard of in the history of the empire. One of the famous rebel *kul*s of the early centuries who staged a rebellion after fleeing palace service, or one of the many Sudanese mutineers who turned on their Turco-Egyptian overseers in the late nineteenth century, may yet prove to have been an Ottoman Spartacus or Toussaint-Louverture. The goals and the precise character of the various recorded events, however, require more investigation relative to slaves and slavery. If we broaden our scope to society as a whole, perhaps the fractiousness, king making, and affiliation with unorthodox Bektashism of the slave-dominated Janissary corps in the sixteenth through seventeenth century can be read as slave resistance rather than economic conflict or elite dissension. Except in frontier zones, including the Ottoman coastline, or in labor operations for

183 For discussions of resistance and cultural survivals, see the articles in Ann J. Lane, ed., *The Debate over Slavery: Stanley Elkins and His Critics* (Urbana, Ill., 1971).

184 Özdeğer, *1463–1640 Yılları*, 126–33; Öztürk, *Askeri Kassama*, 201.

which large groups of captives were assembled, the pattern of Ottoman slaveholding discouraged collective action. In the northern-tier provinces in the eighteenth and nineteenth centuries, most slaves were dispersed as single individuals across scattered households. Collective mobilization was practically out of the question.

Not surprisingly, the most common forms of active resistance were fugitivism and legal and extra-legal appeals against mistreatment. Wherever slavery was practiced, slaves were "a troublesome property."[185] One of their most troublesome features was a tendency to flee. The incidence and costs of fugitivism are not possible to recover at this stage, although the fugitive slave (*kaçkın*, *abık*) seems to have been a common phenomenon. Special hunters (*yavacıs*, or "collectors of strays") were set the task of restoring runaways to their owners. Not surprisingly, males were the typical fugitives, though as a matter of circumstance rather than "nature."[186] Men had greater opportunity than women to secure the multiplicity of confederates and resources necessary to see them safely home. Unless male slaves were chained to galleys, they were permitted wider social and spatial range. Insofar as domestic slaves were concerned, their very maleness meant that they were less closely surveilled than women in any case. Indeed, the job of some male slaves, eunuchs and otherwise, was to make sure the free and slave women of the household did not stray. In any case, as every slaveholding society knew very well, for female slaves, the decision to flee could mean abandoning their children. Societies that trafficked in women could count on motherhood to quash much overt female resistance.

Prior to talk of abolition and universal freedoms in the later nineteenth century, taking flight from a master was a response to mistreatment of oneself rather than a universalized protest against slavery. Newly captured slaves detained together and in proximity to coethnics had the brightest prospects for escape. In a sixteenth-century case from Mostar near Dubrovnik, two female slaves absconded with a male slave to find refuge just across the Ottoman border. Another group, all converts to Islam, made their way by boat to a Venetian-held island, where they resumed their Christian identities.[187] One of the most dramatic escapes was executed to humiliating effect in the late eighteenth century, when European galley slaves overcame a skeleton crew on the flagship of the Ottoman fleet and sailed it safely to Malta.[188] Fugitive traffic could also reverse itself. Europeans were often shocked by the sight of

185 Kenneth M. Stampp, *The Peculiar Institution* (New York, 1956), 86–140.

186 Öztürk, *Askeri Kassama*, 200; Sak, "Konya'da," 193–5; see also Erdem, *Slavery in the Ottoman Empire*, 160–9, on late Ottoman fugitivism.

187 Aktaş et al., *3 Numaralı Mühimme*, 374, 721.

188 Von Hammer, *Geschichte*, 8:237; Danişmend, *İzahlı Osmanlı Tarihi*, 5:215–16; cf. Ahmed Vasıf, *Tarih-i Vasıf* (Istanbul, 1219/1804), 1:207. For a similar escape from Tripoli in the seventeenth century, see Friedman, *Spanish Captives in North Africa*, 65.

fellow Europeans, escapees from Ottoman slavery, making their way back to Ottoman territory to seek out their former keepers.[189]

Appeals within the system against mistreatment are relatively well documented, if one counts paternity suits and other claims arising from female slaves' pregnancy and motherhood. The overlapping authorities of state and master created a competitive space in which slaves might speak and act to recall owners to their supposed ethical code. The state's right to intervene in the event of dire misuse was a more distant reminder of their obligations. A slave's best hope for negotiating this confrontation lay in familiarity with the ethical code, if not with the law itself.

Slaves came into contact with other slaves as well as with dealers, customers, and market officials in the weeks or months before their eventual placement. Once they were in a household, unless they were kept isolated, which was rare, they interacted with other slaves, household members, and neighbors. The Cairo police report discovered by Toledano reveals how an abused Circassian slave girl was able to speak through neighborhood and female networks to gain a modicum of relief.[190] It reveals, too, the politics in play in the exposure of a well-placed transgressor. The girl, called Şemsigül (meaning "sunflower"), suffered for months at the hands of the slave dealer who had impregnated her and, contrary to *ümm-i veled* prescriptions, sold her. Her agonies were compounded by the neglect or complicity of neighbors and guildsmen who could have interceded more decisively. Although she was finally able to tell her story, it was only after terrible abuse. The conflicting interests of the neighborhood and the slave dealers' guild and the inherent biases of the legal system had severely compromised the apparatus of protections.

Slaves' success in garnering favor and improving their life's chances rested in part on the ability to repress memory. Most of the enslaved had surely witnessed the killing or other abuse of relatives and friends in the days of their own capture. Slaves' voices, however, are not often heard in the historical sources. When they are, they tend to be filtered through the formulaic prose of the courtroom. Even then, relatively few cases involving slaves ever found their way to adjudication. Among elite slaves who attained power or position, enslavement's darkest days could be submerged under postemancipation braggadocio, as when Mehmed Hüsrev Pasha turned his own purchase price into a point of honor.[191] For most slaves and former slaves, though, traumatic memories were held in check by society's elaborate rules of engagement. Chief among those were the twin promises of benevolent paternalism and speedy manumission.

189 İnalcık, "Servile Labor," 81, referencing Corneille LeBruyn in the early eighteenth century.
190 Toledano, *Slavery and Abolition*, 54–80; Toledano, "Shemsigul: A Circassian Slave," 59–74.
191 Slade, *Records of Travels*, 1:479.

An etiquette of silence also shielded the system and its victims from recollections of inhumanity. Something of what was at stake in slaves' ability to survive in their new surroundings emerges from an anecdote about male conversation and campaign camaraderie. In the early nineteenth century, the Tatar prince Halim Giray (d. 1823) was living in the town of Çatalca, not far from Istanbul. One evening, a guest regaled the company with the story of a successful Tatar raid in 1769–70 that had burned down a Russian fortress and carried away fifteen thousand prisoners. In the audience was an Ottoman *kadı*, an honored member of the corps of Ottoman judges assigned to duties in the Balkan provinces: "To everyone's amazement, the man, showing 'great embarrassment and confusion,' revealed that he had been one of the captives . . . taken in that raid."[192]

We are not in a position to gauge the lethality of the slave business, much less the extent of the psychological injury sustained by slavery's survivors. Regardless of the resiliency shown by freed slaves in their alien social worlds, the durability of slavery's traumas cannot be discounted. The African child who became the slave maid of the Turkish feminist Halide Edib (d.1964) when Halide was a young girl was a trembling, terrified birthday present from Halide's father. The child, called Reşe, gradually overcame her terror but only after weeks of weeping. She took comfort in singing songs from her homeland until she was no longer able to recall her native tongue.[193] The trauma of enslavement – Reşe had been kidnapped while playing – cannot have been eradicated by comfortable surroundings and a kindly mistress. And, we have only her mistress's word regarding the sisterly relationship between the two; there is no mention in Halide's memoirs of any chastisements inflicted or the involuntary hours that Reşe might have spent attending to the family's whims. In any case, the homey environment Halide describes was hardly every slave's, or even most slaves', lot, permanent or temporary.

Although Ottoman slavery was scarcely comparable in intent or practice to slaveries in North and South America and the Caribbean, it shares with them slavery's most disturbing essentials – the same violent foundations and an ongoing relational distortion built on an imbalance of power. The compliance of all slaves, whether concubines or chattel laborers, proceeded from coercion.[194] Coercion was a muted undercurrent in genteel households and an unambiguous physicality in the less scrupulous, but it was omnipresent regardless of owners' class or station. The mildest masters and mistresses could rely on the actions of their crueler peers to sustain the elements of fear

192 Barbara Kellner-Heinkele, "A Chinggisid and Ottoman: Halim Gerey Sultan," *Altaica* 5 (2001): 71.

193 Halide Edib [Adıvar], *Mor Salkımlı Ev* (Istanbul, 1963), 124. Reşe married and remained in contact with her former mistress.

194 Watson, *Asian and African Systems*, 8.

and insecurity and to make visible the hierarchy that the system's paternalistic face tended to obscure.

If the Ottoman slave story is, in fact, many stories, of different regions, different times, and different social stations, it remains incomplete in whole and in its parts without reference not only to the particular experience of women as slaves but also to the relationship of femaleness to slaveholders and their society.

CHAPTER 5

Meaning and practice

Say a prayer [*al-Fatiha*] for the soul of Zekiye Hanım – upon her God's mercy and forgiveness and heaven's repose – one of the female slaves [*cariye*] of the honorable lady Küçük Kadın Efendi, esteemed consort-wife of the former Şeyhülislam, the late Mekki Efendizade Mustafa Asım Efendi. May 8, 1849.

– Gravestone, Süleymaniye Mosque, Istanbul

They give their slave girls over to their wives' orders, and the dear little wives make them work all day and night, sticking them with a needle when they doze off. These dear wives, who were once household slaves [*halayık*] themselves, call their slave girls [*cariye*] "slut" and "whore."

– *Risale-i Garibe* (ca. 1700)[1]

Slaves and family

The grave of Zekiye Hanım, a female slave of the Mekkizade family, lies in the burial ground of the Süleymaniye, the great mosque and *medrese* complex erected by Süleyman the Magnificent in the mid-sixteenth century. The grave is a template for the meaning and memory of slavery among Ottomans of the elite slaveholding orders.[2] The Mekkizades, with whom Zekiye lived her life in captivity, were an Ottoman first family by reason of wealth, high office, and longevity in both. Mekkizade Mustafa Asım (d. 1846) was the son of a two-time *şeyhülislam*. He himself lived up to the family tradition by heading the religious hierarchy as *şeyhülislam* three times for a total of seventeen years during the modernizing reigns of Mahmud II and Abdülmecid I. A man with strong Nakşbendi connections and sentiments, Mekkizade very likely was the

[1] Hayati Develi, ed., *XVIII. Yüzyıl İstanbul Hayatına dair Risâle-i Garîbe* (Istanbul, 1998), 43.

[2] Mustafa Asım, the son of Mekki Mehmed (d. 1797), served his three terms between 1818 and his death in 1846. Mekkizade's third tenure under Mahmud was allowed to continue under Abdülmecid. On the Mekkizades and the *ulema* aristocracy, see Zilfi, "Elite Circulation," 318–64.

Fig. 14. "Mosque and Tomb of Süleyman [the Magnificent, 1520–66]." Viewed from what is now Istanbul University. Pardoe, *Beauties of the Bosphorus*.

author or inspiration behind Mahmud II's *shari'ah*-infused clothing diatribe of 1818.[3]

The stele inscribed in Zekiye's memory stands among others of varying sizes and ornamentation in commemoration of Ottoman notables and their dependents. It is steps away from the resting place of Süleyman himself, who is buried in a tomb next to that of his wife, previously his slave concubine, Hurrem, or Roxelana as she is also known.[4] At the time of Zekiye's death in 1849 (1265 A.H.), Süleymaniye's gardens had become one of the most prestigious burial spaces in the capital, if not in the empire as a whole.[5]

3 Ergin, *Mecelle*, 1:896–98; see also Chapter 3 in this volume. Mekkizade became *şeyhülislam* for the first time in January 1818 and served until September 1819. Mahmud's ordinance was promulgated in late May 1818. Any one or combination of officials, from the *bostancıbaşı*, the grand vizier, and the *şeyhülislam* to the sultan's preceptor (*imam*) and other palace confidants, not to mention Sultan Mahmud himself, may have been the prime mover behind the document. Mekkizade's role seems likely because of his recent appointment, the fire-and-brimstone attitude of the text, and his Nakşbendi affiliations at a time when polarizing rhetoric and strict *shari'ah* themes were prominent in Nakşbendi-Mujaddidiyya rhetoric. Again, though, such sentiments were by no means confined to the partisans of a single Sufi order. See Abu-Manneh, "The Naqshbandiyya-Mujaddidiyya," 15–16, 24, 32–3, on Mekkizade, the Nakşbendis, and the discourse of orthodoxy in the period.

4 On Hurrem (Roxelana), see Peirce, *Imperial Harem*, 52, 58–65.

5 Hans-Peter Laqueur, *Osmanische Friedhöfe und Grabsteine in Istanbul* (Tübingen, 1993), 57–9; cf. Nicolas Vatin and Stéphane Yerasimos, *Les cimetières dans la ville: Statut, choix et organisation des lieux d'inhumation dans Istanbul intra muros* (Istanbul, 2001).

Zekiye's burial here reveals little about the woman herself except that she was a slave, one of several, belonging to the consort of the former *Şeyhülislam* Mekkizade Mustafa Asım. Given Mekkizade's wealth and position, Zekiye would have been one of a still greater number of slaves attached to the various members of the Mekkizade household. Despite Mekkizade's reputation for tightfistedness in the matter of charities, he was not known to stint on self-signifying luxuries.[6] Charles White noticed in the early 1840s that Mekkizade, "among other singularities and proofs of wealth, never, it is said, wears a waist-shawl twice in the same month."[7] In any case, his high rank called for a fully appointed household. Zekiye's epitaph identifies her as the personal property of the lady known as Küçük Kadın Efendi (literally "Madam Little Lady" or "Young Lady"), by whom Zekiye was evidently valued and probably loved, if her resting place is an indication of Madam Little Lady's regard.

Although dwarfed by the stones that surround it, the dimensions of the monument point to an adult or adolescent deceased. Still, Zekiye may have been very young. As a household slave, she could have been black African or white European (to use contemporary racial categories). Everywhere in the empire, as well as in Iran and Morocco, black and white slaves were harem intimates. Popular and historical accounts recall female slaves primarily in male-centered terms, as the concubines or potential concubines of male family members. Yet most female slaves spent most of their time with other women. Female slaves from toddlers to pensioners served as companions, servants, and often the personal property of the women of the home. Zekiye more than likely had been acquired from the Caucasus region, given the favored position that such women had come to occupy in grandee households since the seventeenth century. Not only in Istanbul but also in Cairo and other cities of the empire, north and south, Circassian and Georgian women were highly priced and prized, as they would continue to be until the final years of the empire.[8] As the property of a great-man household, Zekiye was as likely to have been acquired by gift as through purchase. The gift giver might have been a male or female relative or other household member.

The name Zekiye, the feminine form of "intelligent" or "clever" in Arabic, was one in use among Muslims. It points to its holder's postcapture conversion to Islam. Burial in the precincts of a mosque, especially this one, leaves little doubt of at least nominal Islamization. Otherwise, the name says nothing about Zekiye's origins or how she came to the Mekkizades. When wealthy families had need of slave labor, they sent their personal representatives, usually a relative or trusted retainer, to select and make purchases from local sellers. However, the more important the family, the greater the likelihood that some of its slaves were acquired as gifts. Acquaintances who hoped to cement relations

6 Mustafa Nuri Paşa, *Netayic ül-Vukuat: Kurumları ve Örgütleriyle Osmanlı Tarihi*, ed. Neşet Çağatay (Ankara, 1979–80), 1, pt. 2:311–12.

7 White, *Three Years*, 2:306.

8 Uluçay, *Harem II*, 11–14.

Fig. 15. Grave of the female slave, Zekiye. Photo by Muhammet Sait Yavuz, with my sincerest gratitude for his efforts to photograph the stone, which I had identified in the 1980s. The facing stone has suffered damage in the interim.

with an important officeholder – and could afford some thousands of *akçe*s – looked on the gesture as an investment in reciprocal favors.

Although any number of Marias, Johanneses, Ivans, and Dimitris passed into and out of Ottoman slavery with their Christian names intact, Middle Eastern owners – in common with slaveholders everywhere – conferred new names on their slave acquisitions, taking possession of their identities along with their persons. Female captives, if bound over for sexual use, were subject to an even more presumptive appropriation inasmuch as their owner's ownership extended to their procreative as well as productive capacities. Regardless of an owner's good intentions – to ease a new arrival's integration into the household, for example – slaves' new, local names did away with a remaining trace of their precaptive selves, effectively stamping them as customized, personal property.

In the naming rite that slaveholders arrogated to themselves, male and female owners often played the poet. They chose to confer – to impose – on their female slaves the names of flowers, precious stones, and other "pleasures of life," as Faroqhi terms them.[9] For imperial concubines, endless variations of "rose," "grace," and "delicacy" were always in vogue. Over the course of the empire's six hundred years, even when at war with Iran, the Ottoman dynasty and the palace-connected never abandoned their taste for Persian – the language of poetry and high culture – in female nomenclature. The Persian-derived Mihrimah or Mihrümah ("the light of the moon" or "sun and moon") and Mihrişah ("the light" or "sun of the shah") were perennial favorites for both royal daughters and concubines. In general, though, the names of palace concubines inclined toward rarer concoctions, with flowery Arabic names competing with the customary Persian in the eighteenth and nineteenth centuries.[10]

Fanciful naming, however, was probably not the rule for slave owners generally, still less for the Ottoman Muslim population of free subjects. The naming of freeborn females as well as of slaves who belonged to more modest owners always showed local variability. In Turkish-speaking regions and among the Turkish-speaking diaspora inhabiting the Arab provinces of the Levant, Egypt, and North Africa (the Maghreb), Turkish, Arabic, or Persian designations were always in play. Sometimes they were used alone, at other times in polyglot combination. Referring to the tastes of the palace, Faroqhi points to the emergence of new patterns by the eighteenth century. Increasingly, imperial consorts bore Arabic-derived, historically Islamic names – like Aisha (T., Ayşe), Fatıma, Zeyneb, Esma, Rabia, and Emine, all associated with the family of the Prophet Muhammad – in tandem with prettified nicknames.[11] The slave mother of Ahmed III, for example, was Rabia Gülnuş,

[9] Suraiya Faroqhi, "Quis Custodiet Custodes? Controlling Slave Identities and Slave Traders in Seventeenth- and Eighteenth-Century Istanbul," in Faroqhi, *Stories of Ottoman Men and Women: Establishing Status, Establishing Control* (Istanbul, 2002), 248; also Davis, *Ottoman Lady*, 105, 117; Uluçay, *Harem II*, 18. Cf. Goitein, "Slaves and Slavegirls," 8–9, on medieval Egyptian practice.

[10] War with Iran and confessional retrenchment may account for the increase in Arabic appellations under Ahmed III's successor Mahmud I (1730–54); see Ahmet Akgündüz, *İslâm Hukukunda Kölelik-Câriyelik Müessesesi ve Osmanlı'da Harem* (Istanbul, 1995), 336.

[11] Faroqhi, "Quis Custodiet," 248; Mustafa Çağatay Uluçay, "XVIII. Asırda Harem," *İ. Ü. Edebiyat Fakültesi Tarih Dergisi* 13/17/18 (1962–3), 272; Nejat Göyünç, "Frauen in der

"Rose-Elixir" Rabia, while Ahmed's consorts included Emine Mihrişah and Fatıma Hümaşah (literally "imperial bird of paradise").[12]

Ordinarily, when slaves or free non-Muslims converted to Islam, they passed into their new faith bearing appropriate Muslim appellations.[13] It is revealing that imperial slave women who were released from the palace into freedom (and usually marriage) frequently abandoned the designations of the seraglio. They either adopted Muslim names of their own choosing or held to the Muslim names that they had acquired along the way to becoming Muslims.[14] No stigma attached to former denizens of the palace, at least not prior to the liberal talk of the late nineteenth century. To the contrary, former slave women's palace connections, and the privileges of access that their graduate status conferred, made them prime marriage prospects. Freed slaves who reclaimed the proprietary power of naming regained something of their natal selves along with their physical freedom. For their part, former palace women, regardless of any renaming, clung to their palace identity. The byname "of the palace" (*sarayî* or *saraylı*) signified potential access to imperial favor.[15] It also amounted to an entry ticket into court society, especially in the eighteenth and nineteenth centuries, when royal women and their entourages had latitude for extravagant sociability.[16]

Zekiye's patroness had taken care not only to remember her slave but also to do so in a significant manner, with a modestly elegant stone memorializing Zekiye's ties to her female owner and to the eminent Mekkizades. Perhaps a woman of Küçük Kadın's station in life would not have wanted her appellation – Küçük Kadın is a familial sobriquet rather than a proper name – to be inscribed on anything less than elegant. In the world of Middle Eastern slaveholding, magnanimity of this sort attested to a donor's benevolence – and greater or lesser amounts of self-regard. In any event, acceptance and belonging, if not equality, inhere in the stone's inscription and its placement. It is a reminder of how love and affection, with or without sexual ties, reinforced

Familie Osman und am osmanischen Hof," in Prätor and Neumann, *Frauen, Bilder*, 1:103–7.

12 Uluçay, *Padişahların Kadınları*, is an indispensable source for this sort of information, as are Akgündüz, *İslâm Hukukunda*, 325–47, for the royal consorts and children of specific members of the dynasty, and Abdülaziz Bey, *Osmanlı Âdet, Merasim ve Tabirleri: Âdat ve Merasim-i Kadime, Tabirât ve Muamelât-i Kavmiye-i Osmaniye* (Istanbul, 1995), 2:331–2, 440–9, for names common to different social groups before and after the Tanzimat.

13 Marc David Baer, "Islamic Conversion Narratives of Women: Social Change and Gendered Religious Hierarchy in Early Modern Ottoman Istanbul," *Gender and History* 16, no. 2 (2004): 437. White, *Three Years*, 1:266, and Abdülaziz Bey, *Osmanlı Adet*, 2:449, discuss name giving with regard to black Africans.

14 Uluçay, *Harem II*, 37.

15 In a dispute over a valuable shawl and debt repayment, the complainant is identified only by name and palace connection; see Aykut, *İstanbul Mahkemesi, 121 Numaralı*, 144–5.

16 Esma the Younger, cousin of Selim III and sister of Mahmud II, scandalized the public by her bold and extravagant socializing; Uluçay, *Padişahların Kadınları*, 111–12. See also Faroqhi, *Stories of Ottoman Men and Women*, 44–7.

Ottoman slaveholders' benign self-perceptions and emotional stake in their slavery.

The gravestone and its associations suggest congruities between the Ottoman system and the "family incorporation" model put forward by Miers and Kopytoff for African slavery.[17] The point of departure, however, begins with conceptualizations of the family. Among other things, the continuum that the incorporation model posits between slave and kin, with slaves eventually absorbed into family lineages as recognized, albeit lesser, kin, does not entirely fit the state-regulated Ottoman system and its legal distinctions between slave and free. Nor does the African system of family lineages accord with the Ottomans' – the Middle East's – more supple familism.

The much-invoked metaphor of domestic slaves as junior members of the family puts an idealized gloss on the more complicated reality of master/mistress-slave relationships and the character of the Ottoman family. In many respects, it obscures as much as it explains about the position and role of slaves in relation to the free persons who commanded them. *Family* is, of course, an enormously pliable term. Multiple family-like and en famille dependencies created bonds between otherwise unrelated or distantly related Ottoman subjects in the period. Domestic labor, informal adoption (*evlatlık*), clientage, and apprenticeship were rooted in personal relationships in family settings. The idiom of kinship was liberally deployed. A fellow villager or penurious distant relative became aunt or sister to legitimize entry into the economy and intimacies of the family household.[18] As in other societies of the time, the Ottoman social hierarchy viewed minors of both sexes, and women generally, as family dependents. Domestic slaves in the family labor system were likewise dependents, although they stood at the farthest end of the dependency continuum.

Points of agreement with the incorporation model are nonetheless present in the Ottoman system, at least insofar as household slavery was concerned. Enslaved outsiders were initiated into society through the medium of familial households. And enfranchised slaves, in a society that took emancipation seriously, gave birth to their own freeborn lineages, without lasting taint or stigma. More fundamentally, though, Ottoman slavery's mode of incorporation was confessional rather than family or lineage linked. Conversion to Islam occurred more often than not when household slaves were held in bondage for any length of time. On a more basic level, outsider-converts were incorporated into the empire to become Ottoman subjects. Of course, internally gathered *devşirme kul*s were already subjects, although because of their religious origins, they were outsiders of a sort. The more particular transformation for these converts, setting aside the question of class differentiations for the

[17] Suzanne Miers and Igor Kopytoff, eds., *Slavery in Africa* (Madison, Wis., 1977).

[18] See, e.g., Abdurahman Kurt, "Tanzimat Döneminde Koruyucu Aile Müesseseleri," in Erverdi, Yıldız, Kara et al., *Sosyo-Kültürel*, 2:548–67.

Fig. 16. "Women Going to the Public Bath." A slave or servant carries the bathing accoutrements. Franz Taeschner, *Alt-Stambuler Hof- und Volksleben, ein türkisches Miniaturenalbum aus dem 17. Jahrhundert* (Hannover, 1925).

sake of argument, was from Christian or Jewish outsider to Ottoman Muslim insider. New Muslims, regardless of how recent their conversion, became the social superiors of indigenous Christians and Jews.[19] Religious superiority did

[19] Social acceptance was less forthcoming in the nineteenth century, when the Ottomans were more suspicious of converts' motives.

not guarantee greater wealth. Acceptance as Muslims, however, put converts into the path of public sector employment, the patronage of fellow Muslims, and the considerable benevolence of Islamic charity.[20]

The functional parallel between slaves and kin was reinforced by intimate proximity and affective ties. Under the best of circumstances, the combination helped secure for domestic slaves a place in family life and remembrance. Still, slaves remained a thing apart from true kin. They might be loved and nurtured as sons or daughters but, as salable commodities, they were neither. The popular idiom of marriage was often conveyed in commercial terms – the price of the bride, the selling of daughters, "How much does she cost?" And, as jurists explain, marriage, as a contractual exchange between two parties, has the quality of a business transaction for sexual use.[21] Nonetheless, the free bride possessed rights, recourses, and legal standing that distinguished her, and free females generally, from the enslaved. The distinguishing feature of slavery is understood to have resided less in the personal and demographic advantages that slavery may have furthered than in its moral and psychosocial impress.[22] Free and unfree individuals and institutions converged in some regards, but only the slave was consistently and fundamentally disposable property.

Even when resale was a remote prospect, it remained a defining vulnerability so long as the slave continued in bondage. A *fetva* of Şeyhülislam Çatalcalı Ali in the seventeenth century testifies to slavery's "radical uncertainty"[23] and the evanescence of hope: "If [the slave owner] Zeyd tells [his slave girl] Zeyneb that she is to be free as of forty days before his demise, can he [nonetheless] sell her [and thus abrogate the declaration]?" The response, "[Y]es, he can."[24] Similarly, in an example from the eighteenth century: "If [the female owner] Hind tells her female slave, '[I]f you do not betray me but serve faithfully, you shall be free upon my death.' If the slave [then] acts treacherously, can Hind sell her [regardless of the declaration]?" The *şeyhülislam* answered in the affirmative, as the manumission promise was only conditional. The slave's

[20] However, Bahaeddin Yediyıldız, *Institution du vaqf au xviiiè siècle en Turquie* (Ankara, 1985), 170–1, points out that the class and vocational stipulations of charitable *vakf*s of the eighteenth century cut down on welfare benefits for the genuinely needy. Eyal Ginio's "Living on the Margins of Charity: Coping with Poverty in an Ottoman Provincial City," in Michael Bonner, Mine Ener, and Amy Singer, eds., *Poverty and Charity in Middle Eastern Contexts* (Albany, N.Y., 2004), discusses the relationship between poverty and conversion in Salonica.

[21] Colin Imber, "Women, Marriage, and Property: *Mahr* in the *Behcetü'l-Fetāvā* of Yenişehirli Abdullah," in Zilfi, *Women in the Ottoman Empire*, 86–8; Colin Imber, *Ebu's-suud: The Islamic Legal Tradition* (Stanford, Calif., 1997), 174–5. See also al-Marghinani, *Hedaya*, bk. 2, on marriage; İlber Ortaylı, "Osmanlı Aile Hukukunda Gelenek, Şeriat ve Örf," in Erverdi, Yıldız, Kara et al., *Sosyo-Kültürel*, 2:464; Judith E. Tucker, "*Muftīs* and Matrimony: Islamic Law and Gender in Ottoman Syria and Palestine," *Islamic Law and Society* 1, no. 3 (1994): 294.

[22] Watson, *Asian and African Systems*, 8–9; Thomas Wiedemann, *Greek and Roman Slavery* (Baltimore, 1981), 3–4; Davis, *Slavery and Human Progress*, 14–19; Patterson, *Slavery and Social Death*, 334–42.

[23] Finley, *Ancient Slavery*, 12–13.

[24] Çatalcalı Ali, *Şeyhülislam Fetvaları*, 104.

treachery is taken as a given for the purposes of the question put to the *şeyhülislam*, hence its exact nature is not explained.[25] Promises of this sort could be made and unmade, although slave and mistress might dispute each other's actions and the breaking point in their understanding.[26]

The vulnerability of all slaves to resale arose from two fundamental incapacities. For one thing, slaves lacked real recourse against an owner's caprice. "I love you, I'll never sell you" was dishonest and manipulative if it was not truly meant, but it was not litigable. Also, in contrast to kin, slaves were not entitled to a share in the owner's estate regardless of how much their exertions or acumen had contributed to the wealth at issue. "Don't worry, when I die, you'll be taken care of" had no more force in an Ottoman court of law than it does in inheritance disputes nowadays. For slave women, emancipation sealed by marriage could make the difference between impoverished freedom and entitled socioeconomic standing. However, the legal marriage of freed slaves to their owners – even freed females to male former owners – was exceptional. Slaves could be married off to other slaves or to other free persons, if their owners wished. Because slaves remained slaves regardless of their marital status, any property that they acquired in marriage redounded to the slave owner.

Intimate slavery, concubinage, by itself offered neither legal advantage nor proof against resale. Notwithstanding the bequests, guardianship, and stipends that some slaves acquired, even owners' childbearing slaves, *ümm-i veled*s, were locked out of legal kinship with respect to their owner-consort's family. When an *ümm-i veled* gained freedom on her master's death, her situation could resemble that of other ex-slaves. What could make the difference was her owner-consort's wealth and foresightedness. If the deceased owner had favored her or any of his slaves with an ample bequest, she could be economically viable. As the mother of a child, especially a young one, a recognized *ümm-i veled* could hope that her owner-consort's heirs might elect to give her a home among them. How often such munificence actually materialized is impossible to know. Much of the existing evidence is in the form of legal cases, which, as in any society, are skewed toward conflict. Anecdotal bits, however, show a tendency on the part of families to hold on to those who had connections with them. Unless the estate was that of an official of the realm, heirs were under no official compunction to seek its immediate dissolution. Heirs could wait for years before deciding that it was time to separate out shares. If the deceased's estate was primarily a house and its furnishings, heirs might wish to leave the house intact for the benefit of a surviving parent or care giver. They might do

[25] Dürrizade Mehmed Arif et al., *Netice el-Fetava ma el-Nukul* (Istanbul 1265/1848), 114.

[26] Vows and their intentional or unintentional nullification are treated at length in juridical texts; see al-Marghinani, *Hedaya*, 76–8, 165–72.

so simply because the prospect of dividing up the property created an impasse among survivors.

Although the available sources provide only a sample of *ümm-i veled* reality, the elevation from ordinary female slave to acknowledged mother of a master's child was in many ways a hazardous ascent. At issue in court cases and presumably in conflicts that were resolved informally were precisely those distinctions that set the *ümm-i veled* above other slaves and drew her status closer to that of the free members of the household. Not only did heirs often contest an *ümm-i veled*'s right to emancipation; they also took issue with other props that could stabilize her future. Regarding the ability of such women to fulfill their roles as guardians and caretakers of their own minor children, disputatious heirs contended that the women lacked adequate material resources. Or if the *ümm-i veled* was Christian or Jewish and her owner had been Muslim, her ability or willingness to rear the child appropriately as a Muslim might be challenged even when the child was still a babe in arms. Gifts made to the women during the owner-consort's lifetime were also routinely contested: Had the gifts been witnessed as freely given? Were the items really the master's to give? Were the master's words absolutely unequivocal? [27] Other inheritance controversies arose when the child of an *ümm-i veled* outlived his or her father but predeceased the mother. Under normal circumstances, *ümm-i veled*s were not heirs of the owner-consort. Their children, however, were. On the death of a recognized child, its mother, as the surviving parent, received a share of the child's estate, including some part of whatever the child had inherited from its deceased father or other relatives, including grandparents.[28]

Whether or not an *ümm-i veled*'s claims were supported by the courts, the social value of her pinnacle slave status faded against the assertions of free society. With emancipation, the *ümm-i veled* became a woman without male protection, unless she married. The demise of an owner-consort was supposed to secure her freedom, but it also eliminated the nearest thing she had to a protector. Except for child-care and guardianship stipends – which were temporary and could amount to little – financial security often died along with her master. Given the usual disparity in ages between slaveholders

[27] Genuine gifts, unambiguously bestowed by the master, were legitimately an *ümm-i veled*'s property, as her status was that of a quasi-free (soon to be free) individual who was thus capable of ownership in her own right. For an *ümm-i veled*'s efforts to gain possession of property allegedly given to her as a gift (*hibe*) by her former owner-consort, see İstM 1/32, fol. 49a.

[28] İstM 1/32, fol. 49a, and İstM 1/25, for 1179 Şevval 1766; Kal'a et al., *İstanbul'da Sosyal Hayat 1*, 46–8, 215–16; Düzdağ, *Şeyhülislâm Ebussuûd*, 190; Yenişehirli Abdullah, *Behcet*, 115; Dürrizade Mehmed Arif, *Netice el-Fetava*, 90–1, 113, 116–17; Çatalcalı Ali, *Şeyhülislam Fetvaları*, 109. See also Bogaç Ergene, "Pursuing Justice in an Islamic Context: Dispute Resolution in Ottoman Courts of Law," *The Political and Legal Anthropology Review* 27, no. 1 (2004): 54, for heirs' refutation of claims put forward by the alleged daughter of the deceased and his concubine.

and their young concubines, an *ümm-i veled* could be quite on her own, for good, perhaps, if the deceased had provided for her and for ill if he had not. Marriage and remarriage were the norm for both men and women in Ottoman society. Only wealthy widows and divorcées were able and apparently willing to remain without a mate. Given the specter of poverty and their lack of blood kin, emancipated slave women, like the vast majority of their freeborn sisters, exerted themselves to marry.

A claim registered with the court in Istanbul in 1817 was typical of the imbroglios occasioned by the death of both an emancipated female slave and her child.[29] The case also opens a window onto the normalcy – in their own time – of the families that slavery made. The kin pursuing the estate not only had to prove their relationship to the family member in question but also had to demonstrate that the deceased had been the lawful owner of the contested property. In the 1817 case, a former female slave, Nasna bint Abdullah,[30] became guardian to her son, Mehmed Arif, and trustee of his property. At some point following her death, Mehmed Arif also died. Mehmed Arif might, in fact, have been a grown man by the time of his demise, but he is referred to in the register only by name and relationship, not age. The situation became a matter for the courts when a claim on the estate was put forward by another emancipated slave, a certain Emine bint Abdullah (both she and Nasna bore the common convert's patronym). Emine's claim was based on the fact that she was Nasna's sister and Mehmed Arif's maternal aunt. To establish her rights, Emine argued against her sister Nasna's former owner, who was also a relative of Nasna's deceased ex-slave husband.

In the day-to-day tally of slavery's conditions and exigencies, slave women's experience was bound up with the lives of other women. The epitaph of Zekiye at Süleymaniye points to the multiple ways that friendships and solidarity among slave women could be made or broken. Zekiye's patroness, Küçük Kadın, seems also to have been a slave. Her title of *Küçük*, though literally meaning "little," also has a relational connotation. As a title in the sense of "the young(er)," it was customarily bestowed on the more recent or more junior of two women. The identically named aunt and cousin of Selim III (1789–1808) were styled "Big" (*Büyük*) and "Little" Esma.[31] In Küçük Kadın's life as a concubine, a Büyük Kadın – a senior or prior female personage – had been somewhere on the scene.

The terms *kadın* and *hanım* denote "woman" or "lady." Both words have similar resonance in this period when used as common nouns in narrative discourse. *Hanım*, however, generally carried warmer and often more genteel

[29] Aykut, *İstanbul Mahkemesi, 121 Numaralı*, 95–6.

[30] The name Nasna is queried by the transliterator(s) in Aykut, *İstanbul Mahkemesi, 121 Numaralı*, 95.

[31] Uluçay, *Padişahların Kadınları*, 90–1, 112–13.

weight. As formal titles attached to personal names and honorifics, however, both words have a more checkered history in the connotation of respect. Certainly prior to the eighteenth century, *kadın* in titles customarily signified a female slave,[32] while the title *hanım*, as in "Leyla Hanım" or "Hanım Efendi," applied to free women, yet on Zekiye's gravestone, she, a slave, is called *hanım*. To complicate the matter further, in the eighteenth and nineteenth centuries, princesses of the blood were referred to as Hanım Sultan, not this or that *kadın*. Although the title *hanım* was indeed "adhered to with much jealousy by all free born-ladies,"[33] slave women could be transformed into so-and-so *hanım* if they became free and married well. When a certain Circassian slave woman, Ziba by name, became the wife of a prominent *alim* after having first been the concubine (*müstefreşe*) of another official, she became known as Ziba Hanım. She was an important force in the life of her husband, Çerkes Halil Efendi, who in fact became Mekkizade's replacement as *şeyhülislam* in 1819 after Mekkizade's first tenure.[34]

The household of Şeyhülislam Mekkizade appears to have been polygynist, although it is not entirely certain that his conjugal arrangements were simultaneous. Rumor has it that he was smitten by a female slave of great beauty (and great size, hence the anecdote's survival for more than a century) on a visit to the Istanbul Slave Market. Because he is said to have purchased this girl, the slave known as Küçük Kadın may have been so named because she was literally smaller than the other favorite.[35] Regardless, it is probably the case that Küçük Kadın was a newcomer to the house on her arrival. Her identification as *halile* can mean she eventually became either a consort or wife of Mekkizade.[36] The juxtaposition of *küçük* with *kadın* rather than *hanım* suggests concubinage rather than lawful marriage. However, one finds *halile* used to mean "wife" even in connection with princesses of the blood. For example, Princess Saliha (Saliha Sultan, in Ottoman usage), the daughter of Mahmud II, whose splendid nuptials had recently been celebrated, is identified by a contemporary historian as the *halile* – obviously meaning lawfully married wife – of Damad Halil Rıfat Pasha, on the occasion of the birth of their son in 1835.[37]

32 See Peirce, *Imperial Harem*, 108, and Uluçay, *Harem II*, 11–12, 41–2, for female honorifics in various periods.

33 White, *Three Years*, 2:294.

34 Cevdet, *Tarih*, 11:281–3; Abdülkadir Altunsu, *Osmanlı Şeyhülislâmları* (Ankara, 1972), 181–2. Ziba's impolitic remarks to the wife of Mahmud II's vicious onetime confidant, Halet Efendi, are said to have been the cause of her murder on Halet's orders.

35 The slave in question was said to have been a large-framed girl, with hands and feet the size of a man's; see Halûk Akçam, "Osmanlılarda Cinsellik" (referencing Reşat Ekrem Koçu), *Bravo Dergisi* 23–7 (1983): http://www.halukakcam.com/B6/Notes/OsmanliCinsellik1983.htm (accessed November 6, 2009).

36 Sir James W. Redhouse, *A Turkish and English Lexicon* (1890; repr., Beirut, 1987), 803.

37 Lûtfi Efendi, *Vak'a-nüvis Ahmed Lûtfi*, 4, pt. 5:817, 827.

The disposition of the late Mekkizade's estate does not clear up the puzzle of Küçük Kadın's position. When Mekkizade died in 1846, three years before Zekiye's death and three or more years before Küçük Kadın's presumed commission of Zekiye's gravestone, his estate achieved renown in the annals of grandee wealth. Not only was it of enormous size, but there were no surviving relatives entitled to the bulk of the estate.[38] The quest for clues about the Mekkizade household is hampered by a kind of female-erasure convention employed by Ottoman authors and some contemporary writers. Women often go unmentioned in cases that would seem to warrant their inclusion; for example, fatherless children are designated as orphans (*yetim*) when their mothers are still alive.[39] If Mekkizade left a lawfully wedded wife (*zevce-i menkuha*), contemporaneous accounts might simply have omitted mention of her inheritance position, as the share of a "spouse relict" would have amounted to only a fraction (though still a great deal of money) of Mekkizade's fortune.[40] Mekkizade is known to have been married to the daughter of another *şeyhülislam*, another religious exemplar of storied wealth, Samanizade Ömer Hulusi (d. 1812). She may well have predeceased her husband, or she might have quietly lived on to take her share. Because Mekkizade was childless at the time of his death, and because his father and presumably his mother had died years earlier, the bulk of his riches went into the needy coffers of the state.[41] Whatever Mekkizade's conjugal status was at the time of his death, it is unclear what share, if any, Küçük Kadın might have received. The bulk of the estate fell into the hands of the sultan of the time, Abdülmecid, who assigned the funds to the repair and restoration of the great mosque of Aya Sofya. It seems likely that Küçük Kadın had been left with something, or that the state allotted her a suitable pension. How she actually lived, and with whom, is anybody's guess, however.

It was not uncommon for upper-class women, both freeborn and those who had been in slavery themselves, to acquire and bring up little-girl slaves in the heart of the family. The children were like daughters rather than servants, according to those who encountered the practice. Zekiye may have been such a girl. The rearing process was virtually the same as that involving freeborn daughters, including the selection of husbands for them. There were differences, however. Daughters were legally entitled to the bride gift (*mehr*), which was paid to them by the groom or his family. When a slave was sold rather than

38 Esra Yakut, *Şeyhülislamlık: Yenileşme Döneminde Devlet ve Din* (Istanbul, 2005), 173.

39 See, e.g., Lûtfi Efendi, *Vak'a-nüvis Ahmed Lûtfî*, 2, pt. 3:658; Midhat Efendi, *Üss-i İnkılap*, "Introduction," 19. The Ottoman and modern Turkish (originally Arabic) term *yetim* denotes "orphan" as well as "fatherless child."

40 See Coulson, *Succession in the Muslim Family*, 41.

41 On Mekkizade and Samanizade, see Süreyya, *Sicill-i Osmani*, 3:283, 4:508; [Istanbul] Bab-i Meşihat, *İlmiye Salnamesi* (Istanbul, 1334/1915–16), 557–9, 567–8, 580–2; Altunsu, *Osmanlı Şeyhülislâmları*, 159–60, 167–8, 179–80; Câbî Ömer, *Câbî Târihi*, 2:738–9, 911–12; Mustafa Nuri Paşa, *Netayic*, 1, pt. 2:311–12; Abdurrahman Şeref, *Tarih Söyleşileri (Müsahabe-i Tarihiye)*, ed. Mübeccel Nami Duru (Istanbul, 1980), 226.

given as a gift, the exchange was certainly commercial. The transaction put money into the hands of the slave's owner. The sale price could be considerable, sometimes five or ten times the original sum at purchase. The difference was attributable to the value added by years of instruction in the Ottoman Turkish language and female patrician etiquette. The sale of the slave girl Şehriban, who became the wife of the reformist statesman Ahmed Midhat Pasha (d. 1884), is said to have cost him the head-turning sum of two thousand gold pieces.[42] The family members who had been her surrogate parents were also her owners and sellers. They could congratulate themselves on securing such prominence for their charge. And they could apply their profits to the purchase of another slave apprentice if they wished. In the meantime, their ties to Şehriban and her famous husband were ensured.

Not all girls who were purchased for upper-class households were intended for resale or elite networking. Some were reared in the family for eventual marriage to the son of the house or other relative. In patrilocal Ottoman society, a slave bride, manumitted or not, epitomized anthropology's outsider-bride custom. Brides from outside the kin group or other defined marriage-eligible unit were brought by their husbands to live among the husband's kin and to serve their interests. A slave bride could be expected to be unswervingly amenable to her husband's family and its habits, just as male slaves were for so long thought to make the most tractable and loyal imperial officials. For slave brides, though, the closer analogy was to the marital practice of the imperial palace, which regarded slave concubines as the preferable bearers of future sultans. For elite families as much as for royals, the social alienation that Patterson and others have posited as the distinguishing marker of slavery was here a cardinal virtue.[43] The absence of a slave girl's natal kin meant the absence of maternal-side interference to complicate life for the husband's family.[44] The in-house slave bride combined the best of both worlds in being a product of the groom's family without the encumbrance of blood kin of her own. From the girl's point of view, having no kin meant that there would be no family to see that she was treated well. An Ottoman acquaintance of Charles White defended the practice of outsider brides – without irony – as a way to reinforce family ties. She is "fashioned by our own hands. She regards us as her second parents. She is accustomed to our opinions and mode of

[42] Davis, *Ottoman Lady*, 107.

[43] Patterson, *Slavery and Social Death*, 13; see also Watson, *Asian and African Systems*, 4–6; Meillassoux, *Anthropology of Slavery*. Because of Circassians' tribal ties as well as sheer numbers, many who became a part of Ottoman society sought favors for their relatives, especially in the later nineteenth century, when Circassian immigrants were arriving en masse. Ottomanized Circassians even earlier came to the empire with family members or were sponsored by relatives already residing in the empire. See, e.g., Evliya Çelebi's comments on the Abkhazian ties of his great Abkhazian-Ottoman patron, Melek Pasha, in Dankoff, *Intimate Life*.

[44] Melek Hanım, *Thirty Years*, 128.

life."[45] A hundred years earlier, the poet Nabi (d. 1712) was of like mind when he urged his son to satisfy himself with concubines rather than with a legal wife.[46] His admonition was less about the satisfactions of sexual relations than about the dissatisfactions of family relations, especially on the maternal side.

Any number of Ottoman dignitaries from the sixteenth century through the nineteenth century acquired their wives or concubines in the way that Midhat Pasha had, by means of a household-to-household purchase or gift, with a female relative or acquaintance acting as intermediary. Küçük Esma (Esma the Younger) was one of the most energetic royal intermediaries for her brother Mahmud II, whose situation for a time as the only surviving male of the dynasty gave matchmaking an importance beyond favor seeking.[47] Upper-class women's agency in patrician matchmaking was most pronounced in the nineteenth century, or perhaps one should say that their activities were more transparent thanks to the accounts of female memoirists and European travelers. In their capacity as wives or concubines of Ottoman potentates, upper-class women were procreatively engaged in reproduction. As avocational slave dealers and matchmakers for the rich and powerful, they played a more autonomous role in social reproduction.

Harem-reared slave girls were molded into well-bred and indebted replicas of their wealthy and well-placed mistresses. All was not charity, however. The transformation of little girls from "barbary" into exquisite virginal brides was a manifold investment for any owner. Female owners who were slaves or former slaves had a personal interest in the way the elite slavery story would be told. Associating female slavery with sexual purity and aristocracy elevated the social worth of all those of captive origins. The showcasing of end over means made it possible to rewrite the message of enslavement. Any hint of lowly slave beginnings – every slave had been haggled over at least once – disappeared under elite rhetoric and the silk and jewels that adorned the privileged child slaves of the wealthy. Commenting on a visit with the beautiful Georgian wife of the then foreign minister, Pardoe marveled at how the woman's debased origins – from the perspective of class-conscious Europe – did not show: "you forgot, as you looked upon her, that she had ever been bought at a price, to remember only that she was the wife of one of the great officers of the Empire."[48]

In fact, visitors to grandee harems in nineteenth-century Istanbul were often unable to distinguish among slaves, especially white slaves, and their mistresses.[49] When they could do so, the distinctions seemed slight. Even above-stairs African slaves, who were more likely to be in the position

[45] White, *Three Years*, 2:320–1; cf. Melek Hanım, *Thirty Years*, 126.
[46] Pavet de Courteille, trans., *Conseils de Nabi Efendi à son fils Aboul Khair* (Paris, 1857), 46.
[47] Uluçay, *Padişahların Kadınları*, 120. [48] Pardoe, *City of the Sultan*, 3:55.
[49] Melman, *Women's Orients*, 155; Seng, "Fugitives and Factotums," 160–1.

of maidservant in these settings, had only light duties. They were usually well attired and adorned, and included in outings and celebrations.[50] In the well-ordered household, social differences were signaled by modes of address, both verbal and behavioral, more than by stark material distinctions. Just as slave women hoped one day to be able to revise the account of their mean beginnings, their freeborn rivals sought advantage in insisting on them.

Slave origins were not an ineradicable or institutionalized disability, but they figured in harem competition and could be mean spirited as well as mere banter. A famous jibe by Süleyman's displaced favorite Mahidevran against Hurrem-Roxelana sneered at Hurrem's auction-block origins. "'Sold meat,'" she called her.[51] The difference between a war-captive gift and a public-sale purchase was one of the gradations of slave culture, but in Ottoman society at large, the distinction that really made a difference in women's lives was that between slave and free. Female slaves who became consorts or wives had something to prove to women born to freedom and Ottoman high culture. The proofs lay primarily in a deferential openness to instruction. The tuition by older slaves of young slave charges, the female version of the "slave of a slave" phenomenon,[52] reinforced bonds of dependency as well as the social value of tutored slaves. Like many women of her class, Mekkizade's Küçük Kadın perhaps came to own her slave Zekiye outright once she herself was manumitted. During Küçük's time in the possession of Mekkizade, she might have had the use of Zekiye as her own slave servant. Whether Zekiye had been a gift or a purchase, a strong bond might easily have developed between the two. Rivalries do not seem to have separated them.

Polite society and its discontents

Zekiye's posthumous fate accords with the many portrayals of gentle manners and harmony between upper-class women – freeborn and freed – and their female slave property. Leyla Saz, who was an intimate of the palace during the reigns of sultans Abdülmecid (1839–61) and Abdülaziz (1861–76), expresses strong affection for the girls who passed through her household. She also writes warmly of older slaves, among them her own and her sister's childhood nurses, who remained devoted after years of service and resisted manumission.[53] Womanly concord and the "feminine camaraderie of the harem," however, cannot be taken as the norm for that time or any other.[54] They clearly do

[50] Melek Hanım, *Thirty Years*, 125–6; White, *Three Years*, 2:320; Pardoe, *City of the Sultan*, 1:108–11, 2:258–67.
[51] Peirce, *Imperial Harem*, 59.
[52] I. Metin Kunt, "Kulların Kulları," *Boğaziçi Üniversitesi Dergisi, Hümaniter Bilimler* 3(1975):27–42.
[53] Leyla Saz, *Imperial Harem of the Sultans*, 67–8, 78–80, 87–9.
[54] Melman, *Women's Orients*, 158.

not apply to the imperial harem and the deadly infighting of its rival royal mothers.[55] Below the level of dynastic politics, the notion of concord as the prevailing demeanor of such domestic arrangements also does not hold. The image is tempered by accounts of hurt and conflict in the nineteenth century. This, despite the fact that harmony was thought to have reigned particularly in the nineteenth century and most of all in that century's wealthy households. Given the higher levels of public violence in the seventeenth and eighteenth centuries, including violence against palace women, it is unlikely that the women of elite harems fared better in those centuries. The mixed picture conveyed by the disparate representations of female domesticity calls attention to the important palliative role of strict rules of etiquette and protocols of deference.

Female interactions within the harem, whether or not the man of the house was polygynous, were calibrated to social class, family placement, and household rank. Harem protocol obliged newcomers to show respect for seniorities of age, longevity, and station. As slaves and consorts, women like Küçük Kadın arrived at their position with the advantages of male favor and the disadvantages of their predecessors' prerogatives. As the often-disgruntled divorcée Melek Hanım writes, slave women "were subjected at once to the desires of their master and the terrible jealousy of their mistress."[56]

Leyla Saz, another privileged-class insider of the nineteenth century, concurred with Melek's view, but she was quick to fix some of the blame on the slave girls themselves. The young Circassian slave girls of her day, she said, were supposed to be servants and companions of the lady of the harem, but instead they "do everything to win the master's affection." The problem, according to Saz, was a misplaced sense of entitlement. The girls had been raised since birth with the example of successful compatriots before them. They expected nothing less than the command of their master's affections. The sense of entitlement that Saz speaks of was perhaps peculiar to its time, reflecting a general truth about the late nineteenth century and Circassian girls at the highest end of the trade. In any case, it is not surprising that female slaves in any period did what they could to advance themselves. Nor is it surprising that, even if their intention was to please rather than seduce, their efforts could end in "exciting the jealousy of their mistresses."[57] Saz reflects on female rivalry in slaveholding families with an observation drawn from personal, painful experience. Her own mother was made miserable because of repeated reports about Saz's father's behavior with the slaves of the household.[58]

[55] Peirce, *Imperial Harem*, 55–90.

[56] Melek Hanım, *Thirty Years*, 127; Melek Hanım, who had been married to the Tanzimat statesman Kıbrıslı Mehmed Emin (d. 1871), wrote her recollections after they were divorced; see Davis, *Ottoman Lady*, 80, 124, and 126, on the turbulent marriage of Melek and Kıbrıslı.

[57] Leyla Saz, *Imperial Harem of the Sultans*, 65.

[58] Leyla Saz, *Imperial Harem of the Sultans*, 85.

Even if a female slave had been purchased to be the property and consort of the master, she had no guarantee of uniqueness or permanency in the role. Küçük Kadın had at least one other rival as Mekkizade's consort, the more senior woman who was perhaps known as the Büyük Kadın, with whom to contend or make peace. Whether her arrival was new to the house or simply new to Mustafa Asım's affections, Küçük Kadın's ascent was likely to have been read by her predecessors in the harem as an unflattering judgment on themselves.

Wise junior women made certain to defer to existing wives and favorites. Those who did not, whether slave or free, risked an uncomfortable fall from favor or worse. For slaves, the stakes were high. The consequences of social missteps could, like resale, be life changing. Lawful wives were vulnerable as well. They had to move carefully, lest they lose unrecoverable ground in their husband's regard. Wives also had divorce to fear, although divorce seems to have been less common in upper-class households than among ordinary urban families. The ability to acquire a slave girl allowed the master sexual latitude without the encumbrances of an additional legal wife. Although the position of free women was undercut by the culture of slavery,[59] wives could take comfort in their marital status. So long as they remained lawful wives, they were socially and legally the superior of any concubine. However, because in economic terms divorce was virtually cost free for men – their financial obligation to divorced wives was a bare three months' support plus payment of any outstanding dowry portion (*mehr-i müeccel*) or other debts – a lawful wife's superior social position was fragile.

If Mekkizade's aristocratic wife was still alive during Küçük Kadın's rise, her family connections as the daughter of the very prominent and very rich Samanizade would have helped to shield her from capricious divorce. Samanizade was reportedly so well-off that after provisions for his daughter and charities, he delivered the remainder of his substantial treasures to the sultan. "I have one daughter, your highness's slave [using the word *cariye* to convey his and his daughter's obedient devotion to their sovereign], but what she has from me suffices for her," he wrote to Sultan Mahmud.[60] Samanizade's son-in-law would have been obliged to tread carefully with such a wife. Any new female arrival would have had to accommodate her as well. There is perhaps something to be learned from the account of the first meeting between the second and first wives of the constitutionalist Grand Vizier Ahmed Midhat Pasha. The story of how the young Şehriban bowed to kiss the hand of first wife Fatma Naime resonates with the politics of female power and the link

[59] Ahmed, *Women and Gender in Islam*, 83–101; Ennaji, *Serving the Master*, 1; B[asim] F. Musallam, *Sex and Society in Islam: Birth Control before the Nineteenth Century* (Cambridge, U.K., 1983), 31–6; and Fatima Mernissi, *Dreams of Trespass: Tales of a Moroccan Girlhood* (Reading, Mass., 1994), and *Women's Rebellion and Islamic Memory* (Atlantic Highlands, N.J., 1996), 69–74, 84–90.

[60] Câbî Ömer, *Câbî Târihi*, 2:911–12.

between harem hierarchy and domestic peace.[61] The two women got along well enough during Midhat's active lifetime. It is telling, though, that they did not maintain particularly close relations during Midhat's banishment and imprisonment in Arabia in 1881. Perhaps the absence of the family patriarch had compounded the strains of proximity. The women continued to observe polygamous politesse by asking after each other in their individual letters to Midhat.[62] Had their relationship been truly intimate apart from the man who had made them a unified family, they might have been closer companions in Izmir, where both resided.[63] Their relationship was apparently strained.

The ostensible tranquillity of Midhat Pasha's preexile domestic arrangements was replicated in many upper-class polygynist households, and probably for the same reasons. Female amity was often more a contingent strategy than a viable bond. Women learned to repress the sharper edges of their resentments and apprehensions. In the long run, they might have ultimately prevailed. There is persuasive evidence of the instability of the conjugal bond in early modern Ottoman society, but whether or not a divorce ever took place, maternal and infant mortality reconfigured households willy-nilly. The incidence of early mortality in the eighteenth and nineteenth centuries in the royal family alone gives one pause.[64] Küçuk Kadın, the newcomer on the Mekkizade scene, may well have outlived Mekkizade's wife. Şehriban, Midhat Pasha's young bride, died of tuberculosis shortly after Midhat's death. First wife Fatma Naime lived on as the martyred Midhat's widow and as mother to Şehriban's and Midhat's three children.[65]

Ottoman literature beginning in the Tanzimat increasingly took up themes of slavery, polygamy, and women's social role in the context of patriarchal authority and the structure of the family. The literary turn coincided with the opening up of debate in the political sphere over confessional egalitarianism, the slave trade, and rights in general. Stories set in middle- and upper-class households centered on slave protagonists to explore issues of social justice and inequality. The dramas in which the slaves' (often unhappy) fates unfold have

[61] Davis, *Ottoman Lady*, 90; cf. Pardoe, *City of the Sultan*, 1:106. For household rankings and spatial organization in seventeenth-century Cairo, see Nelly Hanna, *Making Big Money in 1600: The Life and Times of Isma'il Abu Taqiyya* (Syracuse, N.Y., 1998), 146–7.

[62] Davis, *Ottoman Lady*, 89–90, 107–8; Mithat, *Life of Midhat Pasha*, 207–41.

[63] A Western visitor to the two women while they lived together during Midhat's first imprisonment reports that his first wife was "manifestly a lady," while his young second wife sat quietly, appearing dejected and without affect; Emily [Jane Davis] Pfeiffer, *Flying Leaves from East and West* (London, 1885), 16, 19, 20, 21, 22–6. Whether Şehriban was cast down by her subordinate status, saddened at the absence of her husband, or playing the role expected of her is unclear.

[64] Uluçay, *Padişahların Kadınları*, 79–83, 120–8. Of forty-some births credited to Mahmud II's consorts, less than half survived to any age, a fate shared by Ahmed III's equally numerous offspring; and of those who survived, many did not make it past puberty. Of the twenty-three or so children born to Abdülhamid I, only four girls and two boys, including Mahmud II, survived to any age; Yılmaz Öztuna, *II. Sultan Mahmud* (Istanbul, 2006), 4.

[65] Davis, *Ottoman Lady*, 90, 182.

the ring of nonfiction in their portrayal of powerlessness and vulnerability. In their time, they also served as broad metaphors for the tensions in relationships of power in periods of cultural change.[66] Slavery was one of many kinds of subordinations – albeit not the most pressing – that Ottoman thinkers were bestirring themselves to address as the nineteenth century wore on.

The recollections of female relations in polygyny that are met with in biographies and memoirs reprise a narrative thread as old as the Hebrew Bible's Sarah and Hagar: a barren first wife consents to a second wife or suitable concubine in the hope of children to secure her own and her husband's happiness. Any number of marriages and sexual alliances came about in this way wherever polygyny and slave concubinage were practiced. A wife's consent might not have been a ringing endorsement, however. If she herself was the mother of living children, she had to be concerned about her offspring's inheritance prospects and the place they would hold in their father's affections.[67] The concept of barrenness, like that of fatherlessness as orphanhood, was premised on men's unique claims to full personhood. Failure to produce a boy child could define a woman as barren even if she and her husband had living daughters. The designations had to do with the earning power of males and men's religio-cultural responsibilities as family breadwinners and moral guides. With so much legal and social recognition attached to men, their absence was a family calamity. Even so, many households became polygamous or polygynous for reasons having nothing to do with the desire or need for a child.

Notwithstanding the hyperbolic valuing of Ottoman males, Westerners who were privy to Ottoman Muslim family life found some of their other preconceptions challenged. Among other things, they were impressed by the centrality of children in society and the high premium placed on fertility. Charles White, friend to a number of Ottoman dignitaries and an attentive recorder of social relations, did not admit exaggeration when he remarked, "No people in the world are more tenderly attached to their progeny than the Turks."[68] Julia

[66] İsmail Parlatır, *Tanzimat Edebiyatında Kölelik* (1987; repr., Ankara, 1992); H. Emel Aşa, "İlk Türk Kadın Romancısı Fatma Aliye Hanım'ın Romanlarında Aile ve Kadın," in Erverdi, Yıldız, Kara et al., *Sosyo-Kültürel*, 2:650–9; Nükhet Esen, "Türk Ailesindeki Değişmenin Romanımıza Yansımaları," in id., 660–76; Enver Töre, "Türk Ailesindeki Değişmenin Tiyatromuza Yansımaları," in id., 677–700; Deniz Kandiyoti, "Slave Girls, Temptresses, and Comrades: Images of Women in the Turkish Novel," *Feminist Issues* 8 (1988): 35–50; Toledano, *Ottoman Slave Trade*, 272, and Toledano, *Slavery and Abolition*, 122–6; and Sagaster, *"Herren" und "Sklaven,"* esp. 47–130. Parlatır explores the representations of slaves and slavery and notes some of the more optimistic renderings of slaves' fate; on this point, see Aşa, "İlk Türk Kadın," 656–7. Sagaster's valuable study analyzes representative writings of important Tanzimat and post-Tanzimat authors in terms of their own changing attitudes and in the context of slavery's historical meaning in the late empire.

[67] Öztürk, *Askeri Kassama*, 197; Pardoe, *City of the Sultan*, 1:.227. On polygamy in contemporary Turkey, see Pınar İlkkaracan, "Exploring the Context of Women's Sexuality in Eastern Turkey," in *Women and Sexuality in Muslim Societies* (Istanbul, 2000), 232–8; Serim Timur, *Türkiye'de Aile Yapısı* (Ankara, 1972), 93–4.

[68] White, *Three Years*, 2:300, 3:234.

Pardoe, another longtime sojourner, was of the same mind, declaring "strong parental affection... indeed, I may say love of children generally" to be a "distinguishing trait in the Turkish character."[69] Ubicini's concurring observation – that for Ottoman Turks in particular, "a childless home is a curse; a childless wife a disgrace"[70] – drew attention to the inordinate pressure placed on women as bearers of children. A wife was to produce children or make room for women who would.

In most centuries, despite the occasional admiring report, the European view of Muslim family life was both uncomprehending and uncomplimentary. By the opening of the nineteenth century, it had become sharply condemnatory.[71] The polygynous harem, presumed to be the Ottoman and Muslim norm, was decried as an uncivilized abomination. For their part, Ottoman families of every stripe would have been appalled by the rate of child abandonment and social crime in monogamous Christian Europe. Unwanted children and infant abandonment were not unknown in Ottoman society, as Ortaylı and others have shown.[72] However, child abandonment did not approach the epidemic proportions of Europe, where in the 1780s in France alone, forty thousand infants and children annually were left to their fate. In Russia in the 1830s, the figure was five thousand foundlings in just one hospital in St. Petersburg.[73] In the late nineteenth century, Ottoman intellectuals like the novelist and social critic Ahmed Midhat Efendi invoked such statistics in defense of Ottoman culture and Muslim family life.[74] It was a return salvo in the enduring East-West debates over female sexuality, civilization, and society, but it did little to change Western perceptions.

Households undone

Apart from the desire of men and women to have children to love, males were exhorted to fatherhood as a stake in the future and as a demonstration of manhood. For men, however, the costs of childlessness did not mean the loss of economic security, abandonment by a spouse,[75] or the sense of worthlessness that could fall to the lot of childless women. For women who were able to countenance the surrogacy of a cowife or concubine, the rewards could be material security and the chance to share in the upbringing of a beloved child. Given childbed mortality and the eighteenth- and nineteenth-century plagues of typhus and tuberculosis, fertile mothers might end up childless or dead, with barren first wives filling in as mothers.

69 Pardoe, *City of the Sultan*, 1:91–2. 70 Ubicini, *Letters on Turkey*, 1:156.

71 There continued to be exceptions, including Julia Pardoe, Charles White, J. H. A. Ubicini, and Aldolphus Slade, but the view that predominated was hostile and increasingly so.

72 Ortaylı, "Osmanlı Aile," 465; Kurt, "Tanzimat Döneminde," 549–50.

73 Anderson and Zinsser, *A History of Their Own*, 2:246.

74 Kurt, "Tanzimat Döneminde," 550.

75 However, a husband's impotence, if proved, constituted court-granted grounds for divorce.

Still, connubial accord between cowives can have affected only a small proportion of households. Inasmuch as the empire as a whole was home to a monogamous population, for the majority of people, childless marriages were more likely to end in divorce than in polygyny. Even if divorce was less common in some segments of the population, it was a frequent practice in general.[76] Stories of women who gave their approval to the addition of a second wife reflect a reality that continues to the present day, in the polygamous pockets of the United States as well as in Turkey, where it is also officially outlawed, and elsewhere in the Middle East. In the Ottoman context, however, such decisions do not suffice to refute the monogamous preferences of most women and, apparently, most families.[77] Nor can they explain away the troubled domestic dramas that also figure in period sources.

Native memoirists and foreign authors in the eighteenth and nineteenth centuries – de Tott, Slade, Ubicini, Durand de Fontmagne, Melek Hanım, Djavidan Hanım, Leyla Hanım, and Garnett among them – refer to unhappy female cohabitation.[78] A few authors were direct observers. Others merely passed on what they heard from erratically informed locals. Many of the reports betray the "iterative" narration that Said's *Orientalism* famously took to task.[79] Certainly Slade's twice-told tale of an unhappy Georgian concubine who unseated a Turkish wife and then suffered displacement by a Circassian has a generic ring.[80] Indeed, we have heard the story before. Slade, who traveled with the Ottoman navy in the 1820s and 1830s, was apparently alluding to the love life of a grand admiral (*kapudan* pasha) of the time, a man with whom he sailed and came to know, Pabuççuoğlu Ahmed Pasha (d. 1830).[81] Others who wrote about polygyny's woes may well have had Ahmed Pasha's home life in mind, though they need not have. The same set of ethnicities figures in a number of historical and fictional accounts of the later nineteenth century. Female rivalry inhered in harem polygyny, and Georgian, Turkish, and Circassian women were omnipresent in polygynous circles of the eighteenth

[76] Madeline C. Zilfi, "'We Don't Get Along'": Women and *Hul* Divorce in the Eighteenth Century," in Zilfi, *Women in the Ottoman Empire*, 264–96.

[77] Recent polls taken in Turkey, however, indicate wide acceptance of polygamy as a legitimate marital mode. What this might mean regarding women's and men's views of one another in Turkey could do with additional study.

[78] Davis, *Ottoman Lady*, 88–91; de Tott, *Memoirs*, 1, pt. 1:xxvi–xxviii; Slade, *Records of Travels*, 1:140, 150, 353–5; Marie Baronne Durand de Fontmagne, *İstanbul Günleri: İkinci İmparatorluk Döneminde İstanbul'da Fransız Konsolosluğunda Geçen Günler*, trans. İsmail Yerguz (Istanbul, 2007), 288–92; Ubicini, *Letters on Turkey*, 2:183–5; Melek Hanım, *Thirty Years*, 50; Djavidan Hanum [Hanım], *Harem Life by Princess Djavidan Hanum*... (London, 1931), 90–120; Lucy Mary Jane Garnett, *Turkish Life in Town and Country* (London, 1904).

[79] Edward Said, *Orientalism* (New York, 1978), 92–3, 246, 277; İrvin Cemil Schick, "The Women of Turkey as Sexual Personae: Images from Western Literature," in Zehra F. Arat, ed., *Deconstructing Images of "the Turkish Woman"* (New York, 1998), 92.

[80] Slade, *Records of Travels*, 1:140, 150, 353–5; Adolphus Slade, *Slade's Travels in Turkey: Turkey and the Turks, and a Cruise in the Black Sea, with the Capitan Pasha: A Record of Travels* (New York, 1854), 92.

[81] Danişmend, *İzahlı Osmanlı Tarihi*, 5:227–8.

and nineteenth centuries. The autobiographies of Halide Edib and Saz, among others, attest to the commonality of such conflicts and their ethnic mix even in the waning years of legal polygyny.[82] Apart from anecdotal testimony, the legal record is replete with cases of marital dissolution and disappointment. Yet the structural sameness of these dramas may well reflect the reality of similarly constructed families caught in similarly felt dilemmas. The striking sameness of questions asked of muftis century after century further corroborates the timelessness of personal relationships and quandaries.

Ottoman court records and chronicles give evidence of the rancor that clouded the image of domestic tranquility. Two notorious cases, in 1762 and 1810, involved deadly clashes between unrelated women in polygynist, or at least slaveholding, households. The events transpired in households lower down the social ladder than the households known to Western travelogues and Ottoman memoirs. There is evidence of slavery's class distinctions in the experience of both owner and owned here. Both murders apparently involved households that lacked the interpersonal cushioning that great wealth and layers of lightly occupied servants could provide. In the largest households, as in the imperial harem, senior slave women were made responsible, and were compensated accordingly, for disciplining female slaves and servants. Discipline in smaller domiciles was left to the master and mistress. Female homicides at the hands of other female householders were as exceptional as they were publicly sensational.[83] Still, the stabbing deaths (one of them with a meat cleaver) of two wives by apparently angry *cariye*s are a reminder of slavery's violent undertow.

The cryptic summaries that make up the historical record identify the slave women or girls merely as *cariye*s of undisclosed age, one Circassian (*Çerkes*), the other African (*Zenci*). Both are said to have assaulted their mistresses in consequence of reprimands. Precisely what took place to set the women against each other is not part of the stories, although Cabi's account of the meat cleaver incident of 1810 offers additional hearsay details. The victim, the wife of an imam of the Kırkçeşme area of Istanbul, beat or struck (*darb*) the African slave to discipline her for some shortcoming. The slave then seized the cleaver and attacked her mistress with it. In her rage, the slave cut off the woman's hand, all the while shouting: "Is this the hand you beat me with?" According to testimony from neighbors, the victim screamed for mercy and then went silent. The slave was still on the scene when the victim's husband returned to

82 Halide Edib [Adıvar], *Mor Salkımlı Ev* (Istanbul, 1963), and her *Memoirs of Halidé Edib* (New York, n.d.), esp. 203, 206, and 307–8; Saz, *Imperial Harem of the Sultans*, 85–6; Pardoe, *City of the Sultan*, 3:96–7; Djavidan Hanım, *Harem Life*, 92–3.

83 The murder of male owners by male slaves was more common, especially as a part of collective action; see Osman Yıldırım, Vahdettin Atik et al., eds., *85 Numaralı Mühimme Defteri, 1040–1041 (1042)/1630–1631 (1632)* (Ankara, 2002), 168, for the murder of a district governor (*sancak beyi*) by slaves working on ship repairs under his supervision. On crime by or against slaves, see D'Ohsson, *Tableau* 4, no. 2:318–21, 335–8.

find his mutilated wife. Claiming to have been occupied elsewhere, the slave at first denied any knowledge of the murder. She, in fact, suggested that her mistress had been slain by an unidentified friend who had come to the house. "I was in the kitchen cooking. Her friend came and went. That's all I know," she said. This at any rate was the version of the affair that was retailed around the city.[84]

The earlier incident, involving a Circassian slave and the lady of the house, was also a female story. Like the other, it centered on a domestic struggle and convenient kitchen implements. The slave in question was a consignee, the property of an owner who had opted to sell her, as was often done, through a dealer. At the time of the incident, the girl or woman was one of several female slaves, *cariye*s, of unspecified age who were being lodged at the dealer's residence. In keeping with contemporary practice, the at-home arrangement provided a plausible setting for marketing female slaves as chaste and proper. The practice was also an efficient way for the dealer's family, particularly adult females, to participate in the family economy. For all we know, the brains behind the family's slave dealing may have been the lady of the house, with her mate, the dealer, the business's public and formal face.

The role of women of the artisanal classes in the infrastructure of the slave trade was less remarked in the sources than that of wealthy matrons, but the former were indispensable to the gender system and to the sustainment of female slavery in that system. Zarinebaf-Shahr's finding of numerous females among Istanbul's bathhouse owners and managers in the eighteenth century gives evidence of the demand for female workers and for female-specific vocations to support the gender system's social requirements.[85] Although African eunuchs were the prestigious gatekeepers and accoutrements of elite-tier slaveholding, most owners did not have eunuchs to mediate between the male and female worlds.[86] Free women and senior slave women were the nurses, bathers, midwives, seamstresses, examiners, and warders of other women. As the traffic in women became more decentralized in the eighteenth and nineteenth centuries, more business was conducted out of private residences and small warehouses. Wives and other relatives as well as slaves already in residence were perhaps able to play a more active role in the family business.

In the case of the murderous Circassian *cariye* of 1762, the women of the house would have had the use of their transient slave lodgers as they went about instructing them in the work of the household, hygiene, manners, and

[84] Câbî Ömer, *Câbî Târihi*, 1:649–50; Zilfi, "Goods in the Mahalle," 291–5.

[85] Fariba Zarinebaf-Shahr, "The Role of Women in the Urban Economy of Istanbul, 1700–1850," *International Labor and Working-Class History*, no. 60 (2001): 149, notes that at least seventy-three public baths in Istanbul in 1765 were co-owned and/or managed by women.

[86] White, *Three Years*, 2:352, estimated that there were no more than four hundred eunuchs in Istanbul, almost all of them employed by the royal family, in the 1830s and 1840s. De Tott, *Memoirs*, 1, pt. 1:77, remarks that eunuchs were rare in the late eighteenth century, with only the dynasty and very richest households employing them.

the like. Obviously something went terribly wrong. The slave girl is said to have taken violent offense when the dealer's wife tried to discipline her. Exactly what form the chastisement took is not reported. The girl may have been an ordinary consignee, either a new arrival to Istanbul or a slave already resident whose owner chose to use the services of a broker (*dellal*) to resell her. Or the girl may not have been so ordinary, perhaps having already been "a troublesome property" before the fatal encounter.[87] The chronicler Vasıf refers to the slave in disparaging terms, but his judgment of her as hell bound may have been after the fact. Had the girl failed to work out in a previous household? Was her misbehavior in the dealer's house not about that day's scolding but about her larger plight? Just how hard and how often had she been struck? The reports that have come to light thus far do not say.[88]

The slave offenders in both cases were interrogated by the authorities and found guilty. Both were hanged in the open at Istanbul's main Slave Market, "as a warning to other female slaves," according to the official sentences.[89] Perhaps Istanbul's slave population needed such a warning. Anecdotes about female murderers in slaveholding regions – admittedly a small population – hint at a high incidence of slave women among them.[90] Absent real data, we remain in the dark regarding this possibility and what it might tell us. Exemplary punishments meted out to male capital transgressors, whether they were *askeri* or *reaya*, counted on the shock value of corporeal humiliation. Typically the wrongdoer's body was displayed in a locale associated with his social status and the character of his crime. Depositing the body in the transgressor's own occupational space also ensured that the message of swift, absolute punishment would be impressed on peers and passersby. For acts of treason and other high crimes, the severed heads of central government officials and provincial notables came home to roost at the walls of the palace.[91]

Ottoman society, especially urban society, took self-righteous pride in the concealment of women's bodies from public view. The suspended bodies of executed females had more than just voyeuristic impact. In fact, the state's assumption of authority in ordinary homicide cases was somewhat unusual. Islamic law treated homicide as a private matter governed by considerations

87 Kenneth M. Stampp, *The Peculiar Institution: Slavery in the Ante-Bellum South* (New York, 1956), ch. 3, "A Troublesome Property."

88 Mehmed Hâkim "Hâkim Tarihi," TKS Bağdat 233, fol. 143a; Şemdanizade, *Mür'i't-Tevârih*, 2a:41; Vasıf, *Tarih-i Vasıf*, 1:216. Von Hammer, *Geschichte*, 8:246, apparently prefers to translate Vasıf's *ayal* as "children," and thus has the slave murdering the dealer's family rather than his wife.

89 Mehmed Hâkim, "Hâkim Tarihi," fol. 143a; Câbî Ömer, *Câbî Târihi*, 1:649–50.

90 Carl F. Petry has made a similar observation regarding murderers in pre-Ottoman Cairo in the discussion of his paper "Crime without the Blood Money Option? The Paucity of References to Blood Money in Criminal Narratives by Mamluk Historians in Cairo and Damascus," delivered at the Annual Meeting of the Middle East Studies Association, Boston, November 2005.

91 Matei Cazacu, "La mort infâme: Décapitation et exposition des têtes à Istanbul (xve-xix siècles)," in Gilles Veinstein, ed., *Les Ottomans et la mort* (Leiden, 1996), 245–89.

of loss. The victim's heirs were entitled to decide the perpetrator's fate – within legally prescribed limits and alternatives – by way of justice or material compensation. In Ottoman practice, however, the state regularly exercised the right – albeit with *shari'ah* sanction – to impose its own penalties for crimes having wide social or political resonance.[92] The regimes of Mustafa III (d. 1774) and Mahmud II (d. 1839) stood behind the verdicts in both cases. Slave women were not *muhsana* – literally "guarded" or "protected" free women – in particular free, married women. By law they were not entitled to, or responsible for, the bodily modesty normally associated with free women.[93] The harsh didacticism of the hangings was nonetheless a fearsome official response. It was a declaration of ruling-class intolerance for insubordination.

To slaves whose owners brought them to view the punishments, and to those awaiting sale in the cubicles and warehouses of the Slave Market, the hangings laid bare the limits and recourses of paternalism. As for the question of what really happened in the two troubled households, the indictment of the slave women was unproblematized in the historical accounts. In keeping with the hierarchal biases of Ottoman society and reportage, the notion of mitigating circumstances was out of the question. None of the accounts contemplates slavery's structural tensions or the master class's prerogative of force. Certainly there was no allowance for the possibility that these slaves or any slaves might have been resisting egregious treatment or the brutality of enslavement itself.

Sexuality and opportunity

Differences in prescribed gender roles were responsible for the most defining variations in male and female slaves' and ex-slaves' experience, valuation, and personal rights. All women, regardless of skin color, shared certain entitlements and labored under a number of common difficulties and prejudgments. In comparison to race or ethnicity through the early decades of the nineteenth century, restrictions based on gender created more exclusions and structural barriers to women's social access and mobility. The degree to which advantage was outweighed by disadvantage is in large measure the subject of the remainder of this chapter.

Attenuations of absolute slavery, those formal and informal means that brought slaves closer to emancipation, were technically available to all slaves.

[92] J. N. D. Anderson, "Homicide in Islamic Law," *BSOAS* 13, no. 4(1951): 811–28; Peters, *Crime and Punishment*, 38–53; Heyd, *Studies*, 104–6. For the historical expansion of sovereign authority, *örf* (Ar., *'urf*), see *İA*, s.v. "Örf," by Halil İnalcık; Heyd, *Studies*, 267.

[93] Slave women were subject to lighter legal penalites than those imposed on erring free women. On the legal and social meanings of *muhsana* and *muhaddere*, see al-Marghinani, *Hedaya*, 197; Heyd, *Studies*, 109; Peters, *Crime and Punishment*, 61–3. See Peirce, *Morality Tales*, 157–61, for a discussion of the class or status dimensions of the designation *muhaddere* ("respectable woman"). Shatzmiller, *Her Day in Court*, 96–9, though focusing on the Malikis, outlines differences among the Sunni schools of jurisprudence.

For women, though, they were often impractical whatever the year or locale. Women were seldom in a position to negotiate their way to freedom. Even in the nineteenth century, when fixed-term slavery was becoming routine, women rarely had the resources to bargain with their owners for conditional servitude, such as that afforded by the limited-service contract of *mükatebe*. Outside the household economy, employment opportunities for women were limited, at least insofar as gainful and respectable work was concerned. The promise of emancipation in return for a fixed number of years' service (*hizmet*) was one way around the market's dead end. However, for whatever reason, situational or personal, women who managed to sign on to *hizmet* contracts may have been less likely to see the contracts through to emancipation. In an eighteenth-century *fetva*, a female slave's inability to fulfill the terms agreed on ("she is unable to buy out the contract and has no money forthcoming") rendered the contract null and void. The owner, Zeyd (the "John Doe" of *fetva* parlance) therefore regained his precontract rights, including the one that was the crux of the question put to the *şeyhülislam*: "Can Zeyd sell her?" The answer was affirmative. So long as the contract had been in effect, the owner forfeited the right to sell his *mükatebe* slave.[94] Theoretically gender neutral, indeed encouraged by the Qur'an, contractual bargains in practice were almost exclusively a male emancipatory path.[95]

In the past as in the present day, military service was a portal for male advancement. It was true for the freeborn as well as for freedmen and slaves, with and without actual heroics. Inasmuch as women were regarded as the dependents of male guardians and acquired their status from male family members, they benefited from the military advancement of husband or father. The very fact of women's exclusion from military service was also something of a blessing. Contemporaries estimated that only 35 percent of Ottoman soldiers survived the wars of the early nineteenth century.[96] The rate of survival is unlikely to have been much higher in earlier times, even in victory. That being said, military adventurism was a way of life in the early modern era. Women's noncombatant status barred them from the patronage, wealth, and social authority that were warriors' sometime rewards. Yet as civilians in the line of march or fending for themselves on the home front, they faced warfare's terrors and privations.

According to received wisdom, slave women's mobility advantage lay in the realm of sexuality. Theoretically, anywhere that female slaves worked, their sexuality could earn them favors and kinder treatment. But it is in Islamic law's provisions for slave mothers, *ümm-i veled*s, that female slaves'

[94] Dürrizade Mehmed Arif, *Netice el-Fetava*, 111. Sexual relations with a *mükatebe* slave were also prohibited by law.

[95] "Those your right hands own who seek emancipation, contract with them accordingly"; Arberry, *Koran Interpreted*, xxiv:33. The Ottoman *fetva* literature is overwhelmingly concerned with agreements involving male slaves.

[96] White, *Three Years*, 3:8.

advantage is most commonly said to lie. Because the advantage hinged on paternal acknowledgment, however, the value of the provision has to be weighed against its ultimate conditionality.[97] The fact is that paternal disavowals figure prominently in legal actions.[98] We are not able to calculate a failure rate for women whose claims to *ümm-i veled* rights reached the courts. We have no way of knowing how many claims were truly valid in the first place. A common legal dilemma irrespective of the sincerity or insincerity of the litigants arose from uncertainty about the onset of a pregnancy and imperfect knowledge about human gestation. When male owners disavowed paternity, they often contended that the slave or ex-slave had been impregnated by someone else, such as by a husband to whom she was married while a slave or within a short time of being manumitted. The date of the onset of her pregnancy, whether before or after marriage to another man, would determine whether the child was the husband's or the master's.

Toledano's account of the Circassian girl Şemsigül in mid-nineteenth-century Cairo offers the fullest record of an owner's illegal and abusive machinations with regard to a slave who bore his child.[99] Another case brought by an Ethiopian slave woman in Cairo around the same time shows a similar pattern of mistreatment and denial. Like Şemsigül, the woman was able to prove severe abuse at the hands of the slave merchant who had brought her to Egypt, but unlike Şemsigül, she was unsuccessful in the more difficult task of proving her child's paternity.[100] Charles White, writing in the 1840s, asserted that the emancipatory promise of the *ümm-i veled* status was more regularly fulfilled in Istanbul than elsewhere in the nineteenth century and perhaps earlier as well. According to White, the rules were "strictly adhered to in the capital, and generally speaking, in all the Turkish [Ottoman] provinces, except in Egypt."[101] His statement bears directly on conditions in the nineteenth century and on Egypt's exceptionalism under the rule of Mehmed Ali (1805–48) and his successors. The deadly brutality of slave merchants dealing in Egypt's stepped-up African trade in this period was repeatedly decried by witnesses who had experience of the continental passage.[102] Of course, the trade into Egypt was for the benefit of Egypt's nominal Ottoman overseers as well as for the province's semiautonomous regime.

[97] Unlike other schools of Islamic law, the Sunni Hanafi school required the father's explicit declaration for the child to gain legal recognition.

[98] Imber, "Eleven Fetvas," 141–9; Boğaç Ergene, "Pursuing Justice in an Islamic Context: Dispute Resolution in Ottoman Courts of Law," *Political and Legal Anthropology Review* 27, no. 1 (2004): 54.

[99] Toledano, *Slavery and Abolition*, 54–80; Chapter 4 in this volume.

[100] Walz, "Black Slavery in Egypt," 145.

[101] White, *Three Years*, 2:349.

[102] British and Foreign Anti-Slavery Society, *The Anti-Slavery Reporter, under the Sanction of the British and Foreign Anti-Slavery Society*, October 21, 1840, 267–70; October 21, 1840, 270; December 2, 1840, 311; January 13, 1841, 1–3; April 20, 1842, 64; November 29, 1843, 221–2; September 1, 1846, 133–4; October 1, 1846, 154–5; November 2, 1846, 181–3; see also Lane, *An Account of the Manners*, 185–6; White, *Three Years*, 2:293.

The merchants and dealers most implicated in the inhumane treatment of Africans were the trade's wholesalers, the frontline drovers-cum-raiders known as *cellab* or *celeb esirci*s in Ottoman Turkish (Ar. pl., *jellab*). It was they who rounded up and drove sub-Saharan Africans overland to northern markets. Scholars of slavery have long contended that slaves are most vulnerable to bodily harm between capture and the market. It is in that space, they argue, that slaves' humanity is seemingly suspended, and they most partake of the character of commodities. Indeed, the term for their transporters, *cellab*, is the same as that used for dealers in livestock.[103] The intensified importation of slaves – as of sub-Saharan Africans into Egypt and Morocco for use there and beyond in the nineteenth century, of sub-Saharan Africans into Morocco in the early eighteenth century, and of Europeans into the Ottoman heartland throughout the centuries – also aggravated those slaves' commoditized condition and the occasions for inhumane treatment.

Slave trafficking in Istanbul and Cairo may have been comparatively well ordered in many periods, but political upheavals could devastate fragile bureaucratic safeguards. Sudden increases in supply often overwhelmed supervisory mechanisms. The consequent drop in cash value increased the possibility of abuses, as slaves could be had at bargain prices and the circle of buyers widened beyond strict accountability. Prior to the nineteenth century, military campaigns had produced such sudden spikes in supply. In the 1820s, Greek insurrectionary activity led to the sudden and shocking enslavement of several thousand Greek subjects. Those who were declared rebels, often entire communities, were stripped of their *zimmi* protections as indigenous minorities. Official retribution was violent and indiscriminate when some in the population were suspected of collusion in the massacres perpetrated by Greek rebels against Ottoman Muslims and Jews during the uprising. Greek women and children were seized and sold on the market when their kin, neighbors, or even distant compatriots were implicated in the rebellion.[104]

The Crimean War (1853–6) and continuing British abolitionist pressures, especially with regard to the African trade, periodically interrupted the flow of both African and Caucasian slaves to imperial markets. The brutality of Russia's Caucasian offensives in the 1850s and 1860s produced a reversal of the downward trend in white slave imports. In the flight of Circassian refugees, including tens of thousands of peasant slaves legally attached to

[103] Lane, *An Account of the Manners*, 186. Wright's account of slave transport focuses on a number of Saharan peoples (Tuareg, Tebu, or Tibbu) whose domination of particular Saharan routes was among the most cruel and careless of life, including the lives of the slave traders themselves (*Trans-Saharan Slave Trade*, 7–8, 82–6).

[104] For events on Chios and their aftermath, see Slade, *Records of Travels*, 1:57–62; Andrew Wheatcroft, *Infidels: A History of the Conflict between Christendom and Islam* (New York, 2004), 248–52.

Circassian lords, escape from Russian rule did not liberate them from the bonded state. Although many in the Ottoman regime were inclined to recognize their freedom, the slaves' landlord-owners, now resident in the empire, were for a time successful in retaining ownership rights.[105]

The perception of female sexuality as women's own instrument is more problematic than the received historiographical wisdom and than Islamic legal and moral prescriptions would have it. The widespread view of women as quintessentially sexual beings provided the ideological backdrop for the perception of male-female contact as inherently sexually charged, with males the unwitting victims of women's sexual allure.[106] Young boys were regarded as threatening to morals as well, but for the most part, cautions about their seductiveness or sexual appeal were confined to legal and moral admonitions. In practice, young boys were not protectively veiled or segregated out of adult male company.

Grace, charm, and a talent for music are endearing attributes, but in the eyes of many historical beholders, they were indistinguishable from sexual allurements. Such attributes, in fact, lent themselves to sexualization, given the strict rules governing gender relationships in free society. Free women were sequestered for the sake of sexual purity and family honor. Slave women, without family and the right to honor, were quintessential outsiders.[107] They could be offered for sale to any male who could afford the price. Of course, not all male owners availed themselves of concubinage. Some refrained from doing so even when slave women were supplied to them for exactly that purpose.

Sultan Süleyman the Magnificent was a paragon of fidelity during his marriage to Roxelana. He apparently remained faithful to her for more than twenty years, until her death in 1558, despite the powers and temptations of his *Arabian Nights*–like existence.[108] Most men and most households did not aspire to the domestic styles of the rich and famous. In the majority of Ottoman families, monogamous families, most did not possess slaves, either male or female. Nor was monogamy merely a matter of economics, as it is commonly portrayed.[109] Men who might have afforded polygyny did not necessarily take on a slave concubine or an additional wife. Family sensitivities, protective conditions set in the marriage contract, wifely resistance or attachment to one's wife, and the ease of male-initiated divorce combined to make polygyny and

[105] Toledano, *Ottoman Slave Trade*, 148–91; Toledano, *Slavery and Abolition*, 81–111; Erdem, *Slavery in the Ottoman Empire*, 113–24.

[106] Fatima Mernissi, *Beyond the Veil: Male-Female Dynamics in Modern Muslim Society*, rev. ed. (Bloomington, Ind., 1987), 27–45; Peirce, "Seniority, Sexuality, 174–81; Andrews and Kalpaklı, *Age of Beloveds*, 132.

[107] Harald Motzki, "Wal-muhsanatu mina n-nisā'i illā mā malakat aimānukum (Koran 4:24) und die koranische Sexualethik," *Der Islam* 63 (1986): 192–218.

[108] Peirce, *Imperial Harem*, 58–90. [109] Zilfi, "'We Don't Get Along,'" 269.

the acquisition of a concubine or additional wife uncongenial or unnecessary in many cases.[110]

Sexuality was a potent instrument of women's empowerment and survival in the Ottoman world. It is, however, wrongly perceived as singularly female and inevitably advantageous. The misperception is predicated on an urbane slave-holding world. In the minds of its defenders, slavery's authoritarian paternalism was imagined in the tempering context of prosperous stability, scrupulous personal ethics, and efficient legal recourse. But rather than seamless paternalism, domestic slavery was the sum of dubious, unfatherly parts. Much of the interaction between masters and slaves took place in a moral gray zone. The conduct of slave drovers, dealers, masters, and mistresses was largely unseen and often occurred outside the empire's borders. The Circassian Şemsigül, whose *ümm-i veled* case was brought to court in Egypt, was fortunate, to some extent, in her neighbors. In a less residential or settled environment, she might have been abused further or killed, and the authorities would not have known about it or have been legally obligated to care.[111]

Regardless of whether or not individual slaves had to endure terrible mistreatment, they were subject to a volatile captive life. Security and familial integration during slavery may have been tasted only briefly, if at all. The ability of the female slave to employ her sexuality to advantage was most likely to bring only a temporary elevation. Any advancement might disappear overnight because of a rival's triumph, the owner's mere lustful usage, or his death or indebtedness. Ultimately, as an instrument of female agency, sexuality was a thin reed.

The limitations and disadvantages of female sexuality began with the act of enslavement. Although female sexuality afforded women a degree of agency, it was also their most fundamental vulnerability. Historically, it had served as an inducement for the seizure of outsiders' – however defined – wives, sisters, and daughters. In ancient Mesopotamia, home to the earliest records of slavery, the word for "slave girl" predates that for "male slave." Foreign

[110] Although conditions (sing., *şart*) in the marriage contract were generally impermissible according to the Hanafi school of Sunni jurisprudence, they were known to have been employed. The degree to which they were legally enforceable, however, is a different matter. Because polygamy and polygyny were licit according to the Qur'an, an antipolygamy stipulation (e.g., if the husband were to take a second wife, divorce would ensue) seems to have amounted only to a promise on the husband's part, that is, that he would release his first wife if he decided to take a second; see Joseph Schacht, *An Introduction to Islamic Law* (Oxford, 1964), 163, on the nonbinding nature of such stipulations. For other commentaries and evidence of usage, see John L. Esposito, with Natana J. DeLong-Bas, *Women in Muslim Family Law*, 2nd ed. (Syracuse, N.Y., 2001), 22–3; Judith E. Tucker, *In the House of the Law: Gender and Islamic Law in Ottoman Syria and Palestine* (Berkeley, Calif., 1998), 38–9; Jennings, "Women in Early 17th-Century Ottoman Judicial Records: The Sharia Court of Anatolian Kayseri," *JESHO* 18 (1975): 88, 92; Nelly Hanna, "Marriage among Merchant Families in Seventeenth-Century Cairo," in Sonbol, *Women, the Family*, 146–50; Abdal-Rehim Abdal-Rahman Abdal-Rehim, "The Family and Gender Laws in Egypt during the Ottoman Period," in Sonbol, *Women, the Family*, 110–11.

[111] Toledano, *Slavery and Abolition*, 54–80; cf. Erdem, *Slavery in the Ottoman Empire*, 162–3.

females early on emerged as the preferred and numerically preponderant brand of enslaved captive in the ancient Near East and Mediterranean.[112] Except for children and the very old, women were society's least defended and least mobile element. As caretakers of children and the old, their vulnerability and fate were likely to be inseparable from them. If their own men were called to duties elsewhere, women had little hope against the violence of other men, whether foreign attackers or men supposedly of their own kind. Men doing battle with unarmed women, especially women with children, could count on victory. If a well-ordered household was a captive's fate, its reassuring environment dissociated slavery from the aggression that had brought it about and from the wider climate that rewarded such behavior.

The tenuousness of female sexual advantage, however, was not just a function of the enslavement process and masterly caprice. It was also contingent on domestic order in the largest sense. Depredations by urban mobs – usually led and manned by soldiers and paramilitaries – and provincial bandits, which often involved the violation of women, occurred with frightening frequency in the seventeenth century.[113] One of the nastiest incidents ended in the murder of the Grand Vizier Siyavuş Pasha, the son-in-law and former slave of the eminent Köprülü family, who ran afoul of rebellious soldiers. Siyavuş was slaughtered in 1688 at the door of his harem, unsuccessfully defending his family, including his Köprülü wife. Seeing that only some of Siyavuş's women, children, and servants survived the horrors inflicted on the household, a mosque preacher who witnessed the tumult despaired for the lives of innocents: "our families, our children, our property – we're not safe anymore."[114] He had reason to worry, as the rebels had treated the free members of Siyavuş's household as brutally as the slaves and the servants. As a posthumous tribute to Siyavuş lamented, "[T]hey made his property booty and his children slaves." Indeed, the rebels had done just that.[115]

Yet mutineers and bandits were not the only violators of the norms of decency. The state orchestrated its own despoliation of families. Nowhere is

112 Robert McC. Adams, *The Evolution of Urban Society* (Chicago, 1966), 96–7, 102; Davis, *Slavery and Human Progress*, 14; Goody, "Slavery in Time and Space," 20.

113 For various incidents, see von Hammer, *Geschichte*, 5:494–7, 6:470; Naima, *Tarih*, 6:87–8; Mehmed Halife, *Tarih-i Gılmanı*, *TOEM İlaveler 1* (Istanbul, 1340/1924), 13, 49; Thomas Roe, *The Negotiations of Sir Thomas Roe, in His Embassy to the Ottoman Porte from the Year 1621 to 1628 Inclusive* (London, 1740), 114. The attacks on houses and family members that surrounded the fall of Feyzullah Efendi in 1703 were a combination of mob violence and state actions; see Abdülkadir Özcan, ed., *Anonim Osmanlı Tarihi (1099–1116/1688–1704)* (Ankara, 2000), 240–1, 251.

114 Defterdar, *Zübde* (1977–9 ed.), 1:116. For Siyavuş, see Silahdar Mehmed, *Silahdar Tarihi*, 2:332–3; Danişmend, *İzahlı*, 3:463, 5:45–6; and Raşid, *Tarih-i Raşid*, 2:15, although Raşid's and Defterdar's accounts are identical. Compare a similar attack on a residence and harem in Egypt, in Mary Ann Fay, "The Ties That Bound: Women and Households in Eighteenth-Century Egypt," in Sonbol, *Women, the Family*, 167.

115 Hâfız Hüseyin Ayvansarayı, *Mecmuâ-i Tevarih*, ed. Fahri Ç. Derin and Vâhid Çabuk (Istanbul, 1985), 411.

this clearer than in the disposition of slaves on the disgrace of their office-holding male owners. In cases of sovereign displeasure, when dismissal and exile did not suffice, the fallen official's humiliation was taken into his intimate life, stripping him of his slaves along with his ordinary property. Not only the slaves and retainers of the household but also women who were his concubines, including slave mothers of his children and any children who had not been recognized as free, were taken as well. All were inventoried like so much furniture, to be bundled off to the slave market or distributed to favored officials.[116] This further evidence of the culture of violence that surrounded the military-administrative elites continued so long as elite confiscation remained the (unwritten) law of the land. In its time, it promoted bitterness and the desire for revenge. In 1744, after the death of Azımzade Süleyman Pasha, the Ottoman governor of Damascus, the ferocious conduct of the authorities in connection with confiscation proceedings left his servants and loved ones stripped and tortured. Süleyman's nephew cursed the imperial treasurer (*defterdar*) who had overseen the search: "Curse you to hell, you bastard. I have not forgotten what you did to my uncle's women."[117]

The view of sexual appeal as a uniquely female advantage in slavery also disregards the evidence of male liaisons with other males. Homosocial, if not homosexual, relationships between senior males and free and slave male dependents were commonplace. They were partly a consequence of the segregated gender system and the value placed on things male. The same rules of personal conduct and societal organization that exalted maleness and routinely criminalized the casual mixing of unrelated men and women fostered homosocial norms and homoerotic behavior. Appearance and comportment in a young male inspired paternalistic attention. Elite recruitment and mobility operated much as did employment in ordinary crafts and guilds. Both were premised on personal sponsorship. In particular, senior males oversaw judgments of merit. They set the criteria and decided how they were to be met. It behooved dependent males to ingratiate themselves with their superiors. Young boys could not have done otherwise.

The same attractive qualities that propelled certain young men over others of equal or superior merit in one or another vocational track could also spawn less filial attachments, not far removed, if removed at all, from sexual engagement.[118] Young men who became the love objects or prey of men

[116] Slade, *Records of Travels*, 1:442, identifies one of many incidents that occurred in connection with the suppression of the Janissaries in the late 1820s. See also Röhrborn, "Konfiskation," 347; Abraham Marcus, "Privacy in Eighteenth-Century Aleppo: The Limits of Cultural Ideals," *IJMES* 18, no. 2 (1986): 170.

[117] That is, Süleyman al-'Azm; Yüksel, "Vakıf-Müsadere," 404; see also Karl K. Barbir, *Ottoman Rule in Damascus, 1708–1758* (Princeton, N.J., 1980), 31.

[118] Fleischer, *Bureaucrat and Intellectual*, 223, and Fleischer's online comments on H-Turk, "Shehir Oglanları ve Bekar Odaları [web spellings]", October 29, 2001; Peirce, "Seniority, Sexuality," 175; Andrews and Kalpaklı, *Age of Beloveds*, 285–7; Dror Ze'evi, *Producing Desire: Changing Sexual Discourse in the Ottoman Middle East 1500–1900* (Berkeley, Calif.,

in authority, as well as youths whose job it was to play the accommodating acolyte, were as aware of the instrumentality of sexuality as was any slave woman. It is not known how pervasive homosexual encounters and relationships were in Ottoman society. Given the many in-jokes and asides about pederasty among the elites, apparently they were rife.[119] Female life in polygynous harems gave rise to salacious speculation by European travelers, especially male travelers. Their comments, like Slade's on harem women's resorting to "a singular amusement for consolation," were usually brief and uninformed, as befit their lack of direct knowledge.[120] This is not to suggest that female same-sex eroticism and lesbian affairs did not occur, merely that neither their possibility nor their reality spawned the endless commentary associated with male homosexuality.

Any number of stories circulated about seventeenth- and eighteenth-century sultans' attachment to male favorites and lack of zeal for female company. The fact that several rulers – most notably Mahmud I and Osman III – also failed to produce children lent support to the stories. The sexual exploitation of young boys as a feature of urban high and low life, in slave commerce, and provincial banditry was well established.[121] Equally commonplace was the ambiguous role of young boys brought along as attendants on overland campaigns and

2006), 88–91, 156–8; Khaled El-Rouayheb, *Before Homosexuality in the Arab-Islamic World, 1500–1800* (Chicago, 2005); J. W. Wright and Everett K. Rowson, eds., *Homoeroticism in Classical Arabic Literature* (New York, 1997); James A. Bellamy, "Sex and Society in Islamic Popular Literature," in Afaf Lutfi al-Sayyid-Marsot, ed., *Society and the Sexes in Medieval Islam* (Malibu, Calif., 1979), 23–42; Eve Kosofsky Sedgwick, *Between Men: English Literature and Male Homosocial Desire* (New York, 1985), 1–5.

119 Heath W. Lowry, "Impropriety and Impiety among the Early Ottoman Sultans (1351–1451)," *Turkish Studies Association Journal* 26, no. 2 (2002): 29–38. Referring to the prevalence of sodomy among the elites, Evliya Çelebi recounts the tale of a fountain that supposedly stopped running whenever a catamite walked by. Of seventy passersby, sixty-five, according to the fountain's interrupted flow, had been sodomized in their youth; see Dankoff, *Ottoman Mentality*, 119–20.

120 Slade, *Records of Travels*, 2:318. See also Charles Thornton Forster and F. H. Blackburn Daniell, eds., *The Life and Letters of Ogier Ghiselin de Busbecq* (London, 1881), 1:230–2; Judy Mabro, *Veiled Half-Truths: Western Travellers' Perceptions of Middle Eastern Women* (1991; repr., London, 1996), 137.

121 For the various kinds of male-male congress, see Çatalcalı Ali, *Şeyhülislam Fetvaları*, 121; Yıldırım et al., *83 Numaralı Mühimme*, no. 61; Dernschwam, *Tagebuch*, 123, 147, 387; Jennings, *Christians and Muslims*, 128; D'Ohsson, *Tableau*, 4, no. 2, 324–5; Louis Laurent d'Arvieux, *Mémoires du chevalier d'Arvieux... contenant ses voyages à Constantinople, dans l'Asie, la Syrie, la Palestine, l'Égypte, et la Barbarie...*, 6 vols. (Paris, 1735), 4:390–6; G. A. Olivier, *Voyage dans l'Empire Othoman, l'Égypte et la Perse* (Paris, 1801–7), 1:162–4; Jean-Louis Bacqué-Grammont, "Sur deux affaires mineures dans les 'registres d'affaires importantes,'" in Robert Mantran, ed., *Mémorial Ömer Lûtfi Barkan* (Paris, 1980), 1–10; Andrews and Kalpaklı, *Age of Beloveds*, 285–7; Sieur des Joanots Du Vignau, *A New Account of the Present Condition of the Turkish Affairs* (London, 1688), 120; and Slade, *Records of Travels*, 1:176, 230–1. Slade, who was familiar with the issue of homosexuality from his British experience, was less self-righteous about Ottoman practice than were his contemporaries. See Arthur N. Gilbert, "Buggery and the British Navy, 1700–1861," in Wayne R. Dynes and Stephen Donaldson, eds., *History of Homosexuality in Europe and America* (New York, 1992), 132–58.

navy vessels. In an effort to ensure discipline in the military during the wars of the late seventeenth century, the Kadızadeli preacher Vani Efendi saw to it that noncombatant youths would not be allowed to accompany their masters into war. The questionable nature of the practice had for a long time been blatant and did not cease with the Vienna campaign.[122] The institutionalized positioning of dependent youths in the ambit of dominant males, and the reserving of insider women for marital procreation and senior male priority, gave support to the practice. Nonetheless, the demand for outsider women was in no way diminished.

[122] D'Arvieux, *Mémoires*, 4:390–1; Galland, *Journal*, 1:112; Zilfi, *Politics of Piety*, 149.

CHAPTER 6

Feminizing slavery

> A twofold reward in heaven is promised to the man who educates his slave girl, frees her and marries her.
>
> – A *hadith* of the Prophet Muhammad[1]

> Wind of Morning, heartfelt greetings to the one I love convey; [m]ay his life be long, and may his slave be never far away.
>
> – The poet Dâi (fl. 1420)[2]

The market for women

For centuries, the Esir Pazarı, literally "Slave Market," was the commercial center for the selling of male and female slaves in the capital.[3] Only a few doors down from the Istanbul marketplace par excellence, the Covered Bazaar (Kapalı Çarşı),[4] the market shared ground space with one of Istanbul's cathedral mosques, the Nur-i Osmaniye. The mosque, though, had risen only in the 1750s. The Slave Market in one form or another – descriptions of its porches, rooms, and courtyard vary – predated it by more than a century. The Byzantine slave market had apparently stood near the same site.[5] The market was within walking distance of Topkapı Palace and of government headquarters (the Porte), although the sultan and his entitled viziers would have approached it mounted or in carriages, unless they chose to visit incognito.[6]

1 *EI2*, s.v. "'Abd," by R. Brunschvig.

2 Nermin Menemencioğlu and Fahir İz, eds., *The Penguin Book of Turkish Verse* (Harmondsworth, U.K., 1978), 77.

3 The term *esir* (pl., *esirler* or *üsera*), though common usage for "slave" or "enslaved person" in the eighteenth century, most properly refers to captives taken in war.

4 At the time, referred to as the old and new *bedestans* or *bezistans*, literally "cloth markets," although they sold everything from jewelry and weaponry to clothing and sundries; Halil İnalcık, "The Hub of the City: The Bedestan of Istanbul," *IJTS* 1, no. 1 (1979–80): 1–17.

5 Discussions of the market's structure before the 1830s and 1840s, from which most descriptions derive, are cited in Kömürcüyan, *İstanbul Tarihi*, 314–15. See also Toledano, *Ottoman Slave Trade*, 52–3; *DBİA*, s.v. "Esir Pazarı," by Necdet Sakaoğlu; see also Erdem, *Slavery in the Ottoman Empire*, 36, on the structure of the market over time.

6 Topkapı Palace was abandoned as the imperial residence in the latter part of Mahmud II's reign but continued to be used for some official functions.

Fig. 17. "The Mosque of Osmanié [Nur-i Osmaniye] from the Slave Market." Pardoe, *Beauties of the Bosphorus*.

Foreign visitors often confused the Slave Market with the Women's Market (Avrat Pazarı) some distance away.[7] At the Women's Market, women from nearby neighborhoods came to buy and sell food and wares.[8] Foreigners' imperfect knowledge of the city was compounded by the misleading certitudes of equally ill-informed locals, including resident compatriots, who may or may not have realized their error. The muddled identification, however, is reflective of the historical interest in the people – especially European captives and the females among them – who were to be seen in the Slave Market. The confusion also points to another truth, namely that, by the late eighteenth century, if not before, women were not just the majority but the vast majority of slaves bought and sold in the Slave Market and the capital as a whole. The Slave Market's misnomer was less a tourist's gaffe than it at first appears.

Gendering the trade

The range of women's relationships amid conditions of slavery underscores women's centrality as actors and subjects in the long life of slavery in Ottoman

[7] See, e.g., Slade, *Records of Travels*, 2:239, and repeated in his *Slade's Travels*, 193–4.

[8] See P. Ğ. İnciciyan, *XVIII. Asırda İstanbul*, trans. Hrand D. Andreasyan (Istanbul, 1956), 27, for comments on the Avrat Pazarı in the eighteenth century, and John Sanderson, a British envoy, regarding the sixteenth century (qtd. in Peirce, *Imperial Harem of the Sultans*, 329). See also Semavi Eyice, "İstanbul'un Mahalle ve Semt Adları," *Türkiyat Mecmuası* 14 (1965): 210.

lands. The enabling mechanisms behind women's many roles and the shifts in those roles over the centuries had their origins in the changing demographics of enslavement and slave labor. The overall number of slaves, especially as war captives transported to Ottoman lands, is not known and probably not knowable with any certainty. The fluidity of slavery early on makes accurate counting difficult. Frontier exchanges, wholesale ransoming of captives, private transactions outside official reckoning, and the widespread use of conditional slavery arrangements were common practice in the fourteenth, fifteenth, and sixteenth centuries. The frequency of *mükatebe* contracts and other attenuations of absolute slavery points to a multiplicity of slave tenures in early times, as well as a multiplicity of slave meanings. The competing internal demands for ransomable targets, laborers, craftspeople, soldiers, and female menials and reproducers argue for a certain gender balance in the supply of enslaved persons in the expansionist centuries of the empire.

Between the late fifteenth and the late seventeenth centuries, the height of Ottoman imperialism, multiple demands remained in play. Female captives continued to flow into the empire. All slaves, though, came in greater numbers and in a wider variety of ethnicities than had previously been possible. Africans were available in greater numbers after the incorporation of the contiguous Arab lands in the early sixteenth century. Rising Ottoman pressure against the western and northern frontiers exposed additional Slavic regions to Ottoman-sponsored raids. Ransoming continued unabated. The capture of wealthy Europeans of all ages was a lucrative sideline for Ottoman soldiery on the Austrian and Russian fronts. On and around the Mediterranean Sea, hostage taking became more systematized at the hands of European (Christian) and Ottoman and Moroccan (Muslim) pirates, who plundered one another's ships and communities. For Algiers, Tunis, and Tripoli, raiding for ransom targets was an identifying pillar of their regencies through the eighteenth century.[9]

In the high imperial era of the late fifteenth through the early seventeenth centuries, with their elaborate, labor-intensive ceremonial, military bravado, and bureaucratic specialization, slavery showed a pronounced masculine tilt. There was both a robust demand for male slave labor and a glorification of the male slave as a loyal and superior officer of the realm. The adulation of male virtues had powerful social and sexual resonance. In terms of domestic slavery, it affected the gift value of boys relative to girls in this period. In the kind of person-to-person exchanges that were the lifeblood of grandee networking, the father of Grand Vizier Melek Ahmed Pasha (d. 1662) received "as gifts seventy outstanding slave boys and beautiful virgin slave girls" for his own

[9] See Daniel Panzac, *Barbary Corsairs: The End of a Legend*, trans. Victoria Hobson and John E. Hawkes (Leiden, 2005); Valensi, "Esclaves chrétiens," 1267–88, regarding the often limited economic role played by piracy in the North African city-states. See also Palmira Brummett, *Ottoman Seapower and Diplomacy in the Age of Discovery* (Albany, N.Y., 1994), 93–104, on sponsored and unsponsored Ottoman corsair activity.

use or for re-gifting to followers.[10] This kind of scene was played out in countless mansions of the ruling orders as well as in the imperial palace. Gifts of cloth, furs, and gold were relatively sterile in comparison to the rich, lifelong potential afforded by wealth in people. More formally in the period of expansion, the institutional commitment to male slavery reflected the empire's increased manpower needs for its broadened institutionalization and sovereign projection. Male slaves also met the ruling classes' voracious appetite for male dependents to serve in private militarized households.[11]

The mobilization of male war prisoners produced slave laborers by the thousand for countless building and reparation projects throughout the enlarged realm. Insofar as internal recruitment was concerned, the application of the *devşirme* brought in, on average, a thousand or more boys for government service each year of the more than two hundred years – up to the early eighteenth century – in which the levy was applied.[12] As Janissaries and palace servitors, the unfree youths quickly came to represent the ideal slave and servant. The iconic demeanor that overawed European visitors was a favorite motif of Ottoman illustrators as well. The vivid miniatures that focused on the sovereign also depicted his wealth in people in the row upon row of male officials and servants. The portrayal of submissiveness was a commentary on ruling-class masculinity as much as on Ottoman sovereignty.[13] Even when the Janissaries, the soldierly center of *kul* slavery, came to be equated with rebellion and disorder, the image of the sultan's *kul*s as paragons of obedience remained nostalgically in place. Whatever group might be held up as a model, loyalty and deference to seniority remained the lubricants of social relations.

A sense of the value attached to male captives in the sixteenth century and much of the seventeenth can be gleaned from slave prices and ownership data. The findings, however, are scattered over a great deal of Ottoman time and space. Notwithstanding their discontinuity, pricing data suggest gender balance early on rather than the overwhelming female preference that has been taken as a given for virtually all Middle Eastern periods and places. It is worth reexamining price ranges and fluctuations, if only to gain perspective on the hearsay anecdotes that dot Ottoman and European narratives. It is true that virginal beauties at times sold for extraordinary sums. Kömürcüyan, writing in the seventeenth century, mentions that he had heard of girls being sold for a thousand gold florins.[14] In any case, neither the amounts nor the sporadic

10 Dankoff, *Intimate Life*, 272; compare Galland, *Journal*, for the pervasiveness of slaves in social exchange.

11 İnalcık, "Servile Labor," 26.

12 *EI2*, s.v., "Devshirme," by V. L. Ménage. Although the exact date of the last conscription is still debated, it is thought to have taken place in the early 1700s under Ahmed III.

13 On the illustration of submission, if not subservience, see Brummett, "Ceremonies of Submission."

14 Kömürcüyan, *İstanbul Tarihi*, 62.

reports of such sales shed much light on the history of the trade, much less on the fluid conditions of the eighteenth and early nineteenth centuries.

As Sahillioğlu suggested some time ago, as a pricing rule of thumb, the market value of slaves ran parallel to that of real estate.[15] In the seventeenth and eighteenth centuries, a modest dwelling and a modestly favored male or female slave could be purchased for upwards of 1,500 *akçes* each.[16] Smaller quarters in less desirable neighborhoods could cost less, as could an infirm or older slave. A very fine abode, however, and a very well-favored female slave might each be had for five thousand *akçes* in the early centuries and twice that in the later ones.[17] These averages, though, are only that. Above all, the high points and troughs of market prices were reflective of the irregular influx of slaves.

Although individual women could fetch extraordinary sums in high-demand, high-price markets like Istanbul and Cairo, neither the prices nor the numbers of women sold reflected the female market as a whole. The recurring though exceptional superprices of some females relative to males of like age, health, and origin suggest the competitive and speculative value placed on idealized female beauty and fecund possibility. As in other Old World societies, including the internal African market – and in contrast to the Atlantic trade – the price of female slaves, especially at first sale, more often than not exceeded that for males. Nonetheless, a certain amount of gender-neutral variability characterized the Ottoman market.[18] In a sample of Istanbul estates in the seventeenth century, among slaves in the highest price brackets (ten thousand to more than twenty thousand *akçes*), women outnumbered men by a substantial margin (110 to 45). The ratio is in proportion to the number of females to males in the overall sample; roughly a third of both males and females sold for the highest prices. In the next-highest price ranges, the number of females and males in each category tended to run almost even. It is interesting that the highest-priced slave by far in the period was a male, the forty-eight thousand *akçes* for which he was sold being double that for the

[15] On prices over the centuries, see Nicolay, *Nauigations*, 62; Kömürcüyan, *İstanbul Tarihi*, 62; *Anti-Slavery Reporter*, October 21, 1840, 269; January 27, 1841, 19; March 2, 1846, 47; Ubicini, *Letters on Turkey*, 1:146; Bowring, *Report on Egypt*, 99; Saz, *Imperial Harem of the Sultans*, 59–62, 76; Frederick Millingen [Osman Bey, Major Vladimir Andrejevich], *Les femmes de Turquie* (Paris, 1883), 227; Sahillioğlu, "Slaves in the Social," 90–5; Çetin, *Sicillere göre Bursa'da*, 50; Baer, "Slavery and Its Abolition," 172; Toledano, *Ottoman Slave Trade*, 62–80; Schroeter, "Slave Markets and Slavery," 193–5; Davis, *Ottoman Lady*, 116n36; Sak, "Konya'da," 169, 175; Robert Mantran, *Istanbul dans la deuxieme moitié de la XVIIe siècle: Essai d'histoire institutionelle, economique et sociale* (Paris, 1962), 508.

[16] At an exchange rate of 80 *akçes* per (silver) *guruş* in the early seventeenth century and about 120 *akçes* during the eighteenth century. See also Toledano, *Ottoman Slave Trade*, 62, for rates of exchange in the mid-nineteenth century.

[17] Sahillioğlu, "Slaves in the Social," 95.

[18] See James L. Watson and Jack Goody, in Watson, *Asian and African Systems*, 13, 37, on female-male price differentials in Africa. Slade (*Slade's Travels in Turkey*, 295–6) slyly claims that young males cost more than females in his time, a phenomenon he ascribed to the combination of their sexual appeal as boys and usefulness as adults.

closest female.[19] With regard to resold or secondhand slaves who were being sought for general household work, the gap between male and female prices tended to close. Buyers in that market were apt to be looking for acculturation and proved skills.

The lack of reliable age and skills data precludes cross-tabulations of slaves' ages and vocational skills with price brackets. Other than the fact that prepubescent and barely pubescent females were usually those who sold at peak prices, the age distribution in the majority of male and female slave sales might have shown a high correlation between life-cycle stage and social valuation.[20] Even apart from the matter of virginity, which we know carried a premium for young females, do available pricing figures indicate that women lost value more quickly than males?

An analysis of primary slave owners – *askeri* dignitaries and officeholders – and their estates in the fifteenth through the seventeenth centuries argues for there having been greater balance in the social and cultural importance of male and female slaves prior to the eighteenth century. Inventories of ruling-class estates (*tereke*) in Edirne between 1545 and 1659 show a total of 140 slaves. Of the 140, 86 (61 percent) were males, compared with 54 (39 percent) females.[21] Figures for Konya in the seventeenth century show an even larger male-female disparity, with male slaves outnumbering females by almost four to one.[22] Similar findings from the court of Lefkoşa (Nicosia), Cyprus, in the sixteenth and seventeenth centuries led Jennings to question the very notion of a high female-to-male slave norm in those centuries.[23] Bursa and Istanbul estates in the late sixteenth and seventeenth centuries give evidence of more females than males. In Bursa, though, the difference is relatively small, 282 to 201 (16 percent). In Istanbul, the imperial capital and social podium for its potentate households, females outnumbered males 2 to 1 (342 to 171).[24] However, Istanbul's numerous *kul* soldiers and officials attached to the palace and the sultan would not have shown up in these kinds of nondynastic estate inventories. Edirne's contrasting pattern of male dominance may stem from peculiarities of the data or of Edirne's geographical location. In its role as a staging area for both the army and imperial hunting parties, Edirne's labor patterns may have reflected more rustic occupations and the needs of the Ottoman line of march. Like Üsküdar in its role as an Anatolian gateway to the capital, Edirne was a stopping-off point for travelers to and

19 Öztürk, *Askeri Kassama*, 206–9, 214–16. There is no indication that the man was a eunuch, although eunuchs usually fetched higher prices than sexually intact males of like origin and age. However, even eunuchs' elevated price did not approach forty-eight thousand *akçes*. See Hogendorn, "Location of the 'Manufacture' of Eunuchs," 41–68; *Anti-Slavery Reporter*, October 21, 1840, 269; Baer, "Slavery and Its Abolition," 172.

20 See Peirce, "Seniority, Sexuality," 169–96, for life-cycle stages and social roles and expectations of free men and women.

21 İnalcık, "Servile Labor," 27, including his discussion of the study by Ö. L. Barkan.

22 Sak, "Konya'da," 162.

23 Jennings, "Black Slaves and Free Blacks," 560.

24 Özdeğer, *1463–1640 Yılları Bursa*, 122–33; Öztürk, *Askeri Kassama*, 201–2.

from the Balkans. The care, feeding, and rehabilitation of human beings and animals en route may have called for a more masculine workforce in the region.

Estimates of female-male slave ratios give rise to the question of gender bias in the incidence of slaves' premature emancipation and in their social mobility. Much of the information regarding domestic slave numbers derives from the records of posthumous estates. Slaves who were manumitted prior to an owner's death do not appear as property in estate tallies, although former slaves (masc., *ma'tuk*; fem. *ma'tuka*) could be mentioned in other connections. Might female slaves be undercounted in some of the available figures because of premature emancipation? The unduly positive historical and historiographical spin that has been put on the *ümm-i veled* status and female sexuality in general has led to the notion that women were more likely than men to have gained early emancipation. There is no compelling evidence that this was so. One wonders how it could be so given males' greater access to conditional contracts, self-emancipation through flight, and the higher costs of retaining adult male slaves in general. If anything, male slaves were seriously undercounted to begin with. Not just the sultan's and state's *kul* property, who were largely outside the purview of Islamic law (i.e., not slaves in the legal sense), but the invisibles of state maritime operations would not have appeared as slaves in estate data. Both Ottoman and European calculations are prone to overlook the thousands of (male) galley slaves consumed by the great Mediterranean navies and murderous sea battles of the sixteenth and seventeenth centuries.[25] Although galley servitude quickly became standard punishment for indigenous lawbreakers,[26] and the Ottomans employed paid seamen for ship and shore work, their combined numbers were often dwarfed in the earliest centuries by foreign captives and *reaya* draftees.[27] İnalcık's studies of slaveholding led him some time ago to conclude that the ruling class in the early period, in addition to being "the single major group keeping the slave market alive," in fact disposed of more military slaves than any other category of slave.[28]

By the latter half of the eighteenth century, the Ottoman slave trade – the trade of and for the capital and its core northern-tier provinces – had become an increasingly more female-targeted enterprise. Whether for domestic labor or for sexual services, the capture of women fueled enslavement operations. The widened recruitment of European armies and Ottoman failures on the

[25] Peabody, *There Are No Slaves in France*, notes the omission of galley slaves from French calculations of slavery and slave numbers in France through the eighteenth century.

[26] The term for galley slavery, *kürek*, was synonymous with "hard labor" in the postgalley days of the Ottoman navy; individuals sentenced to *kürek* in the eighteenth and nineteenth centuries were destined for hard labor, on the docks or elsewhere.

[27] İpşirli, "XVI. Asrın İkinci Yarısında," 205–7; Aktaş et al., *3 Numaralı Mühimme*, 1:290–1, 318, 413, 550, 681–2.

[28] İnalcık, "Servile Labor," 27.

battlefield from the late seventeenth century onward put many populations beyond the reach of would-be Ottoman captors; it was especially hard for losing armies to capture males. In the empire itself, demand for male slaves waned. Partly in response to problems of supply, the vizier and pasha households of these later times turned more and more to free manpower.[29] The slave system itself did not flag. It was increasingly sustained by great and near-great households operating more as domestic and consumerist space than as cornerstones of an expansionist empire.

The supplanting of military slavery by freeborn recruitment was a process, albeit an uneven one, that was already under way by the opening of the seventeenth century. It did not spell the end of the male slave element in the central elites until the nineteenth century. The careers of Mehmed Hüsrev and his eminent ex-slave protégés in the nineteenth century are proof of both the longevity of the practice and its ultimate extinction. Although the slave soldier phenomenon was dying out in the Ottoman center, it found new traction elsewhere. In Egypt, its nominal Ottoman governor, Mehmed Ali Pasha, employed thousands of enslaved Africans for his army. The experiment ended in failure but only after considerable loss of life.[30] In Morocco, slave soldiery had been a significant institution since the reign of the Alawite dynast Mawlay Ismail (d. 1727). Part black African himself, Ismail built a vast army around thousands of enslaved sub-Saharans.[31] On both shores of the Mediterranean, the use of African males in domestic capacities persisted, with occasional spikes in supply and demand but as a shrinking percentage of the black and white female-dominated slave population overall.

The scale of slave importations as a reflection of the internal demand for females is corroborated by figures from the nineteenth century. Ubicini, drawing from official figures, puts the number of registered slaves in Istanbul at fifty-two thousand in the mid-nineteenth century. Of these, forty-seven thousand were said to have been females.[32] In Cairo at about the same time, the female-to-male ratio was roughly comparable at three to one.[33] Ubicini estimated that slaveholders, almost exclusively Muslim, amounted to some 12 percent

[29] *İA*, s.v. "Reis-ül-Küttâb," by Halil İnalcık; *EI2*, s.v. "Ghulām," by Halil İnalcık; Abou-el-Haj, "Ottoman Vezir and Paşa Households," 438–47; Kunt, *Sultan's Servants*, 97–9.

[30] Fahmy, *All the Pasha's Men*; Sikainga, "Comrades in Arms."

[31] Jamil M. Abun-Nasr, *A History of the Maghrib in the Islamic Period* (Cambridge, U.K., 1987), 230–1; but see Harrak, "Mawlay Isma'il's *Jaysh*," 177–96, who argues that Ismail's army mostly comprised Moroccan-born slaves and manumitted though dependent African Moroccans rather than the new imports from Sudanese lands that European accounts emphasize.

[32] Ubicini, *Letters on Turkey*, 1:145.

[33] Walz, "Black Slavery," 159n70; Tucker, *Women in Nineteenth-Century Egypt*, 167. Meriwether, *Kin Who Count*, 99, surmises a similar distribution for Aleppo. Given Cairo's reliance on Mamluk-slave military households in the seventeenth and eighteenth centuries, the gender distribution of its slave population is likelier than Aleppo to have resembled the central Ottoman pattern.

of Istanbul's Muslim population.[34] The figures are certainly incomplete. There were always many slaves in transit, and many others were sold off the books to avoid taxes and other surveillance. Still, if the ratio of female to male slaves in the nineteenth century reached ten to one, or even only eight or nine to one, the imbalance is not only overwhelming but also a departure from previous central Ottoman practice. The exaggerated imbalance was not a moment but a process. Its ultimate course was arguably decided by the eighteenth century. It moved in line with broad geopolitical trends of Ottoman retrenchment and diminished resources and it was further shaped by transformative disturbances in supply and demand.

The demand for women was robust throughout Ottoman history. It was particularly so among the wealthiest households, the preeminent consumers of multiple wives and consorts and the female servants and slaves to attend them. Such households were concentrated among the official elites – high bureaucrats, military officers, and prominent *ulema*. Wealthier middle class families – mostly Muslims but non-Muslims as well – aspired to the cachet associated with the palace and official elites by seeking to move into the slaveholding ranks. Sometimes they were able to do so, as when supply leveled down prices. Moments of supreme unhappiness for the enslaved, such as occurred during the Greek Revolution in the 1820s, account for the episodic democratization of slave ownership. However, the shift to slavery as *cariye*, female, slavery was also driven by urban and upper-class factors. The demand for female slaves was intimately linked to power. In cities like Istanbul and Cairo (Cairo both before and after the establishment of Mehmed Ali's semi-independent regime in the nineteenth century), the military-administrative elements of the empire's central and provincial governing elites, with their sense of authoritarian entitlement, were most numerous. It was among these groups and in these kinds of milieus that domestic slavery as female slavery was most consistently and tenaciously to be found.[35]

Throughout Ottoman history, men's and women's experience as slaves diverged in a number of ways, though nowhere more crucially than in relation to sexuality and power. Female slaves were excluded from the authoritative exercise of power in the wider community, and they were legally vulnerable to involuntary sexual use. The first disadvantage they shared, with few exceptions, with their free sisters.[36] Their second disadvantage, as sexual beings, however, was uniquely theirs. Other categories of human beings, free and slave, male and female, adult and child, also fell victim to sexual exploitation, but female slaves from the moment of capture were legally subject to the

34 Ubicini, *Letters on Turkey*, 1:145. It is interesting that in the census of 1907, 8 percent of Istanbul's population reported having live-in servants; see Duben and Behar, *Households*, 50.

35 Meriwether, *Kin Who Count*, 99; Tucker, *Women in Nineteenth-Century Egypt*, 167.

36 However, the acceptance of regentlike roles of the *valide*–queen mothers in the seventeenth century reflected a certain amount of authoritative consensus.

disposition of male captors. Many women, perhaps most who survived transport, were not sexually exploited between the time of capture and their appearance on the market. In wartime, women designated as part of the sultan's share of slave booty were likely to be carefully tended. Dernschwam reports that on the eastern European front, girls destined for gifts rather than sale were transported like prize cargo in large panniers slung over pack animals.[37] Their neighbors and compatriots were loaded into carts or forced to walk. Seizure and deracination were brutal in themselves, but they were unquestionably more extreme for captives not bound for the palace. It is, however, worth remembering that the palace itself was prison as well as haven.

The value of both male and female slaves depended on their appearance and fitness. Women's value increased if they were not pregnant and even more if they were young maidens. Nonetheless, sexual mishandling was an inescapable fact of the female slave condition. Contrary to literalist interpretations, the classification of slave women into those intended for light household duties and concubinage (*cariye*s or odalisques), and ordinary and older slave women slated for heavy or nonintimate work (*halayık*, *molada*), reflected market pricing, not sexual destiny.[38] Vocational categories and the price ranges into which dealers slotted their human merchandise did not bind the buyer to employment rules. Odalisques were not legally protected from having to scrub floors on their knees, and *molada*s were not exempt from sexual exploitation. Despite what is today known about sexual violation and exploitation as modes of domination, the notion that only the young and comely are vulnerable to sexual misuse lingers on in the historiography and popular imagination of societies East and West.

Any slave woman could become her master's regular or irregular sexual partner, or she might be given as a gift, to become the sexual partner of her master's or mistress's designee, regardless of her purchase price or in which section of a slave market she had been quartered. And irrespective of how old, young, or plain female slaves might be, male purchasers were entitled to have sexual use of the captive women in their charge. In Leyla Saz's discussion of her beloved father's unfatherly interest in the young slave girls working in the family home, she admits that he probably purchased the girls for their sexual appeal. Saz considered her father's actions "the one venal sin which men permit themselves while still honestly believing that they can do that sort of thing without ceasing to be virtuous."[39] Her reflections may say more about the new critical climate of the post-Tanzimat nineteenth century, not to mention Saz's educated and worldly outlook, than about historical views of upper-class masculinity and male sexual entitlement. Still, she might have

[37] Dernschwam, *Tagebuch*, 241.

[38] Although "cariye" was also used for female slaves in general; for this and other variations, see Peirce, *Imperial Harem*, 132; also *EI2*, s.v., "'Abd."

[39] Leyla Saz, *Imperial Harem of the Sultans*, 85–6.

been speaking of an upstairs-downstairs reality the world over, given the physical vulnerability of female servants everywhere, regardless of the public reputation of their upstairs "betters."[40]

Prostitution and other fine lines

The prostitution of female slaves by dealers and casual buyers was endemic in port cities all over the Mediterranean. At times, urban prostitution may have depended on such utter marginals, although extreme poverty and despair, abusive guardians, and procurers' greed regularly added freeborn women to the supply. The common Ottoman designation for prostitution, *fuhuş*, refers, among other things, to sexual intercourse outside the boundaries of marriage or slave ownership and for profit. The term's specific connotations, however, were context dependent. It could be applied to a variety of sexually construed behaviors, including the mere propinquity of the sexes – irrespective of the individual men's and women's actual conduct – in violation of strict religious norms of gender separation.

Despite the predictable spasm of decrees against prostitution, Istanbul and other Ottoman cities proved incapable of eradicating it.[41] The official commitment behind such efforts is, of course, open to question. Among other factors, those responsible for enforcing the law at street level constituted one of the likely cohorts for sexual misbehavior. Ottoman decrees cited both licensed and unlicensed slave dealers as traffickers in women for unlawful purposes. Two decrees from the late sixteenth and mid-seventeenth centuries repeat the usual warnings, although their litany of prostitutional scams singles out female slave dealers as principal culprits.[42] It is not hard to believe that the worst of female dealers were every bit as bad as the worst of male dealers. The suggestion that women were somehow unique in that regard, however, is unreasonable. For one thing, female dealers were fewer in number. Even if they were recognized dealers with guild affiliation, as women they would always be jealously monitored. To be sure, women operating outside the guilds, as

40 Hill, *Servants and English Domestics*, 44–63; Anderson and Zinsser, *A History of Their Own*, 1:358–61; Mendelson and Crawford, *Women in Early Modern England*, 88–9, 106–7, 268.

41 Zilfi, "Servants, Slaves," 8–9; Şanizade Mehmet Ataullah, *Tarih-i Şanizade* (Istanbul, 1290/1873), 2:151; White, *Three Years*, 2:344; Olivier, *Voyage*, 1:163–4, 4:131–2; Marcus, *Middle East*, 30, 54, 304, 328; Rafeq, "Public Morality in 18th Century Damascus"; Ginio, "Administration of Criminal Justice," 197; Largueche, *Les Ombres de la ville*, 286–313; Lamdan, *A Separate People*, 123, 132–7; Heath W. Lowry, *Ottoman Bursa in Travel Accounts* (Bloomington, Ind., 2003), 100; İbrahim Halil Kalkan, "Prostitution in the Late Ottoman Empire," paper presented at the Annual Meeting of the Middle East Studies Association, Montreal, 2007; Semerdjian, "Sinful Professions," 60–85; Fahmy, "Prostitution in Egypt in the Nineteenth Century," 77–103; Zarinebaf-Shahr, "Women and the Public Eye," 316–18; Seng, "Invisible Women," 248; Vatin and Yerasimos, *Les cimetières*, 13.

42 Kütükoğlu, *Osmanlılarda Narh*, 257–8; Ziya Kazıcı, *Osmanlılarda İhtisab Müessesesi* (Istanbul, 1987), 121–2; Ahmet Refik [Altınay], *Hicrî On Birinci Asırda İstanbul Hayatı: 1000–1100* (Istanbul, 1931), 25–6.

undercapitalized, low-end dealers, were likely to have been prone to dubious transactions. The same, however, could be said for male dealers of this sort, and there were infinitely more of them. The singling out of women in these instances suggests particular individuals at particular moments, perhaps. Yet given the transient male populations that constituted the customer base for prostitutes, it is difficult to imagine that women dealers had the greater access, either to customers or to salable women. The two decrees in question in fact barred women from acting as dealers (*esirci*s) at all. Because the seventeenth-century decree was essentially a copy of the sixteenth-century one, however, women traders, reputable or not, were not easily disposed of.[43]

As with other social legislation, the initiatives behind slavery edicts often arose from disputes in the trade. Freelance and black-market entrepreneurship created problems for licensed slave dealers just as they did for the cloth and clothing guilds. Nonguild dealers evaded taxes and overhead costs by setting up shop out of sight of market regulators. A particular point of contention for the guilds, apart from the costs that freelancers avoided, was competition from what today might be called niche retailers, dealers who specialized in specific areas of the trade or catered to particular clienteles.[44] In 1755, echoing a complaint from a few years previous, a group of slave guild principals – the Steward of Istanbul's Slave Market and senior guildsmen (Esir Pazarı Kethüdası ve *ihtiyarları*) – petitioned to have unlicensed, non-Istanbulite, sellers punished for unauthorized dealings in scattered locations throughout the city.[45] Established merchants were always looking for ways to drive out rivals. The task was made easier when their targets could be identified as social marginals like out-of-towners, foreigners, or women.

Women of virtually every class played key roles in the licit and illicit enslavement of women. At times, women were licensed dealers and duly recognized as such. A seventeenth-century register lists eight females affiliated with the central Slave Market in Istanbul.[46] The decree of 1755 mentions both licensed and unlicensed female brokers (*esir dellalları*), with the latter as the problematic subject. Many more women operated in the shadows of the guild or completely outside of the guild's purview. Women were especially likely to be small-time or occasional dealers, brokers, and harem go-betweens. The last

[43] Kütükoğlu, *Osmanlılarda Narh*, 257; Kal'a et al., *İstanbul Ticaret Tarihi 1*, 92–3; Altınay, *On Altıncı*, 42.

[44] The odd – and erroneous – report that Jews dominated the Istanbul market in the seventeenth century appears to be linked to French informants, who may have relied on identical sources or have generalized from Jewish sellers who had dealings with French speakers. Tournefort, for example, refers to Jews who dealt in the sale of beautiful slave girls whom they instructed in music and dance; Kömürcüyan, *İstanbul Tarihi*, 315. Joseph Pitton de Tournefort (d. 1708), author of *Relation d'un voyage du Levant...* (Lyon, 1717), and Aubry de la Mottraye (d. 1743), author of *Ses voyages en Europe, Asie, et Afrique, depuis 1696, jusqu'en 1725* (The Hague, 1727–32), are frequently cited as authorities.

[45] Kal'a et al., *İstanbul Ticaret Tarihi 1*, 92–3.

[46] Kütükoğlu, *Osmanlılarda Narh*, 257.

Fig. 18. "An Attendant of the Harem of the Grand Signior [Sultan]." A senior slave assigned to keep order among the women of the imperial harem. Dalvimart, *The Costume of Turkey*.

were especially useful when households sought additional slaves or decided to resell one of their own. Female brokers had particular expertise and the kind of access to harem-bound buyers and sellers that male dealers required but had to forgo without female partners or hirelings. Often the wives of dealers, women whose vulnerabilities as matrons and instructors we have already seen, performed those functions.

Some women, perhaps wives of dealers or women operating on their own, earned a living outside the family household as market inspectors of female slaves. Among other functions, they performed physical examinations to assess slaves' health – including pregnancy and fertility issues – and to help sellers determine appropriate price levels. In the same intimate capacity, they also were enlisted to ferret out the less obvious flaws and disabilities that could result in a returned purchase. In the decree of 1755, its clauses regarding unofficial females dealing in the trade – literally unregistered female intermediaries or, less charitably, procuresses[47] – are an additional reminder of the difficulty of determining not only the truth of the charges of women's criminality but also cause and effect in the matter. Certainly, Ottoman guilds of every trade had sought to limit women's right to guild licensing, even standing in the way of widows and surviving daughters who sought to continue in their deceased relative's profession. Part of the strategy of exclusion was to invoke "women" as a category and insist on women's lesser ability or greater immorality. Not surprisingly, most women involved in the slave trade in the period filled only interstitial roles. No doubt some female intermediaries were unsavory. Others operated in as upright a fashion as buying and selling slaves could allow.

Reports of the prostitutional exploitation of female slaves invariably found their way into European travel accounts. Foreign travelers of every origin often had direct knowledge of such matters. Westerners unacquainted with the Ottoman Turkish language, not to mention Ottoman weights and measures, currency, street plans, and the like, necessarily relied on local – though not necessarily indigenous – informants. Newcomers were approached by all sorts of would-be guides. Embassy employees and their white-collar and blue-collar retinues, day laborers, soldiers, sailors, merchantmen, pilgrims, and sightseers were primary consumers as well as occasional purveyors of sex for hire. Parts of Galata and Pera, largely Christian-populated areas across the Golden Horn from Istanbul's Old City, for centuries had a reputation for drunkenness, brawling, and illicit sexual activity, although most of the two suburbs' neighborhoods were home to perfectly respectable Christian, Jewish, and Muslim residences and commerce. In the nineteenth century, many streets became seedier as the number of transients, principally Europeans and Levantines piggybacking on the expansion of European diplomacy and trade, flocked to Galata and Pera for entertainment and lodging. Pardoe viewed Pera in the 1830s as having only two kinds of inhabitants, "the diplomatic and the scandalous."[48] Charles White's scathing judgment that vice and depravity ruled Galata and Pera was not much different from Pardoe's or that of Ottoman authorities. White added with some chagrin that British subjects and British patentees and protégés (*beratlıs*) were the particular "scourge" of both suburbs.[49]

47 That is, *defterden hâric olan nisâ dellâlları*; Kal'a et al., *İstanbul Ticaret Tarihi I*, 93.

48 Pardoe, *City of the Sultan*, 1:54.

49 White, *Three Years*, 3:249, 1:195; Şanizade, *Tarih*, 3:408; H. G. Dwight, *Constantinople, Old and New* (New York, 1915), 184; see also Rosenthal, *Politics of Dependency*, 9, 15. Compare Albert Smith, *Habits of the Turks* (Boston, 1857), 46–7, 54–5, who seconds White's assessment of European patentees, singling out as particularly reprehensible, as White does, "emigrants from Malta and the Ionian Islands." For negative assessments in earlier times, see Louis Mitler, "The Genoese in Galata: 1453–1682," *IJMES* 10, no. 1 (1979): 83–5.

A common form of sexual trafficking occurred when a female slave was purchased in accordance with *shari'ah* law's option-of-defect (*hıyar-ı ayıb*) provision. The option applied to the sale of males as well, but in the case of females, a purchased female slave could be returned to the seller after some days, usually three, if she exhibited a flaw or defect.[50] In accordance with the law, a buyer could demand reimbursement if he or she did so according to the usual "three-day approval option" and if he or she could prove that the defect predated purchase.[51] In the spring of 1817, for example, an agent acting for a local *kadı* who had purchased an African female slave returned the slave to the seller. A dispute arose over the legitimacy of the return, which the buyer claimed was the result of the woman's previously undetected flaws. The woman herself was present in the court by way of demonstration.[52]

Buyers in the Ottoman market often had valid complaints, as when sellers used cosmetics or otherwise misrepresented age or other infirmity.[53] But often, buyer and seller conspired to conceal what was from the outset a prostitution arrangement in the form of a temporary sexual hire.[54] A price-control regulation from the mid-seventeenth century accuses female slave dealers or concessionaires – whose business primarily involved females – of acting as intermediary procurers on behalf of private owners. The women allegedly shopped the girls around "to all manner of non-Muslims, to consular people from Poland and Moldavia, and to other rich non-Muslims."[55] These latter would pay an agreed-on sum as though purchasing the girls. They would then return them within a day or two on the pretext that the girls had not been pleasing in some way, in other words, in connivance with the dealers, invoking the option of defect in order to get or to seem to get their money back. Despite the pinpointing of non-Muslims and foreigners, tricks and ploys were common across the religious and ethnic spectrum. Paid access to females for short-term sexual use, perhaps the classic prostitution, was the mode of foreign, transient, and unmoneyed males.

Orlando Patterson has argued that humiliation and dishonor were intrinsic to the slave's world. In the case of female slaves in Ottoman and Muslim hands, Western visitors showed themselves eager to bear witness. Until 1846 and the closing of the central Slave Market, a visit to the market (if visitors could obtain entry permits) or its environs was a must-see stop on European tours of the East. Not surprisingly, foreign visitors identified most closely with fellow Europeans in captivity. The sixteenth-century traveler de Nicolay

50 Al-Marghinani, *Hedaya*, 258–66.

51 *Üç gün muhayyer*; Aykut, *İstanbul Mahkemesi, 121 Numaralı*, 32.

52 Aykut, *İstanbul Mahkemesi, 121 Numaralı*, 142.

53 Kütükoğlu, *Osmanlılarda Narh*, 257; Rakım Ziyaoğlu, *Yorumlu İstanbul Kütüğü, 330–1983* (Istanbul, 1985), 309. A decree from the seventeenth century prohibited sellers from using makeup on young boys' faces, "like women." The concern was perhaps as much about depravity as disguising blemishes; Altınay, *Hicrî On Birinci*, 25.

54 Ennaji, *Serving the Master*, 32; White, *Three Years*, 2:344.

55 Kütükoğlu, *Osmanlılarda Narh*, 257.

presented an empathic portrait of a solitary captive on display in Istanbul: "I have there seen stripped and 3 times visited in less than an hour, on one of the sides of the Bezestan [Covered Bazaar], a Hungarian maiden, being of thirteen or fourteen years of age, and of beauty indifferent, which in the end was sold unto an old merchant a Turk [Muslim] for four and thirty ducats."[56] De Nicolay's own voyeurism, of course, gives rise to a whole other set of questions. In the seventeenth century, the Polish traveler Simeon recorded a similar scene: "Buyers drew near and uncovered the faces and chests of the young girls . . . and inspected their bodies from head to toe to see whether or not there was a defect."[57] The female slave trade even prior to the reform era seems from time to time to have undergone a certain amount of gentrification, with some of the obvious handling that de Nicolay and Simeon had witnessed more often taking place indoors and out of public view.

In the first half of the nineteenth century, the peripatetic marine Slade was yet another Slave Market tourist. His description – though not his sentiments – is in accord with the others: "The would-be purchaser may fix his eyes on the lady's face, and his hand may receive evidence of her bust." There is no real harm in this, Slade insists, because doing the waltz back in England and France "allows nearly as much liberty."[58] Slade's apologia, however, misses more than one key point. Unlike the slave, the waltzer can disengage or choose not to dance at all. And presumably all of the waltzers arrived at the ball of their own free will. In any case, the analogy of mixed female-male dancing hardly applies to Ottoman gender relations. Nothing resembling the waltz's hands-on, public physicality was permitted to respectable Ottoman women – by definition, free women – in unfamilial mixed company. One suspects that Slade's British readers would not have approved of the comparison either, though on different grounds. With regard to Istanbul's Slave Market and the world the slave owners made, the juxtaposition of commoditized female bodies inside its gates with jealously guarded honorable women outside them is stark and revealing. As Gill Shepherd has observed about gendered slave employment, "[T]he uses to which slaves are put teach us a good deal about what is most valuable in a particular society at a particular time."[59]

For many slaves, their exposure and many-handed indignities would come to an end if and when they were placed in homes or won their freedom. Until then, and if they should ever be subject to resale, the patriarchal promise of care and respect for women did not apply. They could expect to be gawked at

[56] Nicolas de Nicolay, *Dans l'empire de Soliman le magnifique: Navigations into Turkie*, ed. M.-C. Gomez and Stéphane Yerasimos (Paris, 1989), 62. (Spellings here modified by present author.)

[57] Hrand D. Andreasyan, *Polonyalı Simeon'un Seyahatnâmesi (1608–1619)* (Istanbul, 1964), 9.

[58] Slade, *Slade's Travels in Turkey*, 195, and similarly in his *Records of Travels*, 2:242.

[59] Gill Shepherd, "The Comorians and the East African Slave Trade," in Watson, *Asian and African Systems*, 98.

and prodded by prospective buyers, anywhere from the waist up and from the knees down if the rules were followed, and elsewhere if they were not.[60] That treatment was comparatively genteel – only comparatively – and at least subject to some rules of public propriety, in contrast to the sorting-out inspections administered in enslavement zones under the scrutiny of raiders and their confederates.

Like male slaves, female slaves were the personal property of their masters. Unlike males, however, every female slave, of whatever age or provenance and by whatever label, was also her master's sexual property. Women had no right of refusal or appeal with regard to their sexuality, although the law forbade owners to use the women for outright prostitution. The use of males for such purposes was categorically illegal. The notional, if not the legal, line between prostitution and the selling of a female slave to another male, who might sell her to yet another, was whisper thin. Both male and female slaves had recourse to the *shari'ah* courts if they should suffer a disfiguring or disabling physical injury as a result of a master's intentional act. A female slave's sexuality, however, belonged to an alienable category of self. It was not hers to lose, withhold, or contest. Like an injury inflicted by a nonowner on a slave's arm or leg, or the loss of an eye, the loss of virginity counted not as an injury indemnifiable to her but as a loss to her owner. In the winter of 1817, a female owner demanded and received five hundred *guruş*es in compensation for the depreciation in value of her young female slave. The girl, a virgin, had been raped by a man who was subsequently identified and brought to court. Because the girl could no longer be sold for the premium price of a virgin, her owner was entitled to commensurate compensation.[61]

In the literature of Ottoman juristic opinion (*fetva*s), the chapters that touch on slavery are filled with questions about past, present, and future access to female slaves' sexuality. Inquiries were asked and answered about disputed paternity, prostitution, adultery, joint ownership of slaves, marriage, childbirth, violation by someone other than a master, and sexual relations with a wife's slave woman with and without wifely consent.[62] Given the problematic interface between the slave condition and the domestic household, a mufti's expertise often provided litigants with an authoritative opinion to bolster their cases in court.

[60] On the *awra* of slave women, see Müller, *Die Kunst*, 143–50, 190; Camilla Adang, "Women's Access to Public Space according to al-Muhallā bi-l-Āthār," in Manuela Marín and Randi Deguilhem, eds., *Writing the Feminine: Women in Arab Sources* (London, 2002), 77–80, 83.

[61] Aykut, *İstanbul Mahkemesi, 121 Numaralı*, 29. Compare Dürrizade, *Netice el-Fetava*, 582, 589, for the monetary value of slaves and indemnification for their injuries.

[62] Yenişehirli Abdullah, *Behcet el-Fetava*; Düzdağ, *Şeyhülislâm Ebussuûd*, 119–32. For an analysis of Ottoman *şeyhülislams* on these matters, see Colin Imber, *Studies in Ottoman History and Law* (Istanbul, 1996).

Jurisprudential commentaries are another index of the deep involvement of Islamic law with the particularities and contingencies of the pre- and postemancipation world of slaves and slaveholders. In India, after slavery was abolished in the late nineteenth century, translations of Sunni jurisprudential compendia like al-Marghinani's *Hedaya* were published without their original slavery chapters. The expurgated text nonetheless remains interlarded with references to innumerable contingencies arising from slavery. The residue is especially striking where females are concerned, so enmeshed was female slavery with legal decision making in the *shari'ah* context.[63] In Ottoman practice, actual court cases as recorded in the court's daily registers offer additional evidence of the high level of social confusion and conflict provoked by the sexual use of slave women.

Abduction and false enslavement

Callousness toward the peasantry and the urban lower orders and the discriminatory measures that could be taken against them assumed many forms over the centuries. Inequitable legal treatment, duplicative taxation, endemic banditry, and restricted physical and social mobility were some of the obstacles to individual and communal betterment outside the cities.[64] The burden of maltreatment and disadvantage often effaced the line between slave and free. In every century, one of the recurring abuses of the rural populace was the kidnapping of free subjects, Muslim and non-Muslim.[65] Freeborn and freed Muslims were, by law, immune from enslavement, whether they lived inside or outside Ottoman lands. Except for the *devşirme*, which had ended by the early eighteenth century, non-Muslim subjects within the empire were likewise immune.[66] Armies and paramilitary freebooters often rendered the law moot, however. Even when peace reigned, villagers might still have to protect themselves against bands of demobilized soldiers, who were themselves hungry and ill used. The contraction of the empire in the eighteenth and nineteenth centuries created new and perilous borderlands to the east and west. Countless

[63] Al-Marghinani, *Hedaya* (reprint of 1870 edition), 30–41, 59–63. Compare the first Indian edition: *The Hedaya or Guide: A Commentary on the Mussulman Laws*, trans. Charles Hamilton (London, 1791).

[64] On discriminatory fees, see Boğaç A. Ergene, "Costs of Court Usage in Seventeenth- and Eighteenth-Century Ottoman Anatolia: Court Fees as Recorded in Estate Inventories," *JESHO* 45, no. 1 (2002): 34–9; compare Canbakal, *Society and Politics*, 142.

[65] Aktaş, *3 Numaralı Mühimme*, 205, 398, 586–7, 592, 612–13, 626, 634, 653, 682; Aykut, *İstanbul Mahkemesi, 121 Numaralı*, 47, 82–3; Kal'a et al., *İstanbul'da Sosyal Hayat 1*, 46–8; Yıldırım, *85 Numaralı Mühimme*, 46, 72–3, 93, 123–4, 158–9, 187–8, 274–5, 279, 380–1, 398; Faroqhi, *Towns and Townsmen*, 279; İnalcık with Quataert, *An Economic and Social History*, 597; Saydam, "Esir Pazarlarında," 115–34; Vatin, "Une affaire interne," 149–90; Jennings, *Christians and Muslims in Ottoman Cyprus*, 244–5. Regarding Egypt, see Lane, *An Account of the Manners*, 194–5; Heyworth-Dunne, *An Introduction to the History of Education in Modern Egypt*, 33, citing Abdurrahman al-Jabarti.

[66] Collective open rebellion also nullified the non-Muslim (*zimmi*) covenant.

villages that had been insulated in previous decades from such disruption were increasingly exposed to personal and material despoliation.

In the declared and undeclared wars that occupied the Ottoman Empire and Iran during much of the seventeenth and eighteenth centuries, populations on both sides of the border were preyed on by their own and enemy soldiers and irregulars. Because of the mixed message conveyed by the political authorities on the subject of Shiites and the juristic vacillation about whether Shiites were to be treated as true Muslims – and thus protected from enslavement and property confiscation – many Iranian Shiites wound up enslaved to Ottoman captors.[67] On the conclusion of treaties, Ottoman-held captives were to be turned over at designated collection points, usually the local *kadı* court. There the act of emancipation could be recorded and compensations to former captors disbursed. Despite the various binational agreements that sought to restore slaves to their homes by compensating those who had held them captive, many owners refused to relinquish their prizes long after the treaties had become law.[68]

If women and men who had been wrongly seized could find a way to alert the authorities, all was not lost for them. Some managed to make their status known, but exactly how they did so and how many others remained concealed are beyond recovery. In 1743, a girl variously called Şivekâr, meaning "graceful" or "elegant," and Şehriban, perhaps meaning "cultivated" or "urbane" – one of the names probably conferred by her captor – appeared in court in Istanbul.[69] She identified herself both as "a Persian Muslim slave [*acem üserası Müslimlerinden*] liberated by Ottoman decree and the freeborn daughter of freeborn parents Allahvirdi Muhammed Quli and Fatıma" of Tabriz in western Iran.

Unlike the many other war prisoner–slaves caught between formal treaties and recalcitrant captors, Şivekâr's reduction to slavery was more a result of peace than war. Her claims to free status illuminate the resistance displayed by soldiers and booty-seeking opportunists when war suddenly turned to peace and the formerly enslaveable were declared off-limits. Şivekâr's particular plight began in the aftermath of war between the Ottoman and Iranian empires in the 1720s and 1730s. Temporary Ottoman victory resulted in the annexation of Tabriz and the transformation of the city's population from enemy

67 Asım, *Tarih-i Asım*, 303–4, 602–3; Erdem, *Slavery in the Ottoman Empire*, 21–2; and Chapter 4 in this volume. See Masters, "Treaties of Erzurum," 5, regarding Iranian captives sold in Aleppo in 1730 in the aftermath of the Hamadan campaign.

68 E.g., İstM 2/178, fols. 19b–20a, 43b–44a; see also Erdem, *Slavery in the Ottoman Empire*, 20–3, for cases ensuing from the Ottoman-Iranian treaty of 1736, including one captive who had been held for thirty years.

69 Şehribân or Şehrebân, as it appears in the register, though literally meaning "keeper of the city," may be a corruption or misspelling of other Persian words, including *şihrî*, "refined or "urban," and *banu*, "lady." *Şivekâr* can also connote "guileful." My thanks to my colleague Professor Ahmad Karimi-Hakkak for these observations. Midhat Pasha's second wife, originally a slave, was also called Şehriban; see Chapter 5 in this volume.

belligerents to protected subjects.[70] According to Şivekâr's testimony, however, a certain Mustafa Çelebi ibn Abdullah, secretly and contrary to Ottoman law, stole her from Tabriz when she was only a child and took her to Erzurum in Ottoman Anatolia. Given Mustafa Çelebi's convert patronymic *ibn Abdullah*, he was very likely another ex-slave turned slaver. At the time of Şivekâr's testimony, she had been held for more than eight years at the mercy of her captor and others. To evade the authorities, Mustafa had forced her to pretend to be of Georgian Christian origin and thus enslaveable. "When I swore that I was freeborn, he beat me terribly," the girl testified. With witnesses to support her story, she asked the court to confirm her free status. Had Mustafa Çelebi not been run to ground, he more than likely would have continued his subterfuge.[71]

The question of Shiite Muslims' Muslim status had posed problems on an international scale for the Ottoman Empire at least since the sixteenth century, when the wars against Iran's Shiite Safavid dynasty commenced. The hostilities continued on and off for two hundred years, even after the Safavids gave way to rival dynasties midway in the eighteenth century. Ottoman religious authorities had variously ruled on the Iranians as nonbelievers or as the equivalent of nonbelievers because of Iran's treatment of Sunni Muslims generally and Ottoman subjects particularly.[72] Whether grounded in theology or pragmatism, both judgments periodically laid Iran open to the kind of hostage taking and slaving operations that characterized war with Christian Europe. When Iran had the upper hand, as it often did, Ottoman subjects were killed or sometimes enslaved. One can imagine that the Ottomans, who over the centuries had come to know Iran as "the cemetery of the Turks,"[73] would for many reasons have felt entitled to the captives they held. Under ordinary circumstances, neighbors and acquaintances were the eyes and ears of the state in helping to expose illegal slaveholding. Şivekâr's captor had been able to keep her identity concealed at least in part because, in conditions of war, the law and the rules of polite society were often suspended. For the women and men enslaved in those areas and times, emancipation was neither easy nor automatic; in the eighteenth and nineteenth centuries, such areas and times were plentiful.

As for indigenous women, regional banditry, military demobilization, and other causes of civic breakdown made them prey to seizure and enslavement in their own homeland. The numbers may or may not have been great in the overall scheme of things, but villages and families in outlying locales were

[70] Fariba Zarinebaf-Shahr, "Tabriz under Ottoman Rule (1725–1730)," Ph.D. diss., University of Chicago, 1991; Ernest Tucker, "The Peace Negotiations of 1736: A Conceptual Turning Point in Ottoman-Iranian Relations," *TSAB* 20 (1996): 16–37.

[71] İstM 2/183, fols. 42b–43a.

[72] Eberhard [Niewöhner], *Osmanische Polemik*, 68–73.

[73] Sir Paul Rycaut, *The History of the Turkish Empire from the Year 1623 to the Year 1677...* (London, 1680), 1:26; compare Dernschwam, *Tagebuch*, 88.

perennially at risk. Unscrupulous professional slave raiders and even relatives fed the market with children too young or too cowed to make an effective complaint. In 1742, a certain Ayşe, the daughter of Ali, was one of those able to bring a case to court. In the presence of the slave dealer whose ownership rights she sought to have nullified, she testified that she was from the town of Maçukola in the Ohrid subprovince of Ottoman Rumelia (a region now bordering present-day Macedonia and Albania). Like Şivekâr on the other side of the empire, Ayşe told the court that her enslavement was unlawful because she was an Ottoman subject of free origin and a Muslim one at that. She declared that her parents were Ali, son of Hüseyn, son of Süleyman, and his lawful wife, Ayşe, daughter of Mustafa.

The core of Ayşe's suit was that both parents were freeborn inhabitants of the town and that neither she nor they had at any time been of slave status.[74] Two male witnesses from home together with her brother supported her claims. Her captor was a certain Mehmed son of Abdullah, an Istanbul slave dealer and, again, probably of slave origin. His denial of fault amounted to a good-faith purchase defense. He contended that a year and a half earlier he had purchased the girl as his *cariye* for two hundred *guruş*es from a certain Abdi Agha. Mehmed claimed that he had no idea that the girl was freeborn. He does not say how he managed not to know that the girl was of Muslim background. He charged Abdi Agha, who was not present in court, with having misrepresented Ayşe. Because Ayşe was able to prove her status, thanks to her brother and other witnesses, Mehmed was reprimanded and Ayşe was liberated.[75] Although that case had ended, the question of culpability was carried over to a case subsequently brought by Mehmed.

A month after he had surrendered Ayşe, Mehmed returned to court to sue Abdi Agha for the purchase price he had lost by Ayşe's emancipation. Abdi Agha, who is described in vague terms as an official of some standing, again failed to make an appearance. He did, however, designate an agent to act in his behalf. The agent implied that the misrepresenting of Ayşe was the fault of yet another Ottoman officeholder. This phantom figure was also absent from court, although he was identified as a man in the service of Küçük Hasan Pasha, the Ottoman governor of Üsküb (Skopje) in the Macedonian region. It was from Hasan Pasha's man that Abdi Agha claimed to have purchased Ayşe almost two years earlier. In this sitting of the court, the slave owner Mehmed's right to compensation was the point of contention. Because Mehmed produced witnesses who confirmed that he had purchased the girl from Abdi Agha, Abdi, by way of his agent, was reprimanded and ordered to repay Mehmed the full

[74] Even in the sixteenth century, the Ohrid region was notoriously unstable, with villagers who were suspected of collusion with bandits (*eşkiya*) variously enslaved and released by the Ottoman authorities; see Aktaş et al., *3 Numaralı Mühimme*, 460–1, 469–70.

[75] İstM 2/178, fols. 19b–20a, dated Muharrem 1155/1742.

purchase price.[76] If Abdi's version of the chain of events was true, he, in turn, was entitled to pursue a similar action against Hasan Pasha's man.

The court record says nothing about Ayşe's lost years, what exactly befell her during captivity, or how she made a life after being restored to her family. Presumably she did return home, as her brother had argued for her in court. There was no reasonable avenue for Ayşe to seek compensation from her abductors or from the man or men who had exploited her labor and sexual favor. Although *cariye* can simply mean "female slave," its use by Mehmed in this context connotes sexual usage; all that buying and selling seem out of proportion to the hiring of a mere housemaid.

It is possible that Ayşe's family, acting on her behalf, reached an out-of-court settlement with the girl's tormenters, but that is only speculation. What is clear about the ordeal of Ayşe and others like her is that Ottoman officialdom was implicated in the illicit trade in their midst. At worst, officials were directly complicit. At best, they were negligent. Either way, their stewardship of the villagers in Anatolia and the Balkans who were the victims of false enslavement eroded confidence in Ottoman rulership and justice. Hyperbolized Ottoman rhetoric about justice and state power, raising popular expectations, rang all the more hollow in the face of such events. If we accept the facts of Ayşe's case at face value, the ease with which free subjects could be passed from hand to hand by those charged with upholding the law points to a troubling distance between state and subject.

The number of false enslavement cases of this sort may have increased in later centuries as the opportunities for acquiring outsider females in warfare diminished.[77] The apparently growing incidence of false enslavement and female abduction in the eighteenth and nineteenth centuries is explained in part by the ambiguity surrounding the influx of women from the Caucasus region.[78] Of the Circassian women enslaved as *cariye*s in the nineteenth century, a good many were Muslim born. Conversion to Islam had been going on in Circassia for centuries, spurred by the region's Crimean and Ottoman connections. In fact, the free Muslim identity of many such slaves in Istanbul was an open secret.[79] The same illegal pretense allowed many sub-Saharan African Muslims to be swept up in the raids that enslaved their Christian and animist neighbors. Walz's study of slavery in Egypt indicates that some African victims found surprising support for their claims from slave merchants, who testified

[76] İstM 2/178, fols. 43b–44a, dated Safer 1155/1742.

[77] Nuri Adıyeke, "Osmanlı İmparatorluğu'nda Tanzimat Dönemi Evlilikleri," in Kemal Çiçek, ed., *Pax Ottomana: Studies in Memoriam, Prof. Dr. Nejat Göyünç* (Haarlem, 2001), 136–9, regarding the problem in the nineteenth century.

[78] Erdem, *Slavery in the Ottoman Empire*, 22–3, on the knowing enslavement of Muslim Ottomans; and see Dankoff, *Intimate Life*, 273–4, on self-enslavement among the Caucasian Abkhazes in the seventeenth century. Self-enslavement in the Caucasus was attested by numerous Europeans, many of whom had hoped to prove the claim false; see, e.g., DeKay, *Sketches of Turkey*, 278.

[79] Garnett, *Turkish Life*, 78–9; Saz, *Imperial Harem of the Sultans*, 66–8.

to the slaves' bona fides as free Muslims. False enslavement nonetheless remained widespread and recurrent on both sides of the Mediterranean, with some unfortunates enslaved and liberated only to be enslaved again.[80]

The self-enslavement of young women and youths, and the parentally sponsored enslavement of Circassian children, gave Circassian slavery a voluntary aspect not only in the nineteenth century, for which it is best documented, but in earlier centuries as well. Evliya Çelebi, writing about Circassian parents selling their children in the late seventeenth century, makes much of the practice under the heading "A Strange Fact."[81] European travelers in subsequent centuries had a similar reaction. The selling of one's own kinfolk seems to have been judged harshly in the Ottoman population at large, for whom the saying "to go Abkhaz" (*Abaza'ya varmak*) meant "to abase oneself." In contrast to the (exaggerated) voluntary gloss of the Caucasian or Circassian trade, Africans were reputed to fight tooth and nail to escape raiders' nets.[82] In both those non-Ottoman populations, and among some economically fragile communities within the empire, however, self-enslavement and the selling of one's own children occurred with some frequency.[83] If self-enslavement in these cases was an outcome of personal or family desperation, the selling of one's own children within the empire had a murkier etiology. It was often a consequence of poverty, but in some instances, it was the product of need mixed with greed on the part of adult familiars.

The commodification of girl children seems to have been at the root of an episode in the mid-eighteenth century involving false enslavement. Willful deceit on the part of kinsmen is the crux of the story, although the motives behind the deed are unclear. Two Christian girls, Markrit and Katrin, natives of a village near Erzurum, were reportedly secreted from their home by an uncle, the Christian Hovannes (rendered as *Avanis* in the original Ottoman). Hovannes is said to have attempted to pass his nieces off as foreign captives, thus making them lawfully enslaveable. This kind of ruse seems to have been employed with some frequency. The two girls were apparently minors, which could mean that they were five or six years old, in no position to defend themselves. Their uncle or other male in-law – the descriptor *enişte* can mean either – sold them to a ship's captain at Trabzon. Intending to resell the girls elsewhere, the captain transported them west across the Black Sea to a port on what is now the

[80] Walz, "Black Slavery," 147–8. [81] Dankoff, *Intimate Life*, 273.

[82] *Anti-Slavery Reporter*, January 13, 1841, 1–2. Resistance was fierce in the Black Sea zone as well; see Kizilov, "Black Sea and the Slave Trade," 211–35. De Tott's description, *Memoirs*, bk. 1, 2:183–8, of Crimean raiders' burning of villages and hayricks to force inhabitants into the open is further evidence of enslavement as horror rather than opportunity.

[83] White, *Three Years*, 2:290–1; Erdem, *Slavery in the Ottoman Empire*, 50–2; compare Lane, *Manners and Customs*, 194. In contrast to internal Ottoman dynamics, in which self-enslavement was aberrant, self-enslavement was the norm for slavery in the Russian Empire during the sixteenth and seventeenth centuries. And in contrast to the Ottoman policy of enslaving outsiders, the overwhelming majority of Russia's slaves were fellow Russians; Richard Hellie, *Slavery in Russia, 1450–1725* (Chicago, 1982).

Bulgarian coast. The ruse was uncovered, and the captain was apprehended by the police. Other relatives of the girls may have realized what Hovannes was up to and alerted the authorities, or the girls' confinement may have aroused suspicions. No doubt there is more to the tale than appears in the cryptic court entry. At the very least, the case involved the trafficking in free women and an effort on the part of a relative to turn a profit, whatever the precipitating motive.[84]

Women of every sort, not only Muslim-born Circassians but also freeborn Ottoman Muslim women, Turkish and Kurdish, and Ottoman Christians and Jews, were known to be scattered among the slaves of Istanbul's harems and households.[85] That is the meaning of the many cases brought to court by women claiming to have been falsely enslaved. Some of the women in settled harems may have conspired in their own enslavement. Whether they did so before or after the fact, and under what compulsions, remain unclear. Many had settled into their lives as slave servants, too attached to their new homes to seek to reclaim their old lives. If they had been sold by relatives or if their family or village had been destroyed, the lives they had left behind would have had little appeal. Others who were apparently not so content struggled to return to their families and prior lives. The fortunate ones were those who, like Ayşe from Ohrid, had family members able and willing to speak for them in a court of law.

In the second half of the nineteenth century, especially following Abdülmecid's 1857 decree prohibiting the African slave trade throughout the empire,[86] the slave trade was being curbed, at least temporarily, and abolitionism was working its way into public debate. However, the internal enslavement occurring at the time and the arrival of already enslaved Circassians in the 1860s deepened Ottoman slavery's domestic rootedness. The continued bondage of many of the immigrants for a decade or more, and the association

[84] Kal'a et al., *İstanbul Ticaret Tarihi 1*, 38. Young boys also fell victim to enslavement by kin. In 1866, in a case brought against a slave merchant about to transport five Circassian boys to Egypt, four of the five were found to be free Muslims, ages seven to nine, sold into slavery by family members, a paternal uncle in one case and, in the others, an older brother and cousins on the paternal side; Saydam, "Esir Pazarlarında," 127. What role female relatives might have played is not indicated. The men were all male-line kin who may have become the children's guardians if closer relatives such as a father or grandfather had died or abdicated the role. The slave dealer, Arap Süleyman Agha, was probably of sub-Saharan origin, given his identification as *Arap*. On the particulars of the case and the abolitionist and antiabolitionist politics involved, see Erdem, *Slavery in the Ottoman Empire*, 116–21. See also Toledano, *Slavery and Abolition*, 91–2. Although the Circassian slave trade was not subject to the bans and international pressures that affected the trade in Africans, the Ottoman government employed indirect measures, including vigorous policing to detect the sale of free persons, to curtail the Circassian trade as well; Erdem, *Slavery in the Ottoman Empire*, 102–7, 113–16.

[85] Leyla Saz, *Imperial Harem of the Sultans*, 67–8. Garnett, *Turkish Life*, 86, specifically mentions the many Yezidi Kurdish girls serving in Ottoman households in the late nineteenth century.

[86] Erdem, *Slavery in the Ottoman Empire*, 107–13.

of Circassians with slavery in any case, saw Ottoman slavery combine in unwholesome ways with old and new tribal practices regarding abduction, the sale of relatives, and most commonly, the trafficking in women.[87]

Conclusions

Prior to the transformative shifts in the modalities of supply and demand, slave servility was not consistently the province of either gender. Regardless of historical variations in male and female slave numbers and the fact that, over the long term, females tended to be numerically preponderant, male slaves for a long time were among the most prized acquisitions for Ottomans who could afford their keep. Not just men in power but also those who sought to ingratiate themselves with the powerful attached a high value to the possession and gift of males. Male slaves, especially those selected for imperial service and the households of the elites, were centerpieces of imperial culture. For centuries, historical memory and self-promotion by those brought up in and around slave-owning circles lent luster to the idealized image of the slave as the archetypal personal servant and companion – the elite *kul* as the model official and courtier, and the ordinary male *köle* as the exemplary male domestic. In their dominance and pervasiveness, they overshadowed the model of the female slave as the ideal female servant and consort. The fading presence of the model male servant, the *kul* official, along with other social transformations, produced a diminished male slave presence and a reliable pattern, in numerical terms, of female preponderance. It signaled as well a shift in the meaning of slavery, from virtual gender equivalence to a feminization of the institution.

The importance of slavery in Ottoman society, whether in the period of *kapı kulu* preeminence or with the rise in female slavery's proportion and significance, was less a matter of quantity than of social resonance. Among the Ottomans, as elsewhere in Europe and the Mediterranean, society's elite orders disproportionately influenced social norms and values. This is not to deny the role of slaves and former slaves in effecting change. Slaves' resistance and growing sensitivity to international abolitionism in the later nineteenth century helped move the Ottoman system toward greater use of limited-term slavery and contractual emancipation (*mükatebe*) arrangements. Nonetheless, the definition of *enslaveability* and the terms of slaves' use were set down according to the conduct and consent of the elites, what Fischer terms the

[87] See Ortaylı, "Osmanlı Aile," 463–4, on efforts during the Tanzimat to curb female abduction (*kız kaçırma*); Osman Yıldırım et al., eds., *85 Numaralı Mühimme Defteri, 1040–1041 (1042)/1630–1632 (1632)* (Ankara, 2002), 46, 72–3, 93, 123–4, 158–9, 187–8, 274–5, 380–1, 274–5, 279, 398; Peirce, *Morality Tales*, 362–3; Tucker, "*Muftīs* and Matrimony," 293–4; and for the present day, see Yasa, *Kız Kaçırma*; Paul Stirling, *Turkish Village* (London, 1965), 193–4, and Paul J. Magnarella, *Anatolia's Loom: Studies in Turkish Culture, Society, Politics and Law* (Istanbul, 1998), 65–6, 133. Abductions involving the sexual compromising of heiresses were common in contemporaneous Ireland, where they served extortive purposes more than romance; Hufton, *Prospect*, 271.

"iron law of oligarchy."[88] The importance of officials of slave origin always derived not from mere numbers but from the interplay among imperial favor, individual eminence, and the ability to capture high office.

The conceptual link between male and slave was always tenuous. The masculinity of sovereignty was underscored by the exclusion of women from authoritative office. The sovereign was male as were his deputies. The discourse of order invested the males of households and officialdom with the authorized power of precedence, seniority, and religious sanction. The decline in the imperial slave element and of the quasi-slave public official occurred in tandem with an emerging, male-centered discourse of rights. The widening of the conceptual distance between male and slave was an inevitable consequence of Mahmud II's abandonment of political execution and confiscation, the enshrinement of essentially male confessional egalitarianism in Tanzimat reform edicts, the appointment of non-Muslim males to state office, and the ongoing erasure of legal distinctions between Muslim and non-Muslim males. One can argue that many of these rights and recognitions implicitly encompassed women. The argument for women's rights, however, was one that had to be made separately and latterly, as occurred in Europe and the United States as well as in the empire.

The chief impediment to a gender-neutral reading of, for example, Gülhane or the Edict of 1856 was the continued replenishment of gendered social legislation and moralist discourse on women's special, socially harmful nature. The reform decrees of Mahmud II and the Tanzimat were not promulgated on a neutral social slate. They were informed by the pedagogy of social legislation, the hundreds of restrictive and deprecating pronouncements on the category of "women." Social life was never clearly demarcated by these prescriptions, but the discourse on women had disproportionate power to shape social behavior and to influence the emerging parameters of rights. Overall, the sumptuary restrictions and moral injunctions that lasted into the Tanzimat and beyond barely bothered about non-Muslim men but clung fast to women.

Throughout the nineteenth century, the quintessential servile being was a slave. All over the Mediterranean, the enslaved might be from the Caucasus or Africa; different decades and different regions saw variant ethnic and color ratios. The relationship between blackness and Africanness in the northern-tier provinces and in other distinctive regions – in whole or in part the Arabian Peninsula, the Persian Gulf and Indian Ocean littorals, Egypt, Libya, Tunisia, Algeria, and Morocco – must still be sorted out according to their specific histories, including the evolution of racial attitudes.

The historiographical and anthropological generalizations that make a single racialized story, an African story, out of the different peoples, slave subjugations, rulerships, and racial and ethnic mixtures of the Mediterranean over the centuries are not without value. They alert us to identities and attitudes current

[88] David H. Fischer, *Albion's Seed: Four British Folkways in America* (New York, 1989), 5, 896.

in the late nineteenth century and thereafter. However, they have little to tell us about the far greater number of places and times in the Ottoman era when black Africans did not constitute the dominant element among slaves. Race or ethnicity was not the cornerstone on which Mediterranean slavery, much less Ottoman slavery, was built. But either-or has never been a satisfactory model for explaining human relations in historical time. The question of how the femaleness of slavery intersects with ethnicity still awaits the many answers that will ensue from regional investigations. In the meantime, it must be said that in the eighteenth and nineteenth centuries, the slave of the Ottoman slave owner was a woman and that slavery itself was increasingly female. The *kul*-harem paradigm of elite dependency and Ottoman statecraft has great utility in explaining elite reproduction and dynastic longevity,[89] but it is more the case that, by the dawn of the Tanzimat, the paradigm had become disaggregated, leaving in place not just harem slavery but also female slavery.

Although most slaves in the nineteenth century were employed as domestic workers – with women's sexuality at the disposal of owners – whether owners chose to use it, sell it, marry it, or marry it off – the persistence of slavery, the lack of will to stamp it out, was entangled in the normative weight and reality of women's subservience, with or without religious rhetoric. It was also a function of elite politics. The exchange of women was crucial to the social reproduction of the dynasty and its central elite supporters. The ramifications of slavery's feminization and female exchange form the subject of the chapter that follows.

[89] See esp. Toledano, *Slavery and Abolition*, 20–53, and more recently, Ze'evi, "Kul and Getting Cooler," 177–95.

CHAPTER 7

Men are *kanun*, women are *shari'ah*

> Bring me a slave girl [*cariye*] who has been brought up in the city since childhood, and I will make her the sultan's chief consort.
>
> – Sultan Mahmud II's sister, after the death of his chief consort in childbirth, 1809[1]

> To say "family" is to mean woman.
>
> – Şemseddin Sami, 1879[2]

Longevity

In its imperial neighborhood with its imperial licenses and certified guildsmen vendors, Istanbul's downtown Slave Market symbolized slavery's place in the empire and the culture of the capital. That is, it did so until Sultan Abdülmecid ordered it closed in December 1846.[3] The Slave Dealers' Guild (Esirci Esnafı) was effectively disestablished in the same stroke. With the end of the central market and of the guild's official monopoly, the trade lost its institutional center and its overt government sanction. Competition and rival locations had always challenged the guild's monopoly. Any number of commercial inns (*hans*) and residences throughout the Old City picked up the pieces of the trade without the worry of jealous surveillance. Some dealers operated outside the law. Others continued within the kind of legality that taxpaying confers; otherwise, they, too, carried on at a distance from the government.

Some of the larger and more lasting slave-selling enterprises that still stood in the 1860s could be found in the Tophane district near dockside and in the

1 Cabi Ömer, *Câbî Târihi*, 1:443. Mahmud's sister, Dürrişehvar, who was considerably older than Mahmud, had been born when their father, Abdülhamid I, was still a prince.

2 Şemseddin Sâmî, *Kadınlar*, ed. İsmail Doğan (Ankara, 1996), 24.

3 Erdem, *Slavery in the Ottoman Empire*, 95–9, analyzes the motives behind the ruling. Although the government tended to explain the closure as a reform in the interests of maltreated slaves, sales merely dispersed around the city, and the government continued to collect taxes on them. Erdem questions reformist readings of the closure on the grounds that decentralization potentially worsened slaves' situation by making government and guild oversight even more scant than it had been previously.

row of shops across from the Süleymaniye Mosque.[4] Private houses of the sort that produced Midhat Pasha's second wife and other slave girls "brought up like daughters" to be married off for money or favor were part of a more genteel and clandestine trade, a family matter and yet not.[5] For many years following 1846, slave dealing and slave owning remained forces in the capital and in the empire. However, the public face of the trade was far less public, thanks to the closure of the Esir Pazarı and subsequent restrictions on open trading.

The distancing of the state from slavery and the slave trade served the interests of the government regardless of whether modernizers or conservatives were in power. Direct confrontation with the social and religious forces of antiabolitionism was avoided. At the same time, slavery's unseemly showcase was no longer able to attract European notice and opprobrium. As international abolitionists recognized, however, the Ottomans proved far more amenable to curbing the trade in African slaves than to curbing the Circassian trade, much less the practice of slavery, white or black. Stripped of government sanction, diminished by dwindling supply and growing ideological unease, and beset by international agreements and covenants, slavery was a much-reduced institution in its last half century. It nonetheless remained a living institution until the end of the empire.[6] Throughout, the dynasty and like-minded members of the religious, bureaucratic, and military elites continued to be the primary consumers of slaves and defenders of slavery.

The weakened but prolonged life of slavery as social practice testifies to the tenacity of the institution and to the crosscurrents of Ottoman politics. The tortuous pathways of social experience, domestic opinion, and international politics in slavery's end years are beyond the scope of the present study.[7] Those decades, after the Crimean War (1853–6), belong to a far different historical moment. They were punctuated by cascading secessionism in the Balkan provinces and profoundly shaped not just by foreign pressure but also by foreign conquest and other direct interventions.[8] They were also

4 Frederick Millingen, "On the Negro Slaves in Turkey," *Journal of the Anthropological Institute of Great Britain and Ireland* 8 (1870–1): xcii.

5 See Chapter 5, on "Slaves and family," in this volume.

6 Slavery was not explicitly outlawed by decree even under the Republic of Turkey. However, in 1933, within a year of its entry into the League of Nations, Turkey endorsed the prohibition by ratifying the League of Nations Convention on the Suppression of Slavery; see Erdem, *Slavery in the Ottoman Empire*, xix; and Patrick Manning, *Slavery and African Life: Occidental, Oriental, and African Slave Trades* (Cambridge, U.K., 1990), 12.

7 The Slave Market's closure was followed in 1847 by a ban on the African trade in the Persian Gulf and in 1857 by an empire-wide prohibition on the fresh importation of African slaves and, more obliquely, on intercontinental transfers within the empire. The Circassian trade was also hobbled but through less direct means. On the vicissitudes of the slave trade after the closure of the Esir Pazarı, see Erdem, *Slavery in the Ottoman Empire*, 94–124.

8 Toledano, *Ottoman Slave Trade*, 249–67; Tucker, *Women in Nineteenth-Century Egypt*, 173–7; Ricks, "Slaves and Slave Traders," 279–89. Intervention by Great Britain included maritime

Fig. 19. "Circassian Slaves in the Interior of a Harem." With black eunuch. Walsh and Allom, *Constantinople and the Scenery of the Seven Churches*.

distinguished by slaves' own rising consciousness and greater assertions on behalf of emancipatory rights.[9] Ottoman resistance to outright abolition relates chiefly to that later history, to its unique political figures and movements, not least the Young Ottomans, constitutionalists, Abdülhamid II (r. 1876–1909), and the Young Turks, and to the foreign and domestic crises that beset decision makers and public opinion. Nevertheless, in the matter of slavery, the two periods arguably reflect continuity as well as rupture.

Antiabolitionist sentiment and the lack of discomfiture about the perpetuation of slavery in its various forms were rooted in the period with which the present study is concerned. As reflected in the practice and discourse of the capital, Ottoman attitudes toward slavery, and cultural continuities between the periods, call attention to the partiality of the analytical categories – reform and reformism, conservatism and modernity – by which Ottoman history of the eighteenth and nineteenth centuries has been imagined. The gendered dimensions of the attachment to slavery offer an additional gloss on the period and on the categories that inform its historiography.

Historians of slavery and the late Ottoman Empire have commonly viewed Ottoman resistance to emancipation – "laying the axe to the root"[10] – as the product of three overlapping imperatives: national sovereignty, cultural defense, and religious sanction. In the 1840s and thereafter, as European pressure against slavery became more pointed, it was important for imperial leaders to appear to stand up against foreign bullying as a matter of sovereignty with respect to a very domestic issue. The empire was already yielding vital ground – literally and figuratively – on numerous other fronts. Resistance to blanket abolition was especially apt for a practice that the Ottomans regarded not only as woven into the fabric of society but also defensible on humane grounds, although politicians and thinkers after the mid-nineteenth century increasingly decried the abominations of the slave trade per se.

The religious or *shari'ah* defense had deeper resonance. Culture and sovereignty were themselves conceptualized as inherently and necessarily Islamic. More directly, slavery was understood to carry scriptural sanction. The licitness of slavery was attested by its Qur'anic recognition as a social fact, by the Prophet Muhammad's possession of slaves and his clear admonitions regarding the treatment of slaves, and by *shari'ah* law's scrupulous elaboration of the rules of engagement regarding slaves and slave owners in society. A call for the eradication of slavery would conceivably create a

interdictions of the Persian Gulf trade (affecting slave dealing in Iran and India as well as in Ottoman lands), the provision of sanctuary to fugitive slaves, and restrictive measures imposed in Egypt after the British takeover in 1882.

9 Petitions for freedom and politically conscious slave flight were on the rise in the period; Erdem, *Slavery in the Ottoman Empire*, 159–60. Detailed episodes from the later nineteenth century are provided in Toledano, *As If Silent and Absent*.

10 The phrase is attributed to the British abolitionist Joseph Sturge, who stressed the importance of abolishing slavery rather than just the slave trade; Temperley, *British Anti-Slavery*, 65.

religious backlash in an already delicate climate. The abolition of slavery in 1846 in the Regency of Tunis by the unilateral declaration of its governor Ahmed Bey owed to the courage and careful politics of the ruler himself. It was also aided by favorable economic and political conditions and by supportive *ulema*. Over the long term, though, all of that was not enough to erase slavery from Tunisia, where it continued to exist. Slavery's resilience there, according to Larguèche, owed to the fact that it "functioned above all as a component of the lifestyle of socially dominant groups."[11] His observation is relevant to the rest of the slave-owning Mediterranean as well.

Interest and consumption

The religious defense of slavery cannot be detached from the wider circumstances of the religious intelligentsia in the nineteenth century. The *ulema* had gone from enjoying indulgence and favor during much of Selim III's and Mahmud II's reigns to relative marginalization as a corporate force during the Tanzimat era (1839–76). Both Selim and Mahmud had assiduously courted members of the *ulema* in order to dissipate opposition to their innovations.[12] The *ulema* were too diverse a body to incline toward any one political camp, but Mahmud's overtures succeeded in winning broad *ulema* and student support for the dissolution of the Janissaries. Individual *ulema* intellectuals were indispensable in shaping subsequent reform efforts. Without continued assistance or quiescence on the part of many of the *medrese* trained – and their sons and grandsons – the Tanzimat could not have gone forward. Nonetheless, the distinctiveness and distinction of the *ulema* as an elite body pale in comparison to their pre-Tanzimat standing.

The *ulema*'s real and perceived losses over the course of the forty years of the Tanzimat were compounded by deep resentment, shared by others in society, over the reduced sphere of *shari'ah* law and/or their own place in the

11 Abdelhamid Larguèche, *L'Abolition de l'esclavage en Tunisie à travers les archives, 1841–1846* (Tunis, 1990), 37. The views of prominent Tunisian *ulema*, who concurred with Ahmed Bey's emphasis on Islamic law's "marked tendency toward the extension of liberty" (Larguèche, *L'Abolition*, 66), warrant further study in the context of juristic opinion in the capital; for a brief but cogent statement regarding the nature of the debate in Istanbul in the 1860s, see Ali Suavi, "Esir ve Cariye Alım Satımı," in M. Kaplan, İ. Enginün, and B. Emil, eds., *Yeni Türk Edebiyatı Antolojisi* (Istanbul, 1978), 2:569–72. On the Tunisian context, see L. Carl Brown, *The Tunisia of Ahmad Bey, 1837–1855* (Princeton, N.J., 1974), 321–5; Khelifa Chater, "Islam et réformes politiques dans la Tunisie du XIXème siècle," *Maghreb Review* 13, nos. 1–2 (1988): 77–83; Erdem, *Slavery in the Ottoman Empire*, 89–90, 115–17, and 150; Julia A. Clancy-Smith, *Rebel and Saint: Muslim Notables, Populist Protest, Colonial Encounters (Algeria and Tunisia, 1800–1904)* (Berkeley, Calif., 1994), 87, 157, 320.

12 In addition to gifts and emoluments for *medrese* professors and middle-level *kadı*s, both rulers awarded scores of honorary ranks – titles and privileges without actual office – and patronage opportunities to men at the highest levels of the *kadı* (judicial) career. To build up a reform party in the *ulema*, one of their more controversial strategies had been to bypass the *ulema*'s seniority queues and promote their own favorites by imperial decree. See Zilfi, "Elite Circulation" and "A Medrese for the Palace."

new era.[13] The two pillars of religious power and patronage, namely education and the law, were increasingly undermined by Tanzimat reforms. New schools independent of both the *medrese* curriculum and the *ulema*'s supervision siphoned off students and resources. The secularization of commercial and criminal law and the construction of dedicated courts did much the same with regard to the law, thereby depriving the *ulema* of their accustomed institutional monopolies. The edicts, ordinances, and codes of which the sultan's legislation, *kanun*, was comprised had always existed as an adjunct to *shari'ah* and theoretically in concert with it. Increasingly, *kanun* and *shari'ah* became more separate, with different sources of thought and practice, and different bodies of experts and practitioners, although admittedly the lines between them were neither straight nor consistently evident.[14]

The paradigm of religious-secular bifurcation that has often been invoked to characterize the culture wars of the reform era can be faulted for overstating the secular nature of the period and for the very notion of clear-cut bifurcation or duality.[15] With regard to the law, *shari'ah* concepts and premises suffused ostensibly secular juristic practice throughout the reform era.[16] In addition, members of the *ulema* were tapped for policy-making roles in government institutions even when secularly trained personnel seemed called for.[17] Although secular legislation, *kanun*, in the reform years was more religiously hued than has been thought, some fields of law were exempted from the contest from the outset. The jurisdictional realms of family law and personal status, which did so much to define women's experience and expectations, were not subject to the revamping and codification that affected other subcategories of civil law as well as criminal law. Indeed, family law was pointedly omitted from the grand opus of civil law of the nineteenth century, the *Mecelle-i*

13 Berkes, *Development of Secularism*, 169–72; Christoph K. Neumann, *Das Indirekte Argument: Ein Plädoyer für die Tanzīmāt vermittels der Historie* (Münster, 1994), 124.

14 Peters, *Crime and Punishment*, 71–133; Avi Rubin, "Ottoman Modernity: The *Nizamiye* Courts in the Late Nineteenth Century," Ph.D. diss., Harvard University, 2006; Rubin, "Legal Borrowing and Its Impact on Ottoman Legal Culture in the Late Nineteenth Century," *Continuity and Change* 22, no. 2 (2007): 279–303.

15 Berkes, *Development of Secularism*, 106–10; and also on these points, Christoph K. Neumann, "Bad Times and Better Self: Definitions of Identity and Strategies for Development in Late Ottoman Historiography, 1850–1900," in Fikret Adanır and Suraiya Faroqhi, eds., *The Ottomans and the Balkans: A Discussion of Historiography* (Leiden, 2002), 58–9.

16 Ruth A. Miller, *Legislating Authority: Sin and Crime in the Ottoman Empire and Turkey* (New York, 2008), esp. 72–8; Miller, "Apostates and Bandits: Religious and Secular Interaction in the Administration of Late Ottoman Criminal Law," *SI* 97(2003): 155–78.

17 The *ulema*'s representation in the new educational and judicial organs gave scope to religion and the religious class in Tanzimat and post-Tanzimat institutions. See David Kushner, "The Place of the Ulema in the Ottoman Empire during the Age of Reform (1839–1918)," *Turcica* 19 (1987): 51–74; Miller, "Apostates," 172–8. The intellectual and political standpoint of the religious establishment over the course of the nineteenth century and into the twentieth, however, was far from static; see İsmail Kara, "Turban and Fez: *Ulema* as Opposition," in Elisabeth Özdalga, ed., *Late Ottoman Society: The Intellectual Legacy* (London, 2005), 162–200; Karpat, *Politicization*, 114–15.

Ahkâm-i Adliye (Collection of Judicial Ordinances), the last of whose sections or books (*kitab*) was completed in 1876.[18] Like slavery, the core concerns of family law and thus of women's lives in the period – marital relations and the marriage contract, divorce, separation, alimony, dowries and marital debt, child custody, child support – remained encrusted in the *shari'ah* and within the purview of *ulema* practitioners. Progressive legislation in the nineteenth century, such as the establishment of gender parity for daughters with regard to the inheritance of landed property, meant that women's status was part of the period's discourse of rights. Nonetheless, the *shari'ah*-buttressed edifice of family control remained intact.[19]

The matter of slavery's abolition threatened a deep excision, not only from the body of society but also from the domain of the *shari'ah* and of the several thousand men in Istanbul alone who were its current and future interpreters and advocates. On the most basic level, too, the *ulema*'s stake in slavery was bound up in the juristic training that lent them status as exponents of the law. The slave-free divide in law was as fundamental to the *ulema*'s professional claims as were the particulars of prayer, marriage, and the fractional math of inheritance shares. The intransigence over slavery, already an official position in Mahmud II's reign, compares to the somewhat later focus on women's status and veiling.[20] Circling the wagons in slavery's defense produced a lower-key exchange, but both issues were fodder for the same East-West-inflected discourse.[21]

Along with the high military and administrative ranks, members of the *ulema* were among the most consistent users of female slaves. An ostentatious

[18] The *Mecelle-i Ahkâm-i Adliye* (Istanbul, 1305/1887) is concerned with transactions between people (*muamalat*) according to Hanafi jurisprudence. The commission of jurists that produced the compilation was headed by the great *alim* turned bureaucrat, Ahmed Cevdet Pasha (d. 1895). An English translation, originally published in 1901 in Nicosia, Cyprus, is *The Mejelle, Being an English Translation of Majallahel-Ahkam-i-Adliya and a Complete Code on Islamic Civil Law*, trans. C. R. Tyser (Lahore, 1980). On the *Mecelle* and other codifications and reforms, see Shaw and Shaw, *History of the Ottoman Empire*, 2:65–8; Berkes, *Development of Secularism*, 160–9; Davison, *Reform in the Ottoman Empire*, 234–69.

[19] Of the legal reforms affecting women, most did not bear on core women's issues, especially the degree to which they were considered legal minors requiring male guardianship. See, e.g., Ze'evi, *Producing Desire*, 73, regarding the 1858 Criminal Code's gender-equalizing provisions; but see Tuba Demirci and Selçuk Akşin Somel, "Women's Bodies, Demography, and Public Health: Abortion Policy and Perspectives in the Ottoman Empire of the Nineteenth Century," *Journal of the History of Sexuality* 17, no. 3 (2008): 377–420, on *shari'ah* compatibility in the new criminal code on the subject of abortion; and Nicole A. N. M. van Os, "Polygamy before and after the Introduction of the Swiss Civil Code in Turkey," in Touraj Atabaki, ed., *The State and the Subaltern: Modernization, Society and the State in Turkey and Iran* (London, 2007), 179–98.

[20] Although there is disagreement over the sequence of public or official discussions regarding abolition, women, and the religious minorities, it seems clear that women's rights, not to mention gender equality, followed the debates over minority rights and slavery. For a different view, see, e.g., Toledano, *Ottoman Slave Trade*, 275.

[21] Ahmed, *Women and Gender*, 144–68, on "The Discourse of the Veil" and the notion of the fusion of women and culture.

libertine like the Rumelia Kadıasker Damadzade Murad Mehmed (d. 1778), an embarrassment to his more moderate peers, was not typical of *ulema* slave owners.[22] He was, however, representative of the arrogance and sense of entitlement that characterized too many of the privileged cadres. Far more common among the *ulema* were the sundry deputy judges (*naib*s) and *kadı*s of the middle and lower judgeship ranks who traveled to and from their posts accompanied by a sole wife, a female relative or two, and one or more female slaves.[23] Many of their slaves were probably concubines or potential concubines. Others may simply have been acquired as servants and continued to work as such for the ladies of the house. Still others may have been the purchased or inherited property of the mothers and mothers-in-law who were often in these suites.[24] Whatever functions the slaves fulfilled, they seem to have been de rigeur in such households.

Sexual braggarts like Damadzade Murad exemplified the polygynist license that some religious figures took to be their special right if not a badge of religiosity.[25] The ill-fated *şeyhülislam*, Feyzullah (d. 1703), was particularly forthcoming about his conjugal prowess. The father of fifteen surviving children, Feyzullah made it plain in his autobiography that each of the fifteen had been born of a different mother.[26] Among his wives was the daughter of the Kadızadeli preacher Vani Mehmed, who until his disgrace was Feyzullah's great patron and benefactor.[27] In contrast to Feyzullah's fall from grace – for nepotism among other things – it was Damadzade's high living rather than his political excesses that was the cause of his ill repute. Among other

[22] As did the Mekkizades, the Damadzade family had numerous high *ulema* officials to its credit. Süreyya, *Sicill-i Osmani*, 3:271, 4:358–9; Cevdet, *Tarih*, 2:97–9; de Tott, *Memoirs*, 1:40–51.

[23] The term *naib* here refers to judge-substitutes, *medrese* graduates who served in small judgeships in place of nominal officeholders. For the functions of the *naib* in the later context of the Tanzimat, see Jun Akiba, "A New School for Qadis: Education of the Sharia Judges in the Late Ottoman Empire," *Turcica* 35 (2003): 125–63.

[24] For example, *ulema* in transit between Istanbul and posts in Rumelia and Anatolia in the 1740s included: the *kadı* of Sofia, traveling with female family members and an unspecified number of *cariyes*; a *kadı* of the Rumelia *kadı* corps with his wife, mother-in-law, and two *cariyes*; the *kadı* of Akçakızarlık with his wife, mother-in-law, adult daughter, and two *cariyes*; a *kadı* named Abdülaziz with his wife, three children, three *cariye*s, and some servants; the *naib* of Tatarpazarı with his mother, wife, four *cariye*s, and two small children; the *naib* of Çirmen with his wife, son, a *cariye*, and three servants (*hizmetkâr*); a certain Hüseyin Efendi, with his mother Hadice, wife Emine, sister Esmihan, and *cariye* Rukiyye; a *kadı* named İbrahim with his wife, three children, and three *cariye*s; a *kadı* named Mehmed Sadık with three *cariyes* and three little children (no mention of a wife); the *naib* of Yanya with his wife Fatıma, mother-in-law Hadice, a daughter, and six *cariye*s; a *naib* acting for the *kadı* of Istanbul in Uzuncaabad, with his wife, mother-in-law, daughter, and two *cariye*s. See Kal'a et al., *İstanbul'da Sosyal Hayat 1*, 4, 22, 32–3, 53, 75–6, 80–1, 82–3, 200–1, 202, 238.

[25] Damadzade was matched by a bureaucratic contemporary, el-Hajj Mehmed Emin Recai Efendi, who observed strict rules of prayer and fasting but was "inclined to using his slaves as concubines," and thus left more than eighteen children ("orphans") at his death; Cevdet, *Tarih*, 2:149–50.

[26] Ahmed Türek and Farih Çetin Derin, "Feyzullah Efendi'nin Kendi Kaleminden Hal Tercümesi," *Tarih Dergisi* 24 (March 1970): 91.

[27] Zilfi, *Politics of Piety*, 215–20.

scandals, Damadzade was reportedly unable to recognize by sight all of his numerous children. Once prodded, however, he apparently did recall their mothers.[28]

Although the economic interests of slavery's defenders in this part of the Ottoman world do not compare to the economic and social investment of the planter class in the Americas, many individuals and families profited from the slave trade. Part of the potency of religious justifications of slavery was the resonance of the religious idiom in nonreligious venues. The great strength of conservative *ulema* and political figures derived from their ability to mobilize support within the wider population. Members of the public whose attachment to slavery was more economic than theological (e.g., drovers, dealers, and the infrastructure of slave transport) joined forces with the theological and cultural opposition in standing against abolition. Such a conjuncture occurred in the late 1850s, when Red Sea and Indian Ocean slave traders at Jidda added lethal violence to their demonstrations against the Ottoman government and European economic interests.[29] Economic objections played a lesser role in Istanbul than on the imperial peripheries of North Africa and the Arabian Peninsula. However, Istanbul, regardless of the makeup of its own slaving elements, could not afford to ignore antiabolitionist sentiment rising up from the provinces, especially when questions of religious authority and political legitimacy were so much in play.

At bottom, Ottoman dynastic legitimacy rested on its Islamic character. With or without other lines of antiabolitionist reasoning, the ruling elites could not appear to reject scripture and the practice of the Prophet. Since slavery had not been outlawed in the Prophet's time, it was difficult to argue for abolition against the conservative voices raised against outright emancipation. Many aspects of Sultan Mahmud's and the Tanzimat's policies were religiously suspect as it was. Ottoman Muslims had already been asked to change much about themselves without, many thought, reaping benefit. Attacks on the integrity of Mahmud II and the Tanzimat leadership – for their Westernizing, centralizing, modernizing, or secularizing impulses – were routinely presented in terms of religio-moral deviation. Islamic identity itself appeared to be at risk. It seemed to many that the reformist faction disrespected if not discarded the differentiating categories on which Islamic society and its values were founded. Not just the difference between Muslim and non-Muslim, but the notion of an Islamic realm (*Dar el-Islam*), superior to the external infidel foe, had been effaced by the terms of equality that the Ottomans were obliged to concede to

[28] De Tott, *Memoirs*, 1, pt. 1:46. Whether Damadzade intended a joke in his exchange with de Tott, his comment about his family was more boast than apology.

[29] Ahmed Cevdet [Pasha], *Tezâkir*, ed. Cavid Baysun, 2nd ed. (Ankara, 1986), 1:"Tezkire 12"; Michael Christopher Low, "Empire and the Hajj: Pilgrims, Plagues, and Pan-Islam," *IJMES* 40 (2008): 276–7. On attitudes in Arabia and religious opposition, see Lewis, *Race and Slavery*, 80–2; Toledano, *Ottoman Slave Trade*, 129–35; Erdem, *Slavery in the Ottoman Empire*, 86–7.

European allies, adversaries, and trading partners.[30] Recalcitrance over abolition was part of a more general posture taken by elements of the elites and the population at large against the disequilibrium of change, especially change that threatened to transgress on the family and household.

The frozen premises of sumptuary ordinances played a role in the formation – and expression – of Muslim public opinion. They helped prepare the ground for the notional conflation of religion and tradition, a habit of mind that in some quarters intensified over the course of the nineteenth century. As Berkes observed, religion "began to be identified unconsciously with that which is unchanging and, hence, separate from or opposed to that which is changing."[31] The cultural justification of slavery was thus inevitably – and often opportunistically – enmeshed with religion. However, the sense of slavery as an ordained right was, in the cultural context, further sharpened into a matter of necessity. Some apologists portrayed the possession of slaves as essential for the maintenance of the Ottoman family. Free, wage-earning employees supposedly could not rise to the appropriate level of fidelity, whereas slaves would be selflessly protective of their families' material and reputational welfare. Slaves could be entrusted with the most intimate relations of the household, particularly to guarantee the gender system of the idealized upper-class family. Such rationales notwithstanding, it is closer to the truth to say that the danger posed by emancipation had less to do with the integrity of "the Ottoman family" than with sustaining the hierarchical order and trappings of status by which many elite families – wealthy and officially connected – secured or sought to secure their social dominance.[32]

Large households of the extended-family or compound-conjugal type were a minority in Ottoman life. They were a minority even among the governing elites in the late eighteenth and early nineteenth centuries.[33] The view that

30 On the concept of an equality of sovereignty, see Thomas Naff, "Ottoman Diplomatic Relations with Europe in the Eighteenth Century: Patterns and Trends," in Thomas Naff and Roger Owen, eds., *Studies in Eighteenth Century Islamic History* (Carbondale, Ill., 1977), 97–8.

31 Berkes, *Development of Secularism*, 109.

32 Family transformation in late nineteenth-century Egypt has been the subject of a growing literature on economic change and the demise of slavery and military households as preconditions for the bourgeoisification of elite families. See, e.g., Mary Ann Fay, "From Warrior-Grandees to Domesticated Bourgeoisie: The Transformation of the Elite Egyptian Household into a Western-Style Nuclear Family," in Doumani, *Family History in the Middle East*, 77–97; Kenneth M. Cuno, "Ambiguous Modernization: The Transition to Monogamy in the Khedival House of Egypt," in Doumani, *Family History in the Middle East*, 247–69; Beth Baron, *Egypt as a Woman: Nationalism, Gender, and Politics* (Berkeley, Calif., 2005); Lisa Pollard, "The Family Politics of Colonizing and Liberating Egypt, 1882–1919," *Social Politics* 7, no. 1 (2000): 47–79. The transition to monogamy is linked to the Egyptianization of the family and of national politics as conscious distancings from Ottoman political and cultural hegemony. In *Egypt as a Woman*, Baron sees the demise of slavery and its impact on elite self-identity as particularly central to such processes (17–39).

33 On the prevalence of the simple conjugal family, see Duben and Behar, *Istanbul Households*, 48–86, 243; Marcus, *Middle East*, 197; Haim Gerber, "Social and Economic Position of Women in an Ottoman City, Bursa, 1600–1700," *IJMES* 12 (1980): 241; Meriwether, *Kin Who Count*, 69–82.

slavery's end would jeopardize Ottoman domestic life cannot have applied to the 80 to more than 90 percent of families who neither lived in large households nor counted on the buffer of slaves to ensure gender segregation and the honor of the family.[34] If such values were upheld in those households, the task fell to family members and the labor of free, wage workers. For a small but socially resonant subset of the population, the imperial dynasty at its summit, abolition had more portentous implications. Slave ownership and the acquisition of dependents were signposts and scaffolding for estimable social position. Not for the sake of slave owning as such but to anchor the social order for which it stood, slavery's most committed defenders sought to link slave ownership and other badges of wealth and status to the moral authority of Islam and tradition. To that extent, antiabolitionism replicated the stratification strategy of sumptuary legislation.

Sovereign distinction

The top-down reforms of the late eighteenth century and the nineteenth century had the advantage of expeditiousness. The rulers commanded and the populace was obliged to comply. The disadvantage, for good or for bad, was the persistence of views and values that countered the new institutions, rules, and appearance of things. An abiding value whose usefulness the state continued to endorse even after jettisoning turbans and caftans was the material representation of central government power. To distinguish officials as representatives of the state and monarchy, Sultan Mahmud's clothing reforms had been amended to ensure that officials would not be confused with the ordinary populace. Gold and silver braiding, tassels of varying lengths and threads, distinctive colors, and the occasional diamond perked up the elite fez and jacket in the 1830s and thereafter.[35] Unlike official dress, the ownership of slaves was a matter of personal choice, not a government fiat. It was nonetheless an elite social marker, give or take a sprinkling of ownership outside elite circles.

Elite households possessed slaves for many reasons. In Gill Shepherd's apt understatement, slaves were "property with a wide range of potential uses."[36] Apart from adventitious owning as a result of inheritance or gift, slaveholders acquired slaves much as they did other high-status possessions, in expectation of a social or cultural return. Slave ownership – or simply participating in the transfer of slaves by sale or bestowal without owning them for any length of time oneself – was also about associations with past and current power

[34] According to Duben and Behar, *Istanbul Households*, 50, live-in servants (an unknown percentage of them slaves) were found in only 8 percent of Istanbul households registered in 1907; regarding household types in the nineteenth and early twentieth centuries, see also 55–62. It would be interesting to know the rate of slaveholding in upper-class households headed by women, although their possession of slaves may have been the result of inheritance rather than a preference for unfree over free employees.

[35] Lûtfi, *Tarih*, 2–3:425. [36] Shepherd, "Comorians and the East African Slave Trade," 99.

wielders. So long as the sultans preferred slaves as palace servants and slave-origin women as the mothers of their children, the model of the imperial household would be fixed in fact as well as in memory. And so long as the dynasty maintained its legitimacy, slaveholding would continue to project an aura of distinction.[37] But more than mere status consumption, the slave was an unambiguous sign of the right of some people to command the fate of others.

In the dynasty's continued use of women "to communicate with," the traffic in women moved into and out of the palace.[38] Sultans like Selim, Mahmud, and Abdülmecid, reformist in some senses but clearly not in others, were little different from their predecessors or from their fiercely autocratic successor, Abdülhamid II, in the deployment of females to cement bonds with hand-picked military and civilian officials. Some female gifts were princesses of the dynasty, although royal women in the nineteenth century had certain rights of refusal as well as wealth independent of their husbands. The true female gifts were slave women, unwitting exemplars of what Weiner calls "the paradox of keeping-while-giving."[39] The female slave (*cariye*) made up for any dearth of marriageable royal sisters and daughters. All three sultans, like others before and after them, made political alliances through marriage. They assimilated brothers-in-law, nephews-in-law, and/or sons-in-law into monarchist tradition and networks by means of the female gift, a tie with which to bind.[40]

In the early nineteenth century, when the dynasty seemed in danger of producing only viable daughters rather than sons, royal sisters and aunts energetically shopped for consorts for Mahmud and Abdülmecid during each's sultanate. All royals had an interest in perpetuating the dynasty, but because dynastic succession after the early seventeenth century devolved on the eldest prince of the house, sisters had a special interest in seeing a brother rather than an uncle or cousin accede to the throne. In Mahmud's case, after the death of his cousin and brother in 1808, he was, for a number of years, the dynasty's only surviving prince. His sisters did what other royal sisters had done before them. This time, though, the survival of the family was at stake rather than the ascendancy of this or that dynastic branch. Older sister Esma (d. 1848) provided Mahmud with Bezmialem, the Caucasian slave girl who, brought up under Esma's wing, became the mother of Sultan Abdülmecid.[41]

37 A point also made by Toledano, *Slavery and Abolition*, 53.

38 Claude Lévi-Strauss, *The Elementary Structures of Kinship* (1949; repr., Boston, 1969), 496; although it was generally young women who were communicated. On the palace as a gift economy in and of itself, see François Georgeon, "Le Ramadan à Istanbul," in François Georgeon and Paul Dumont, eds., *Vivre dans l'Empire Ottoman: Sociabilités et relations intercommunautaires (xviiie-xxe siècles)* (Paris, 1997), 57.

39 Annette B. Weiner, *Inalienable Possessions: The Paradox of Keeping-while-Giving* (Berkeley, Calif., 1992).

40 However, Mahmud in particular took into consideration his daughters' wishes and dispensed with the childhood betrothals that had marked imperial women's marriages in the seventeenth and eighteenth centuries; see Uluçay, *Harem II*, 92–3.

41 White, *Three Years*, 1:184. It was in Esma's residence that Mahmud spent his last illness and died; Anıl and Gencer, *İkinci Sultan Mahmut*, 86–7.

Fig. 20. "The Sultana in the State [*Araba*], Constantinople." Said to represent Esma, the sister of Mahmud II, departing from her palace on the Golden Horn. Walsh and Allom, *Constantinople and the Scenery of the Seven Churches.*

If the sixteenth century was the age of the royal consort and the seventeenth that of the queen mother,[42] the nineteenth was the province of the royal sister.

The social meaning of slaves as the marker of wealth in the form of people was primarily an artifact of monarchy. The contours and import of slavery, though, reached beyond the abode of the dynasty. Slaveholding was a practice and an aspiration among elite families at various levels of wealth and power. As scholars of Ottoman and other Middle Eastern slaveries well know, one of the difficulties of gauging the extent and sincerity of abolitionist sentiment is the absence of close studies of the public and private writings of statesmen and thinkers. Also lacking are the biographical particulars that enable historians to perform Namierite calculations of personal backgrounds and interests against public utterances and ideology. However, where biographical information beyond career details does exist in relative abundance, as it does for many eighteenth- and nineteenth-century figures, it is rarely joined to the analysis of the political. Certainly policy makers are not reducible to their personal lives, but their personal lives can direct our attention to the extent and limits of their values.

On the issue of slavery, similarities in marital and other personal behavior on the part of ostensible political rivals point to greater social conformity than their public standpoints would suggest. Incongruity between word and deed is perhaps best exemplified by Midhat Pasha, although he was far from alone among Tanzimat notables.[43] Despite impeccable credentials as a progressive, not only as a constitutionalist but also as an advocate for girls' education,[44] he gave and received gifts of slaves even while proclaiming distaste for the institution.[45] He is credited with a bold attempt in 1876 to pressure Sultan Abdülhamid II into setting a national example by emancipating the slaves of the palace. According to his son and biographer, Midhat aimed to have slavery abolished entirely, on the grounds that it was "a scandal and a disgrace to the empire."[46] Others regarded his move as a mere political ploy, an attempt to embarrass Abdülhamid rather than to advance the cause of abolition.[47] The two possibilities are not mutually exclusive. Midhat's real Jeffersonian moment, however, is reflected in his purchase of a *cariye* to become his second wife.

42 As Peirce has established in *Imperial Harem* and elsewhere.

43 According to Davis, *Ottoman Lady*, 93, the well-regarded reformist minister of education of the later nineteenth century, Sami Paşazade Subhi Pasha (d. 1888), had "ten wives and concubines." His father, Sami Pasha, also generously polygynous, had "innumerable sons"; Mardin, *Genesis*, 233.

44 Sema Uğurcan, "Tanzimat Devrinde Kadının Statüsü," in Hakkı Dursun Yıldız, ed., *150. Yılında Tanzimat* (Ankara, 1992), 502. Midhat also established mixed Muslim-Christian schools during his governorships in the European provinces; Mithat, *Life of Midhat Pasha*, 141–4.

45 Erdem, *Slavery in the Ottoman Empire*, 128, 131.

46 Mithat, *Life of Midhat Pasha*, 104–15; but see Erdem, *Slavery in the Ottoman Empire*, 126–7, for an analysis of discrepancies between the English and Ottoman versions of Ali Haydar Mithat's narrative regarding his father's views and aims.

47 Erdem, *Slavery in the Ottoman Empire*, 126–8.

The new sociability of international diplomacy set the stage for the disparity between public performance and private conduct in the lives of Ottoman officials. Polygamy, or rather monogamy, had become a barometer of reformism almost as soon as Mahmud II threw open the doors to regular embassies and social connection. In the first decades of the nineteenth century, when European envoys and their spouses began to exchange visits with their Ottoman hosts and when Ottoman diplomats ventured abroad with their families, the question of polygamy and concubinage inevitably arose. Sensitive to European views, men of the reformist circles took care to give the appearance of monogamy. Some Europeans were under the impression that the principal reformers were living monogamous, bourgeois lives. Others knew differently.[48] Many such dignitaries were, strictly speaking, monogamous. However, like the upper echelons of the governing class, for whom the ownership of female slaves was the norm, men of reformist repute did not forgo the use of concubines in addition to or in place of a legal wife. Mustafa Reşid (d. 1858), the first of the Tanzimat triumvirs and author of the Gülhane Rescript, kept several concubines in addition to his legal and very visible wife.[49] Because elite families were not immune to war, pestilence, and early mortality, especially maternal mortality, yesterday's married man was tomorrow's widower and seeming celibate. However, slave concubinage apparently remained rife, with or without future marriage for the women in question.

A defense of slavery by another of the Tanzimat oligarchs, Mehmed Fuad Pasha (d. 1869), highlights the impasse between Ottoman mores and Western expectations. In a conversation with visitors from the French diplomatic community in the late 1850s, Fuad hoped to dispel Western misperceptions of Ottoman slavery's disrepute and detriment by identifying as a daughter-in-law a young woman, formerly a slave, who had been reared in the family since childhood.[50] The great reformer's emphasis on the social mobility and easeful lives of his son's wife and many other female slaves inadvertently revealed the political neutrality of slaveholding. "Traditional" households could be found across the Ottoman political spectrum. The various

48 Austen Henry Layard, *Sir A. Henry Layard, G.C.B, D.C.L.: Autobiography and Letters from His Childhood until His Appointment as H. M. Ambassador at Madrid...*, ed. Sir Arthur Otway (London, 1903), 2:51–2, 94–5. Layard concluded that "enlightened men" like Mustafa Reşid, Ali, and Fuad pashas, whom he had known since the 1830s, had only one wife. For an opposing view, see Frederick Millingen, "The Circassian Slaves and the Sultan's Harem," *Journal of the Anthropological Society of London* 8 (1870–1): cxix. In any case, Layard's observation begs the question of polygyny and concubinage. Although Layard believed that the statesman and man of letters Ahmed Vefik Pasha (d. 1891) and his diplomat father Ruheddin Efendi were both monogamous and without male or female slaves in their households, his description of Ruheddin's residence is filled with references to its numerous attendants, including harem women, and other servants. See also Slade, *Records of Travels*, 2:361–2, on Reşid Mehmed, grand vizier from 1829 to 1833; Davis, *Ottoman Lady*, 88–94.

49 G. L. Dawson Damer, *Diary of a Tour in Greece, Turkey, Egypt, and the Holy Land* (London, 1841), 1:175; White, *Three Years*, 1:306–7; Davis, *Ottoman Lady*, 93–4.

50 Durand de Fontmagne, *İstanbul Günleri*, 308–10.

historiographical descriptors – conservative, reformist, modernist, traditionalist, and their hybrids – that have been used to label the politics of Ottoman movers and shakers tend to lose their defining edges in the face of female slavery and its defenders.[51]

Fuad Pasha's defense also laid open the female-centeredness not only of slavery in the period but also of the mildness defense itself. Elite households and the imperial palace rather than the slave trails of the Sudan and the Caucasus were the heart of his argument, but in conjuring up the household, romantic displacement was the order of the day. It was the treatment of female slaves, specifically the white Circassian and Georgian slaves of elite households, that Fuad and more intransigent apologists relied on to suggest slavery's beneficent face. It is telling that Istanbul apologists made a point of distinguishing Istanbul's practice from "the misery and suffering that slaves experience in the Egyptian region."[52] There, slave owning occurred more widely in the population, beyond the governing classes, and the brutalities of the African trade were closer at hand. Apart from the rhetorical and moral invisibility of black African slaves, who were ubiquitous in many of the same households of the day, Fuad's defense testifies to the impress of power, disproportionate and unequal, however well or badly slaves' lives might turn out.

Fuad's apologetics also suggest the asymmetrical possibilities of elite male conjugation – the older man with a very young consort or bride and the free man with a slave mate. Although it is unclear what the age difference may have been between the young daughter-in-law and Fuad's son, May-December liaisons were a more common reality than was the rich, happy ex-slave wife.[53] Access to females was a cornerstone of elite male privilege and entitlement. The villa in which Fuad entertained foreign guests into the 1860s held numerous female slaves, all of them in attendance on the then lady of the house,[54] but all accessible to some extent to the master and his sons. The men's relationships with the women may, in fact, have met the highest standards of both Ottoman and Western propriety. Nonetheless, the enslavement of outsider women for the uses of the governing class was an open advertisement of the gender of extreme dependency. In nineteenth-century male relationships, the idea of men's having a master was shedding its positive connotations. Where women were concerned, however, the staying power of female slavery and the patriarchal household argued for the normalcy of women's being mastered.

[51] But see Karpat, *Politicization*, 358–9, for more nuanced terminology for the complex politics of Tanzimat statesmen and intellectuals.

[52] The remark is that of the nineteenth-century man of letters, Ahmed Midhat Efendi, in his *Üss-i İnkılâp*, written for Abdülhamid II and first published in 1877–8; a modern Turkish version is *Üss-i İnkılâp*, ed. Tahir Galip Seratlı (Istanbul, 2004), 2:149.

[53] Marriage data from the end of the nineteenth century and beginning of the twentieth century reveal a substantial age gap between husband and wife under normal circumstances, and "the later the [man's] marriage the larger the age-gap," especially when the bride was a virgin as opposed to a widow or divorcée; Duben and Behar, *Istanbul Households*, 127–33.

[54] Boulden, *An American among the Orientals*, 91–7.

Slaveholding was about free women and class location as well as about male dominion and aspirations. The interface between elite women's supervision and slave women's labor bears on the relational domination by which women acceded to male-led social hierarchies and participated in their making and maintenance. After Fuad Pasha died, his widow was one of the most important of such aristocratic brokers, carrying on a lucrative business for some years.[55] The wife of Ali Pasha (d. 1871), the third of the Tanzimat triumvirs, was apparently also an active participant in the trade.[56] Elite women's active role in the slave trade provided independent income, but an immediate economic return was arguably secondary to the prospect of other gains. Women who brokered governing-class marriages for their female slaves were perhaps compensating for their own exclusion from power in other, more public arenas. But the social space created by matrimonial sponsorship and continuing intimacy as former owners (and even potential heirs) did not merely support a parallel, empowered female universe. In expanding elite women's social environment, slave owning offered an important point of entry to the decision-making precincts of peer households and factions. Western observers in the late eighteenth century and the nineteenth century were surprised at how much power elite women, as well as royals, exercised behind the scenes. "Petticoat power," as some called it, "is much more considerable than one would presume." Apart from the power of feminine pleas on behalf of banished or imprisoned relatives, many an official owed his promotion – or his fall – to "petticoat interest."[57]

Although women were disadvantaged relative to men of the same class, elite women – and wealthy or high-status women in general – enjoyed advantages relative to some junior men and certainly relative to junior or dependent women. Social elevation and privilege were attainable attributes rather than closed preserves. However, most slaves were not able to find elite status outside their owners' protective aura. Slave women who succeeded in rising above the common lot of captives had opportunities to supervise the labor of other women. Wealthy free women, especially royal women, were empowered from the outset. Sultan Mahmud was heard to say about his strong-minded older sister Esma that had she been born a man, she, rather than he, would have been sultan.[58] Esma did not become sultan, but she was her brother's confidante, and she shared his ability to make use of the productive and reproductive labor of subordinate women.[59] Finding consorts for her brother was only one such

[55] Millingen, "Circassian Slaves," cxiv, who identifies her only as "Behieh," probably for "Behice."

[56] That is, Mustafa Reşid Pasha, Fuad Pasha, and Ali Pasha. Saz, *Imperial Harem*, 63.

[57] Olivier, *Voyage dans l'Empire Othoman*, 1:170. Cf. Slade, *Records of Travels*, 2:316; de Tott, *Memoirs*, 1, pt. 1:154–5.

[58] Anıl and Gencer, *İkinci Sultan Mahmut*, 84. With the deaths of Selim III and Mustafa IV, there was talk of placing Esma on the throne instead of Mahmud. Members of the *ulema* provided religious objections, but lay officials were equally keen to quash the idea.

[59] Claire C. Robertson and Martin A. Klein, "Women's Importance in African Slave Systems," in Claire C. Robertson and Martin A. Klein, eds., *Women and Slavery in Africa* (Madison, Wis., 1983), 12–16.

activity. The many palaces over which she and other royal women presided in the eighteenth and nineteenth centuries ran on female and male slave labor, and the females were available, as the males were not, for marital gift giving to the powerful.[60]

Esma and other women of the dynasty, especially princesses of the blood, were shielded from the kitchen combat that could erupt between working-class free women and the female slaves under their supervision. Nonetheless, female-on-female violence also occurred in the palace and *konak* (mansion) classes. When it did, class and status had a way of tempering punishments. A high-profile incident in 1817–18 draws attention to, among other things, the singular advantages of status and connection. At the time, the incident shone an unwelcome light on the Mekkizades, as the villain of the piece was the daughter of the late Şeyhülislam Mekki Mehmed and thus also the sister of Mekkizade Mustafa, who at the time was poised to become the next *şeyhülislam*. His sister's misadventure is another female slave story but of an uncommon kind inasmuch as the slave masters in this case were aristocratic daughters rather than vulnerable tradespeople.

Most of the chroniclers do not identify the daughter of Mekki Mehmed by name.[61] They tend to refer to her cryptically as Mekki's daughter, sometimes adding her wifely connection. She was, in fact, the wife of a former *kadı* of Bursa, Arif Mehmed, one of the many sons of the notorious Damadzade Murad. Elsewhere she is called Lebibe Hanım. Her ill fame had its start in her relationship with Züleyha Hanım, the daughter of another prominent official, the by then deceased chronicler and onetime head of the nascent foreign ministry, Ahmed Vasıf Efendi (d. 1806). The women, who were neighbors, were discovered in compromising circumstances in Lebibe's house by Lebibe's own slave woman. When the slave reprimanded the two and threatened to expose them, Lebibe – with or without the aid of Züleyha – seized the woman, shaved her head, and dispatched her in her underclothes to a hospital for lepers. Presumably, the women expected or hoped that the slave would not be heard from again. And presumably there was more violence in the attack and more money to buy silence than the spare narrative discloses.

Unfortunately for Lebibe and Züleyha, the ruse failed and, not surprisingly, came to the attention of the authorities. The two women cannot have overcome the slave, bundled her out of the house and onto a boat, and then had her transported over the water to Üsküdar without the help of confederates. The incident probably was bruited about locally before it came to the notice of Sultan Mahmud. The two women were banished in considerable disgrace to different rural destinations. Lebibe's husband Arif Mehmed, doubly disgraced, was forced into exile with his wife, who was charged with outrageous

[60] The extravagance of the princesses' minicourts amid rising imperial debt was a cause of concern and bitterness among Tanzimat officials.

[61] These observations are necessarily tentative, pending further research in manuscript versions of the chronicles and other documents of the time.

obscenity. Outrageous or not, all were pardoned within a matter of months, thanks to the women's contrition and the intercession of Lebibe's brother, Mekkizade Mustafa, who became *şeyhülislam* for the first time in early 1818.[62]

The incident confirms the insecurity that could topple a slave's world, but it also invites speculation about justice in the larger sense. In some respects, the system of slave protections worked. Those who cruelly mistreated their bondswoman were found out and punished. However, the entire event transpired in the late months of 1817 and early 1818, a period that saw sumptuary restrictions on women and minorities tightened and punishments made more severe. They were also years in which the Ottoman war against the puritanical Wahhabis in Arabia was reaching its climax. As *şeyhülislam*, Mekkizade was to provide Mahmud with invaluable religious support against the movement and its defeated Saudi leadership.[63]

In the Züleyha-Lebibe incident, it is not the nasty punishment meted out to the tattletale *cariye* – if tattletale is what she was – that draws our attention. It is instead the light penalty imposed on persons who, in Sultan Mahmud's own words, were guilty of "outrageous obscenity."[64] By contrast, men and women of the lower orders who violated clothing minutiae were subjected to caning, imprisonment, or worse. The lapses and indiscretions of the privileged with regard to their monarch could be capital offenses. However, when the privileged mistreated their social inferiors they scarcely merited a slap on the wrist.[65] It is no wonder that elite stakeholders and those who hovered at the edges of elite belonging were reluctant to disown the perquisites of entitlement, their *askeri* edge, even after the *askeri-reaya* divide was being bridged by the Tanzimat's equalizing pronouncements and policies.

To be sure, Fuad Pasha's stark characterization of traditional society as sharply divided between ruler and ruled painted a false picture of historical reality.[66] Still, it may not have misstated the governing orders' own worldview. The architects of the Tanzimat were committed to a new order and a more inclusive social vision but never to the extent of destroying the elitist, patriarchal character of the social hierarchy. They had that particular

[62] Cevdet, *Tarih*, 10:239–40; Şanizade, *Tarih*, 2:362–3. Arif Mehmed also received promotions in later years, rising to titular chief justice of Anatolia, although he subsequently ran into difficulties allegedly because of ties to the Janissary-affiliated Bektaşi dervish order; Süreyya, *Sicill-i Osmani*, 3:271.

[63] Mekkizade as *şeyhülislam* was in office to issue the *fetva* authorizing the execution of Abdullah ibn Saud and his confederates; Cevdet, *Tarih*, 11:57–62; Şanizade, *Tarih*, 3:15–17, 59.

[64] *Bu ihanet-i fahişesinden naşi*; Cevdet, *Tarih*, 10:240.

[65] The Damadzades were notorious for more than the antics of Damadzade Murad and their Mekkizade daughter-in-law. In the mid-1770s, another member of the family, identified as Murad's brother, one Mehmed Tahir, beat and stabbed innocent groundskeepers who questioned his and his friends' presence on the sultan's meadow. Mehmed Tahir, a *medrese* professor at the time, only spent a month or two in exile thanks to the intercessions of his family, including his brother Murad, which resulted in a pardon from Abdülhamid I. Cevdet *Tarih*, 2:17–18.

[66] See Chapter 1, "Seeing like the Ottoman state," p. 11, in this volume.

continuity in common with their more absolutist political rivals,[67] although they were less keen on the egregious bowing and scraping that the royal party demanded of subordinates.[68] It becomes less surprising, then, to recall the strong links between Ottoman officials stationed in the provinces and their penchant for slaveholding, especially female slaveholding. In the nineteenth century, social reproduction via the slave consort, preferably the Circassian or Georgian consort, reinforced the social distance between rulers and ruled. Among some of the ruling class at least, that distance was underscored not just by hegemonic male access to multiple females but also by ethnically selective conjugal choices. Whether or not conjugal strategies were always ethnically tinged – Arab averse in North Africa and anti-Anatolian Turkish and Kurdish at Istanbul – female slaves provided ruling elements with a "social species" with which to replicate themselves.[69] When slavery's defenders built their arguments around female slavery, concubinage, and the household, they did so not just because those categories were most defensible on mildness grounds. Rather, their frame of reference was female slavery because female slavery was the foundation on which Ottoman slaveholding rested. Male military slaves, agricultural slaves, eunuchs, and domestics of all kinds came and went. Indeed, in many times and places they disappeared entirely. Not so female slaves, as domestics and as concubines, not until the end of the empire itself.

Continuity in ruling rites and social practice remained a closely held value throughout the reform era. However, it was far from uniformly applied. State efforts to stabilize women's attire while permitting masculine dress to follow its own Westernized course remind us of the discriminating deployment of continuity or tradition as Islamic values. Slavery was sustained by a similar bow to continuity. Yet the retention of female slavery, notably elite-driven harem slavery, did not just capitalize on the force and promise of timelessness. Female slavery was, to be sure, a metaphor in the service of the patriarchal household and masculine authority. But female slavery was also a social relationship based in reality. Slaveholding was living proof of societal hierarchy and of the monarchical tradition that held it in place. Indeed, the value of slavery lay in its association with authority relations of all kinds, in a period when Ottoman rulership, and sovereignty itself, were so much in peril.

67 Ortaylı, *İmparatorluğun En Uzun Yüzyıl*, 171.

68 For some years during the height of the Tanzimat, prostrations and other extreme servile obeisances were discouraged, but they were restored by Sultan Abdülaziz after the deaths of Fuad and Ali pashas; Mithat, *Life of Midhat Pasha*, 62–3; Necdet Kurdakul, *Tanzimat Dönemi Basınında Sosyo-Ekonomik Fikir Hareketleri* (Ankara, 1997), 256.

69 Meillassoux, *Anthropology of Slavery*, 193.

Abbreviations

AHR	*American Historical Review*
BSOAS	*Bulletin of the School of Oriental and African Studies*
CSSH	*Comparative Studies in Society and History*
DBİA	*Dünden Bugüne İstanbul Ansıklopedisi*
EI2	*Encyclopaedia of Islam, 2nd edition*
İA	*İslam Ansiklopedisi*
IJMES	*International Journal of Middle East Studies*
IJTS	*International Journal of Turkish Studies*
IS	*Islamic Studies*
İstM	İstanbul Müftülüğü
JAOS	*Journal of the American Oriental Society*
JESHO	*Journal of the Economic and Social History of the Orient*
JNES	*Journal of Near Eastern Studies*
JTS	*Journal of Turkish Studies*
Ktp.	Kütüphane (Library)
MES	*Middle Eastern Studies*
OA	*Osmanlı Araştırmaları*
OTAM	*Ankara Üniversitesi Osmanlı Tarihi Araştırma ve Uygulama Merkezi Dergisi*
SI	*Studia Islamica*
TID	*Tarih İnceleme Dergisi*
TOEM	*Tarih-i Osmani Encümeni Mecmuası*
TKS	Topkapı Sarayı Kütüphanesi/Topkapı Palace Library, Istanbul
TSAB	*Turkish Studies Association Bulletin*
TSAJ	*Turkish Studies Association Journal*
TveT	*Tarih ve Toplum*
WI	*Die Welt des Islams*
ZDMG	*Zeitschrift der Deutschen Morgenländischen Gesellschaft*

Selected works

Abdal-Rehim, Abdal-Rehim Abdal-Rahman. "The Family and Gender Laws in Egypt during the Ottoman Period." In *Women, the Family*, ed. Sonbol, 96–111.

Abdülaziz Bey. *Osmanlı Âdet, Merasim ve Tabirleri: Âdat ve Merasim-i Kadime, Tabirât ve Muamelât-i Kavmiye-i Osmaniye*. 2 vols. Istanbul, 1995.

Abdullah, Yenişehirli. *Behcet el-Fetava ma Nukul*. Istanbul, 1266/1849.

Abir, Mordechai. "The Ethiopian Slave Trade and Its Relation to the Islamic World." In *Slaves and Slavery*, ed. Willis, 2:123–36.

Abou El-Fadl, Khaled. "The Use and Abuse of 'Holy War.' Review of James Turner Johnson, *The Holy War Idea in Western and Islamic Traditions* (University Park, PA, 1997)," Carnegie Council Resource Library, http://www/cceia.org/viewMedia.php/prmID/216.

Abou-El-Haj, Rifa'at 'Ali. *Formation of the Modern State: The Ottoman Empire Sixteenth to Eighteenth Centuries*. Albany, N.Y., 1991.

———. "Ottoman Attitudes toward Peace Making: The Karlowitz Case," *Der Islam* 51 (1974): 131–7.

———. "The Ottoman Vezir and Paşa Households, 1683–1703: A Preliminary Report." *JAOS* 94 (1974): 438–47.

Abou Hadj, Rifaat [Rifa'at 'Ali Abou-El-Haj]. "The Ottoman Nasihatname as a Discourse over 'Morality.'" In *Mélanges Robert Mantran*, edited by Abdeljelil Temimi. Zaghouan, 1988, 17–29.

Abu-Manneh, Butrus. "The Naqshbandiyya-Mujaddidiyya in the Ottoman Lands in the Early 19th Century." *WI*, n.s., 22 (1982): 1–36.

Abun-Nasr, Jamil M. *A History of the Maghrib in the Islamic Period*. Cambridge, U.K., 1987.

Adams, Robert McC. *The Evolution of Urban Society*. Chicago, 1966.

Adang, Camilla. "Women's Access to Public Space according to al-Muhallā bi-l-Āthār." In *Writing the Feminine: Women in Arab Sources*, edited by Manuela Marín and Randi Deguilhem. London, 2002, 75–94.

[Adıvar], Halide Edib. *Memoirs of Halidé Edib*. New York, n.d.

———. *Mor Salkımlı Ev*. Istanbul, 1963.

Adıyeke, Nuri. "Osmanlı İmparatorluğu'nda Tanzimat Dönemi Evlilikleri." In *Pax Ottomana*, ed. Çiçek, 121–49.

Ahmed, Leila. *Women and Gender in Islam*. New Haven, Conn., 1992.

Akarlı, Engin. "Gedik: Implements, Mastership, Shop Usufruct, and Monopoly among Istanbul Artisans, 1750–1850." *Wissenschaftskolleg-Jahrbuch* (1984–85): 223–32.

______. "Punishment, Repression and Violence in the Marketplace: Istanbul, 1730–1840." Paper presented at the Annual Meeting of the American Historical Association. Washington, D.C., January 2004.

Akçam, Halûk. "Osmanlılarda Cinsellik." *Bravo Dergisi* 23–7 (1983), http://www.halukakcam.com/B6/Notes/OsmanliCinsellik1983.htm.

Akdağ, Mustafa. *Türkiye'nin İktisadî ve İctimaî Tarihi.* 2 vols. Istanbul, 1974.

Akgündüz, Ahmed. *İslâm Hukukunda Kölelik-Câriyelik Müessesesi ve Osmanlı'da Harem.* Istanbul, 1995.

______. *Şer'iye Sicilleri Mahiyeti, Toplu Kataloğu ve Seçme Hükümler.* 2 vols. Istanbul, 1988–9.

Akiba, Jun. "A New School for Qadis: Education of the Sharia Judges in the Late Ottoman Empire." *Turcica* 35 (2003): 125–63.

Aksan, Virginia H. "Ottoman Political Writing, 1768–1808," *IJMES* 25 (1993): 53–69.

______. *An Ottoman Statesman in War and Peace: Ahmed Resmi Efendi,* 1700–1783. Leiden, 1995.

______. *Ottoman Wars, 1700–1870: An Empire Besieged.* Harlow, U.K., 2007.

Aksan, Virginia H., and Daniel Goffman, eds. *The Early Modern Ottomans: Remapping the Empire.* Cambridge, U.K., 2007.

Aktaş, Necati, et al., eds. *85 Numaralı Mühimme Defteri (1040–1041/1042/1630–1631/1632).* Ankara, 2002.

Aktaş, Necati, Nezihi Aykut, Mücteba İlgürel, and Mehmet İpşirli, et al., eds. *Dîn-i Hümâyûn Sicilleri Dizisi I: 3 Numaralı Mühimme Defteri (966–967/1558–1560).* 2 vols. Ankara, 1993.

Aktepe, M. Münir. *Patrona İsyanı (1730).* Istanbul, 1958.

Alexandris, Alexis. "The Greek Census of Anatolia and Thrace (1910–1912): A Contribution to Ottoman Historical Demography." In *Ottoman Greeks in the Age of Nationalism,* ed. Gondicas and Issawi, 45–76.

Ali Efendi, Çatalcalı. *Fetava-i Ali Efendi.* 2 vols. Istanbul, 1305/1887.

Ali Efendi [Çatalcalı]. *Şeyhülislam Fetvaları,* translated by İbrahim Ural. N.p., 1995.

Aliye, Fatma. *Cevdet Paşa ve Zamanı.* Istanbul, 1332/1914.

Allen, W. E. D., and Paul Muratoff, eds. *Caucasian Battlefields: A History of the Wars on the Turco-Caucasian Border, 1821–1921.* Cambridge, U.K., 1953.

al-Marghinani, 'Ali ibn Abi Bakr. *The Hedaya: Commentary on the Islamic Laws,* translated by Charles Hamilton. 1791. Reprint, New Delhi, 1985.

______. *The Hedaya or Guide: A Commentary on the Mussulman Laws,* translated by Charles Hamilton, edited by Standish Grove. 2nd ed. 1873. Reprint, Lahore, 1957.

Alpkaya, Gökçen. "Tanzimat'ın 'Daha az Eşit' Unsurları: Kadınlar ve Köleler," *OTAM* 1, no. 1 (Haziran 1990):1–10.

[Altınay], Ahmet Refik. *Felâket Seneleri.* Istanbul: 1332/1916–17.

______. *Hicrî On Birinci Asırda İstanbul Hayatı*: 1000–1100. Istanbul, 1931.

______. *Hicrî On İkinci Asırda İstanbul Hayatı (1100–1200).* Istanbul, 1930.

______. *Hicrî On Üçüncü Asırda İstanbul Hayatı (1200–1255).* Istanbul, 1932.

______. *Kadınlar Saltanatı.* Istanbul, 1332/1913–14.

______. *Lâle Devri.* Ankara, 1973.

______. *On Altıncı Asırda İstanbul Hayatı (1553–1591).* Istanbul, 1935.

______. *Onuncu Asr-i Hicri'de İstanbul Hayatı (961–1000).* Istanbul, 1333/1914–15.

Altunsu, Abdülkadir. *Osmanlı Şeyhülislâmları.* Ankara, 1972.

And, Metin. *Osmanlı Şenliklerinde Türk Sanatları*. Ankara, 1982.

Anderson, Bonnie S., and Judith P. Zinsser. *A History of Their Own: Women in Europe from Prehistory to the Present*. 2 vols. 1988. Reprint, New York, 2000.

Anderson, J. N. D. "Homicide in Islamic Law." *BSOAS* 13, no. 4 (1951): 811–28.

Anderson, Sonia P. *An English Consul in Turkey: Paul Rycaut at Smyrna, 1667–1678*. Oxford, 1989.

Andreasyan, Hrand D., trans. *Polonyalı Simeon'un Seyahatnâmesi (1608–1619)*. Istanbul, 1964.

Andrews, Walter G., and Mehmet Kalpaklı. *The Age of Beloveds: Love and the Beloved in Early-Modern Ottoman and European Culture and Society*. Durham, N.C., 2005.

Anhegger, Robert. "Osmanlı Devleti'nde Hiristiyanlar ve İç Tartışmaları." *Tarih ve Toplum* 8, no. 47 (November 1987): 17–20.

Anıl, Yaşar Şahin, and Meltem Gencer. *Sultan İkinci Mahmut*. Istanbul, 2006.

Anonymous. "Kadın-I." *TveT* (1984): 32–9.

Apak, Melek Sevüktekin, Filiz Onat Gündüz, and Fatma Öztürk Eray. *Osmanlı Dönemi Kadın Giyimleri*. Ankara, 1997.

Arat, Zehra F., ed. *Deconstructing Images of "the Turkish Woman."* New York, 1998.

Arberry, A. J., trans. *The Koran Interpreted*. New York, 1955.

Arif, Dürrizade Mehmed. *Netice el-Fetava ma el-Nukul*. Istanbul, 1265/1848.

Arıkan, V. Sema, ed. *III. Selim'in Sırkâtibi Ahmed Efendi tarafından Tutulan Rûznâme*. Ankara, 1993.

Aristarchi Bey, [Grégoire]. *Législation ottomane, ou, recueil des lois, réglements, ordonnances, traités, capitulations et autres documents officiels de l'Empire Ottoman*. 7 vols. Constantinople, 1873–88.

Artan, Tülay. "Architecture as a Theatre of Life: Profile of the Eighteenth-Century Bosphorus." Ph.D. diss., Massachusetts Institute of Technology, 1988.

Aşa, H. Emel. "İlk Türk Kadın Romancısı Fatma Aliye Hanım'ın Romanlarında Aile ve Kadın." In *Sosyo-Kültürel*, ed. Erverdi, Yıldız, Kara et al., 2: 650–9.

Asım, Küçük Çelebizade İsmail. *Tarih-i Asım*. Vol. 6 of Raşid, *Tarih-i Raşid*. Istanbul, 1282/1865.

Ata, Tayyarzade Ahmed Ataullah. *Tarih-i Ata*. 5 vols. [Istanbul, 1875–6.]

Atayı, Nevizade. *Zeyl-i Şakaik*. 2 vols. in 1. Istanbul, 1268/1851–2.

Atıl, Esin. *Levni and the Surname: The Story of an Eighteenth-Century Ottoman Festival*. Istanbul, 1999.

Atış, Sarah. "Telling Tales in the Mirror of Culture: A Comparison of Aarne Tale Type 709, 'Snow White,' and Eberhard-Boratav Tale Type 167, 'Nar Tanesi.'" Paper presented at Türk Dil Kurumu, 3. Uluslar Arası Türk Dil Kurultayı, Ankara, 1996.

Austen, Ralph A. "The Mediterranean Islamic Slave Trade out of Africa: A Tentative Census." *Slavery and Abolition* 13 (1993): 214–48.

Ayalon, David. *Eunuchs, Caliphs and Sultans: A Study in Power Relationships*. Jerusalem, 1999.

Aykut, Şevki Nezihi, ed. *Şer'iyye Sicillerine göre İstanbul Tarihi: İstanbul Mahkemesi 121 Numaralı Şer'iyye Sicili*. Istanbul, 2006.

Aynur, Hatice. "Ottoman Literature." In *The Cambridge History of Turkey*, ed. Faroqhi. 3:481–520.

Ayvansarayı, Hâfız Hüseyin. *Mecmuâ-i Tevarih*, edited by Fahri Ç. Derin and Vâhid Çabuk. Istanbul, 1985.

Bacqué-Grammont, Jean-Louis. "Sur deux affaires mineures dans les 'registres d'affaires importantes,'" In *Mémorial Ömer Lûtfi Barkan*, edited by Robert Mantran. Paris, 1980, 1–10.

Baer, Gabriel. "Slavery and Its Abolition." In *Studies in the Social History of Modern Egypt*, 161–89.

______. *Studies in the Social History of Modern Egypt*. Chicago, 1969.

Baer, Marc David. *Honored by the Glory of Islam: Conversion and Conquest in Ottoman Europe*. Oxford, 2008.

______. "Honored by the Glory of Islam: The Ottoman State, Non-Muslims, and Conversion to Islam in Late Seventeenth-Century Istanbul and Rumelia." Ph.D. diss., University of Chicago, 2001.

______. "Islamic Conversion Narratives of Women: Social Change and Gendered Religious Hierarchy in Early Modern Ottoman Istanbul." *Gender and History* 16, no. 2 (2004): 425–58.

Bailey, Frank Edgar. *British Policy and the Turkish Reform Movement: A Study in Anglo-Turkish Relations, 1826–1853*. Cambridge, Mass., 1942.

Barbir, Karl K. "One Marker of Ottomanism: Confiscation of Ottoman Officials' Estates." In *Identity and Identity Formation*, edited by Baki Tezcan and Karl K. Barbir, 135–51.

______. *Ottoman Rule in Damascus, 1708–1758*. Princeton, N.J., 1980.

Baron, Beth. *Egypt as a Woman: Nationalism, Gender, and Politics*. Berkeley, Calif., 2005.

Bartholdy, J. L. S. *Voyage en Grèce, fait dans les années 1803 et 1804*, translated by A. Du Coudray. 2 vols. Paris, 1807.

Başaran, Betül. "Remaking the Gate of Felicity: Policing, Migration, and Social Control in Istanbul at the End of the Eighteenth Century, 1789–1793." Ph.D. diss., University of Chicago, 2006.

Bellamy, James A. "Sex and Society in Islamic Popular Literature." In *Society and the Sexes in Medieval Islam*, edited by Afaf Lutfi al-Sayyid-Marsot. Malibu, Calif., 1979, 232–42.

Ben-Naeh, Yaron. "Blond, Tall, with Honey-Colored Eyes: Jewish Ownership of Slaves in the Ottoman Empire." *Jewish History* 20 (2006): 73–90.

______. *Jews in the Realm of the Sultans: Ottoman Jewish Society in the Seventeenth Century*. Tübingen, 2008.

______. "Moshko the Jew and His Gay Friends: Same-Sex Sexual Relations in Ottoman Jewish Society." *Journal of Early Modern History* 9 (2005): 79–105.

Bennett, Judith M. "Misogyny, Popular Culture, and Women's Work." *History Workshop Journal* 31 (1991): 166–88.

______. "Women's History: A Study in Continuity and Change." *Women's History Review* 2, no. 2 (1993): 173–84.

Berkes, Niyazi. *The Development of Secularism in Turkey*. New York, 1998.

Berlin, Ira. *Many Thousands Gone: The First Two Centuries of Slavery in America*. Cambridge, Mass., 1998.

Bill, James A., and Robert Springborg. *Politics in the Middle East*. Boston, 1979.

Bilmen, Ömer Nasuhi. *Hukukı İslâmiyye ve Istılahatı Fıkhiyye Kamusu*. 8 vols. Istanbul, n.d.

Blassingame, John W. *The Slave Community: Plantation Life in the Antebellum South*. New York, 1972.

Blumi, Isa. "Undressing the Albanian: Finding Social History in Ottoman Material Cultures." In *Ottoman Costumes*, ed. Faroqhi and Neumann, 157–80.

Bon, Ottaviano. *The Sultan's Seraglio: An Intimate Portrait of Life at the Ottoman Court*, edited by Godfrey Goodwin. London, 1996.

Bonner, Michael, Mine Ener, and Amy Singer, eds. *Poverty and Charity in Middle Eastern Contexts*. Albany, N.Y., 2004.

Boogert, Maurits H. van den. *The Capitulations and the Ottoman Legal System: Qadis, Consuls and Beratlıs in the 18th Century*. Leiden, 2005.

———. "Redress for Ottoman Victims of European Privateering: A Case against the Dutch in the Divan-i Hümayun (1708–15)." *Turcica* 33 (2001): 91–118.

Bouhdiba, Abdelwahab. *Sexuality in Islam*, translated by Alan Sheridan. 1975. Reprint, London, 1998.

Boulden, James E. P. *An American among the Orientals, including an Audience with the Sultan and a Visit to the Interior of a Turkish Harem*. Philadelphia, 1855.

Bourdieu, Pierre. *Distinction: A Social Critique of the Judgement of Taste*, translated by Richard Nice. Cambridge, Mass., 2000.

Bowen, Donna Lee. "Muslim Juridical Opinions concerning the Status of Women as Demonstrated by the Case of *'Azl*." *JNES* 40, no. 4 (1981): 323–8.

Bowring, Sir John. *Report on Egypt and Candia, 1823–1838, under the Reign of Mohamed Ali*. New ed. London, 1998.

Bozkurt, Gülnihâl. *Gayrimüslim Osmanlı Vatandaşlarının Hukukî Durumu*, 1839–1914. Ankara, 1989.

———. "Köle Ticaretinin Sona Erdirilmesi Konusunda Osmanlı Devletinin Taraf Olduğu İki Devletlerarası Anlaşma." *OTAM* 1, no. 1 (1990): 45–77.

Braude, Benjamin."International Competition and Domestic Cloth in the Ottoman Empire, 1500–1650." *Review* 2 (1979): 437–51.

Braude, Benjamin, and Bernard Lewis, eds., *Christians and Jews in the Ottoman Empire: The Functioning of a Plural Society*. 2 vols. New York, 1982.

British and Foreign Anti-Slavery Society. *Anti-Slavery Reporter*. London, 1840–.

Brockopp, Jonathan E. *Early Mālikī Law: Ibn 'Abd al-Hakam and His Major Compendium of Jurisprudence*. Leiden, 2000.

Brown, L. Carl. *The Tunisia of Ahmad Bey, 1837–1855*. Princeton, N.J., 1974.

Brummett, Palmira. "Ceremonies of Submission and the Containment of Violence in 16th and 17th Century Ottoman Narrative and Imagery." Paper presented at Annual Meeting of the American Historical Association. Washington, D.C., January 2004.

———. *Ottoman Seapower and Diplomacy in the Age of Discovery*. Albany, N.Y., 1994.

Bukhari, Muhammad ibn Ismail. *Al-Sahih*. Vol. 3, http://www.usc.edu/schools/college/crcc/engagement/resources/texts/muslim/search.html.

Bulut, R. "İstanbul Kadınlarının Kıyafetleri ve II. Abdülhamid'in Çarşafı Yasaklaması." *Belgelerle Türk Tarihi Dergisi*, no. 48 (2001): 33–5.

Burke, Edmund, ed. *Struggle and Survival in the Modern Middle East*. Berkeley, Calif., 1993.

Busbecq, Ogier Ghislen de. *Turkish Letters*. London, 2001.

Câbî Ömer Efendi. *Câbî Târihi*, edited by M. Ali Beyhan. 2 vols. Ankara, 2003.

Canbakal, Hülya. *Society and Politics in an Ottoman Town: 'Ayntāb in the Seventeenth Century*. Leiden, 2007.

Çavuşoğlu, Semiramis. "The Kadızadelis: An Attempt of Şeri'at-Minded Reform in the Ottoman Empire." Ph.D. diss., Princeton University, 1990.

Cazacu, Matei. "La mort infâme: décapitation et exposition des têtes à Istanbul (xve–xix siècles)." In *Les Ottomans et la mort*, ed. Veinstein, 245–89.

Çetin, Osman. *Sicillere göre Bursa'da İhtida Hareketleri ve Sosyal Sonuçlar*, 1472–1909. Ankara, 1994.
Cevdet (Paşa), Ahmed. *Tarih-i Cevdet*. 12 vols. Istanbul, 1309/1891.
______. *Tezâkir*, edited by Cavid Baysun. 2nd ed., 4 vols. Ankara, 1986.
Chamberlain, Michael. *Knowledge and Social Practice in Medieval Damascus*, 1190–1350. Cambridge, U.K., 1994.
Chapoutot-Remadi, Mounira. "Femmes dans la ville mamluke. *JESHO* 38, no. 2 (1995): 145–64.
Chater, Khelifa. "Islam et réformes politiques dans la Tunisie du XIXème siècle." *Maghreb Review* 13, no. 1–2 (1988): 77–83.
Chatterjee, Indrani, and Richard M. Eaton. *Slavery and South Asian History*. Bloomington, Ind., 2006.
Çiçek, Kemal. "Living Together: Muslim-Christian Relations in Eighteenth-Century Cyprus as Reflected by the Sharī'a Court Records." *Islam and Christian-Muslim Relations* 4, no. 1 (1993): 36–64.
______. "Osmanlılar ve Zimmiler: Papa Pavlos'nun İslâm'a Hakareti ya da Renklere İsyanı." In *Kıbrıs'tan Kafkasya'ya*, ed. Çiçek and Saydam, 135–62.
______. "Tanzimat ve Şer'iat: Namaz Kılmayan ve İçki İçenlerin Takip ve Cezalandırılması hakkında Kıbrıs Muhassılı Mehmet Tal'at Efendi'nin İki Buyuruldusu." *Toplumsal Tarih* 3, no. 15 (1995): 22–7.
______, ed. *Pax Ottomana : Studies in Memoriam, Prof. Dr. Nejat Göyünç*. Haarlem, 2001.
Çiçek, Kemal, and Abdullah Saydam. *Kıbrıs'tan Kafkasya'ya Osmanlı Dünyasında Siyaset, Adalet ve Raiyyet*. Trabzon, 1998.
Clancy-Smith, Julia A. *Rebel and Saint: Muslim Notables, Populist Protest, Colonial Encounters (Algeria and Tunisia, 1800–1904)*. Berkeley, Calif., 1994.
Clarence-Smith, William Gervase. *Islam and the Abolition of Slavery*. London, 2006.
______, ed. *The Economics of the Indian Ocean Slave Trade in the Nineteenth Century*. London, 1989.
Colley, Linda. *Captives*. New York, 2002.
______. *The Ordeal of Elizabeth Marsh: A Woman in World History*. New York, 2007.
Cook, Michael. *Commanding Right and Forbidding Wrong in Islamic Thought*. Cambridge, U.K., 2001.
______. *Forbidding Wrong in Islam: An Introduction*. Cambridge, U.K., 2003.
Corrigan, Philip. "On Moral Regulation." *Sociological Review* 29 (1981): 313–37.
Coulson, N[oel] J[ames]. *Succession in the Muslim Family*. Cambridge, U.K., 1971.
Courteille, Pavet de, trans. *Conseils de Nabi Efendi à son fils Aboul Khair*. Paris, 1857.
Craven, Elizabeth, Baroness. *A Journey through the Crimea to Constantinople*. New York, 1970.
Cunningham, Allan. *Collected Essays*, edited by Edward Ingram. London, 1993.
Cuno, Kenneth M. "African Slaves in 19th-Century Rural Egypt." *IJMES* 41 (2009): 186–8.
______. "Ambiguous Modernization: The Transition to Monogamy in the Khedival House of Egypt." In *Family History in the Middle East*, ed. Doumani, 247–69.
Cuthell, David Cameron. "The Muhacirin Komisyonu: An Agent in the Transformation of Ottoman Anatolia, 1860–1866." Ph.D. diss., Columbia University, 2005.
Dalvimart, Octavian. *The Costume of Turkey*. London, 1804.
Damer, G. L. Dawson. *Diary of a Tour in Greece, Turkey, Egypt, and the Holy Land*. 2 vols. London, 1841.

D'Amora, Rosita. "Some Documents concerning the Manumission of Slaves by the Pio Monte della Misericordia in Naples (1681–1682). *Eurasian Studies* 1, no. 1 (2002): 37–76.

Danışman, Zuhuri, ed. *Koçi Bey Risalesi*. Istanbul, 1972.

Danişmend, İsmail Hami *İzahlı Osmanlı Tarihi Kronolojisi*. 2nd rev. ed., 6 vols. Istanbul, 1971–2.

Dankoff, Robert. *The Intimate Life of an Ottoman Statesman: Melek Ahmed Pasha (1588–1662)*. Albany, N.Y., 1991.

———. *An Ottoman Mentality: The World of Evliya Çelebi*. Leiden, 2004.

Darling, Linda T. *Revenue-Raising and Legitimacy: Tax Collecting and Finance Administration in the Ottoman Empire*, 1550–1660. Leiden, 1996.

d'Arvieux, Louis Laurent. *Mémoires du chevalier d'Arvieux... contenant ses voyages à Constantinople, dans l'Asie, la Syrie, la Palestine, l'Égypte, et la Barbarie*... 6 vols. Paris, 1735.

Dávid, Géza. "Manumissioned Female Slaves at Galata and Istanbul around 1700." In *Frauen, Bilder*, ed. Prätor and Neumann, 1:229–36.

———. "Manumitted Male Slaves at Galata and Istanbul around 1700." In *Ransom Slavery*, ed. Dávid and Fodor, 183–91.

Dávid, Géza, and Pál Fodor, eds. *Ransom Slavery along the Ottoman Borders: Early Fifteenth-Early Eighteenth Centuries*. Leiden, 2007.

Davis, David Brion. *The Problem of Slavery in Western Culture*. Ithaca, N.Y., [1966].

———. *Slavery and Human Progress*. 1984. Reprint, New York, 1986.

Davis, Fanny. *The Ottoman Lady: A Social History from 1718–1918*. New York, 1986.

Davis, Robert C. *Christian Slaves, Muslim Masters: White Slavery in the Mediterranean, the Barbary Coast, and Italy, 1500–1800*. New York, 2003.

Davison, Roderic H. *Reform in the Ottoman Empire, 1856–1876*. 2nd ed. New York, 1973.

———. "Turkish Attitudes Concerning Christian-Muslim Equality in the Nineteenth Century." *AHR* 59 (1954): 844–64.

De Amicis, Edmondo. *Constantinople*, translated by Caroline Tilton. New York, 1878.

De Bruyn, Cornelis. *A Voyage to the Levant, or Travels in the Principal Parts of Asia Minor, the Islands of Scio, Rhodes, Cyprus, &c*, translated by W. J. Reizen. London, 1702.

Decker, Catherine H. "Regency Fashion." http://regencyfashion.org.

DeKay, James E. *Sketches of Turkey in 1831 and 1832*. New York, 1833.

Demirci, Tuba, and Selçuk Akşin Somel. "Women's Bodies, Demography, and Public Health: Abortion Policy and Perspectives in the Ottoman Empire of the Nineteenth Century." *Journal of the History of Sexuality* 17, no. 3 (2008): 377–420.

Denny, Frederick M. *Islam and the Muslim Community*. San Francisco, 1987.

Deringil, Selim. "Redefining Identities in the Late Ottoman Empire: Policies of Conversion and Apostasy." In *Imperial Rule*, edited by Alexei Miller and Alfred J. Rieber. Budapest, 2004, 107–32.

Dernschwam, Hans. *Hans Dernschwam's Tagebuch einer Reise nach Konstantinopel und Kleinasien (1553/55)*, edited by Franz Babinger. Munich, 1923.

Develi, Hayati, ed. *XVIII. Yüzyıl İstanbul Hayatına dair Risâle-i Garîbe*. Istanbul, 1998.

Diez, Heinrich Friedrich von, ed. and trans. *Ermahnung an Islambol, oder Strafgedicht des turkischen Dichters Uweissi uber die Ausartung der Osmanen*. Berlin, 1811.

Djavidan Hanum, [Hanım]. *Harem Life by Princess Djavidan Hanum*... London, 1931.

D'Ohsson, Mouradgea. *Tableau général de l'Empire Othoman*. 7 vols. Paris, 1788–1824.

Douglas, Mary, and Baron Isherwood. *The World of Goods: Towards an Anthropology of Consumption*. 1979. Reprint, London, 1996.
Doumani, Beshara. "Endowing Family: Waqf, Property Devolution, and Gender in Greater Syria, 1800–1860." *CSSH* 40, no. 1 (1998): 3–41.
Doumani, Beshara, ed. *Family History in the Middle East: Household, Property, and Gender*. Albany, N.Y., 2003.
Drescher, Seymour, and Stanley L. Engerman, eds. *A Historical Guide to World Slavery*. Oxford, 1998.
Duben, Alan, and Cem Behar. *Istanbul Households: Marriage, Family, and Fertility, 1880–1940*. Cambridge, U.K., 1991.
Durand de Fontmagne, Marie, Baronne. *İstanbul Günleri: İkinci İmparatorluk Döneminde İstanbul'da Fransız Konsolosluğunda Geçen Günler*, translated by İsmail Yerguz. Istanbul, 2007.
Durkheim, Émile. *Émile Durkheim on Morality and Society: Selected Writings*, edited by Robert N. Bellah. Chicago, 1973.
Dürrizade Mehmed Arif, et al. *Netice el-Fetava ma el-Nukul*. Istanbul, 1265/1848.
Du Vignau, Sieur des Joanots. *A New Account of the Present Condition of the Turkish Affairs*. London, 1688.
Düzdağ, M. Ertuğrul. *Şeyhülislâm Ebussuûd Efendi Fetvaları Işığında 16. Asır Hayatı*. Istanbul, 1972.
Dwight, H. G. *Constantinople, Old and New*. New York, 1915.
Eisenstein, Zillah R. *The Female Body and the Law*. Berkeley, Calif., 1988.
Eldem, Edhem. *French Trade in Istanbul in the Eighteenth Century*. Leiden, 1999.
______. "Urban Voices from Beyond: Identity, Status and Social Strategies in Ottoman Muslim Funerary Epitaphs of Istanbul (1700–1850), in *The Early Modern Ottomans*, ed. Aksan and Goffman, 233–55.
Elkins, Stanley M. "The Slavery Debate." *Commentary* 60 (1975): 40–54.
El-Leithy, Tamer. "Coptic Culture and Conversion in Medieval Cairo, 1293–1524." Ph.D. diss., Princeton University, 2005.
Elliot, Henry G. *Some Revolutions and Other Diplomatic Experiences*. New York, 1922.
Elliot, Matthew. "Dress Codes in the Ottoman Empire: The Case of the Franks." In *Ottoman Costumes*, ed. Faroqhi and Neumann, 103–23.
El-Rouayheb, Khaled. *Before Homosexuality in the Arab-Islamic World, 1500–1800*. Chicago, 2005.
Enault, Louis. *Constantinople et la Turquie*. Paris, 1855.
Engerman, Stanley, Seymour Drescher, and Robert Paquette, eds. *Slavery*. Oxford, 2001.
Ennaji, Mohammed. *Serving the Master: Slavery and Society in Nineteenth-Century Morocco*. New York, 1999.
Ercan, Yavuz. "Osmanlı İmparatorluğunda Gayri Müslimlerin Giyim, Mesken ve Davranış Hukuku." *OTAM* 1, no. 1(1990): 117–25.
______. *Osmanlı Yönetiminde Gayrimüslimler: Kuruluştan Tanzimat'a kadar Sosyal, Ekonomik ve Hukuki Durumları*. Ankara, 2001.
Erdem, [Y.] Hakan. "'Do Not Think of the Greeks as Agricultural Labourers': Ottoman Responses to the Greek War of Independence." In *Citizenship and the Nation-State in Greece and Turkey*, edited by Faruk Birtek and Thalia Dragonas. London, 2005, 67–84.
______. *Slavery in the Ottoman Empire and Its Demise*, 1800–1909. London, 1996.
Ergene, Boğaç A. "Costs of Court Usage in Seventeenth- and Eighteenth-Century Ottoman Anatolia: Court Fees as Recorded in Estate Inventories," *JESHO* 45, no. 1 (2002): 2–39.

———. *Local Court, Provincial Society and Justice in the Ottoman Empire: Legal Practice and Dispute Resolution in Çankırı and Kastamonu (1652–1744)*. Leiden, 2003.

———. "On Ottoman Justice: Interpretations in Conflict (1600–1800)." *Islamic Law and Society* 8, no. 1 (2001): 52–87.

———. "Pursuing Justice in an Islamic Context: Dispute Resolution in Ottoman Courts of Law." *Political and Legal Anthropology Review* 27, no. 1 (2004): 51–71.

Ergin, Osman Nuri. *Mecelle-i Umur-i Belediye*. 5 vols. Istanbul, 1338/1922.

Ergut, Ferdan. *Modern Devlet ve Polis: Osmanlı'dan Cumhuriyet'e Toplumsal Denetimin Diyalektiği*. Istanbul, 2004.

Ertuğ, Nejdet. *Osmanlı Döneminde İstanbul Deniz Ulaşımı ve Kayıkçılar*. Ankara, 2001.

Erverdi, Ezel, Hakkı Dursun Yıldız, İsmail Kara et al., eds. *Sosyo-Kültürel Değişme Sürecinde Türk Ailesi*. 3 vols. Ankara, 1992.

Esen, Nükhet. "Türk Ailesindeki Değişmenin Romanımıza Yansımaları." In *Sosyo-Kültürel*, ed. Erverdi, Yıldız, Kara et al. 2:660–76.

Esposito, John L., with Natana J. DeLong-Bas. *Women in Muslim Family Law*. 2nd ed. Syracuse, N.Y., 2001.

Evin, Ahmet Ö. "The Tulip Age and the Definitions of 'Westernization.'" In *Türkiye'nin Sosyal ve Ekonomik Tarihi (1071–1920)*, edited by Osman Okyar and Halil İnalcık. Ankara, 1980, 131–45.

Evliya Çelebi. *Evliya Çelebi Seyahatnâmesi*, edited by Tevfik Temelkuran and Necati Aktaş. 8 vols. Istanbul, 1976–82.

Ewald, Janet J. "Slavery in Africa and the Slave Trades from Africa." *AHR* 97 (April 1992): 465–85.

Eyice, Semavi. "İstanbul'un Mahalle ve Semt Adları hakkında bir Deneme." *Türkiyat Mecmuası* 14 (1964): 199–216.

Fahmy, Khaled. *All the Pasha's Men: Mehmet Ali, His Army, and the Making of Modern Egypt*. Cambridge, U.K., 1997.

———. "Prostitution in Egypt in the Nineteenth Century." In *Outside In: On the Margins of the Modern Middle East*, edited by Eugene L. Rogan. London, 2002, 77–103.

Fargues, Philippe. "Family and Household in Mid-Nineteenth-Century Cairo." In *Family History in the Middle East*, ed. Doumani, 23–50.

Faroqhi, Suraiya N. "Black Slaves and Freedmen Celebrating, Aydın, 1576." *Turcica* 21–3 (1991): 205–15.

———. "Declines and Revivals in Textile Production." In *The Cambridge History*, ed. Faroqhi, 3:356–75.

———. "From the Slave Market to Arafat: Biographies of Bursa Women in the Late Fifteenth Century." *TSAB* 24, no. 1 (2000): 3–20.

———. "Labor Recruitment and Control in the Ottoman Empire (Sixteenth and Seventeenth Centuries)." In *Manufacturing in the Ottoman Empire*, ed. Quataert, 13–57.

———. *Making a Living in the Ottoman Lands, 1480–1820*. Istanbul, 1995.

———. "Migration into Eighteenth-Century 'Greater Istanbul' as Reflected in the Kadı Registers of Eyüp." *Turcica* 30 (1998): 163–83.

———. "Quis Custodiet Custodes? Controlling Slave Identities and Slave Traders in Seventeenth- and Eighteenth-Century Istanbul." In *Stories of Ottoman Men and Women: Establishing Status, Establishing Control*. Istanbul, 2002, 245–63.

———. *Stories of Ottoman Men and Women: Establishing Status, Establishing Control*. Istanbul, 2002.

______. *Subjects of the Sultan: Culture and Daily Life in the Ottoman Empire*. London, 2005.

______. *Towns and Townsmen of Ottoman Anatolia: Trade, Crafts and Food Production in an Urban Setting*. Cambridge, U.K., 1984.

Faroqhi, Suraiya N., ed. *The Cambridge History of Turkey*. Vol. 3, *The Later Ottoman Empire*, 1603–1839. Cambridge, U.K., 2006.

Faroqhi, Suraiya N., and Christoph K. Neumann, eds. *Ottoman Costumes: From Textiles to Identity*. Istanbul, 2004.

Fay, Mary Ann. "From Warrior-Grandees to Domesticated Bourgeoisie: The Transformation of the Elite Egyptian Household into a Western-Style Nuclear Family." In *Family History in the Middle East*, ed. Doumani, 77–97.

______. "The Ties That Bound: Women and Households in Eighteenth-Century Egypt." In *Women, the Family*, ed. Sonbol, 155–72.

______. "Women and Households: Gender, Power, and Culture in Eighteenth-Century Egypt." Ph.D. diss., Georgetown University, 1993.

______. "Women and *Waqf*: Property, Power, and the Domain of Gender in Eighteenth-Century Egypt." In *Women in the Ottoman Empire*, ed. Zilfi, 28–47.

Fendoğlu, Hasan Tahsin. *İslâm ve Osmanlı Hukukunda Kölelik ve Câriyelik*. Istanbul, 1996.

Fierro, Maribel. "Idra'ū l-Hudūd bi-l-Shubuhāt: When Lawful Violence Meets Doubt." *Hawwa* 5 (2007): 208–38.

Fındıkoğlu, Ziyaeddin. *Tanzimat 2*. Ankara, 1999.

Findley, Carter V. "The Acid Test of Ottomanism: The Acceptance of Non-Muslims in the Late Ottoman Bureaucracy." In *Christians and Jews*, ed. Braude and Lewis, 1:340–68.

______. *Bureaucratic Reform in the Ottoman Empire: The Sublime Porte, 1789–1922*. Princeton, N.J., 1980.

______. "La Soumise, la subversive: Fatma Aliye, romancière et féministe." *Turcica* 27 (1995): 153–76.

______. *Ottoman Civil Officialdom: A Social History*. Princeton, N.J., 1989.

Finkel, Caroline. *Osman's Dream: The Story of the Ottoman Empire 1300–1923*. New York, 2005.

Finley, Moses I. *Ancient Slavery and Modern Ideology*, edited by Brent D. Shaw. Princeton, N.J., 1998.

Finley, Moses I., ed. *Classical Slavery*. 1987. Reprint, London, 2003.

Fischer, David H. *Albion's Seed: Four British Folkways in America*. New York, 1989.

Fisher, Alan. "Chattel Slavery in the Ottoman Empire." *Slavery and Abolition* 1 (1985): 25–45.

______. "The Sale of Slaves in the Ottoman Empire: Markets and State Taxes on Slave Sales." *Boğaziçi Üniversitesi Hümaniter Bilimler Dergisi* 6 (1978): 149–74.

______. "Studies in Ottoman Slavery and Slave Trade, II: Manumission." *JTS* 4 (1980): 49–56.

Fisher, Allan G. B., and Humphrey J. Fisher. "Slavery amongst the Muslims of Africa." In *Slavery, a Comparative Perspective*, ed. Winks, 108–15.

Fleischer, Cornell. *Bureaucrat and Intellectual in the Ottoman Empire: The Historian Mustafa Âli, 1541–1600*. Princeton, N.J., 1986.

Flemming, Barbara. "Die Vorwahhabitische Fitna im Osmanischen Kairo 1711." In *İsmail Hakkı Uzunçarşılı'ya Armağan*. Ankara, 1976, 55–65.

Fodor, Pál. "Piracy, Ransom Slavery and Trade: French Participation in the Liberation of Ottoman Slaves from Malta during the 1620s." *Turcica* 33 (2001): 119–34.

Fogel, Robert W., and Stanley L. Engerman. *Time on the Cross: The Economics of American Negro Slavery*. Boston, 1974.

Forster, Charles Thornton, and F. H. Blackburn Daniell, eds. *The Life and Letters of Ogier Ghiselin de Busbecq*. 2 vols. London, 1881.

Fortna, Benjamin C. *Imperial Classroom: Islam, the State, and Education in the Late Ottoman Empire*. New York, 2002.

Friedman, Ellen G. *Spanish Captives in North Africa in the Early Modern Age*. Madison, Wis., 1983.

Frierson, Elizabeth B. "Women in Late Ottoman Intellectual History." In *Late Ottoman Society*, ed. Özdalga, 135–61.

Fukusawa, Katsumi. *Toilerie et commerce du Levant, d'Alep à Marseille*. Paris, 1987.

Gallagher, John, and Ronald Robinson. "The Imperialism of Free Trade." *Economic History Review*, 2nd ser., 6, no. 1 (1953): 1–15.

Galland, Antoine. *Journal d'Antoine Galland pendant son séjour à Constantinople, 1672–1673*, edited by C. Schefer. 2 vols. in 1. Paris, 1881.

Garnett, Lucy M. J. *Turkish Life in Town and Country*. New York, 1904.

Gautier, Théophile. *Constantinople*. New York, 1875.

Genç, Mehmet. "Ottoman Industry in the Eighteenth Century: General Framework, Characteristics and Main Trends." In *Manufacturing in the Ottoman Empire*, ed. Quataert, 59–86.

Gencer, Bedri. "The Rise of Public Opinion in the Ottoman Empire (1839–1909)." *New Perspectives on Turkey* 30 (2004): 115–54.

Genovese, Eugene D. *Roll, Jordan, Roll: The World the Slaves Made*. New York, 1974.

Georgeon, François. "Le Ramadan à Istanbul." In *Vivre dans l'Empire Ottoman: Sociabilités et relations intercommunautaires (xviiie–xxe siècles)*, by François Georgeon and Paul Dumont. Paris, 1997, 31–113.

Gerber, Haim. *Economy and Society in an Ottoman City: Bursa, 1600–1700*. Jerusalem, 1988.

———. "Social and Economic Position of Women in an Ottoman City, Bursa, 1600–1700." *IJMES* 12 (1980): 231–44.

Gershoni, Israel Y., Hakan Erdem, and Ursula Wocöck, eds. *Histories of the Modern Middle East: New Directions*. Boulder, Colo., 2002.

Gibb, E. J. W. *A History of Ottoman Poetry*. 6 vols. 1900–9. Reprint, London, 1958–67.

Gibb, H. A. R., and Harold Bowen. *Islamic Society and the West*. Vol. 1, *Islamic Society in the Eighteenth Century*. 2 parts. London, 1950–7.

Gibb, H. A. R., and J. H. Kramers, eds. *Shorter Encyclopaedia of Islam*. Ithaca, N.Y., 1953.

Gilbert, Arthur N. "Buggery and the British Navy, 1700–1861." In *History of Homosexuality in Europe and America (Studies in Homosexuality)*, edited by Wayne R. Dynes and Stephen Donaldson. New York, 1992, 132–58.

Ginio, Eyal. "The Administration of Criminal Justice in Ottoman Selânik (Salonica) during the Eighteenth Century." *Turcica* 30 (1998): 185–209.

———. "Living on the Margins of Charity: Coping with Poverty in an Ottoman Provincial City." In *Poverty and Charity in Middle Eastern Contexts*, ed. Bonner, Ener, and Singer, 165–84.

______. "Piracy and Redemption in the Aegean Sea during the First Half of the Eighteenth Century." *Turcica* 33 (2001): 135–47.

Glazer, Mark. "Women Personages as Helpers in Turkish Folktales." In *Studies in Turkish Folklore, in Honor of Pertev N. Boratav*, edited by İlhan Başgöz and Mark Glazer. Bloomington, Ind., 1978, 98–109.

Göçek, Fatma Müge. *Rise of the Bourgeoisie, Demise of Empire: Ottoman Westernization and Social Change*. New York, 1996.

Goffman, Daniel. "Ottoman *Millets* in the Early Seventeenth Century." *New Perspectives on Turkey* 11 (1994): 135–58.

Goitein, S. D. "Slaves and Slavegirls in the Cairo Geniza Records." *Arabica* 9 (1962): 1–20.

Golombek, Lisa. "The Draped Universe of Islam." In *Content and Context of Visual Arts in the Islamic World*, edited by Pricilla O. Soucek. University Park, Pa., 1988, 25–38.

Gölpınarlı, Abdülbaki. *Mevlânâ'dan sonra Mevlevîlik*. Istanbul, 1953.

Gondicas, Dimitri, and Charles Issawi, eds. *Ottoman Greeks in the Age of Nationalism: Politics, Economy, and Society in the Nineteenth Century*. Princeton, N.J., 1999.

Goody, Jack. "Slavery in Time and Space." In *Asian and African Systems of Slavery*, ed. Watson, 16–42.

Göyünç, Nejat. "Frauen in der Familie Osman und am osmanischen Hof." In *Frauen, Bilder*, ed. Prätor and Neumann, 1:103–7.

Gradeva, Rossitsa. *Rumeli under the Ottomans, 15th–18th Centuries: Institutions and Communities*. Istanbul, 2004.

Greene, Molly, ed. *Minorities in the Ottoman Empire*. Princeton, N.J., 2005.

Grenville, Sir Henry. *Observations sur l'état actuel de l'Empire Ottoman*, edited by Andrew S. Ehrenkreutz. Ann Arbor, Mich., 1965.

Guboglu, M[ihail]. *Paleografia şi Diplomatica Turco-Osmană: Studiu şi Album*. Bucharest, 1958.

Gutman, Herbert G. *The Black Family in Slavery and Freedom, 1750–1925*. New York, 1976.

Habermas, Jürgen. *The Structural Transformation of the Public Sphere: An Inquiry into a Category of Bourgeois Society*, translated by Thomas Burger. 1989. Reprint, Cambridge, Mass., 1991.

Hagen, Gottfried. "Legitimacy and World Order." In *Legitimizing the Order*, ed. Karateke and Reinkowski, 55-83.

Hakim, Mehmed. "Hâkim Tarihi." Istanbul, TKS, Bağdat nos. 231 and 233.

Hallaq, Wael B. *Ibn Taymiyya against the Greek Logicians*. Oxford, 1993.

Halman, Talat S. *Süleyman the Magnificent Poet*. Istanbul, 1987.

Hamadeh, Shirine. "The City's Pleasures: Architectural Sensibility in Eighteenth-Century Istanbul." Ph.D. diss., Massachusetts Institute of Technology, 1999.

______. *The City's Pleasures: Istanbul in the Eighteenth Century*. Seattle, 2007.

Hambly, Gavin R. G., ed. *Women in the Medieval Islamic World: Power, Patronage, and Piety*. New York, 1998.

Hamid, Abdul Ali, ed. *Moral Teachings of Islam: Prophetic Traditions from "al-Adab al-Mufrad" by Imam al-Bukhari*. Walnut Creek, Calif., 2003.

Hammer-Purgstall, Joseph von. *Geschichte des Osmanischen Reiches*. 10 vols. Pest, 1827–35.

Hanna, Nelly. *Habiter au Caire: La maison moyenne et ses habitants au XVIIe et XVIIIe siècles*. Cairo, 1991.

———. *Making Big Money in 1600: The Life and Times of Isma'il Abu Taqiyya*. Syracuse, N.Y., 1998.

———. "Marriage among Merchant Families in Seventeenth-Century Cairo." In *Women, the Family*, ed. Sonbol, 143–54.

Harrak, Fatima. "Mawlay Isma'il's *Jaysh al-'Abīd*: Reassessment of a Military Experience." In *Slave Elites*, ed. Toru and Philips, 177–96.

Hatem, Mervat. "The Politics of Sexuality and Gender in Segregated Patriarchal Systems: The Case of Eighteenth- and Nineteenth-Century Egypt." *Feminist Studies* 12 (1986): 251–74.

Hathaway, Jane. *Beshir Agha: Chief Eunuch of the Ottoman Imperial Harem*. London, 2005.

———. "Marriage Alliances among the Military Households of Ottoman Egypt." *Annales Islamologiques* 29 (1995): 133–49.

Hay, Douglas. "Property, Authority and the Criminal Law." In *Albion's Fatal Tree: Crime and Society in Eighteenth-Century England*, edited by Douglas Hay et al. London, 1975, 16–63.

Hearn, Jeff. "From Hegemonic Masculinity to the Masculinity of Men." *Feminist Theory* 5, no. 1 (2004): 49–72.

Hellie, Richard. "Recent Soviet Historiography on Medieval and Early Modern Russian Slavery." *Russian Review* 35, no. 1 (1976): 1–32.

———. *Slavery in Russia, 1450–1725*. Chicago, 1982.

Heyd, Uriel. "The Ottoman 'Ulemā and Westernization in the Time of Selīm III and Maḥmūd II." *Scripta Hierosolymitana* 9 (1961): 63–96.

———. *Studies in Old Ottoman Criminal Law*, edited by V. L. Ménage. Oxford, 1973.

Heywood, Colin. "A Buyuruldu of A.H. 1100/A.D. 1689 for the Dragomans of the English Embassy at Istanbul." In *The Balance of Truth: Essays in Honour of Professor Geoffrey Lewis*, edited by Çiğdem Balım-Harding and Colin Imber. Istanbul, 2000, 125–44.

Heyworth-Dunne, J[ames]. *An Introduction to the History of Education in Modern Egypt*. London, 1939.

Hill, Aaron. *A Full and Just Account of the Present State of the Ottoman Empire in All Its Branches*. . . London, 1733.

Hill, Bridget. *Servants and English Domestics in the Eighteenth Century*. Oxford, 1996.

Hızır İlyas Ağa, Hafız. *Tarih-i Enderun: Letaif-i Enderun, 1812–1830*, translated by Cahit Kayra. Istanbul, 1987.

Hogendorn, Jan S. "The Location of the 'Manufacture' of Eunuchs." In *Slave Elites*, ed. Toru and Philips, 41–68.

Howard, Douglas A. "Ottoman Historiography and the Literature of 'Decline' of the Sixteenth and Seventeenth Centuries." *Journal of Asian History* 22 (1988): 52–77.

Hufton, Olwen. *The Prospect before Her: A History of Women in Western Europe*. 1995. Reprint, New York, 1998.

Hughes, Diane Owen. "Sumptuary Law and Social Relations in Renaissance Italy." In *Disputes and Settlements: Law and Human Relations in the West*, edited by John Bossy. Cambridge, U.K., 1983, 69–99.

Hunt, Alan. *Governance of the Consuming Passions: A History of Sumptuary Law*. New York, 1996.

———. *Governing Morals: A Social History of Moral Regulation*. Cambridge, U.K., 1999.

Hunwick, John. "Islamic Law and Polemics over Race and Slavery in North and West Africa (16th–19th Century)." In *Slavery in the Islamic Middle East*, ed. Marmon, 43–68.

______. "The Religious Practices of Black Slaves in the Mediterranean Islamic World." In *Slavery on the Frontiers of Islam*, ed. Lovejoy, 149–71.

Hunwick, John, and Eve Troutt Powell, eds. *The African Diaspora in the Mediterranean Lands of Islam*. Princeton, N.J., 2002.

Hurewitz, J. C., ed. *The Middle East and North Africa in World Politics: A Documentary Record*. 2nd rev. ed., 2 vols. New Haven, Conn., 1975.

İlkkaracan, Pınar. "Exploring the Context of Women's Sexuality in Eastern Turkey." In *Women and Sexuality in Muslim Societies*, edited by Pınar İlkkaracan. Istanbul, 2000, 229–44.

Imber, Colin. *Ebu's-suud: The Islamic Legal Tradition*. Stanford, Calif., 1997.

______. "Eleven Fetvas of the Ottoman Sheikh ul-Islam 'Abdurrahim." In *Islamic Legal Interpretation : Muftis and Their Fatwas*, ed. Muhammad Khalid Masud, Brinkley Messick, and David S. Powers. Cambridge, Mass., 1996, 141–9.

______. "The Hanafi Law of Manumission: A Problem in the Fatwas of Dürrizade Mehmed 'Arif." Typescript, personal copy.

______. "'Involuntary' Annulment of Marriage and Its Solution in Ottoman Law." In *Studies*, 217–51.

______. *The Ottoman Empire, 1300–1650: The Structure of Power*. Basingstoke, U.K., 2002.

______. *Studies in Ottoman History and Law*. Istanbul, 1996.

______. "Women, Marriage, and Property: Mahr in the *Behcetü'l-Fetāvā* of Yenişehirli Abdullah." In *Women in the Ottoman Empire*, ed. Zilfi, 81–104.

______. "Zinā' in Ottoman Law." In *Studies*, 175–206.

İnalcık, Halil. "Adâletnâmeler." *Belgeler* 2 (1965): 49–145.

______. "The Hub of the City: The Bedestan of Istanbul." *IJTS* 1, no. 1 (1979–80): 1–17.

______. "Osmanlılarda Raiyyet Rüsûmu." *Belleten* 23 (1960): 575–610.

______. *The Ottoman Empire: The Classical Age 1300–1600*. London, 1973.

______. "The Policy of Mehmed II toward the Greek Population of Istanbul and the Byzantine Buildings of the City." *Dumbarton Oaks Papers*, nos. 23–4 (1969–70): 231–49.

______. "Servile Labor in the Ottoman Empire " In *The Mutual Effects of the Islamic and Judeo-Christian Worlds: The East European Pattern*, edited by A. Ascher et al. New York, 1979, 25–52.

______. "Süleyman the Lawgiver and Ottoman Law." *Archivum Ottomanicum* 1 (1969): 105–38.

İnalcık, Halil, with Donald Quataert, eds. *An Economic and Social History of the Ottoman Empire, 1300–1914*. Cambridge, U.K., 1994.

İnciciyan, P. Ğ. *XVIII. Asırda İstanbul*, translated by Hrand D. Andreasyan. Istanbul, 1956.

Inikori, J. E. "The Origin of the Diaspora: The Slave Trade from Africa." *Tarikh* 5 (1978): 1–19.

İpşirli, Mehmet. "XVI. Asrın İkinci Yarısında Kürek Cezası İlgili Hükümler." *İ.Ü.E.F. Tarih Enstitüsü Dergisi* 12 (1981–2): 203–48.

İstanbul Müftülüğü. Istanbul, Turkey. Şer'iye Mahkemeleri Sicilleri (İstanbul, Bâb, Ahi Çelebi, Kasım Paşa, Galata, Üsküdar, Mahmud Paşa Mahkemeleri).

Itzkowitz, Norman. "Eighteenth Century Ottoman Realities." *SI* 16 (1962): 73–94.

______. "Mehmed Raghib Pasha: The Making of an Ottoman Grand Vezir." Ph.D. diss., Princeton University, 1959.

Jahn, Karl. *Türkische Freilassungserklärungen des 18. Jahrhunderts (1702–1776).* Naples, 1963.

———. "Zum Loskauf christlicher und türkischer Gefangener und Sklaven im 18. Jahrhundert." *ZDMG* 111, no. 1 (1961): 63–85.

Jennings, Ronald C. "Black Slaves and Free Blacks in Ottoman Cyprus, 1590–1640." *JESHO* 30 (1987): 286–302.

———. *Christians and Muslims in Ottoman Cyprus and the Mediterranean World, 1571–1640.* New York, 1993.

———. *Studies on Ottoman Social History in the Sixteenth and Seventeenth Centuries: Women, Zimmis and Shariah Courts in Kayseri, Cyprus and Trabzon*, edited by Suraiya Faroqhi. Istanbul, 1999.

———. "Women in Early 17th-Century Ottoman Judicial Records – The Sharia Court of Anatolian Kayseri." *JESHO* 18 (1975): 53–114.

Jirousek, Charlotte. "Ottoman Influences in Western Dress." In *Ottoman Costumes*, ed. Faroqhi and Neumann, 231–51.

Johansen, Baber. "The Valorization of the Human Body in Muslim Sunni Law." *Princeton Papers* 4 (Spring 1996): 70–112.

Jung, Mahomed Ullah ibn S., ed. *The Muslim Law of Inheritance, Compiled from Original Arabic Authorities with Arabic Text... and Their English Translation.* Lahore, n.d.

Jwaideh, Albertine, and J. W. Cox. "The Black Slaves of Turkish Arabia during the 19th Century." *Slavery and Abolition* 9, no. 3 (1988): 45–59.

Kadivar, Mohsen. "An Introduction to the Public and Private Debate in Islam." *Social Research* 70, no. 3 (2003): 659–80.

Kafadar, Cemal. *Between Two Worlds: The Construction of the Ottoman State.* Berkeley, Calif., 1995.

———. "Janissaries and Other Riffraff of Ottoman Istanbul: Rebels without a Cause?" In *Identity and Identity Formation*, ed. Tezcan and Barbir, 113–34.

Kal'a, Ahmet, et al., eds. *İstanbul Külliyâtı, İstanbul Ahkâm Defterleri: İstanbul Esnaf Tarihi 1.* Istanbul, 1997.

———. *İstanbul Külliyâtı, İstanbul Ahkâm Defterleri: İstanbul'da Sosyal Hayat 1.* Istanbul, 1997.

———. *İstanbul Külliyâtı, İstanbul Ahkâm Defterleri: İstanbul'da Sosyal Hayat 2, 1755–1765.* Istanbul, 1998.

———. *İstanbul Külliyatı, İstanbul Ahkâm Defterleri: İstanbul Ticaret Tarihi 1 (1742–1779).* Istanbul, 1997.

———. *İstanbul Külliyâtı: İstanbul Esnaf Birlikleri ve Nizamları I.* Istanbul, 1998.

Kalkan, İbrahim Halil. "Prostitution in the Late Ottoman Empire." Paper presented at the Annual Meeting of the Middle East Studies Association, Montreal, 2007.

Kandiyoti, Deniz A. "Bargaining with Patriarchy." *Gender and Society* 2, no. 3 (1988): 274–90.

———. "Emancipated but Unliberated? Reflections on the Turkish Case." *Feminist Studies* 13, no. 2 (1987): 317–38.

———. "Slave Girls, Temptresses, and Comrades: Images of Women in the Turkish Novel." *Feminist Issues*, no. 8 (1988): 35–50.

Kara, İsmail. "Turban and Fez: *Ulema* as Opposition." In *Late Ottoman Society*, ed. Özdalga, 162–200.

Karal, Enver Ziya. *Selim III'ün Hat-tı Hümayunları.* Ankara, 1946.

Karateke, Hakan T., and Maurus Reinkowski, eds. *Legitimizing the Order: The Ottoman Rhetoric of State Power*. Leiden, 2005.

Karpat, Kemal H. *Ottoman Population, 1830–1914: Demographic and Social Characteristics*. Madison, Wis., 1985.

______. *The Politicization of Islam: Reconstructing Identity, State, Faith, and Community in the Late Ottoman State*. New York, 2001.

Kasaba, Reşat. *The Ottoman Empire and the World Economy: The Nineteenth Century*. Albany, N.Y., 1988.

Katib Çelebi. *Fezleke-i Tarih*. 2 vols. Istanbul, 1286/1870.

Kātib Chelebi [Katib Çelebi]. *The Balance of Truth*, translated by Geoffrey L. Lewis. London, 1957.

Kazıcı, Ziya. *Osmanlılarda İhtisab Müessesesi*. Istanbul, 1987.

Keddie, Nikki R., and Beth Baron, eds. *Women in Middle Eastern History: Shifting Boundaries in Sex and Gender*. New Haven, Conn., 1991.

Keller, Gottfried. *Kleider Machen Leute*. Stuttgart, 1986.

Kellner-Heinkele, Barbara. "A Chinggisid and Ottoman: Halim Gerey Sultan." *Altaica* 5 (2001): 69–80.

Kern, Karen M. "The Prohibition of Sunni-Shi'i Marriages in the Ottoman Empire: A Study of Ideologies." Ph.D. diss., Columbia University, 1999.

Khoury, Dina Rizk. "Drawing Boundaries and Defining Spaces: Women and Space in Ottoman Iraq." In *Women, the Family*, ed. Sonbol, 173–87.

Kizilov, Mikail B. "The Black Sea and the Slave Trade: The Role of Crimean Maritime Towns in the Trade in Slaves and Captives in the Fifteenth to Eighteenth Centuries." *International Journal of Maritime History* 17, no. 1 (2005): 211–36.

Kızıltan, Mübeccel. *Fatma Aliye Hanım: Yaşamı, Sanatı, Yapıtları, ve Nisvan-i İslam*. Istanbul, 1993.

______. "Türk Kadın Hakları Mücadele Tarihinde Fatma Aliye Hanım'ın Yeri." *Kuram* 1 (1993): 83–93.

Kızıltan, Mübeccel, and Tülay Gençtürk, eds. *Atatürk Kitaplığı Fatma Aliye Hanım Evrakı Kataloğu-1*. Istanbul, 1993.

Klebe, Fritz. "Kleidervorschriften für Nichtmuslimische Untertanen des Turkischen Reiches im 16. Jahrhundert." *Der Neue Orient* 7, no. 4 (1920): 169–71.

Klein, Martin A. "State of the Field: Slavery." Annual Meeting of the Organization of American Historians. Boston, 2004.

[Koçu], Reşat Ekrem. *Osmanlı Muahedeleri Kapitülâsiyonlar, 1300–1920, ve Lozan Muahedesi, 24 Temmuz 1923*. Istanbul, 1934.

______. *Osmanlı Tarihinde Yasaklar*. Istanbul, 1950.

Kolchin, Peter. *American Slavery, 1619–1877*. New York, 1993.

Kömürcüyan, Eremya Çelebi. *İstanbul Tarihi: XVII. Asırda İstanbul*, edited and translated by Hrand D. Andreasyan. Istanbul, 1952.

Kortantamer, Tunca. "Nabi'nin Osmanlı İmparatorluğunu Eleştirisi." *TID* 2 (1984): 83–116.

______. "17. Yüzyıl Şairi Atayı'nın Hamse'sinde Osmanlı İmparatorluğu'nun Görüntüsü." *TID* 1 (1983): 61–105.

Köse, Osman. "XVIII. Yüzyıl Sonları Rus ve Avusturya Savaşları esnasında Osmanlı Devletinde bir Uygulama: İstanbul'da İçki ve Fuhuş Yasağı." *Turkish Studies/Türkoloji Dergisi* 2, no. 1 (2007): 104–23.

Kravets, Maryna. "From Nomad's Tent to Garden Palace: Evolution of a Chinggisid Household in the Crimea." In *History and Society in Central and Inner Asia*, edited by Michael Gervers, Uradyn E. Bulag, and Gillian Long. Toronto, 2005, 47–57.

Kuban, Doğan. *Istanbul: An Urban History*. Istanbul, 1996.

Kunt, İ. Metin. "Ethnic-Regional (*Cins*) Solidarity in the Seventeenth-Century Ottoman Establishment." *IJMES* 5 (1974): 233–9.

———. "Kulların Kulları." *Boğaziçi Üniversitesi Dergisi, Hümaniter Bilimler* 3 (1975): 27–42.

———. "State and Sultan up to the Age of Süleyman: Frontier Principality to World Empire." In *Süleyman the Magnificent*, ed. Kunt and Woodhead, 3–29.

———. *The Sultan's Servants: The Transformation of Ottoman Provincial Government, 1550–1650*. New York, 1983.

———. "Transformation of *Zimmi* into *Askerî*." In *Christians and Jews*, ed. Braude and Lewis, 1:55–67.

Kunt, İ. Metin, Sina Akşin et al., eds. *Türkiye Tarihi 3: Osmanlı Devleti 1600–1908*. Istanbul, 1988.

Kunt, İ. Metin, and Christine Woodhead, eds. *Süleyman the Magnificent and His Age: The Ottoman Empire in the Early Modern World*. London, 1995.

Kurdakul, Necdet. *Tanzimat Dönemi Basınında Sosyo-Ekonomik Fikir Hareketleri*. Ankara, 1997.

Kurt, Abdurahman. "Tanzimat Döneminde Koruyucu Aile Müesseseleri." In *Sosyo-Kültürel*, ed. Erverdi, Yıldız, Kara et al., 2:548–67.

Kurt, İhsan. "Atasözlerinde Aile." In *Sosyo-Kültürel Değişme Sürecinde Türk Ailesi*, ed. Erverdi, Yıldız, Kara et al. 3 vols. Ankara, 1992, 2:626–49.

Kuru, Selim S. "Sex in the Text: Deli Birader's Dâfi'ü'l-gumûm ve Râfi'ü'l-humûm and the Ottoman Literary Canon." *Middle Eastern Literatures* 10 (2007): 157–74.

Kushner, David. "The Place of the Ulema in the Ottoman Empire during the Age of Reform (1839–1918)." *Turcica* 19 (1987): 51–74.

Kut, Günay. "Veysi'nin Divanında Bulunmayan bir Kasidesi Üzerine." *Türk Dili Araştırmaları Yıllığı-Belleten* (1970).

Kütükoğlu, Mübahat. *Osmanlılarda Narh Müessesesi ve 1640 Tarihli Narh Defteri*. Istanbul, 1983.

Lamdan, Ruth. *A Separate People: Jewish Women in Palestine, Syria and Egypt in the Sixteenth Century*. Leiden, 2000.

La Mottraye, Aubry de. *Ses voyages en Europe, Asie, et Afrique, depuis* 1696, *jusqu'en* 1725. 3 vols. The Hague, 1727–32.

Lane, Ann J., ed. *The Debate over Slavery: Stanley Elkins and His Critics*. Urbana, Ill., 1971.

Lane, Edward William. *An Account of the Manners and Customs of the Modern Egyptians: The Definitive 1860 Edition*. Cairo, 2003.

Laqueur, Hans-Peter. *Osmanische Friedhöfe und Grabsteine in Istanbul*. Tübingen, 1993.

Larguèche, Abdelhamid. *L'Abolition de l'esclavage en Tunisie à travers les archives, 1841–1846*. Tunis, 1990.

———. *Les Ombres de la ville: Pauvres, marginaux et minoritaires à Tunis (XVIIIème et XIXè siècles)*. Manouba, Tunisia, 1999.

La Rue, George Michael. "The Frontiers of Enslavement: Bagirmi and the Trans-Saharan Slave Routes." In *Slavery on the Frontiers of Islam*, ed. Lovejoy, 31–54.

Latifi, [Hatibzade Abdullatif]. *Evsaf-i İstanbul*, edited by Nermin Süner [Pekin]. Istanbul, 1977.

Layard, Austen Henry. *Sir A. Henry Layard, G.C.B, D.C.L.: Autobiography and Letters from His Childhood until His Appointment as H. M. Ambassador at Madrid . . .*, edited by Sir Arthur Otway. 2 vols. London, 1903.

Le Gall, Dina. *A Culture of Sufism: Naqshbandīs in the Ottoman World, 1450–1700*. Albany, N.Y., 2005.

Le Gall, Michel, trans. "Translation of Louis Frank's *Mémoire sur le commerce des nègres au Kaire, et sur les maladies auxquelles ils sont sujets en y arrivant* (1802)." In *Slavery in the Islamic Middle East*, ed. Marmon, 69–88.

Lerner, Gerda. *The Creation of Patriarchy*. Oxford, 1986.

Lévi-Strauss, Claude. *The Elementary Structures of Kinship*. 1949. Reprint, Boston, 1969.

Levy, Avigdor. "The Officer Corps in Sultan Mahmud II's New Ottoman Army, 1826–1839." *IJMES* 2 (1971): 21–39.

Lewis, Bernard. *The Emergence of Modern Turkey*. 3rd ed. Oxford, 2002.

______. *The Jews of Islam*. Princeton, N.J., 1984.

______. "Ottoman Observers of Ottoman Decline," *IS* 1 (1962): 71–87.

______. *Race and Slavery in the Middle East: An Historical Enquiry*. 1990. Reprint, Oxford, 1992.

______. "Slade on Turkey." In *Türkiye'nin Sosyal ve Ekonomik Tarihi (1071–1920)*, edited by Osman Okyar and Halil İnalcık. Ankara, 1980, 215–25.

Lewis, Reina. *Rethinking Orientalism: Women, Travel and the Ottoman Harem*. New Brunswick, N.J., 2004.

London Society for the Mitigation and Abolition of Slavery in the British Dominions. *Anti-Slavery Reporter*. London, 1827–36.

Lopashich, Alexander. "A Negro Community in Yugoslavia." *Man* 58 (1958): 169–73.

Lovejoy, Paul E., ed. *Slavery on the Frontiers of Islam*. Princeton, N.J., 2004.

Low, Michael Christopher. "Empire and the Hajj: Pilgrims, Plagues, and Pan-Islam." *IJMES* 40 (2008): 269–90.

Lowry, Heath W. "Impropriety and Impiety among the Early Ottoman Sultans (1351–1451)." *TSAJ* 26, no. 2 (2002): 29–38.

______. *Ottoman Bursa in Travel Accounts*. Bloomington, Ind., 2003.

Lûtfi Efendi, Ahmed. *Vak'a-nüvis Ahmed Lûtfî Efendi Tarihi*, edited by M. Münir Aktepe. Vols. 10–15. Ankara, 1988–93.

Lûtfî Efendi, Ahmed. *Vak'anüvîs Ahmed Lûtfî Efendi Tarihi*, edited by Yücel Demirel. 8 vols. in 4. Istanbul, 1999.

Lutfi, Huda. "Manners and Customs of Fourteenth-Century Cairene Women: Female Anarchy versus Male Shar'i Order in Muslim Prescriptive Treatises." In *Women in Middle Eastern History*, ed. Keddie and Baron, 99–121.

Lybyer, Albert C. *The Government of the Ottoman Empire in the Time of Suleiman the Magnificent*. 1913. Reprint, New York, 1966.

Mabro, Judy. *Veiled Half-Truths: Western Travellers' Perceptions of Middle Eastern Women*. 1991. Reprint, London, 1996.

Mackie, Louise W. "Ottoman Kaftans with an Italian Identity." In *Ottoman Costumes*, ed. Faroqhi and Neumann, 219–29.

Magnarella, Paul J. *Anatolia's Loom: Studies in Turkish Culture, Society, Politics and Law*. Istanbul, 1998.

Mann, Michael. *The Sources of Social Power*. 2 vols. Cambridge, U.K., 1986–.

Manning, Patrick. *Slavery and African Life: Occidental, Oriental, and African Slave Trades*. Cambridge, U.K., 1990.

Manning, Patrick, ed. *Slave Trades, 1500–1800: Globalization of Forced Labour*. Brookfield, Vt., 1996.

Mantran, Robert. *Histoire d'Istanbul*. Paris, 1996.

Marcus, Abraham. *The Middle East on the Eve of Modernity: Aleppo in the Eighteenth Century*. New York, 1989.

———. "Privacy in Eighteenth-Century Aleppo: The Limits of Cultural Ideals." *IJMES* 18, no. 2 (1986): 165–83.

Marcus, Jacob R. *The Jew in the Medieval World*. 1938. Reprint, New York, 1974.

Mardin, Ebül'ulâ Mardin. *Huzur Dersleri*. 3 vols. in 2. Istanbul, 1951–66.

Mardin, Şerif. "Center-Periphery Relations: A Key to Turkish Politics?" *Daedalus* 102 (1973): 169–91.

———. *The Genesis of Young Ottoman Thought: A Study in the Modernization of Turkish Political Ideas*. 1962. Reprint, Syracuse, N.Y., 2000.

———. "Some Notes on an Early Phase in the Modernization of Communications in Turkey." *CSSH* 3, no. 3 (1961): 250–71.

———. "Super Westernization in Urban Life in the Ottoman Empire in the Last Quarter of the Nineteenth Century." In *Turkey: Geographic and Social Perspectives*, edited by Peter Benedict et al. Leiden, 1974, 403–46.

Marmon, Shaun E., ed. *Slavery in the Islamic Middle East*. Princeton, N.J., 1999.

Marsot, Afaf Lutfi Al-Sayyid. "Marriage in Late Eighteenth-Century Egypt." In *The Mamluks in Egyptian Politics and Society*, edited by Thomas Philipp and Ulrich Haarmann. Cambridge, U.K., 1998, 282–9.

Martal, Abdullah. "19. Yüzyılda Kölelik ve Köle Ticareti." *TveT* 121 (Ocak 1994): 13–22.

Masters, Bruce A. "The Treaties of Erzurum (1823 and 1848) and the Changing Status of Iranians in the Ottoman Empire." *Iranian Studies* 24 (1991): 3–15.

———. *Christians and Jews in the Ottoman Arab World: The Roots of Sectarianism*. Cambridge, U.K., 2001.

Masud, Muhammad Khalid, Brinkley Messick, and David S. Powers, eds. *Islamic Legal Interpretation: Muftis and Their Fatwas*. Cambridge, Mass., 1996.

Matar, Nabil I. *Britain and Barbary, 1589–1689*. Gainesville, Fla., 2005.

———. *Turks, Moors, and Englishmen in the Age of Discovery*. New York, 1999.

Mauss, Marcel. *The Gift: The Form and Reason for Exchange in Archaic Societies*, translated by W. D. Halls. London, 1990.

Mazower, Mark. *Salonica, City of Ghosts: Christians, Muslims and Jews, 1430–1950*. New York, 2005.

McCarthy, Justin. *The Ottoman Peoples and the End of Empire*. London, 2001.

Mecelle-i Ahkâm-i Adliye. Istanbul, 1305/1887.

Mehmed Halife. *Tarih-i Gılmanı. TOEM İlaveler 1*. Istanbul, 1340/1924.

Mehmed Paşa, Defterdar Sarı. *Zübde-i Vekayiât*, edited by Abdülkadir Özcan. Ankara, 1995.

———. *Zübde-i Vekayiat (Olayların Özü)*, edited by Abdülkadir Özcan. 3 vols. Istanbul, 1977–9.

Mehmed Tahir, Bursalı. *Osmanlı Müellifleri*, translated by A. F. Yavuz and I. Özen. 3 vols. Istanbul, 1972–5.
Meillassoux, Claude. *The Anthropology of Slavery*. Chicago, 1991.
Melek Hanım [Melek-Hanum]. *Thirty Years in the Harem, or, the Autobiography of Melek-Hanum, Wife of H. H. Kıbrızlı-Mehemet-Pasha*. New York, 1872.
Melman, Billie. *Women's Orients: English Women and the Middle East, 1718–1918*. 1992. Reprint, Ann Arbor, Mich., 1995.
Memon, Muhammad Umar, ed. and trans. *Ibn Taimīya's Struggle against Popular Religion*. The Hague, 1976.
Mendelson, Sara, and Patricia Crawford. *Women in Early Modern England, 1550–1720*. Oxford, 1998.
Menemencioğlu, Nermin, and Fahir İz, eds. *The Penguin Book of Turkish Verse*. Harmondsworth, U.K., 1978.
Meriwether, Margaret L. *The Kin Who Count: Family and Society in Ottoman Aleppo, 1770–1840*. Austin, Tex., 1999.
Mernissi, Fatima. *Beyond the Veil: Male-Female Dynamics in Modern Muslim Society*. Rev. ed. Bloomington, Ind., 1987.
———. *Dreams of Trespass: Tales of a Moroccan Girlhood*. Reading, Mass., 1994.
———. *Women's Rebellion and Islamic Memory*. Atlantic Highlands, N.J., 1996.
Meyân, A. Faruk, trans. *Birgivî Vasiyetnâmesi'nin Kâdızâde Şerhi*. Istanbul, 1977.
Micklewright, Nancy. "Public and Private for Ottoman Women of the Nineteenth Century." In *Women, Patronage, and Self-Representation in Islamic Societies*, edited by D. Fairchild Ruggles. Albany, N.Y., 2000, 155–76.
Midhat Efendi, Ahmet [Ahmed]. *Üss-i İnkılap: Kırım Muharebesinden II. Abdülhamid Han'ın Cülûsuna kadar*, translated by Tahir Galip Seratlı. 2 vols. Istanbul, 2004.
Miers, Suzanne, and Igor Kopytoff, eds. *Slavery in Africa*. Madison, Wis., 1977.
Miller, Pavla. *Transformations of Patriarchy in the West*, 1500–1900. Bloomington, Ind., 1998.
Miller, Ruth A. "Apostates and Bandits: Religious and Secular Interaction in the Administration of Late Ottoman Criminal Law." *Studia Islamica* (2003): 155–78.
———. *Legislating Authority: Sin and Crime in the Ottoman Empire and Turkey*. New York, 2008.
Millingen, Frederick [Osman Bey, Major Vladimir Andrejevich]. "The Circassian Slaves and the Sultan's Harem." *Journal of the Anthropological Society of London* 8 (1870–1): cix–cxx.
———. *Les femmes en Turquie*. Paris, 1883.
———. "On the Negro Slaves in Turkey," *Journal of the Anthropological Institute of Great Britain and Ireland* 8 (1870–71): lxxxv–xcvi.
Mithat, Ali Haydar. *The Life of Midhat Pasha*. 1903. Reprint, New York, 1973.
Mitler, Louis. "The Genoese in Galata: 1453–1682," *IJMES* 10, no. 1 (1979): 71–91.
Mitter, Ulrike. "Unconditional Manumission of Slaves in Early Islamic Law: A Hadīth Analysis." *Der Islam* 78 (2001): 35–72.
Montagu, Mary Wortley. *Letters from the Levant during the Embassy to Constantinople 1716–1718*. New York, 1971.
Morgan, Edmund S. *The Puritan Family: Religion and Domestic Relations in Seventeenth-Century New England*. New York, 1966.
Motika, Raoul, and Michael Ursinus, eds. *Caucasia between the Ottoman Empire and Iran, 1555–1914*. Wiesbaden, 2000.

Mottahedeh, Roy, and Kristen Stilt. "Public and Private as Viewed through the Work of the *Muhtasib*." *Social Research* 70, no. 3 (2003): 735–48.

Motzki, Harald. "Wal-muhsanatu mina n-nisā'i illā mā malakat aimānukum (Koran 4:24) und die koranische Sexualethik." *Der Islam* 63 (1986): 192–218.

"Mühimme Defteri." No.111. Chicago, University of Chicago, Regenstein Library. Ottoman Archive, vol. 44.

Müller, Hans. *Die Kunst des Sklavenkaufs nach arabischen, persischen und türkischen Ratgebern vom 10. bis 18. Jahrhundert*. Freiburg im Breisgau, 1980.

Mumcu, Ahmet. *Osmanlı Devletinde Siyaseten Katl*. Ankara, 1963.

Murphey, Rhoads. "The Veliyuddin Telhis: Notes on the Sources and Interrelations between Koçi Bey and Contemporary Writers of Advice to Kings." *Belleten* 43 (1979): 547–71.

Murray, John. *Handbook for Travellers in Turkey in Asia, including Constantinople, the Bosphorus, Dardanelles, Brousa and Plain of Troy*. New rev. ed. London, [1871].

Musallam, B[asim] F. *Sex and Society in Islam: Birth Control before the Nineteenth Century*. Cambridge, U.K., 1983.

Mustafa Âli, Gelibolulu. *Görgü ve Toplum Kuralları üzerinde Ziyâfet Sofraları (Mevâidü'n Nefâis fi Kavâidi'l Mecâlis)*, edited by Orhan Şaik Gökyay. 2 vols. Istanbul, 1978.

Nabi Efendi, *Conseils de Nabi Efendi à son fils Aboul Khair*, translated by Pavet de Courteille. Paris, 1857.

Naff, Thomas. "Ottoman Diplomatic Relations with Europe in the Eighteenth Century: Patterns and Trends." In *Studies in Eighteenth Century Islamic History*, edited by Thomas Naff and Roger Owen. Carbondale, Ill., 1977, 88–107.

Naima, Mustafa. *Tarih-i Naima*. 6 vols. Istanbul, 1280/1863–4.

Necipoğlu, Gülru. *Architecture, Ceremonial, and Power: The Topkapı Palace in the Fifteenth and Sixteenth Centuries*. Cambridge, Mass., 1991.

Neumann, Christoph K. "Bad Times and Better Self: Definitions of Identity and Strategies for Development in Late Ottoman Historiography, 1850–1900." In *The Ottomans and the Balkans: A Discussion of Historiography*, edited by Fikret Adanır and Suraiya Faroqhi. Leiden, 2002, 57–78.

———. *Das Indirekte Argument: Ein Plädoyer für die Tanzīmāt vermittels der Historie*. Münster, 1994.

———. "How Did a Vizier Dress in the Eighteenth Century?" In *Ottoman Costumes*, ed. Faroqhi and Neumann, 181–217.

———. "Political and Diplomatic Developments." In *The Cambridge History of Turkey*, ed. Faroqhi, 44–62.

Nicolay, Nicolas de. *Dans l'empire de Soliman le magnifique: Navigations into Turkie*, edited by M.-C. Gomez and Stéphane Yerasimos. Paris, 1989.

———. *The Nauigations into Turkie*. 1585. Reprint, Amsterdam, 1968.

[Niewöhner], Elke Eberhard. *Osmanische Polemik gegen die Safawiden im 16. Jahrhundert nach arabischen Handschriften*. Freiburg im Breisgau, 1970.

Nuri Paşa, Mustafa. *Netayic ül-Vukuat: Kurumları ve Örgütleriyle Osmanlı Tarihi*, edited by Neşet Çağatay. 4 vols. in 2. Ankara, 1979–80.

Ocak, Ahmet Yaşar. *Osmanlı Toplumunda Zındıklar ve Mülhidler (15.–17. Yüzyıllar)*. Istanbul, 1998.

———. "XVII. Yüzyılda Osmanlı İmparatorluğu'nda Dinde Tasfiye (Püritanizm) Teşebbüslerine bir Bakış: 'Kadızâdeliler Hareketi.'" *Türk Kültürü Araştırmaları* 17–21 (1979–83): 208–25.

Ochsenwald, William. "Muslim-European Conflict in the Hijaz: The Slave Trade Controversy, 1840–1895." *MES* 16, no. 1 (1980): 114–26.
O'Fahey, R. S. "Slavery and Society in Dar Fur." In *Slaves and Slavery in Muslim Africa*, ed. Willis, 2:83–100.
Okandan, Recai G. *Âmme Hukukumuzun Ana Hatları*. Istanbul, 1957.
Olivier, G. A. *Voyage dans l'Empire Othoman, l'Égypte et la Perse*. 6 vols. Paris, 1801–7.
Orhonlu, Cengiz. "Derviş Abdullah'ın Darussaade Ağaları hakkında bir Eseri: Risale-i Teberdariye fi Ahval-i Daru's-Saade." In *İsmail Hakkı Uzunçarşılı'ya Armağan*. Ankara, 1976.
Ortaylı, İlber. *İmparatorluğun En Uzun Yüzyılı*. Istanbul, 1983.
______. "Osmanlı Aile Hukukunda Gelenek, Şeriat ve Örf." In *Sosyo-Kültürel*, ed. Erverdi, Yıldız, Kara et al., 2:456–67.
______. *Osmanlı Toplumunda Aile*. Istanbul, 2000.
Osmân Agha de Temechvar. *Prisonnier des infidels: Un soldat ottoman dans l'empire des Habsbourg*, edited by Frédéric Hitzel. [Paris], 1998.
Owen, Roger. *The Middle East in the World Economy, 1800–1914*. Rev. ed. London, 1993.
Özcan, Abdülkadir, ed. *Anonim Osmanlı Tarihi (1099–1116/1688–1704)*. Ankara, 2000.
Özcan, Tahsin. "Osmanlı Mahallesi Sosyal Kontrol ve Kefalet Sistemi," *Marife* 1, no. 1 (2001): 129–51.
Özdalga, Elisabeth, ed. *Late Ottoman Society: The Intellectual Legacy*. London, 2005.
Özdeğer, Hüseyin. *1463–1640 Yılları Bursa Şehri Tereke Defterleri*. Istanbul, 1988.
Özkaya, Yücel. "XVIII. Yüzyıl İkinci Yarısına ait Sosyal Yaşantıyı Ortaya Koyan bir Belge." *OTAM* 2 (Ocak 1991): 303–20.
Öztürk, Necati. "Islamic Orthodoxy among the Ottomans in the Seventeenth Century with Special Reference to the Qādī-zāde Movement." Ph.D. diss., University of Edinburgh, 1981.
Öztürk, Said. *Askeri Kassama ait Onyedinci Asır İstanbul Tereke Defterleri*. Istanbul, 1995.
P Art and Culture Magazine. "Fashion at the Ottoman Court." Issue 3.
Pakalın, Mehmet Zeki. *Osmanlı Tarih Deyimleri ve Terimleri Sözlüğü*. 3 vols. Istanbul, 1946–54.
Pamuk, Şevket. *A Monetary History of the Ottoman Empire*. Cambridge, U.K., 2000.
______. *The Ottoman Empire and European Capitalism: Trade, Investment, and Production, 1820–1913*. Cambridge, U.K., 1987.
Panaite, Viorel. *The Ottoman Law of War and Peace: The Ottoman Empire and Tribute Payers*. New York, 2000.
Pankhurst, Richard. "Ethiopian and Other African Slaves in Greece during the Ottoman Occupation." *Slavery and Abolition* 1, no. 3 (1980): 339–44.
Panzac, Daniel. *Barbary Corsairs: The End of a Legend*, translated by Victoria Hobson and John E. Hawkes. Leiden, 2005.
______. *La peste dans l'Empire Ottoman, 1700–1850*. Louvain, 1985.
______. *Les corsaires barbaresques: La fin d'une épopée, 1800–1820*. Paris, 1999.
Pardoe, Julia. *The Beauties of the Bosphorus: Illustrated in a Series of Views of Constantinople and Its Environs from Original Drawings by W[illiam] H. Bartlett*. London, 1838.
______. *The City of the Sultan, and Domestic Manners of the Turks, in 1836*. 2nd ed., 3 vols. London, 1838.
Parish, Peter J. *Slavery: History and Historians*. New York, 1989.

Parla, Jale. *Babalar ve Oğullar: Tanzimat Romanında Epistemolojik Temelleri.* Istanbul, 1990.

———. *Efendilik, Şarkiyatçılık, Kölelik.* Istanbul, 1985.

Parlatır, İsmail. *Tanzimat Edebiyatında Kölelik.* 1987. Reprint, Ankara, 1992.

Peabody, Sue. *There Are No Slaves in France: The Political Culture of Race and Slavery in the Ancien Régime in France.* New York, 1996.

Peirce, Leslie P. *The Imperial Harem: Women and Sovereignty in the Ottoman Empire.* New York, 1993.

———. *Morality Tales: Law and Gender in the Ottoman Court of Aintab.* Berkeley, Calif., 2003.

———. "Seniority, Sexuality, and Social Order: The Vocabulary of Gender in Early Modern Ottoman Society." In *Women in the Ottoman Empire*, ed. Zilfi, 169–96.

Peters, Rudolph. "The Battered Dervishes of Bab Zuwayla: A Religious Riot in Eighteenth-Century Cairo." In *Eighteenth-Century Renewal and Reform in Islam*, edited by Nehemia Levtzion and John O. Voll. Syracuse, N.Y., 1987, 93–115.

———. *Crime and Punishment in Islamic Law: Theory and Practice from the Sixteenth to the Twenty-First Century.* Cambridge, U.K., 2005.

Petry, Carl F. "Crime without the Blood Money Option? The Paucity of References to Blood Money in Criminal Narratives by Mamluk Historians in Cairo and Damascus." *Annual Meeting of the Middle East Studies Association.* Boston, November 2005.

Pfeiffer, Emily [Jane Davis]. *Flying Leaves from East and West.* London, 1885.

Philipp, Thomas. *Acre: The Rise and Fall of a Palestinian City, 1730–1831.* New York, 2001.

Philipp, Thomas, and Ulrich Haarmann, eds. *The Mamluks in Egyptian Politics and Society.* Cambridge, U.K., 1998.

Piterberg, Gabriel. *An Ottoman Tragedy: History and Historiography at Play.* Berkeley, Calif., 2003.

Pollard, Lisa. "The Family Politics of Colonizing and Liberating Egypt, 1882–1919." *Social Politics* 7, no. 1 (2000): 47–79.

Porter, David. *Constantinople and Its Environs in a Series of Letters from Constantinople.* 2 vols. New York, 1835.

Porter, James, Sir. *Observations on the Religion, Law, Government, and Manners of the Turks.* 2nd ed. London, 1771.

Powell, Eve M. Troutt. *A Different Shade of Colonialism: Egypt, Great Britain, and the Mastery of the Sudan.* Berkeley, Calif., 2003.

———. "Slaves or Siblings? 'Abdullah al-Nadim's Dialogues about the Family." In *Histories of the Modern Middle East: New Directions*, edited by Israel Gershoni, Hakan Erdem and Ursula Wocöck. Boulder, Colo., 2002, 155–65.

Prätor, Sabine, and Christoph K. Neumann, eds. *Frauen, Bilder und Gelehrte: Studien zu Gesellschaft und Künsten im Osmanischen Reich–Festschrift Hans Georg Majer.* 2 vols. Istanbul, 2001.

Quataert, Donald. "Clothing Laws, State and Society in the Ottoman Empire, 1720–1829." *IJMES* 29 (1997): 403–25.

———. "Janissaries, Artisans and the Question of Ottoman Decline, 1730–1826." In *Workers, Peasants and Economic Change*, ed. Quataert.

Quataert, Donald, ed. *Consumption Studies and the History of the Ottoman Empire, 1550–1922.* Albany, N.Y., 2000.

______. *Manufacturing in the Ottoman Empire and Turkey, 1500–1950.* Albany, N.Y., 1994.

______. *Workers, Peasants and Economic Change in the Ottoman Empire, 1730–1914.* Istanbul, 1993.

Rafeq, Abdul-Karim. "Public Morality in 18th-Century Ottoman Damascus." *Revue du monde musulman et de la Méditerranée* 55–6 (1990): 180–96.

Ramsaur, Ernest Edmondson. *The Young Turks: Prelude to the Revolution of 1908.* Princeton, N.J., 1957.

Raşid, Mehmed. *Tarih-i Raşid.* 6 vols. Istanbul, 1282/1865.

Rasim, Ahmed. *Resimli ve Haritalı Osmanlı Tarihi.* 4 vols. in 2. Istanbul, 1326–30/1908–12.

Raymond, André. "Architecture and Urban Development: Cairo during the Ottoman Period, 1517–1798." In *Problems of the Modern Middle East in Historical Perspective*, edited by John Spagnolo. Reading, U.K., 1992, 211–27.

______. "The Residential Districts of Cairo's Elite in the Mamluk and Ottoman Periods (Fourteenth to Eighteenth Centuries)." In *The Mamluks in Egyptian Politics*, ed. Philipp and Haarmann, 207–23.

Redhouse Press. *Yeni Türkçe-İngilizce Sözlük.* 1968. Reprint, Istanbul, 1979.

Redhouse, Sir James W. *A Turkish and English Lexicon.* 1890. Reprint, Beirut, 1987.

Reindl-Kiel, Hedda. "Mord an einer Haremsdame." *Münchner Zeitschrift für Balkankunde* 7–8 (1991): 167–89.

Ricks, Thomas M. "Slaves and Slave Traders in the Persian Gulf, 18th and 19th Centuries: An Assessment." In *Slave Trades*, 1500–1800, ed. Manning, 279–89.

Robertson, Claire C., and Martin A. Klein. "Women's Importance in African Slave Systems." In *Women and Slavery in Africa*, ed. Robertson and Klein, 3–25.

Robertson, Claire C., and Martin A. Klein, eds. *Women and Slavery in Africa.* Madison, Wis., 1983.

Roche, Daniel. *The Culture of Clothing: Dress and Fashion in the "Ancien Régime,"* translated by J. Birrell. Cambridge, U.K., 1994.

Roe, Thomas. *The Negotiations of Sir Thomas Roe, in His Embassy to the Ottoman Porte from the Year 1621 to 1628 Inclusive.* London, 1740.

Röhrborn, Klaus. "Konfiskation und Intermediäre Gewalten im Osmanischen Reich." *Der Islam* 55, no. 2 (1978): 345–51.

Rosenthal, Steven T. *The Politics of Dependency: Urban Reform in Istanbul.* Westport, Conn., 1980.

Rubin, Avi. "Legal Borrowing and Its Impact on Ottoman Legal Culture in the Late Nineteenth Century." *Continuity and Change* 22, no. 2 (2007): 279–303.

______. "Ottoman Modernity: The *Nizamiye* Courts in the Late Nineteenth Century." Ph.D. diss., Harvard University, 2006.

Rubin, Uri. "'Al-Walad li-l-firash': On the Islamic Campaign against 'Zina'." *Studia Islamica* 78 (1993): 5–26.

Rycaut, Sir Paul. *The History of the Turkish Empire from the Year 1623 to the Year 1677 . . .* 2 vols. London, 1680.

Sabean, David Warren. *Kinship in Neckarhausen, 1700–1870.* Cambridge, U.K., 1998.

Sagaster, Börte. *"Herren" und "Sklaven": Der Wandel im Sklavenbild türkischer Literaten in der Spätzeit des Osmanischen Reiches.* Wiesbaden, 1997.

Sahillioğlu, Halil. "Slaves in the Social and Economic Life of Bursa in the Late 15th and Early 16th Centuries." *Turcica* 17 (1985): 43–112.

Said, Edward. *Orientalism.* New York, 1978.

Sajdi, Dana. "A Room of His Own: The 'History' of the Barber of Damascus (fl.1762)." *MIT Electronic Journal of Middle East Studies* 4 (2004): 19–35.

Sajdi, Dana, ed. *Ottoman Tulips, Ottoman Coffee: Leisure and Lifestyle in the Eighteenth Century*. London, 2007.

Sak, İzzet. "Konya'da Köleler: 16. Yüzyıl Sonu – 17. Yüzyıl." *OA* 9 (1989): 159–97.

Sakaoğlu, Necdet. "Osmanlı Giyim Kuşamı ve 'Elbise-i Osmaniyye.'" *TveT* 8, no. 47 (1987): 36–41.

Salzmann, Ariel C. "The Age of Tulips: Confluence and Conflict in Early Modern Consumer Culture (1500–1730)." In *Consumption Studies*, ed. Quataert, 83–106.

Sami, Mustafa, Hüseyn Şakır, Mehmed Subhi. *Tarih-i Sami ve Şakır ve Subhi*. Istanbul, 1198/1783.

Sâmî, Şemseddin. *Kadınlar*, ed. İsmail Doğan. Ankara, 1996.

Şanizade Mehmed Ataullah. *Tarih-i Şanizade*. 4 vols. in 1. Istanbul, 1290/1873.

Sariyannis, Marinos. "'Mobs,' 'Scamps' and Rebels in Seventeenth-Century Istanbul: Some Remarks on Ottoman Social Vocabulary." *IJTS* 11 (2005): 1–15.

Saydam, Abdullah. "Esir Pazarlarında Yasak Ticaret: Hür İnsanların Satılması." In *Kıbrıs'tan Kafkasya'ya*, ed. Çiçek and Saydam, 115–34.

———. "Kamu Hizmeti Yaptırma ve Suçu Önleme Yöntemi olarak Osmanlılarda Kefâlet Usûlü." In *Kıbrıs'tan Kafkasya'ya*, ed. Çiçek and Saydam. Trabzon, 1998, 98–115.

Saz, Leyla [Leyla Hanım]. *The Imperial Harem of the Sultans: Daily Life at the Çırağan Palace during the 19th Century*, translated by Landon Thomas. Istanbul, 1994.

Scarce, Jennifer M. *Women's Costume of the Near and Middle East*. London, 2003.

Schacht, Joseph. *An Introduction to Islamic Law*. Oxford, 1964.

Schick, İrvin Cemil. "Representation of Gender and Sexuality in Ottoman and Turkish Erotic Literature." *TSAB* 28, no. 1–2 (2004): 81–103.

———. "The Women of Turkey as Sexual Personae: Images from Western Literature." In *Deconstructing Images of "the Turkish Woman,"* ed. Arat, 83–100.

Schroeter, Daniel J. "Slave Markets and Slavery in Moroccan Urban Society." *Slavery and Abolition* 13 (1993): 185–213.

Scott, James C. "Domination and the Arts of Resistance." In *Slavery*, ed. Engerman, Drescher, and Paquette, 366-70.

———. *Seeing Like a State: How Certain Schemes to Improve the Human Condition Have Failed*. New Haven, Conn., 1998.

Sedgwick, Eve Kosofsky. *Between Men: English Literature and Male Homosocial Desire*. New York, 1985.

Segal, Ronald. *Islam's Black Slaves: The Other Black Diaspora*. New York, 2001.

Şemdanizade Süleyman, Fındıklılı. *Şem'dânî-zâde Fındıklılı Süleyman Efendi Târihi Mür'i't-Tevârih*, edited by M. Münir Aktepe. 3 vols. Istanbul, 1976–81.

Semerdjian, Elyse. *"Off the Straight Path": Illicit Sex, Law, and Community in Ottoman Aleppo*. Syracuse, N.Y., 2008.

———. "Sinful Professions: Illegal Occupations of Women in Ottoman Aleppo, Syria." *Hawwa* 1, no. 1 (2003): 60–85.

Seng, Yvonne J. "Fugitives and Factotums: Slaves in Early Sixteenth-Century Istanbul." *JESHO* 39 (1996): 136–69.

———. "Invisible Women: Residents of Early Sixteenth-Century Istanbul." In *Women in the Medieval Islamic World*, ed. Hambly, 241–68.

______. "A Liminal State: Slavery in Sixteenth-Century Istanbul." In *Slavery in the Islamic Middle East*, ed. Marmon, 25–42.

Seni, Nora. "Ville ottomane et représentation du corps feminin." *Les Temps Modernes* 41 (1984): 66–95.

Şeref, Abdurrahman. *Tarih Konuşmaları*. Istanbul, 1978.

______. *Tarih Söyleşileri (Müsahabe-i Tarihiye)*, edited by Mübeccel Nami Duru. Istanbul, 1980.

Sersen, William John. "Stereotypes and Attitudes towards Slaves in Arabic Proverbs: A Preliminary View." In *Slaves and Slavery in Muslim Africa*, ed. Willis, 1:92–105.

Sevin, Nureddin. *On Üç Asırlık Türk Kıyafet Tarihine bir Bakış*. Istanbul, 1973.

Şeyhi Mehmed. "Vekayı-i Fuzela (Zeyl-i Zeyl-i Atayı)." Istanbul. Süleymaniye Ktp., Hamidiye 939/1.

Shaham, Ron. "Jews and the Sharī'a Courts in Modern Egypt." *SI* 82 (1995): 113–36.

______. "Masters, Their Freed Slaves, and the *Waqf* in Egypt (Eighteenth-Twentieth Centuries)." *JESHO* 43, no. 2 (2000): 162–88.

Shalit, Yoram. *Nicht-Muslime und Fremde in Aleppo und Damaskus im 18. und in der ersten Hälfte des 19. Jahrhunderts*. Berlin, 1996.

Shatzmiller, Maya. *Her Day in Court: Women's Property Rights in Fifteenth-Century Granada*. Cambridge, Mass., 2007.

Shaw, Stanford J. *Between Old and New: The Ottoman Empire under Sultan Selim III, 1789–1807*. Cambridge, Mass., 1971.

______. "The Ottoman Census System and Population, 1831–1914." *IJMES* 9 (1978): 325–38.

Shaw, Stanford J., and Ezel Kural Shaw. *History of the Ottoman Empire and Modern Turkey*. 2 vols. Cambridge, U.K., 1977.

Shepherd, Gill. "The Comorians and the East African Slave Trade." In *Asian and African Systems*, ed. Watson, 73–99.

Shields, Sarah. "Take-Off into Self-Sustained Peripheralization: Foreign Trade, Regional Trade and Middle East Historians." *TSAB* 17, no. 1 (1993): 1–23.

Shinder, Joel. "Career Line Formation in the Ottoman Bureaucracy, 1648–1750: A New Perspective." *JESHO* 16 (1973): 217–37.

Shuval, Tal. "Households in Ottoman Algeria." *TSAB* 24, no. 1 (2000): 41–64.

Sikainga, Ahmad Alawad. "Comrades in Arms or Captives in Bondage: Sudanese Slaves in the Turco-Egyptian Army, 1821–1865." In *Slave Elites in the Middle East*, ed. Toru and Philips, 197–214.

Silahdar Fındıklılı Mehmed Ağa. *Silahdar Tarihi*. 2 vols. Istanbul, 1928.

Slade, Adolphus. *Records of Travels in Turkey, Greece, &c., and of a Cruise in the Black Sea, with the Capitan Pasha, in the Years 1829, 1830, and 1831*. 2 vols. London, 1833.

______. *Slade's Travels in Turkey: Turkey and the Turks, and a Cruise in the Black Sea, with the Capitan Pasha: A Record of Travels*. New York, 1854.

Smith, Albert. *Habits of the Turks*. Boston, 1857.

Somel, Selçuk Akşin. *The Modernization of Public Education in the Ottoman Empire, 1839–1908: Islamization, Autocracy, and Discipline*. Leiden, 2001.

Sonbol, Amira El-Azhary, ed. *Beyond the Exotic: Women's Histories in Islamic Societies*. Syracuse, N.Y., 2005.

______. *Women, the Family, and Divorce Laws in Islamic History*. Syracuse, N.Y., 1996.

Sonyel, Salahi R. "The Protégé System in the Ottoman Empire." *Journal of Islamic Studies* 2 (1991): 56–66.
Spry, William J. J. *Life on the Bosphorus: Doings in the City of the Sultan.* London, 1895.
Stampp, Kenneth. *The Peculiar Institution: Slavery in the Ante-Bellum South.* New York, 1956.
Stillman, Yedida K., and Nancy Micklewright. "Costume in the Middle East." *Middle East Studies Association Bulletin* 26, no. 1 (1992): 13–38.
Stirling, Paul. *Turkish Village.* London, 1965.
Stoianovich, Traian. *Between East and West: The Balkan and Mediterranean Worlds.* 4 vols. New Rochelle, N.Y., 1992–5.
Stowasser, Barbara Freyer. *Women in the Qur'an, Traditions, and Interpretation.* New York, 1994.
Suavi, Ali. "Esir ve Cariye Alım Satımı." In *Yeni Türk Edebiyatı Antolojisi*, edited by M. Kaplan, İ. Enginün, and B. Emil. 2 vols. Istanbul, 1978, 2:569–72.
Süleyman, Kanuni Sultan. *Divan-i Muhibbi.* Istanbul, 1308/1890–1.
Süreyya, Mehmed. *Sicill-i Osmani.* 4 vols. Istanbul, 1308–15/1891–7.
Swartz, David. *Culture and Power: The Sociology of Pierre Bourdieu.* Chicago, 1997.
Taeschner, Franz. Alt-Stambuler Hof- und Volksleben, ein türkisches Miniaturenalbum aus dem 17. Jahrhundert. Hannover, 1925.
Takvim-i Vekayı. Istanbul, 1247–77/1831–60.
Tan, M. Turhan. *Tarihî Fıkralar.* Istanbul, 1962.
Tanzimat I: *Yüzüncü Yıldönümü Münasebetile.* Istanbul, 1940.
Tatarcık Abdullah. "Nizam-i Devlet hakkında Mütalaat." *TOEM*, no. 41 (1332/1916–17): 257–84.
Temperley, Howard. *British Antislavery, 1833–1870.* Columbia, S.C., [1972].
———. *England and the Near East: The Crimea.* Hamden, Conn., 1964.
Terzioğlu, Derin. "Sufi and Dissident in the Ottoman Empire: Niyāzī-i Mısrī (1618–1694)." Ph.D. diss., Harvard University, 1999.
Tezcan, Baki. "*Dispelling the Darkness*: The Politics of 'Race' in the Early Seventeenth-Century Ottoman Empire in the Light of the Life and Work of Mullah Ali." In *Identity and Identity Formation*, ed. Tezcan and Barbir, 73–95.
Tezcan, Baki, and Karl K. Barbir, eds. *Identity and Identity Formation in the Ottoman World: A Volume of Essays in Honor of Norman Itzkowitz.* Madison, Wis., 2007.
Timur, Serim. *Türkiye'de Aile Yapısı.* Ankara, 1972.
Toledano, Ehud R. *As If Silent and Absent: Bonds of Enslavement in the Islamic Middle East.* New Haven, Conn., 2007.
———. "Attitude to Slavery during the Tanzimat." In *150. Yılında Tanzimat*, ed. Yıldız, 303–24.
———. "The Imperial Eunuchs of Istanbul: From Africa to the Heart of Islam." *MES* 20, no. 3 (1984): 379–90.
———. *The Ottoman Slave Trade and Its Suppression, 1840–1890.* Princeton, N.J., 1982.
———. "Shemsigul: A Circassian Slave in Mid-Nineteenth-Century Cairo." In *Struggle and Survival in the Modern Middle East*, edited by Edmund Burke. Berkeley, Calif., 1993, 59–74.
———. *Slavery and Abolition in the Ottoman Middle East.* Seattle, 1998.
Töre, Enver. "Türk Ailesindeki Değişmenin Tiyatromuza Yansımaları." In *Sosyo-Kültürel*, ed. Erverdi, Yıldız, Kara et al., 2:677–700.

Toru, Miura, and John Edward Philips, eds. *Slave Elites in the Middle East and Africa: A Comparative Study*. London, 2000.

Tott, [François] Baron de. *Memoirs of Baron de Tott*. 2 vols. in 4 pts. 1785. Reprint, New York, 1973.

Tournefort, Joseph Pitton de. *Relation d'un voyage du Levant*... 3 vols. Lyon, 1717.

Tritton, A. S. *The Caliphs and Their Non-Muslim Subjects: A Critical Study of the Covenant of 'Umar*. London, 1970.

Tucker, Ernest. "The Peace Negotiations of 1736: A Conceptual Turning Point in Ottoman-Iranian Relations," *TSAB* 20 (1996): 16–37.

Tucker, Judith E. "The Fullness of Affection: Mothering in the Islamic Law of Ottoman Syria and Palestine." In *Women in the Ottoman Empire*, ed. Zilfi, 232–52.

______. *In the House of the Law: Gender and Islamic Law in Ottoman Syria and Palestine*. Berkeley, Calif., 1998.

______. "*Muftīs* and Matrimony: Islamic Law and Gender in Ottoman Syria and Palestine." *Islamic Law and Society* 1, no. 3 (1994): 265–300.

______. *Women in Nineteenth-Century Egypt*. Cambridge, U.K., 1985.

Tuğlacı, Pars. *Türkiye'de Kadın/Women in Turkey*. 3 vols. Istanbul, 1984–5.

Tuncer, Hadiye, ed. *Yavuz Sultan Selim Han Kanunnamesi*. Ankara, 1987.

Türek, Ahmed, and Farih Çetin Derin. "Feyzullah Efendi'nin Kendi Kaleminden Hal Tercümesi." *Tarih Dergisi* 24 (March 1970): 69–92.

Tyan, Émile. *Histoire de l'organisation judiciaire en pays d'Islam*. 2 vols. Paris, 1938–43.

Tyser, C. R., trans. *The Mejelle, Being an English Translation of Majallahel-Ahkam-i-Adliya and a Complete Code on Islamic Civil Law*. Lahore, 1980.

Ubicini, J. H. A. *Letters on Turkey: An Account of the Religious, Political, Social, and Commercial Condition of the Ottoman Empire*... 2 vols. 1856. Reprint, New York, 1973.

Uğur, Ali. *The Ottoman 'Ulemā in the Mid-17th Century: An Analysis of the Vakā'i'u'l-Fuzalā of Mehmed Şeyhī Ef.* Berlin, 1986.

Uğurcan, Sema. "Tanzimat Devrinde Kadının Statüsü." In *150. Yılında Tanzimat*, ed. Yıldız, 497–510.

Újvary, Zsuzsanna J. "A Muslim Captive's Vicissitudes in Ottoman Hungary (Mid-Seventeenth Century)." In *Ransom Slavery*, ed. Dávid and Fodor, 141–67.

Ullman, Manfred. *Der Neger in der Bildersprache der arabischen Dichter*. Wiesbaden, 1998.

Uluçay, M[ustafa] Çağatay. *Harem II*. Ankara, 1992.

______. "XVIII. Asırda Harem." *İ. Ü. Edebiyat Fakültesi Tarih Dergisi* 13/17/18 (1962–3): 269–74.

______. *Padişahların Kadınları ve Kızları*. Ankara, 1980.

Umur, Suha. "Kadınlara Buyruklar." *TveT* 10, no. 58 (1988): 13–15.

Ünver, A. Süheyl. "XVIIinci Yüzyıl Sonunda Padişaha bir Layiha." *Belleten* 33 (1969): 21–34.

Ursinus, Michael. *Grievance Administration (Şikayet) in an Ottoman Province: The Kaymakam of Rumelia's 'Record Book of Complaints' of 1781–1783*. London, 2005.

Uşakizade, İbrahim. *Lebensbeschreibungen berühmter Gelehrten und Gottesmänner des Osmanischen Reiches im 17. Jahrhundert*, edited by Hans Joachim Kissling. Wiesbaden, 1965.

Uzunçarşılı, İsmail Hakkı. "Asâkir-i Mansûre'ye Fes Giydirilmesi hakkında Sadr-i *Âzamın* Takriri ve II. Mahmud'un Hatt-ı Hümayunu." *Belleten* 70 (1954): 223–30.

———. *Osmanlı Devleti Teşkilâtından Kapukulu Ocakları I.* 1943. Reprint, Ankara, 1988.

———. *Osmanlı Devletinin İlmiye Teşkilâtı.* Ankara, 1965.

———. *Osmanlı Tarihi.* Ankara, 1973.

Valensi, Lucette. "Esclaves chrétiens et esclaves noirs à Tunis au xviiie siècle." *Annales* 22 (1967): 1267–88.

van Os, Nicole A. N. M. "Polygamy before and after the Introduction of the Swiss Civil Code in Turkey." In *The State and the Subaltern: Modernization, Society and the State in Turkey and Iran*, edited by Touraj Atabaki. London, 2007, 179–98.

Vasıf, Ahmed. *Tarih-i Vasıf.* 2 vols. in 1. Istanbul, 1219/1804.

Vatin, Nicolas. "Une Affaire interne: Le sort et la libération de personnes de condition libre illégalement retenues en esclavage sur le territoire ottoman (XVI siècle)." *Turcica* 33 (2001): 149–90.

Vatin, Nicolas, and Stéphane Yerasimos. *Les cimetières dans la ville: Statut, choix et organisation des lieux d'inhumation dans Istanbul intra muros.* Istanbul, 2001.

Veblen, Thorstein. *The Theory of the Leisure Class.* New York, 1994.

Veinstein, Gilles. "La voix du maître à travers les firmans de Soliman le Magnifique." In *Soliman le Magnifique et son temps*, ed. Veinstein, 127–44.

Veinstein, Gilles, ed. *Les Ottomans et la mort.* Leiden, 1996.

———. *Soliman le Magnifique et son temps.* Paris, 1992.

Vitkus, Daniel J., ed. *Piracy, Slavery, and Redemption: Barbary Captivity Narratives from Early Modern England.* New York, 2001.

Volney, C.-F. *Voyage en Syrie et en Égypte.* 2 vols. Paris, 1799.

Von Schlegell, Barbara Rosenow. "Sufism in the Ottoman Arab World: Shaykh 'Abd al-Ghanī al-Nābulsī (d.1143/1731)." Ph.D. diss., University of California, Berkeley, 1997.

Walby, Sylvia. *Theorizing Patriarchy.* Oxford, 1990.

Wallerstein, Immanuel. *The Modern World-System II: Mercantilism and the Consolidation of the European World-Economy, 1600–1750.* New York, 1980.

Walsh, Robert. *A Residence at Constantinople.* 2 vols. London, 1836.

Walsh, Robert, and Thomas Allom. *Constantinople and the Scenery of the Seven Churches of Asia Minor, Illustrated in a Series of Drawings from Nature by Thomas Allom.* 2 vols. London, n.d.

Walz, Terence. "Black Slavery in Egypt during the Nineteenth Century as Reflected in the Mahkama Archives of Cairo." In *Slaves and Slavery in Muslim Africa*, ed. Willis, 2:137–60.

Watson, James L., ed. *Asian and African Systems of Slavery.* Oxford, 1980.

Weigert, Gideon. "A Note on the Muhtasib and Ahl al-Dhimma." *Der Islam* 75 (1998): 331–7.

Weiner, Annette B. *Inalienable Possessions: The Paradox of Keeping-While-Giving.* Berkeley, Calif., 1992.

Weiss, Gillian. "Back from Barbary: Captivity, Redemption, and French Identity in the Seventeenth- and Eighteenth-Century Mediterranean." Ph.D. diss., Stanford University, 2002.

Wheatcroft, Andrew. *Infidels: A History of the Conflict between Christendom and Islam.* New York, 2004.

White, Charles. *Three Years in Constantinople, or Domestic Manners of the Turks in 1844.* 2 ed., 3 vols. London, 1846.

Wiedemann, Thomas. *Greek and Roman Slavery.* Baltimore, 1981.

Willis, John Ralph, ed. *Slaves and Slavery in Muslim Africa.* 2 vols. London, 1984–5.

Winks, Robin W., ed. *Slavery: A Comparative Perspective: Readings on Slavery from Ancient Times to the Present.* New York, 1972.

Woodhead, Christine. "Perspectives on Süleyman." In *Süleyman the Magnificent*, ed. Kunt and Woodhead, 164–90.

Wright, John. "Morocco: The Last Great Slave Market?" *Journal of North African Studies* 7 (2002): 53–62.

______. *The Trans-Saharan Slave Trade.* London, 2007.

Wright, J. W., and Everett K. Rowson, eds. *Homoeroticism in Classical Arabic Literature.* New York, 1997.

Wright, Walter L. *Ottoman Statecraft: The Book of Counsel for Vezirs and Governors.* 1935. Reprint, Westport, Conn., 1971.

Yakut, Esra. *Şeyhülislamlık: Yenileşme Döneminde Devlet ve Din.* Istanbul, 2005.

Yasa, İbrahim. *Kız Kaçırma Gelenekleri ve Bununla İlgili Bazı İdârî Meseleler.* Ankara, 1962.

Yediyıldız, Bahaeddin. *Institution du vaqf au xviiiè siècle en Turquie.* Ankara, 1985.

Yi, Eunjeong. *Guild Dynamics in Seventeenth-Century Istanbul: Fluidity and Leverage.* Leiden, 2004.

Yıldırım, Osman, et al., eds. *85 Numaralı Mühimme Defteri, 1040–1041 (1042)/1630–1632 (1632).* Ankara, 2002.

Yıldırım, Osman, Vahdettin Atik et al., eds. *83 Numaralı Mühimme Defteri (1036–1037/1626–1628): Özet, Transkripsiyon, İndeks, ve Tipkibasim.* Ankara, 2001.

Yıldırım, Osman, Vahdettin Atik et al., eds. *85 Numaralı Mühimme Defteri, 1040–1041 (1042)/1630–1631 (1632).* Ankara, 2002.

Yıldız, Hakkı Dursun, ed. *150. Yılında Tanzimat.* Ankara, 1992.

Yücel, Yaşar. *Osmanlı Devlet Teşkilâtına dair Kaynaklar.* Ankara, 1988.

______, ed. *Kitâb-i Müstetâb.* Ankara, 1974.

Yüksel, Hasan. "Vakfiyelere göre Osmanlı Toplumunda Aile." In *Sosyo-Kültürel Değişme*, ed. Erverdi et al., 2:468–503.

______. "Vakıf-Müsadere İlişkisi (Şam Valisi Vezir Süleyman Paşa Olayı)." *Osmanlı Araştırmaları* 12 (1992): 399–424.

Yusuf Ali, Abdullah, ed. and trans. *The Holy Qur'an: Text, Translation and Commentary.* New York, 1988.

Zarinebaf-Shahr, Fariba. "The Role of Women in the Urban Economy of Istanbul, 1700–1850." *International Labor and Working-Class History*, no. 60 (2001): 141–52.

______. "Tabriz under Ottoman Rule (1725–1730)." Ph.D. diss., University of Chicago, 1991.

______. "Women and the Public Eye in Eighteenth-Century Istanbul." In *Women in the Medieval Islamic World*, ed. Hambly, 301–24.

Ze'evi, Dror. "*Kul* and Getting Cooler: The Dissolution of Elite Collective Identity and the Formation of Official Nationalism in the Ottoman Empire." *Mediterranean Historical Review* 11, no. 2 (1996): 177–95.

______. *Producing Desire: Changing Sexual Discourse in the Ottoman Middle East 1500–1900.* Berkeley, Calif., 2006.

Zilfi, Madeline C. "The Diary of a Müderris: A New Source for Ottoman Biography," *Journal of Turkish Studies*, 1 (1977): 157–74.

———. "Elite Circulation in the Ottoman Empire: Great Mollas of the Eighteenth Century." *JESHO* 26 (1983): 318–64.

———. "Goods in the Mahalle: Distributional Encounters in Eighteenth-Century Istanbul." In *Consumption Studies*, ed. Quataert, 124–41.

———. "The *İlmiye* Registers and the Ottoman *Medrese* System prior to the Tanzimat." In *Collection Turcica III: Contributions à l'histoire économique et sociale de l'Empire Ottoman*, edited by J.-L. Bacqué-Grammont and P. Dumont. Louvain, 1983, 309–27.

———. "The Kadızadelis: Discordant Revivalism in Seventeenth-Century Istanbul." *JNES* 45, no. 4 (1986): 251–69.

———. "A *Medrese* for the Palace: Ottoman Dynastic Legitimation in the Eighteenth Century." *JAOS* 113, no. 2 (1993): 184–91.

———. "Muslim Women in the Early Modern Era." In *The Cambridge History of Turkey*, ed. Faroqhi, 3:226–55.

———. "Osmanlı'da Kölelik ve Erken Modern Zamanda Kadın Köleler." In *Osmanlı*, edited by Halil İnalcık. 12 vols. Ankara, 1999, 5:474–9.

———. *The Politics of Piety: The Ottoman Ulema in the Postclassical Age (1600–1800).* Minneapolis, 1988.

———. "Servants, Slaves, and the Domestic Order in the Ottoman Middle East." *Hawwa* 2, no. 1 (2004): 1–33.

———. "Thoughts on Women and Slavery in the Ottoman Era and Historical Sources." In *Beyond the Exotic*, ed. Sonbol, 131–8.

———. "'We Don't Get Along'": Women and Hul Divorce in the Eighteenth Century." In *Women in the Ottoman Empire*, ed. Zilfi, 264–96.

———. "Whose Laws? Gendering the Ottoman Sumptuary Regime." In *Ottoman Costumes*, ed. Faroqhi and Neumann, 125–41.

———. "Women and Society in the Tulip Era, 1718–1730." In *Women, the Family*, ed. Sonbol, 290–303.

Zilfi, Madeline C., ed. *Women in the Ottoman Empire: Middle Eastern Women in the Early Modern Era*. Leiden, 1997.

Ziyaoğlu, Rakım. *Yorumlu İstanbul Kütüğü, 330–1983*. Istanbul, 1985.

Zürcher, Erik J. *Turkey, a Modern History*. London, 1993.

Żygulski, Zdzisław. *Ottoman Art in the Service of the Empire*. New York, 1992.

Index

Cambridge Studies in Islamic Civilization

Titles in the series:

POPULAR CULTURE IN MEDIEVAL CAIRO *Boaz Shoshan*

EARLY PHILOSOPHICAL SHIISM: THE ISMAILI NEOPLATONISM OF ABŪ YA'QŪB AL-SIJISTĀNI *Paul E. Walker*

INDIAN MERCHANTS IN EURASIAN TRADE, 1600–1750 *Stephen Frederic Dale*

PALESTINIAN PEASANTS AND OTTOMAN OFFICIALS: RURAL ADMINISTRATION AROUND SIXTEENTH-CENTURY JERUSALEM *Amy Singer*

ARABIC HISTORICAL THOUGHT IN THE CLASSICAL PERIOD *Tarif Khalidi*

MONGOLS AND MAMLUKS: THE MAMLUK–ĪLKHĀNID WAR, 1260–1281 *Reuven Amitai-Preiss*

HIERARCHY AND EGALITARIANISM IN ISLAMIC THOUGHT *Louise Marlow*

THE POLITICS OF HOUSEHOLDS IN OTTOMAN EGYPT: THE RISE OF THE QAZDAĞLIS *Jane Hathaway*

COMMODITY AND EXCHANGE IN THE MONGOL EMPIRE: A CULTURAL HISTORY OF ISLAMIC TEXTILES *Thomas T. Allsen*

STATE AND PROVINCIAL SOCIETY IN THE OTTOMAN EMPIRE: MOSUL, 1540–1834 *Dina Rizk Khoury*

THE MAMLUKS IN EGYPTIAN POLITICS AND SOCIEITY *Thomas Philipp and Ulrich Haarmann (eds.)*

THE DELHI SULTANATE: A POLITICAL AND MILITARY HISTORY *Peter Jackson*

EUROPEAN AND ISLAMIC TRADE IN THE EARLY OTTOMAN STATE: THE MERCHANTS OF GENOA AND TURKEY *Kate Fleet*

REINTERPRETING ISLAMIC HISTORIOGRAPHY: HARUN AL-RASHID AND THE NARRATIVE OF THE 'ABBĀSID CALIPHATE *Tayeb El-Hibri*

THE OTTOMAN CITY BETWEEN EAST AND WEST: ALEPPO, IZMIR, AND ISTANBUL *Edhem Eldem, Daniel Goffman, and Bruce Masters*

A MONETARY HISTORY OF THE OTTOMAN EMPIRE *Sevket Pamuk*

THE POLITICS OF TRADE IN SAFAVID IRAN: SILK FOR SILVER, 1600–1730 *Rudolph P. Matthee*

THE IDEA OF IDOLATRY AND THE EMERGENCE OF ISLAM: FROM POLEMIC TO HISTORY *G. R. Hawting*

CLASSICAL ARABIC BIOGRAPHY: THE HEIRS OF THE PROPHETS IN THE AGE OF AL-MA'MŪN *Michael Cooperson*

EMPIRE AND ELITES AFTER THE MUSLIM CONQUEST: THE TRANSFORMATION OF NORTHERN MESOPOTAMIA *Chase F. Robinson*

POVERTY AND CHARITY IN MEDIEVAL ISLAM: MAMLUK EGYPT, 1250–1517 *Adam Sabra*

CHRISTIANS AND JEWS IN THE OTTOMAN ARAB WORLD: THE ROOTS OF SECTARIANISM *Bruce Masters*

CULTURE AND CONQUEST IN MONGOL EURASIA *Thomas T. Allsen*

REVIVAL AND REFORM IN ISLAM: THE LEGACY OF MUHAMMAD AL-SHAWKANI *Bernard Haykel*

TOLERANCE AND COERCION IN ISLAM: INTERFAITH RELATIONS IN THE MUSLIM TRADITION *Yohanan Friedmann*

GUNS FOR THE SULTAN: MILITARY POWER AND THE WEAPONS INDUSTRY IN THE OTTOMAN EMPIRE *Gábor Ágoston*

MARRIAGE, MONEY AND DIVORCE IN MEDIEVAL ISLAMIC SOCIETY *Yossef Rapoport*

THE EMPIRE OF THE QARA KHITAI IN EURASIAN HISTORY: BETWEEN CHINA AND THE ISLAMIC WORLD *Michal Biran*

DOMESTICITY AND POWER IN THE EARLY MUGHAL WORLD *Ruby Lal*

POWER, POLITICS AND RELIGION IN TIMURID IRAN *Beatrice Forbes Manz*

POSTAL SYSTEMS IN THE PRE-MODERN ISLAMIC WORLD *Adam J. Silverstein*

KINGSHIP AND IDEOLOGY IN THE ISLAMIC AND MONGOL WORLDS *Anne F. Broadbridge*

JUSTICE, PUNISHMENT, AND THE MEDIEVAL MUSLIM IMAGINATION *Christian Lange*

THE SHIITES OF LEBANON UNDER OTTOMAN RULE *Stefan Winter*